SALES SECRETS

THE WORLD'S TOP SALESPEOPLE SHARE THEIR SECRETS TO SALES SUCCESS

BRANDON BORNANCIN

Sales Secrets — The World's Top Sales Experts Share Their Secrets To Success

To order more copies for you or your team, please visit **https://www.brandonbornancin. com**

First Edition—November 2020

DEDICATION

I hope this book inspires you like it has for me to utilize your God-given talents to make an extraordinarily positive impact on the world.

This book is dedicated to the four most important sales of my life.

My wife, Danielle. I went through four years of endless sales prospecting, pitching, and objection handling to finally get my wife, Danielle, to go out with me. It was the longest deal I ever worked on with a treacherous sales cycle. Well, you know what they say...the greatest things in life never come easy. Now I get to spend the rest of my life with one of the most amazing, beautiful, and inspiring women in the world. I can't wait to build a family together with you and teach our future kids everything we've learned on this crazy journey. Future kids—you can do anything in this world if you work hard for it and do whatever it takes! Everything we do is for you so you better appreciate it! Don't forget.

My employees at Seamless.AI. The most difficult deal of my life was risking it all for years trying to invent Seamless.AI to help the world connect to opportunity and positively impact 1 billion people. I want to thank all of our 100+ employees at our company. This book would never have been made possible without the entire team. We always knew we could sell this amazing product but selling investors to invest in our prototype so we could build it took years of rejection, and rise and grind hell. After pitching 347 VCs, 297 heart-breaking NOs….we were able to survive and thrive. Now we get to positively impact the world together. The lesson here is to JUST NEVER QUIT and don't let anyone tell you that you can't do something!

My fans on Linkedin & Social Media. I always wanted to share with you everything I learned on my journey in sales and entrepreneurship so that you can maximize your potential and hopefully do it much smarter and better than I ever could. It all started with posting really bad sales tips and videos five years ago on Linkedin, to now having millions of viewers and followers each month. I will never forget having less than a hundred fans, and will never take you for granted. Your likes, comments, and shares are the fuel to my fire every day. Everything I post is to inspire you to accomplish more than you ever thought was possible or had in you. Thank you for all of your support, I couldn't do it without you!

My Customers & Investors. Without our customers, we wouldn't have the money to support the business. Without the money to support the business, we would have never received the funding from investors. Every day I wake up obsessed to help you win "President's Club" and our highly coveted Seven Figure Club Award. I am so grateful that you invested your hard earned money in our products, and I promise you we will give it our all to never let you down.

FOREWORD

KEITH ROSEN

November 6, 2006. The New York Marathon. On this blistering, sticky day, Paul Tergat surged one last time, breaking the tape only one heartbeat before the defending champion, Hendrick Ramaala, fell across the finish line. After more than two hours of running, the 2006 New York City Marathon came down to a final sprint and a *third of a second*. One of the closest finishes in race history.

Now fast forward to today. You're at work. After hours of emails, meetings, reports, reviews, sales calls, prospecting, personal responsibilities, and the daily problems to resolve, you sprint towards the end of another high intensity, fast-moving day. But what is presented to you next, is your defining moment.

You can call it quits. After all, you did your job. No one will question that. Or, you can push yourself. One last, not overly, time-consuming step; one last effort, one last point of reflection. And then, like that, your next sale was a direct result of that final effort which moved the sale over the finish line. You won.

These are the one-percenters. And this book is about learning what they do so you can become one yourself and part of this exclusive group of Quota Crushers.

In *Sales Secrets,* serial entrepreneur and founder of Seamless.AI Brandon Bornancin has diligently and deliberately mined the worldwide sales leadership community of thought leaders to unearth diamonds of universally applicable, superior sales wisdom and strategies shared by the talented and visionary thought leaders included in this book from experts like Gary Vaynerchuck, Jordan Belfort, Ryan Serhant, Jeffrey Gitomer and more.

When talking to Brandon about this book and why he was compelled to write it, Brandon realized, "Great salespeople don't always do different things. They just do things differently. And this was something my team personally needed to identify and implement to prove its validity, which we did."

Brandon shares these same strategies in this brilliant compilation of sales wisdom from hundreds of unique, pioneering sales leaders.

While counterintuitive, *Sales Secrets* (which features the top 1% in sales) isn't about being #1 or winning the race. It's about being *your* #1, your best, to win *your* race, and achieve your sales goals. And when you open yourself up to the strategies outlined in this book, breakthroughs will occur, as your superpowers will be revealed.

So, what does It take to become part of the exclusive, top 1%?

While the gap between average and great is wide and deep, taking the leap from good to great isn't as daunting as you may think. From a scientific perspective, there are more than three million differences between your genome and anyone else's. On the other hand, we are all 99.9% the same, DNA-wise. By focusing on these minor, yet significant differentiators, you can upgrade your very DNA, or at least your sales DNA to produce exponential results.

Think of the compound effect. How one seemingly small or insignificant activity, compounded over time, will build upon another activity or result, to the point where a greater measurable impact or result has been produced.

What if you can do one thing 1% better each day? A task, a thought, an activity, a conversation. Multiplied over time, what would that mean to you? It could be as simple as:

- Asking one more question to a prospect or customer.
- Making one more call or courteous call to a customer to ensure you're proving exemplary customer service.
- Refining one more step in your sales process and presentations.
- Delivering one more presentation.
- One more skill to develop.
- Scripting and sending one more follow up email.
- Looking for one more person to help.
- Engaging in one more social media activity.
- One more coaching conversation.
- One more article to read or skill to practice.
- One more entry in your CRM.
- One more hour to plan another day.
- One more rep in the gym.
- One more mile in your run.

Just *one — more — step,* one final surge, one shift in thinking, one trigger event, that gives you one-third of a second lead. What would that mean today and tomorrow?

Salespeople must always remember that *you* are the lifeline of your company and your business. Simply, nothing happens, and no additional job functions are needed until a sale is made.

Yet, the exponential impact of technology is something that we cannot ignore in this book. It is what prospects use to find out information about a company, a product or service, and even a salesperson. It can also speed up sales cycles, improve, and automate lead generation and provide in-depth, relevant information about prospects that will facilitate effective, even autonomous selling activities.

Regardless of how automated and efficient you can make your sales process, there will always be the core, fundamental truth when it comes to professional selling.

People still buy from people. For every organization, you still need to nurture prospects, close deals and hit your quota. It's how you complement, integrate, leverage, and develop this symbiotic relationship that will make you part of the top 1%. And in today's technologically advanced, hyper-competitive marketplace, well-rounded, highly skilled, and technologically advanced salespeople are essential; making you more valuable to your company and customers.

Sales Secrets gives you the edge over your competition by upgrading your skill set, mindset, and strategies to maximize your sales and find financial freedom. This is where your journey begins; and how you can transform from a salesperson and into a sales champion.

Just like the compound effect, take one chapter at a time. One idea, one change, one activity, one step at a time to build upon. Remember, you don't have to be great at selling to start. But you have to start to be great at selling.

This book is your blueprint, your lynchpin, to build an exceptional sales career. So, grab your best running shoes, start your coaching and training, and in your rear-view mirror, watch your competition eat your dust as you race past your sales quota and towards greater success.

Welcome to your path to the top 1%.

Table of Contents

INTRODUCTION

My name is Brandon Bornancin, and everything I've accomplished from selling over $100M in sales for Google & IBM to launching multiple 8-figure companies from the ground up has been achieved one of two ways:

1) **Trial and error**

2) **Reading and executing**

One of these ways I've learned will multiply your success, while the other can minimize it.

Unfortunately, I learned this the hard way.

When my father worked tirelessly to help our family go from rags to riches in sales, he did it all by trial and error.

I modeled his approach in several areas of my life, including the first seven-figure adtech company I started at age 18 for the online gambling industry. That's when the craziest journey of my life started all because of Texas Hold 'Em.

I was gearing up to go to college and Texas Hold 'Em was hitting the U.S. by storm, and I was obsessed with it. I wanted to make millions becoming an expert at online poker and I thought if I simply played a lot, eventually, I would make a ton of money.

Boy was I wrong. Months of playing online poker went by and I was stuck in the same vicious cycle... winning some but losing more than anything. When I would lose, the losses were devastating and I would lose it all.

All of my hard-earned money from my endless workweeks would disappear in a nanosecond. As a high school kid at the time making only $7-10 an hour, those hits really added up and destroyed not only my bank account but my morale too!

After each loss at the tables, I kept asking myself, "Is this really the best way to do this?"

I felt like I was going insane. I knew there had to be a smarter way to get better at playing online poker besides trial and error, losing everything I owned.

I even remember asking all my friends, what is the secret to making a lot of money playing poker? How do I maximize my gains and cut my losses?

They all said the same thing… "You have to play a lot of online poker and eventually you'll get better."

I just didn't buy it. I couldn't believe this was the only way to achieve success.

Fast forward a month later, I was lucky enough to watch a Tony Robbins online seminar and I decided to attend because I was looking for the keys to become a success in life.

Little did I know that one speech would change my life forever.

I remember Tony's speech like it was yesterday where he was screaming out loud, "If you want to achieve success, all you have to do is model those who have achieved success!"

That's when I had the big epiphany.

My friends always told me that if I wanted to become great at online poker, all I have to do is play as much as possible. After hearing Tony speak, I realized that trying to become successful at anything by trial and error was a fool's game, and my friends were all WRONG!!!

After watching that training, I knew exactly what I needed to do. All I needed to do was find the top Texas Hold 'Em players and model everything they do.

When I got out of the Tony Robbins training, I started researching all the top poker players such as Phil Gordon, Doyle Brunson, Daniel Negreanu, Mike Caro, David Sklansky, Jared Tendler, Alton Hardin, and many others. Throughout my research, I noticed they all published various poker books.

That's when my second epiphany hit me.

All of these experts in Texas Hold 'Em spent decades becoming masters of their craft, then spent years documenting their expertise in their books. Now all I have to do is spend $20 to buy it, read it, and get all the cheat codes?

Are you kidding me?!?

I would've paid $100,000 to meet with Doyle Brunson, Phil Gordon, or Daniel Negreanu and get 1-on-1 coaching, yet, here we are, with a $20 book that documents everything they know about making millions playing poker.

After buying Doyle Brunson's book, I went all-in to master everything he was teaching. I started reading, writing, documenting, taking notes, and learning all the different poker strategies. I created notecards, odds sheets, betting systems, seat placement charts, audio recordings, word documents, you name it. By the time I was done with the book, the whole thing was highlighted in yellow and completely marked up.

I was ready to hit the tables with a new perspective and the next time I played Texas Hold 'Em, instead of losing a few hundred dollars that night, I went home making the most I ever made in a session, over $750.

That's when I realized that knowledge is power, and the more knowledge you have, the more money you can make.

I immediately went and bought ten more books on how to master playing Texas Hold 'Em from all the different poker experts.

After studying for weeks and reading everything I could find, I finally went back to the tables and made my biggest trophy yet, over $10,000 in one day!

That's when it really hit me. Tony Robbins was exactly right.

"If you want to achieve success, all you have to do is model the people who have already achieved success."

You just have to buy the books, courses, and training from these experts and learn everything you can from them. Then go and execute what they teach you!

Anything you want to achieve, you just have to learn from and model the experts!

After consistently winning multiple poker games, I realized there was a bigger opportunity than simply playing poker.

After becoming a successful poker player, I decided to build an advertising technology company for the gambling industry, and it ended up generating millions in sales every year.

Fast forward to a few years into my entrepreneurship career, the gambling industry crashed, I launched a second company called EnMobile that failed, losing millions, and I had to quit entrepreneurship for the time being and go all-in on taking a career in sales.

When I started full-time in sales, I realized the best way to maximize my success is to study and model what the most successful salespeople do every day.

I went to Barnes and Noble and Borders Books at the time (Amazon just launched and didn't have many books at the time) and I bought every possible sales book in the store.

From Zig Ziglar, to Brian Tracy, Jill Konrath, Tom Hopkins, and more. I bought all the books and started reading, studying, and taking as many notes as possible.

As I became obsessed with learning, I progressed in my sales career and my sales income increased with it.

Year-after-year I continued to double my income.

The more knowledge I gained, the more money I made in sales. It was almost an instant domino effect.

When I became a millionaire again selling for IBM & Google, it was because of two reasons:

1) **I had the sales lists of everyone I needed to sell to (From building Seamless.AI).**

2) **I had all the sales knowledge to sell to the list.**

It took me hundreds of sales books and nearly a decade of endless research.

I remember sitting in my office one night with stacks and stacks of books, thinking to myself, "I wish there was just one book that summarized all the sales secrets from the world's top sales experts."

After scouring hundreds of google searches, websites, book stores, I couldn't find a single book compiling all the world's top salespeople and their #1 secret to success.

It was at that moment I decided I needed to step up and write this book to help others accomplish the same results I did but in one-tenth of the time.

That's when I told myself "You know what, I'm going to interview the world's top salespeople and write this book myself."

Over the last two years, I've interviewed hundreds of world-class top sales performers for my book, Sales Secrets.

The guests range from entrepreneurial icons like Jordan Belfort (aka the Wolf of Wallstreet), Gary Vaynerchuck, and Ryan Serhant, to sales legends like Tom Bilyeau, Jeffrey Gitomer, and Trish Bertuzzi.

For many of my guests, it's their first time agreeing to speak in a one to two hour interview. This unique perspective helped make Sales Secrets one of the greatest sales books and podcasts of all time.

This book contains the top sales secrets, strategies, tools, and tactics you won't find anywhere else. It also includes secrets from previous guests and life lessons from new ones that you may have never met before.

What makes the book different is my obsession to uncover the sales secrets that you can put into action right away to increase your results. If I can't test something and see the results for myself, I'm not interested in it.

Everything in this book has been tested and applied to my own sales process to validate the concepts. I've used hundreds of the strategies and tactical advice documented in this book and applied it throughout our sales process, such as prospecting, pitching, high-stakes negotiations, fundraising, recruiting, multi-million dollar business deals, and across both large and small sales opportunities of all sizes.

I created this book to share with you all of the secrets to sales from world-class salespeople who have been there and done it.

The lessons I've learned have made me millions and saved me years of wasted time, money, effort, and frustration.

This book has changed my life, and I hope it does the same for you.

ABOUT THE AUTHOR

Brandon Bornancin is a serial salesperson (sold over $100M in sales), a two-time multimillion-dollar technology entrepreneur, motivational sales speaker, and 18x sales author obsessed with helping you maximize your sales results.

Pictured Above: Brandon consulting with experts like Gary Vaynerchuk, Grant Cardone, Jeffrey Gitomer, Ryan Serhant, and thousands of others.

Mr. Bornancin is currently the CEO & Founder at Seamless.AI, a software platform that delivers the world's best sales leads with the first real-time B2B sales search engine powered by artificial intelligence. Seamless.AI helps salespeople, marketers, and entrepreneurs globally find accurate emails, cell phone numbers, and pitch intelligence for any professional in the world. Seamless.AI helps over 50,000 (and counting) companies flood their calendars and generate millions in sales.

Pictured above: Brandon speaking to thousands on the art and science of building a predictable, repeatable, and scalable sales machine at Demo Day.

Mr. Bornancin is the author of *Sales Secrets* and podcast host of "Sales Secrets", where he interviews the world's best sales experts on their top secrets to sales success podcast host of "Sales Secrets".

Mr. Bornancin is also the author of over 15 sales books and the box set series famously known as *The Seven Figure Sales System*. In *The Seven Figure Sales System,* he reveals THOUSANDS of pages of proven sales scripts, strategies, and secrets that he has battle-tested throughout his career to generate over $100M in sales and build two multimillion-dollar companies. Rather than taking years or decades for you to learn these sales secrets on your own or by going through trial-and-error which is very costly to do, he's compacted everything he's learned into a sales system composed of over 15 books, training courses, and his powerful list building automation platform known as Seamless.AI.

Brandon Bornancin is also heavily involved in the community, helping spread awareness for whole-food, plant-powered living and for organizations supporting Alzheimer's disease, cancer, heart disease, diabetes, and many others. He lost his mother to Alzheimer's disease when he was in college and believes the food we consume can prevent the world's deadliest diseases.

He currently resides in Columbus, Ohio, and New York, New York with his wife Danielle Demming.

You can learn more about Brandon Bornancin at

https://www.brandonbornancin.com.

PITCHING

#1 Messaging Matters

KEVIN DORSEY

"I study people. Because no matter what niche, and no matter what product, you're still gonna sell to a person. You still have to convince a person to change their behavior because of your communication style."

ABOUT KEVIN DORSEY:

Kevin Dorsey, the VP of Inside Sales at PatientPop Inc., is a SaaS consultant, speaker, consultant, expert sales leader, and self-proclaimed avid swearer. He has been named Sales Development Executive of the Year, a Top 100 Sales Coach, and an InsideSales Top 10 Sales Leader.

Kevin was the Director of Sales and Marketing at H.U.M.A.N. Healthy Vending, which then turned into Snack Nation where he was VP of Sales. Next, he moved to ServiceTitan, a small company that blew up and is just crushing it in its space. And now, he's stepped in as the VP of Inside Sales at PatientPop.

One of the most interesting aspects of Kevin is his ability to successfully build, develop, and lead stellar sales teams across various industries. From selling food in a box to cloud- based software for home service companies to growth platforms for healthcare providers.

Those who know Kevin say he is ridiculously smart and focuses on helping people to improve all-around, not just at sales. He is known for his strong leadership skills which bring tremendous value to teams as well as being a trustworthy person who cares more about others than himself. In his latest role, he is said to have moved all of PatientPop's KPIs forward in his first 90 days alone! Kevin has a love for sales and the sales process and reveals his top sales secret below.

At the end of one of my first months at PatientPop, my team needed a boost. I wrote a three email cadence, kind of like an end-of-the-month special and delivered it to the AE's and AA's. Keep in mind, I was new so I didn't have a ton of industry knowledge yet. However, I had developed an understanding of people and how to communicate with them.

My team looked at the emails and said, "Oh, KD, these are cheesy, man. These emails won't work." I replied, "Well, you don't have a better one, so go for it." And they sent it out. On the first day, three extra deals popped. The second day, two more. The third, the last day of the month, four more.

The team was sitting there going, "How does this shit work?"

MESSAGING MATTERS

What have I learned going from industry to industry to industry throughout my career? Messaging matters more than anything else.

If you make 50 calls and I make 50 calls, and messaging doesn't matter, we would always have the same results. But we don't. If you're writing shitty emails, it doesn't matter how many you send out. If you have a shitty script, it doesn't matter how many calls you make. If you have poor training, it doesn't matter how good the script is—period.

The secret to writing effective messaging, no matter what industry you are in, is to study people and learn how they think—learn their language patterns and rhetoric; learn their core motivators, and learn effective copywriting. You have to understand how to drive emotion and how to communicate.

If you don't have the right formula, the right tone, the right messaging, the right value prop, the right questions, and the confidence to ask for the sale, the rest doesn't matter. And that's the secret of the 1%: proper messaging.

HOW TO CREATE PROPER MESSAGING

So how do you optimize your messaging? Here's what I've learned.

Understand the Core Motivators of Human Beings

First, you have to understand the core motivators of human beings.

If you ask a lot of people what motivates them, most will say, "Money." But that is bullshit. Money does not motivate most people. If it did, everyone would hit quota. Period. A second common answer is financial security but that's not it either.

The truth is, it's just security.

But, many salespeople don't know this. They approach selling with a "thrive" mindset. "I'm going to make things better. I'm going to make it bigger. I'm going to make it faster. I'm going to get you more results." Human beings, our brains don't work to thrive. Security is the core motivating driver. You have to find out what security means to your target persona and un-sell the status quo around it.

For example, at SnackNation, I was working with HR representatives at companies. For them, security meant lower turnover, lower worker's comp, lower benefit costs, and things like that. So when I was talking to prospects in HR, if I could break down why putting pretzels in a tub was not leading to that security—I'd created a real need for my product.

So first you need to identify the core motivators of your target personas.

Study Copywriting

Next, it goes one level deeper to study the language. If I could give a tip to any salesperson out there, start studying copywriting. When you study copy, you understand how to create emotion and need from the written word. And if you can do that in writing, you can do it anywhere. I believe every sales team in this country should have a professional copywriter on their team. That's who should be writing the scripts, emails, etc.

To learn more about people and copywriting, I recommend you study, read books, take courses, and listen to calls. Never stop learning. Gary Keller, Eben Pagan, and Frank Kern have good courses. The Ultimate Sales Letter by Dan Kennedy is a classic. Methods of Persuasion by Nick Kolenda is a must-read. And there's hundreds more books and courses out there. Amazon is my search engine, not Google. Go out on the hunt.

FOLLOW THE FORMULA

Now putting it all together. You have to craft a message that resonates with people. So most of my scripts now are relatively "fill in the blank," because I have the following formula.

Industry

First, I start with the industry. Every company is targeting industries and there are typically going to be five to six. So, for example, with SnackNation, it was SaaS, Finance, Banking, and Marketing. At ServiceTitan the target industries were Plumbing, HVAC, Electric ... so you write your messaging by industry because each industry is going to use different languages. Then, you identify the personas within the industry. When I say personas, I mean what is the role of the people you need to talk to?

For example, let's say I am trying to sell a sales assistance software product. The industry I am selling to is healthcare and our target persona is the VP of Sales.

The Problem We Solve

Next, identify the problems you solve for each persona. There should be at least three or four. Then, find out what they are doing to solve them right now.

Using the example above, a problem the VP of Sales is facing is they need to acquire more users to hit quota. When they hit quota, their job is safe, they gain a good reputation, they gain security. I'd work on finding out what my prospects are doing now to achieve that goal. Let's say a particular prospect is sending outbound emails, running demos, having reps make 70 to 80 calls per day, having a trainer work with marketing. You would then reveal how your product can help the VP of Sales with each of their activities.

STFW

Now after you show them you can solve the problem, imagine the customer asking, "So the fuck what?" Why should they care, right? This is where you tell them what you are going to deliver that helps them reach their overall goal.

From the example above, you would tell them, it's going to increase your conversion rate and enable you to hit and surpass your quota.

The Gap Question

Next are the gaps. In this situation, the gap is how do you get from your product to the benefit? How do you ensure a customer understands the value? To close the gap, you use strategic questions that expose them.

For example, the rep above could say, "Imagine your reps going into a demo. Rep A is going in blind. Rep B has the five latest Twitter posts, two of their *TechCrunch* articles, three of their LinkedIn profiles, and an article that was written in *Forbes* in front of them. Now, they can use that information throughout the demo. Do you think maybe your conversion rates would go up if you had a demo running like that? Let me know if you want to talk."

You showcase how your product works in a story and ask the prospect a suggestive question about the benefit.

I do not believe in discovery questions. Most discovery questions are wrong and are a waste of time. Like, you have to earn the right to get into discovery questions. Gap questions allow you to build curiosity and sell your product without actually selling it.

VALUE PROPOSITION

Lastly, the value proposition should go along these lines:

I think our solution might make sense. Your (gap-percent to quota is causing) (pain-a deficit in revenue). Our company was designed to (oppo gap—give your reps the intel they need to better understand their prospects and close more deals). (Benefit—This enables more reps to attain and even exceed their quotas, lifting your total attainment and revenue sustainably). Could we set up some time tomorrow to talk about this further, to see if we could help you?

And that's the formula. While it's not always easy, if you work hard in the right areas, you get better results from it. It's really that simple.

I know if I'm putting in this much work to get the messaging right and I'm still not getting them all, people that aren't really trying, won't be able to keep up... they can't. So, get your messaging right. Learn your prospects. Ask the right questions. Study copywriting. Study rhetoric. Study language. Shit, study people, and you'll surely be a better salesperson.

Want to learn more from Kevin Dorsey? Follow him on: LinkedIn: linkedin.com/in/kddorsey3

#2 Facts Don't Sell, Stories Do

MIKE ADAMS

"Humans don't want facts. We want stories."

ABOUT MIKE ADAMS:

Mike Adams is an engineer turned sales leader. He taught himself storytelling 'on the job' while selling and managing sales teams in the United Kingdom, Russia, India, China, Vietnam, Indonesia, Malaysia, and Australia. He has worked for several major international corporations such as Schlumberger, Siemens, Nokia, and Halliburton.

Since 2014, Mike has been helping companies find and develop their own stories through his storytelling consulting practice. Mike is the author of the best-selling book, *Seven Stories Every Salesperson Must Tell.*

Continue reading to learn more about what Mike sees as the seven most essential stories every salesperson should use to be successful.

I grew up in Tasmania, a small island just south of Australia. I actually came into sales quite late in life as my education was in electrical and mechanical engineering. Out of school, I got what I considered my dream job—I was hired by an oil and gas services company and had the opportunity to work all over the world. I worked in China, Malaysia, and Indonesia, running electronic surveys on oil wells.

As a technical expert, I eventually had the opportunity to go to London where I worked on some new software that my employer was trying to sell to oil and gas companies.

One day, I get called into my manager's office where he says, "Mike, we have this great career opportunity. We want you to go to Norway and sell software." Initially, I said no, thinking my wife who was eight months pregnant at the time would not want to move. And to be honest, I wasn't sure how interested I was in sales. After talking it over with my wife, though, she was dead set on moving to Norway—and so we did.

In all reality, I likely would not have stayed in sales had it not been for some dumb luck. Upon moving to Norway, I wasn't really cutting it as a new salesperson. I was more technically-orientated and knew I could always fall back on my engineering background if this whole sales thing didn't pan out.

But for whatever reason, the stars aligned perfectly for me and I ended up selling the biggest deal in our company my first year. It was pure luck. I just happened to meet the right person, at exactly the right time. While I knew I may not yet have all the technical skills I needed to be a great salesperson, that deal helped boost my confidence and gave me a reason to continue selling. I eventually moved to Russia where I ran a sales team and continued to harness my craft.

In time, my family and I decided to move back to Australia to be closer to my father who was ill. The move back home meant that I would have to find a new gig, which ultimately meant doing sales in a different industry. I ended up getting a job in telecommunications—an industry I knew nothing about. By this time, I had started to realize the value of storytelling and began using stories as a way to compensate for my lack of industry knowledge. That was the very beginning of my journey into storytelling, which has since become the basis for how I approach sales.

THE VALUE OF STORYTELLING

As I have already alluded to, I believe that to be a good salesperson, you also have to be a good storyteller. While it took me 10 years to fully realize the value of storytelling, once I did, it changed everything. As humans, we don't want facts, we want stories. Your competitors can all spew the same set of facts but none of them have the same story to tell. Your story is what makes you unique.

What Makes a Good Business Story?

Oftentimes, people think they know how to tell a good story, but they are actually missing some major pieces. When telling a business story, there are three main points to keep in mind.

1) **A story is a sequence of related events**

2) **A story has to be unpredictable or include a surprising twist**

3) **A story has to make a relevant business point, otherwise, you're wasting people's time**

If you can do these things as you develop your story, you can start to master business storytelling.

SEVEN STORIES EVERY SALESPERSON SHOULD DEVELOP

In my book, *Seven Stories Every Salesperson Must Tell*, I go into much greater detail about the seven basic stories that should be in every salesperson's arsenal but here I'll provide a brief overview of each.

CONNECTION STORIES

Personal Story:

Your personal story is designed to help build rapport and trust with your prospects. It should be about who you are and why you do what you do. It's also important to add something personal about yourself, with the goal that what you share will spark your prospect to share something about themselves. Every human has an interesting story and we love to know about other humans. Use this exchange to get to know your prospect on a more personal level.

Company Story:

Every salesperson should be able to tell their company story as a narrative. In this story, your purpose is to explain why your company exists and how it came to be. Your company story can really help distinguish you from your competition so it is an important part of building a solid relationship with your prospect.

Key Team Member Story:

The key staff story is about someone else in your company that your prospect needs to know about. When you tell this story, your prospect can start to build trust with this person before they even meet them. If you're on a reasonably sized deal, your prospect will need to get to know more than just you, which is why this story is important. You need your prospect to trust more than just you so you'll need to purposely collect stories from the other people that are important to the deal.

PRIMARY STORIES

Insight Story:

The insight story is the discovery story. It is intended to show how you or your company reached a major business discovery and how you proved it. This story can also be called the researcher's story. The purpose of this story is to take your prospect on a journey from not knowing how an important business challenge could be solved, then illustrating how you figured it out. This is where you show them the Eureka moment.

Success Story:

Success stories should be told in six parts, or what I refer to as "events." To best illustrate a success story, let me share an example. When I wrote my book, *Seven Stories Every Salesperson Must Tell*, I had a lady help me at the beginning. I'd written a bunch of stories, and she helped me get the book formalized. One of her pieces of advice was to not send my manuscript everywhere because people would have all sorts of opinions that would change the book. I opted to ignore her advice because I wanted to hear from other salespeople. So I sent it around and connected with a guy named David Masover, an ex-Silicon Valley software sales leader who had written a couple of books on sales processes.

David decided that he was going to become a sales coach and wanted to use LinkedIn to connect with salespeople all over the world. He didn't find that so easy at the start, however.

Around this time, I sent David a copy of my manuscript. A week after sending him a copy, I receive an email from David that says, "Mike, this is brilliant. I've been in sales for 20 years and I've written two books on sales processes but I never thought about using stories like this. Today, I did a combination of my personal story and company story. Long story short, it led to a business deal. This is amazing. I am now changing my sales process to incorporate stories." I replied saying that we should do a video conference where I could coach him on his personal story. He agreed and with my support, David now has more clients than he knows what to do with—he's done brilliantly.

Now, let's break this story down into the six events I mentioned above. The first event is David in his original setting. The second event is when David encounters a problem—not being able to connect with prospects. The third event is when he encounters me—his guide, the person who will ultimately help solve his problem. The fourth event is "the plan" that I am able to offer him (a new approach to sales). Through this plan, David is able to avoid failure, which is the fifth event. Ultimately, through the plan I offered him, David is able to succeed and grow his clientele. Succeeding is the sixth and final event.

If you tell your success stories with these six parts, I guarantee that your future client will listen with absolute interest because you're telling a story about someone else like them.

CLOSING THE DEAL STORIES

Value Story:

The value story is the story that explains to your future client what you're like to deal with, how ethical you are, and how you behave, even when things go wrong. This is the story your client needs to hear when signing any kind of significant deal. As big decisions like these are often made by a committee rather than an individual, your value story needs to convince all of the important players that your company is the right one for the job.

Teaching Story:

The final story is the teaching story, which is related to the value story. In many cases, the person you have been dealing with throughout the entire sales process will need to become your internal sponsor when presenting the deal to other stakeholders. You essentially need to teach them how to sell on your behalf to get the deal across the finish line.

Again, you'll find more detailed information on these seven stories in my book but this should give you some ammunition on how to get started.

Want to learn more from Mike Adams? Follow him on: Website: MySevenStories.com

#3 Leading With Passion, Closing With Quirk

JULIANO SARINELLI

"Burger King. That's what people call me and it's a term of endearment because you never know how I might end up getting a sale. I've sold people talking to them about pancakes."

ABOUT JULIANO SARINELLI:

Juliano Sarinelli is the Senior Sales Development Manager at Reciprocity, Inc. Prior to that, he was the Head of Sales Development at Plastiq in San Francisco.

Juliano graduated from San Francisco State University with a Bachelor's degree in City/ Urban, Community, and Regional Planning. His go-getter attitude can be traced back to his time at SF State when he was on the Cum Laude Dean's list every semester. After college, he joined Bridgestone as a sales executive, where he exceeded his quota right off the bat and continued to do so for three consecutive years. In an effort to expand his impact, Juliano was moved into the position of SMB and New Business Sales Manager where he increased the annual store revenue by over $1M.

Juliano's outstanding performance hasn't gone unnoticed. In 2018, he was named a "Sales Development Leader" by InsideSales.com. Additionally, in 2017, he was the President's Club Winner at Zenefits, holding the highest average quota of the entire sales team.

Amongst his direct reports and peers, Juliano is known to be a born leader with extremely high integrity, a person with relentless perseverance, and the type of manager who will go to war for you. His superiors say he quickly earns the respect of organizations due to his great energy and insane production. He is a person who always leads the pack with a mentality and process that has been said to "set the golden standard."

Sales is so much more than numbers on paper or achieving goals. It is a noble quest to find the people in your industry that need your solution. The problem is that people have walls up against salespeople. Everyone has their walls up because we live in a society where we are bombarded with sales pitches at every turn. From scrolling through our social media feeds to listening to music, to emails, and beyond.

So how have I been able to achieve remarkable success in sales despite these walls? How do I break through the barriers to help people who need the solutions I offer? For me, it comes down to focusing on one goal: being memorable.

In Order to be Remarkable, You Must First be Memorable

My top sales secret is to make yourself memorable. To be memorable, you have to be different in some way. You have to stand out from the dozens of other sales calls a person receives. To do that, think about what most sales pitches are like. I don't need to look beyond the messages in my LinkedIn inbox to see that most sales pitches are self-serving, robotic, non-personal attempts that put forth minimal effort.

You can't be that person if you want to be remarkably successful. You have to be different by being "in there." If you're just "going through the motions," you're never going to be truly successful. Instead, you have to make every interaction count by being fully present and dynamic in your conversations.

I once was talking to a prospect who lived in an area that had just been buried under nine feet of snow. Now, where I'm from, it doesn't snow like that so I have no idea what that is like. But I said, "I'm pretty sure in HR you don't need to go to work in that much snow. I couldn't be sure, but I feel like it should be in the Constitution." And she said, "You know what. You're so funny," and she was open to what I had to say. I won her trust, I stood out, and that's what she actually wanted. Someone she could trust to take a leap of faith with. You have to be that person.

HOW CAN YOU BECOME THAT ONE SALESPERSON NO ONE CAN FORGET?

How do I do it? Here are the actionable steps I have learned that can help you break the mold and make a lasting impression.

Know Yourself

Becoming memorable is going to be different for everyone but it always starts the same way. You have to be true to yourself, know yourself, and commit to truly helping your prospects. People can sniff out inauthenticity and ulterior motives in a split-second through a person's tone and approach. So first you need to figure out who you are.

When I'm looking for SDRs, I actually look for people who have been through some sort of existential crisis to discover who they are. It takes hard work and you have to put yourself through uncomfortable challenges but once you know and are honest with yourself, you can identify your purpose and work towards it with total transparency.

People can sense if you know yourself and are honest, and it establishes a sense of trust. So if you aren't really sure about yourself yet, get out there and put yourself in a variety of situations. Don't be afraid to fail because there will be lessons in every failure. Set high goals and work your tail off to achieve them. You will discover yourself in the process and can build the finesse you need to be good at sales and anything else you set your mind to.

Bring the Passion

Once you are grounded in who you are, you need to stay true to yourself. Are you passionate about sales and helping match people to solutions? Then you are in the right business. You have to care and have to want to be the most passionate person out there. There's this saying I like, and it might be played out, but I like it. It says, "I don't want them to love me or fear me but be afraid of home much they love me." You can only achieve that if you come with passion.

Be Unique and Candid

The next step is to ask yourself, "Who can I really help with this product or service?" Once you get them on the phone or in a meeting, be honest. Don't try to pretend like you have a connection with them yet. Introduce yourself, tell them why you are calling, be yourself, and throw some whimsy in there to make them smile. I've closed deals talking about pancakes, my favorite lunch meat, and even closed a $30,000 deal talking about Sasquatch vs. Bigfoot!

One time, I spoke to a lady about payroll and I wanted her to try a demonstration of my company's product.

She said, "I want something that's very simple to use, but I want to be able to use this as an admin in a very robust way."

I said, "Look, have you ever watched those YouTube videos of life hacks where they are MacGyvering things? Where they take a paperclip and a piece of bubblegum and suddenly have a parachute?"

She said, "Yeah."

So I said, "It's just like one of those videos where you see a pineapple. Super simple, but then through the art of fruit origami it looks like Princess Diana after four minutes. If you get on this demonstration, they'll show you how to do that. Your people will be able to see and use this tool very easily, like being able to eat a pineapple. But you, as the admin, will be able to make fruit like Edible Arrangements."

It caught her so off guard and she laughed so hard and just said, "Yeah, let's go for it."

So the lesson here is don't take yourself too seriously and approach conversations with a light heart and open mind. Use analogies, tongue-in-cheek examples, and randomness to get people out of their shell.

Know Your Industry and Audience

Next, SDRs really need to know their industry. More than the products, you need to know who you are selling to and if your product will truly benefit them. You have to know the lay of the land and who your product will fit with so you don't waste their time. Your client's time is precious to them and you don't want to build a reputation of being a time-waster. How? Put in the research. Nowadays, you can find out what you need to know about someone to have a meaningful conversation with about 10 minutes of research on LinkedIn. Further, in time, you will gain a clear understanding of who exactly is in your prime target audience. Speed up the process by analyzing data and asking those around you.

Keep Learning

The last thing I recommend is to be an avid learner. Read as much as you possibly can. The more you continue to learn, the more smart, interesting, and relatable you will become. I recommend reading both books about your profession and books about stuff you are just interested in.

For example, I bought a hunting book recently by Steve Rinella, he's like the Mark Twain of hunting. I've never been hunting but I wanted to go. I read the first 20 pages and learned more tidbits than I've learned from a lot of sales books.

One of the things he said was to always trust your gear. I took that to mean when you leave that mountaintop, don't think that you left it because your shoe was peeling, or your sales force wasn't working, or outreach or sales was bad. At the end of the day, the only variable is you. I truly believe that. I was thinking, wow, this guy's talking about shooting a buffalo next to the Copper River in Alaska, but I'm getting tech stack knowledge out of this. And that's the way that I've been approaching it.

I know work and life can be busy but I recommend seeking out new knowledge and information as often as you can. Even if you can't finish a book, you may be able to get something super helpful in the first 20 pages.

Be Memorable and Become Remarkable

To be remarkable at sales is no easy task. You have to put your whole self out there and all your efforts into continuously improving. If you put any less than 110%, you'll be just like everyone else. Lastly, you can't lose yourself because that is the only thing that makes you stand out!

Want to learn more from Juliano Sarinelli? Follow him on: LinkedIn: linkedin.com/in/jsarinelli

#4 Dollarizing the Deal

ROB JEPPSEN

"Your prospects have to tell you their problem with their own mouth. If it does not cross their lips, if they don't say it, you don't have the right to solve it."

ABOUT ROB JEPPSEN:

Rob is the CEO and Founder of Xvoyant, the world's number one sales improvement platform. He's also a keynote speaker, the host of The Sales Leadership Podcast, a well sought-out sales coach, a serial entrepreneur, the winner of more than 15 Stevie Awards, and the recipient of the Salesforce Surfboard Award for best utilizing their technology to win new business.

Rob attended college at Brigham Young University where he earned his BA in marketing. In the following years, he worked at several companies and gained sales and technology experience before co-founding Allegiance Technologies. Allegiance provided feedback management and customer/ employee retention systems.

Next, he took on the role of Chief Strategy Officer at Primary Intelligence, an enterprise- class sales intelligence solution company. He directed the company's focus, strategic development, and corporate positioning. Another notable position was with Zions Bank as the Sr. Vice President of Sales, where he spent 10 years helping to lead a team of about 300 commercial bankers.

Now, Rob has used the culmination of his experience and knowledge to launch Xyovant, where he's providing leaders with insights using predictive analytics to fix the broken sales coaching model.

Those who know Rob say he is one of the most talented people they've ever met, a person who practices what they preach, and someone with a remarkable ability to connect and engage with audiences. Further, he and his team at Xvoyant are said to be rewriting the handbook on successful coaching.

There's a lot of things you have to do to be successful in sales, and there are no silver bullets. So, whoever is reading this, I hope you know that you have to string secrets together. But here is the one tip that has helped me more than anything else.

Dollarizing the deal

Dollarization is the process of putting a dollar value on the impact of either solving a prospect's problem or creating a result they care about. It is calculating the impact so you can say a statement like, "If we solve this problem, your company will earn $150,000 more per year and $450,000 over three years."

So many times businesses haven't ever dollarized their goals. When you take them through the process, they thank you because you have now given them a pathway to win internally. Further, they begin to trust you because you've helped them figure out something important to their business.

HOW TO DOLLARIZE YOUR PROSPECT'S PRIORITIES

How can you facilitate dollarization with your prospects?

Dollarization can be simple. You just need to ask your prospect the following five questions:

1) **What's the problem you want to solve or the result you want to achieve?**

2) **What's the value of solving the problem or creating the desired result?**

3) **What do you want the value to be?**

4) **What's the value of the difference?**

5) **What's the value of the difference over time (three years)?**

You need those five answers. Once you get them, you will know what your prospect's priority is, why they're working on it, what the current state is, what the future state is, and what the value of the difference is immediately and over three years. And, oftentimes, you get way more information and inspire awesome dialogue which can help you solve their problem.

Since most companies don't dollarize their goals, the value is usually bigger than they imagined. This sets you up to help them achieve that value with your help. I can't tell you how many of my customers sign multi-year contracts not because I ask for it but because we dollarize it annually in the first place.

So work on getting comfortable with the dollarization structure. It's a simple five-step process and you're not going to have a list in front of you, so you need to get good at the business acumen.

Tips on Dollarization-in-Action

Here are some tips to help with the dollarization process throughout your sales process: The Prospect's Priorities Come First You can only be valuable in two ways as a salesperson. You can solve a problem someone cares about or achieve a result they care about. It's not important that it's a problem or a result, the important thing is that they care about it. If you try to change someone's priorities, you're probably going to crash and burn. So you need to talk with prospects and connect with them so they open up and tell you what they actually care about. And it's not enough to know what the priority is but why it matters and the impact it has on the organization.

Sit On Your Product

Note, the initial conversation should have nothing to do with your product or service. You're not pitching yet, and you shouldn't have even said what you do. Instead, you want to slow down and discover the problems first. Only if you find a problem you can solve, that is worth your time to solve, should you pitch your solution that includes your product or service.

Create Urgency

Once a client has answered all five questions, you can dig deeper and create urgency with the following three questions:

- When do you want this to happen?
- What happens when this happens?
- What happens if this doesn't happen?

The first question puts the problem on a timeline that you can use when offering your solution. The second opens the prospect up about the things driving them to achieve the goal. The third uncovers the negative consequences of doing nothing, which can also inspire action.

Gain Pre-Commitment

If you decide that the problem at hand is one you can solve and one that is worth solving, then you can use an approach like this as a bridge to gain a pre-commitment: "Okay, you're looking for this kind of improvement. We've helped a number of people do that and, as I listen to what you're looking for, you seem like a really good candidate for us to show you. So my question is if we can show you how you could do this within your desired timeframe, what's your interest level?"

Using Dollarization in Price Negotiations

Lastly, a common objection as you come to the very end of a deal is the prospect comes back and tries to beat you up on the price. When that happens, the conversation can go along these lines:

You say, "Oh, that's too bad. I thought we were solving an X-dollar problem." And they say, "We are."

You respond, "So, if you think that this little amount is too much to invest for this big of a problem, what do you think the appropriate investment is to solve that problem?" And I shut up and I look them in the eye.

Then, a follow up can be, "You know, if you only have this much, maybe it would be better to solve a smaller problem."

The dollarized value of the solution helps to justify the investment. So if you dollarize the deal early, it helps to take that price objection off the table late in the sale.

In summary, dollarizing your deals using the process described above can help you to learn your prospect's priorities in-depth. Understanding those priorities, the dollar value they can bring in the long- and short-term, and what that means to the organization is a powerful key you can use to unlock more deals.

Want to learn more from Rob Jeppsen? Follow him on:
LinkedIn: linkedin.com/in/robjeppsen
Website: xvoyant.com

#5 The Art of Asking Great Questions

TIM WACKEL

"It's a real passion of mine that once you finally get a meeting, shut the hell up and don't waste your prospect's time asking questions that are only beneficial to you. Figure out where they're at, what they want to accomplish and what's getting in their way—then wrap your solution into their ideas."

ABOUT TIM WACKEL:

With more than 20 years of sales leadership experience, Tim Wackel is one of the world's most popular business speakers. His success has been built on a lifetime of tremendous achievements and first-hand experiences. He was once recognized as the number one producer in a 10,000 person sales organization, helped lead a Silicon Valley startup through a successful IPO, and directed a $50 million sales organization for a Fortune 500 Company.

Tim is the founder and president of The Wackel Group, a training and consulting firm focused on driving business results for clients. His list of clients includes organizations such as Allstate, Cisco, Hewlett Packard, Wells Fargo, Philips Medical Systems, and Raytheon, in addition to many professional and trade associations.

Through his vast knowledge and experience, Tim helps businesses see just how simple sales can be when you have a plan—and that's what he helps create. Actionable and insightful sales plans that simplify the sales process.

Anyone that's been in sales for any length of time knows that to be successful, you have to put in the work. Sure, there's always dumb luck and being in the right place at the right time but to stay aboard the inevitable sales rollercoaster, you have to commit to excellence—and that's not an easy thing to do. Throughout my career, I've experienced great highs and really, low, lows. Through the good times and bad, I've committed to putting in the work, which has paid dividends. There's an old saying that I remind myself of frequently that says, "I love going the extra mile because there's just not much traffic there."

Every day, I try to challenge myself and think about what I can do differently which will make a positive impact on my customers and prospects. But that's no secret—every salesperson knows this to be true on some level. It's really just a matter of how committed you are and how driven you are to succeed.

So, what is my top sales secret then? While there's no replacing hard work and dedication, to become an elite sales leader you have to be able to ask great questions. And I'm not talking about what *you* think are great questions. Research shows that 86 percent of today's B2B buyers report being asked the same mind-numbing, self-serving, manipulative questions by salespeople time after time. "What's your budget?" "Who's the decision maker?" If you find yourself asking these kinds of self-serving questions, stop. Stop now.

It's a real passion of mine that once you finally get a meeting, shut the hell up and don't waste your prospect's time asking questions that are only beneficial to you. Figure out where they're at, what they want to accomplish and what's getting in their way—then wrap your solution into *their* ideas. Three Tips on How to Ask Great Questions:

1) Imitate Sales People You Admire:

Like any skill in sales, learning how to ask quality questions takes practice. One of the best ways to hone this skill is to learn by example. Make an effort to watch and listen to the salespeople you admire and take note of how they ask questions. The more you're exposed to quality questioning, the more it will rub off on how you interact with prospects. So, tag along when you can on sales calls and make a concerted effort to imitate the successful salespeople around you.

2) Do Your Due Diligence:

Thanks to Google and YouTube, there's no shortage of advice on how to develop great sales questions. Leverage online channels like blogs and podcasts to find quality sales questions, check out YouTube videos and be willing to inundate yourself on the topic. Even as a sales veteran, I must own a dozen books focused on asking great sales questions. Books like Tom Freese's *Secrets of Question-Based Selling* are great resources to reference that I highly recommend.

Ultimately, you'll find that every piece of information you absorb will help stimulate your thinking. While you won't walk away from any individual book or YouTube video as an expert, the content you consume will help you generate new ideas. And sales is all about new ideas and getting creative.

3) Add Context to Your Questions:

If you look at people that are excellent interviewers, such as those that make their living interviewing celebrities and VIPs, they don't just log question after question after question; they add context to their questions. When you add context to your question, it gives the person you're speaking with the reason behind why you're posing the question in the first place. Doing this also enables you to position yourself as a subject matter expert by leveraging pertinent data and research.

Take this example—I go to a sales executive and say "A recent report published by *Harvard Business Review* says 80 percent of new business opportunities today require at least five failed attempts to connect, yet 83 percent of salespeople report giving up after just three failed tries. Given this information, what initiatives or plans do you have in place to help your team capitalize on this opportunity?"

This is what I mean by adding context to a question. You've forced the sales executive to slow down and consider something they may not have otherwise. And, you've provided data to reinforce your expertise. Instead of interrogating your prospect with a barrage of questions, now you've started a conversation. This type of two-way dialogue will enable you to learn how to deliver the best solution to your prospect. Leveraging What You Learn:As you get better at asking the questions that matter, you'll find more and more ways to leverage what you learn. In my career, I've discovered that one of the main keys to success is to make your ideas *their ideas.* Through your line of questioning, you will likely uncover pain points they never knew existed. As such, quality questions help plant seeds that compel prospects to find innovative solutions.

Here's an example. Let's say a prospect comes to you simply requesting an estimate to redesign their website. As part of your discussion, you ask what they are doing with SEO and pay-per-click. They respond that they hadn't considered those things but because of the questions you posed, you've now planted a seed! As you prepare your proposal, you now have a better understanding of the full scope of their needs. Because you had the patience to ask the right questions, you'll be able to deliver a *customized* solution that hits on exactly what they need.

Key Takeaways:

To help identify the questions that work the best, I'm a big proponent of building a question bank library. Start with three key questions and try them out on a prospect. What response did you get? Did your question lead to greater engagement or a blank stare? Over time, continue adding questions to your library and figure out which ones are the winners and which ones are the losers. Developing a library of great sales questions is about trial and error so don't be afraid to test new material. Additionally, this may go without saying, but I can't emphasize enough the importance of sales and meeting preparation. Put in the time upfront to research your prospect so that you know what questions to ask. If you're wasting your prospect's time by asking questions that you could answer by visiting their website, don't bother asking the question. Your prospect will thank you in the end and you will thank yourself.

Ultimately, while there are several skills that make a top sales professional, developing quality questions is—in my opinion—the most important. If you showed up on my doorstep and the only skill you had was asking great questions, I would pick you on my team.

Want to learn more from Tim Wackel? Follow him on:
Website: timwackel.com
Twitter: Twitter.com/timwackel
LinkedIn: linkedin.com/in/timwackel/
YouTube: youtube.com/user/TimWackel

#6 Stop Force-Feeding Your Prospects

CHRIS BEALL

"Set the table but don't reach over, grab their fork, and stick food in their mouth. Let them get intrigued by the dishes on the plate and help themselves."

ABOUT CHRIS BEALL:

Chris Beall is the CEO at ConnectAndSell where he helps to deliver a week's worth of live business conversations in one hour. He also has over 15 patents and was the winner of the Technology of the Year Award. Chris specializes in strategy, business design, founding startups, startup management, business development, go-to-market planning and execution, software architecture, and design.

Chris began his adulthood journey in college where he earned his BAE in physics from Arizona State University. From there, he held many roles from a Resident Visitor at AT&T Bell Laboratories and the Director of Software Development at Unisyn, Inc. to the Chief Technology Officer at Cadis and CEO at EVP Products. In June of 2011, Chris joined ConnectAndSell, Inc. as the Chief Product Officer, and in January of 2014, he became the CEO; the position he holds today.

With over 35 years of experience participating in early-stage software startups, Chris consistently focuses on creating and taking to market simple products that can be used successfully the first time they are touched, without any need for a manual or course. He believes that the value of key software is letting the computer do what it does well to free up human potential.

Those who know Chris say he is, hands down, one of the most interesting business leaders in the industry, with an unmatched ability to derive insights from various business processes and circumstances. He is said to be someone who people listen to carefully, and who has an unflinching capacity to take action and absorb adversity.

One of the biggest deals I ever closed was worth $120 million for a product that was only about 10 weeks old. Now how did I manage to do that? I went to the lunchroom of the company I was prospecting, in their headquarters, and I sat there day after day, listening to conversations and talking to people.

Finally, one day, an opportunity came up. The local guys were having a problem that allowed me to get my product in the door. I was very open with them and shared some stuff that the other guys wouldn't share. The next thing you know, we're doing an OEM deal that started small and then steamrolled into $120 million. There was no force-fit selling there. I was patient, curious, and waited for the right opportunity to present them with a fitting solution.

What I've grown to believe after doing this stuff for about 40 years is that the competitive nature that salespeople have is both a blessing and a curse. It's a blessing because you need a big motor to drive you and to do all the work. There's lots of work to be done in sales so you have to have that motor. But it's a curse because it can cause you to push too hard and leave your prospects in the dust.

STAY CURIOUS

When we approach somebody as a salesperson, by instinct, they are going to back away and tell us things that aren't true— just to get away from us. But sales can be much easier if our attitude is based on very, very pure curiosity.

We have to take our desire to sell and put it on the shelf, making sure that's not part of the deal. Keep the energy like you want the deal but you can't want the deal. I didn't show up to the company that won me that $100+ million deal, pitching my product out of the gate. But I did show up every single day to the lunchroom waiting for the right moment. While that may not be feasible for every prospect, the approach behind it is.

Our role is to just find out if we can help the person and to do it efficiently while having fun. And if they don't want it or aren't a good fit, that's okay. Move on. However, if they do show interest, create space for them to become curious and pursue you for your solution.

HOW TO GET PEOPLE CURIOUS ABOUT YOUR OFFERING

So how do you get people to become curious about your offering and pursue you?

Cultivate a Curiosity Mindset

You must set the tone by being relaxed, open-minded, and ready to explore. Become authentically interested in what's going on in the prospect's life and business and accept that it's entirely possible the person or company doesn't need what you have. I always envisioned sales as a form of search, you're searching to find a situation where the sale is very straightforward, where the fit is good, where the value is good, and where you're not forcing anything. You shouldn't really want to sell your product to somebody when it's a forced-fit.

Don't Talk About the Product in the Initial Conversation

When contacting a prospect, all you want to do is put something in front of them that might make them curious. But no matter how many times they ask you more about your offering, don't talk about it during that initial contact. Instead, say, "You know, I've learned the hard way that an ambush conversation like this is inappropriate and unfair to both you and to my product. Now is next Wednesday at 2:00 or next Thursday at 3:00 better for you?"

Go Into the Meeting With an Open Mind

When you go to the meeting, keep a very open mind and don't over-research. Further, don't assume you know everything and don't think you're going to drive them down a path. Just be curious, but don't be afraid to express what it is that you're doing that is unique and then let them confess their interest. If they confess that they're interested in what you have, let them lead with their questions.

Be ready to talk business

When it comes time to talk business in B2B, you've got to understand business so you can have meaningful conversations. If you can't read a P&L or understand the balance sheet, and if you don't know what strategy is and what it means, then you'll use empty words that will drive away real prospects. So brush up on your business understanding.

Cut Your Losses

Lastly, you don't really know anything until you have a conversation with somebody, so be ready to have lots and lots of conversations and don't worry about how they go. Run with the ones that are great and move on from the ones that aren't.

I find that the big issue with salespeople is that our big motor makes us want to drive the conversation where we want it to go. But if we do that, we'll get resistance forever. Once you stop, the resistance goes away. So set the table but don't reach over, grab their fork, and stick food in their mouth. Let them get intrigued by the dishes on the plate and help themselves.

Want to learn more from Chris Beall? Follow him on:
LinkedIn: linkedin.com/in/chris-beall-7859a4
Website: connectandsell.com

#7 Adapt and Win

DANIEL DISNEY

"Adaptability was one of the biggest lessons I learned early on and it helped me to really carve out the career I have."

ABOUT DANIEL DISNEY:

Daniel Disney is the Founder and Owner of The Daily Sales, a popular website and sales blog with more than 150,000 followers worldwide. In addition, Daniel is a sales expert, international keynote speaker, and social selling trainer from London with more than 15 years' experience. He is on a mission to help as many people as possible learn how to sell using LinkedIn.

Daniel has generated over £25,000,000 in revenue directly from LinkedIn leads, gained over 450,000+ LinkedIn followers, and runs LinkedIn's most popular publication for salespeople.

His career began back in 2002 when he worked as a sales supervisor at Homebase for four years. Next, he spent four years as a sales manager at B&Q, followed by two years as an area sales manager for Avon, and two years as a regional sales manager for 3AAA. In 2014, Daniel pivoted to head of sales at New Horizons Computer Learning Centers and it was during this time he began sharing his sales knowledge through blogs and memes. After about two years, Daniel moved to the Training Room as head of sales while continuing to share content in his spare time. One year later, The Daily Sales took off and he was able to focus on it full-time.

Today, Daniel reaches over 10,000,000 people every month through The Daily Sales where he shares sales tips, sales training, humor, blogs and content relevant to anyone and everyone working in sales. He also recently released his first book, The Million- Pound LinkedIn Message, which is available on Amazon.

Those who know Daniel say his dedication and diligence to his profession is a testament to the company he has built from scratch. His Social Selling Masterclass is said to be extremely useful for teams due to Daniel's extensive knowledge on techniques that can be applied to businesses. He is praised for being a speaker/trainer who "made it" and doesn't only talk about his theory but real, actionable tips.

Imagine that you have a goal to gain 5 to 10 pounds of muscle so you go on the search for a personal trainer.

The first one you meet with gives you a diet and workout plan without asking you any questions. He doesn't know your goal and doesn't seem to care. He has a "perfect solution" that he gives all his clients and believes it works for everyone. After reviewing the plan, you realize it's for weight loss and won't help you meet your goal. Needless to say, you start looking for another trainer.

The next trainer you meet talks and talks... and talks. You're there for an hour, hardly get a word in, and make up an excuse to leave. While he had a more customized plan, you don't want to deal with all of the talking on an ongoing basis.

The third trainer is friendly and open. He is curious about you, shares your sense of humor, and seems to respect your time. He finds out about your needs and customizes a plan for your goal. Plus, you get out of there and on with your day in about 30 minutes.

Which one would you choose?

YOUR SALES PROCESS SHOULDN'T BE COOKIE CUTTER

My top sales secret comes down to this, you have to adapt to your individual customers. When I go into businesses to train teams, many of them are treating all of their prospects the same, like trainer one in the example above. They are on a sort of autopilot sales mode where they have the same robotic pitch no matter what. Unfortunately, that greatly hinders their effectiveness. Sure, it may work every once in a while as even a broken clock is right twice per day but it's not working smart. If you want to optimize your success, it's important to understand that every customer is different and you need to treat them accordingly, like trainer number three. You don't need a certain personality and it doesn't require doing anything difficult or complex. You just need to stop for a second, put the selling and pressure on the back burner, focus on the individual, and cater to them during the interaction. Adaptability is one of the key skills I observe in all of the best salespeople I've met and it has helped me to advance in my career.

HOW TO ADAPT TO YOUR CUSTOMERS

How do you start adapting to your customers?

The key is to test the waters in the first few minutes of your conversations. Figure out what kind of person they are by looking at factors like:

- Do they like to talk a lot or do you need to dig for the information?
- How is their posture?
- What sort of language are they using?
- Are they well-spoken or more casual in their language style?
- What is most important to them? What do they want to talk about?
- Do they like to joke around and laugh?
- Do they swear?

It's important to observe all of these little details about a person's personality so you can craft your approach accordingly. For example, if you've got someone who is not swearing and you start swearing, you may offend them. But if they are swearing, you may build rapport by also swearing. If you bring high energy and the other person is very low energy, you may overwhelm them. However, if your energy is low to a high energy person, your message may not resonate. So try and pick up as much as you can and then mirror it so you can get your message across as clearly and effectively as possible.

Today, we have advantages that we didn't have back when I first started in sales thanks to technological advancements. Now, you can go onto social media platforms and start to research these things about people through their content and profiles before engaging with them. And if they make video content, you can learn even more.

Adapt and Win

In conclusion, every buyer, every decision-maker, every person you encounter is going to be different. For everyone reading this, I hope you take this message with you the next time you are back on the phone or back in meetings. If you want to win, you can't go in with the same approach every time. You have to test the waters and mirror your prospects. It may be beneficial to transform the way you sit, the way you talk, what you talk about, and the language you use. Take a step back and speak their language and style. Get in their shoes and help them find the solution they are really looking for.

Want to learn more from Daniel Disney? Follow him on:
LinkedIn: linkedin.com/in/danieldisney
Personal Website: danieldisney.net
Company Website: thedailysales.net
LinkedIn—Daily Sales Blog:
linkedin.com/company/the-daily-sales

#8 Bet Your Money on the Mobilizers

CRAIG ELIAS

"You make big decisions with your heart.
You make the little decisions with your head."

ABOUT CRAIG ELIAS:

Craig Elias is the creator of Trigger Event Selling™, and the Chief Catalyst of SHiFT Selling, Inc. For nearly 20 years, Craig has used Trigger Event strategies to become a leading sales performer, including his time at WorldCom where he became the #1 salesperson within six months of joining the company. Craig's Trigger Event strategies won him a million-dollar prize in a global "Billion-Dollar Idea" pitch competition and earned his company the distinction of being one of Silicon Valley's 40 hottest companies.

Craig has been featured in global publications like The New York Times, the Wall Street Journal, Nikkei Marketing Journal, Business 2.0, The Globe and Mail, the National Post, Sales and Marketing magazine, Venture Magazine, Calgary Inc., and many more.

I attended the University of West Ontario where I was actually on track to get a degree in computer science. Sometime during my first or second year, I took a business course called Business 257. I loved it. As I'm absorbing everything I can from this course, I'm faced with a major decision—do I want to spend all day in front of a computer or all day in front of people? Ultimately, I decided to shift my entire career focus and ended up with something called a cross-disciplinary degree. It was the best of both worlds as it allowed me to pursue my new-found passion for business but also my love for technology.

During college, I put myself through school by working at a very popular bar. This was during the 80s and I was easily bringing in $1,500 a week. Despite the nice paycheck, I knew I needed to get a "real job". A guy I worked with at the bar told me about an inside sales job with a company called Aircraft Marine Products (AMP) so I went in for an interview. During the interview, the lady interviewing me asks, "Why do you want this job?" I tell her that I want the job so that I can eventually become an outside salesperson. She bluntly explains that only engineers become outside salespeople and that likely won't be in the cards for me. I left thinking there was absolutely no way I was ever going to get the job... I'm not sure how or why, but I landed the job. Call it dumb luck or fate, but she apparently saw something in me that convinced her to hire me. Interestingly enough, within my first 60 days on the job, I was asked to transition to outside sales—go figure! Apparently none of their engineers were ready to be in sales so the head of national sales (who happened to be married to the woman who originally interviewed me) asked me to take on the role. And that is how my career in sales got started.

3 QUESTIONS TO ASK WHEN TAKING OVER NEW ACCOUNTS

As a young salesperson just starting out, I had a lot to learn. One of the biggest challenges I had to overcome early on was figuring out how to effectively take over accounts or transition to new territories without losing clients. I learned from my mistakes and developed these three questions, which I would pose to the highest level decision-maker I could reach.

1) **What did (former account lead's first name) do really well that I should keep doing?**

2) **What does my competition do really well that I should start doing?**

3) **What is no one doing that you wished everyone would do?**

Through these questions, I learned a ton about my accounts and what I needed to do to keep them happy. This was a crucial building block in my professional development.

Why Relationships Matter

As I'm taking over new accounts and territories, there is one major account on Vancouver Island that I'm desperate to get in with. The major challenge with this particular account was that it was not easy to get to—it required a ferry ride and a three-and-half-hour journey.

The first time I made the trek to the island was on a Wednesday. When I was there, I told them that I would be back every other Wednesday. Knowing how long it took to get there, no one believed I would be back every other week. But I was determined to prove them wrong…

I soon learned that they went mountain biking on Wednesday nights and, being a mountain biker myself, decided to join them. Through these bike rides, I began to foster relationships with the engineers. What I noticed over time was that because I had something in common with them, they were more inclined to share new opportunities with me than my competitors. In less than a year, they went from being a $60,000 account to a $3 million account!

This idea of sharing common experiences as a way of forging meaningful relationships was a major revelation for me. One way to describe this phenomenon is a technique called the Johari window. The Johari window suggests that the more you have in common with someone, the more likely they are to choose you over someone else. I encourage every salesperson to keep this in mind as you develop relationships with clients.

Timing Is Everything

I eventually went on to earn my executive MBA and then went to work for WorldCom where I became their #1 seller in less than six months. Twenty-one days after I became the #1 salesperson, WorldCom admitted to conducting accounting fraud. Talk about bad timing!

After that news hit, I couldn't get anyone to buy from me. I then began to truly reflect on my luck as a salesperson. When was I good? When was I great? When was I just unstoppable as a salesperson?

It was at this moment that I began to understand the importance of timing and I learned three key lessons that became career-changing.

The first thing I figured out was that a lot of my success was due to me showing up during the "window of dissatisfaction." This is when a prospect is thinking of changing but they haven't defined the problem or started designing a solution yet. If you get to this person before your competition, on average, you'll get their business 74% of the time.

The second thing I realized is that there are three buying modes—the status quo, the window of thinking, and searching for alternatives. Within these buying modes, there are three events that move a prospect from one mode to the next. The first event happens when your prospect realizes they want to change. Just because they want to change, though, doesn't mean they will—there needs to be a second event where they can afford to change.

Once they can afford to change, they then have to be able to justify the decision to other people. By paying attention to these three distinct events, I was able to become much more effective as a salesperson.

The third thing I learned that became completely transformational for me was to stop focusing on the deals I had lost and instead focus on the deals I had won. I came up with this approach that is now called a "Won Sales Analysis." This approach is focused entirely on analyzing the deals you win as a means to replicate your best customers.

These learnings went on to shape my career in invaluable ways and helped lay the foundation for where I am today. It also brings me to my sales secret...

Are You Targeting Motivated Prospects?

I've always believed that selling is all about timing which is why my sales secret is to only sell to people that are motivated to change. I believe that you should focus your efforts on what I call "mobilizers." Mobilizers are people that are new in their roles; they are vice presidents or higher and they have money, authority, or influence.

Why focus on mobilizers you ask?

Research shows that 40% of all decision-makers that are new in their roles will make a million dollars worth of decisions within their first 90 days. If you only sell to those that are motivated, you're way more likely to be successful. With this small window of opportunity, I believe you have about 45 days to reach your targeted mobilizers.

How to Effectively Sell to Mobilizers: Keep Tabs on People Changing Jobs:

The first thing you'll want to establish is an effective means to keep track of your mobilizers. I use LinkedIn for this. I have 27,000 people in my network and every week, hundreds of them change jobs and become a VP of sales. You can also keep track of the bounced emails you receive as this is often an indication that someone has changed roles. Whatever way you go about it, make sure you have an ongoing list of mobilizers that you can tap into.

Make The Seven-Second Sales Call:

Once you have your list, you'll then want to make what I term the seven-second sale. This call is all about describing your value in seven seconds. The secret is to use words that take away your prospect's pain. As an analogy, think of what you're selling as a painkiller, not a vitamin. The words you use should reduce, minimize, or eliminate your prospect's pain. (e.g. "I can eliminate your inventory write-downs." Or, "I can reduce the vendor incompatibility in your infrastructure."

Data tells us that people are ten times more likely to act in order to avoid a negative than they are to move toward a positive so use this information to your advantage. The goal of your call is to get your prospect to simply ask "how" you can help them. Once you have piqued their interest, you know you have accomplished your objective.

Follow Up Every Two Days:

For the prospects you aren't able to connect with via phone, I recommend waiting two days before following up. And when you do follow up, shoot them an email in case email is their preferred method of communication. From there, follow up every two days, switching up the channel each time.

Like I have mentioned already, selling is all about timing. The more you can focus your efforts on those most motivated to buy, the more successful you will be. Don't waste your time on those you know aren't ready for change. Zero in on your mobilizers and keep on the pressure.

Want to learn more from Craig Elias? Follow him on:
Website: shiftselling.com
LinkedIn: linkedin.com/in/craigelias

#9 Negotiating the Respect Contract

RICHARD HARRIS

"Failure is what drives success."

ABOUT RICHARD HARRIS:

Richard Harris is the Founder of The Harris Consulting Group and the Director of Sales Training & Consulting Services for Sales Hacker. He is recognized as a Top 25 Inside Sales Leader, sales trainer, public speaker, and trusted advisor.

Richard has consulted with a wide range of organizations including start-ups, mid-size companies, and global organizations. Some of the companies Richard has consulted with include Mashery (acquired by Intel), Spanning (acquired by EMC), Outbound Engine, TopOpps, Village Voice Media, Riverdeep (acquired by Houghton Mifflin Harcourt), PC Guardian (acquired by Acco Brands), DotNext Inc., Telecom Inc., and Yozio.

Throughout his career, Richard has been viewed as a trusted and respected source for all things sales and he continues to embark his wisdom on those around him. Despite many challenges along the way, Richard remained resilient and has proven that you can overcome anything if you are truly focused on succeeding.

At a fairly early age, I knew I wanted to pursue business in some way, shape, or form. Growing up in Macon, Georgia, my interest in business was driven largely by my parents—my mom in particular. She sold advertising for cable television and eventually became a stockbroker. I remember when I was about 15-years-old I bought my first stock. This was the '80s and I bought stock in MTV. I only invested a few hundred dollars but I remember the excitement I felt as I watched that investment grow.

Fast forward a few years and as I entered college at the University of Arizona, I knew I wanted to pursue a degree in business. During my last semester at school, I got a part- time job at the Gap; this seemed like the perfect opportunity as I had always envisioned myself working in management at the retail clothing giant. When I interviewed, I even told them I wanted to move into a management position. That was my master plan anyway—a plan that quickly back-fired...

Within a very short time, I was fired from my part-time gig. I remember pleading with my boss to keep me on staff. He reluctantly agreed to keep me, but only on an on-call basis, meaning I worked the shifts no one wanted. I came in early and stayed late to prove my value.

Around this time, Gap Kids had come along and they were opening a store in Denver. Not letting my previous roadblock stand in my way, I applied for a management position and, to my surprise, I got it! While it was not the exact path I had envisioned, my initial failure ultimately drove me to success. That first management position at Gap Kids is really what kick started my career. Looking back, I don't think any of it would have happened had I not been fired in the first place. Getting fired was the motivation I needed to strive for success. In many ways, overcoming adversity and failure has been a common theme throughout my life and career...

Overcoming Adversity— Time and Time Again

After Gap Kids, I went to work for a company in Denver called Westword. Westword was an alternative, hippie-like weekly paper, and my job was to sell classified ads. After a period of relative success, I became frustrated that I was not getting the promotions I thought I deserved. I even threatened to quit to go get my MBA. Instead (and after a lively exchange), my manager convinced me to stay and offered me a position in Cleveland. He told me I could earn a "real-world" MBA with on the job experience. So I moved to Cleveland for a couple of years and absolutely crushed it. They eventually transferred me to San Francisco (a place I had always wanted to live) and I continued to experience great professional success.

Despite my success in sales, personally, I was at one of my lowest points ever. I remember waking up one day utterly depressed to the point where I literally could not get out of bed. I think a part of me had always been depressed but this was the first time I openly acknowledged it; I simply could not go on as I had been for so many years. At that point, I threw myself into therapy and ended up quitting my job at the paper. Even though I had been wildly successful, I couldn't handle the pressure and I didn't know how to create a proper work/life balance. In many ways, that was a major turning point in my life. I came to realize that I needed help and it was OK to ask for support. That realization gave me the strength I needed to power through the many highs and lows that would characterize the next few chapters of my career.

A Dose of Reality

After taking the time I needed to deal with my depression, I got involved with a few startups. Then the dot-com bubble hit. At the time, I had just taken a new job then literally got laid off six weeks later. That turned out to be a blessing as I soon went to work for a company called The Learning Company.

Over the next several years, I had the opportunity to work with some great companies like PC Guardian and Mashery, but I also had to learn to ride the wave. Through various acquisitions and legal issues (not mine personally), I was laid off at a few different points in my career but always managed to get back on my feet—even if that meant taking two steps backward to move forward. After about two decades in the tech space, I got into consulting, which brings me to where I am today.

Along the way, I learned on several occasions that I needed to check my ego at the door and to give other people an opportunity to have an opinion. I realized that I didn't always have to be the smartest person in the room—which was a challenging concept for me to embrace. Sometimes, you have to let other people have the mic. As a salesperson, that may be a difficult thing to do, but over time you will learn that it will pay dividends. Not only will it allow you to learn from other people, but it will also teach you a lesson in respect, which brings me to my sales secret...

The Respect Contact

One of the most important lessons I've learned throughout my career and something I constantly teach is that to be successful, you have to earn the right to ask questions. It's great if you have a good pitch and a good product, but until you earn the right to ask questions, you're never going to be as successful as you could be.

I often talk about something I call the "respect contract." The respect contract is something you establish at the beginning of a conversation and grants you permission to ask the questions you want to ask. For example, I'll often start off a conversation saying something like, "My goal of this conversation is simply this—I want to get a frame of reference. I don't know if we're going to do business together. Maybe we will. Maybe we won't. If we do, great. If we don't, let's walk away friends so I don't have to send you checking in, reaching out, touching base emails. You don't want to get them. I don't want to send them."

Establishing a respect contract upfront enables you to ask the questions you want to ask and also provides your prospect with an out if what you're selling really isn't a good fit. It also gives you the opportunity to be candid and not waste your time on your prospect's time.

With your respect contract, your main objective is to invite a conversation. Once your prospect feels comfortable, they are far more willing to share—and that is the part you want to happen. The sharing and exchange of information are how you move a deal forward.

While it is a relatively simple concept, a respect contract is crucial in helping you build trust. The more you can do to build mutual trust and respect upfront, the more value you will gain from your conversation. Just remember, you want to use your respect contract to earn the right to ask the questions that matter—if you can earn that right, the results will follow.

And, if you fail in your first few attempts, keep trying. If life has taught me anything, it is that failure drives success. Always keep pushing.

Want to learn more from Richard Harris? Follow him on:
Website: theharrisconsultinggroup.com
LinkedIn: linkedin.com/in/rharris415

#10 Don't Just Make Calls, Make Smart Calls

ART SOBCZAK

"The only way to cut through the clutter is to have a message that is going to resonate with the person and what's going on in their world, right at that very moment."

ABOUT ART SOBCZAK:

Art is an award-winning author who has delivered content-rich inside sales and cold calling training programs for over three decades. His latest book, Smart Calling, hit #1 in Amazon.com's Sales category its first day and was named "Top Sales Book" in 2010. In 2012, Art also received the Lifetime Achievement Award from the American Association of Inside Sales Professionals for his contribution to the sales community.

Through authoring, speaking, and creating content-rich inside sales and cold calling training programs and resources, Art has helped hundreds of thousands of sales pros to say the right things that cut through the noise and sell.

An entrepreneur at heart, Art knew he wanted to run his own business since his college days. However, he was getting married after graduation and needed some real-life experience and income. He began his career as a telemarketer in the Bell System Sales Center where he received his first formal inside sales training.

While Art excelled in the role, he didn't take to corporate politics. At the ripe age of 23, he quit, partnered with a co-worker, and started a consulting business. After learning many lessons, losing his partner, and stepping back into a 9-5 role with American Express, he decided he needed to restart his consulting business the right way and on his own. That's what he did and has now been running Business By Phone Inc. for over 36 years!

Art is known as one of the greatest sales trainers around. His books are said to be must- reads for any sales pro. Further, his common sense and practical approach is said to be effective and easy to implement.

I get calls almost every day from salespeople who have no idea who I am but get right into their pitch. Just last week a guy calls me and says, "Yeah, I'd like to speak with the person who is in charge of your shipping." I reply, "My shipping of what?" He says, "The shipping of whatever that you might ship there." I ask, "Do you know anything at all about what we do?" He answers, "Well no, not really. Business by phone, probably something with phones."

Nothing gets by this guy, right?

So I say, "So you really didn't do any research, you don't know what I do, but you're going to ask me about my shipping." He goes, "Yeah, pretty much. What kinds of things do you ship?" I insist, "I mean, it really doesn't phase you at all that you know nothing about me?" He says, "No, just wondering what you ship." So I say, "Okay. I really don't ship anything. For what I do, I use a fulfillment service." In my opinion, the absolute biggest mistake in sales is calling up a prospect and blindly pitching without knowing anything about the person that you're calling. It becomes solely a numbers game with no strategy, skill, or craft which leads us to my top sales secret.

Always Get Information Before You Give It

It really isn't rocket science, and it's the same thing that I've been teaching for years. You need to know something about the person that you're calling before you call them. Further, you need to craft, tailor, and personalize your message so it is relevant to them and what's going on in their world. I call it making a "smart call."

The Numbers Game vs. Research Debate

Now, there are people out there who subscribe to the numbers game type of mentality where they believe they don't need to waste time doing research. Instead, you just bang out those calls, you know 100 calls, 1,000 calls per day, or whatever.

Well, here's the rebuttal to that approach. Number one—if you don't know anything about the person that you're calling, you're pretty much going to have a generic type of pitch or presentation. You are solely playing the numbers game.

Number two—some people say that bad calls do not reflect badly on an organization. I tend to disagree. If you leave a horrible voice mail, that's going to stick in their mind and say a couple of things. First, geez I can't believe that XYZ Company is doing that. Another is, I'm never going to take that call again.

Today, we are bombarded with, depending on what research you look at, anywhere between 300 to 3,000 messages per day. And we're only reacting or responding to a couple of them.

The only way to cut through the clutter is to have a message that is going to resonate with the prospect and what's going on in their world, right at that very moment. You've got to give some indication, right away, that you're different than every other salesperson out there who is trying to get a piece of their time, and you don't have a whole lot of time to do that.

HOW TO MAKE SMARTER CALLS

Common sense and human nature say we're going to be interested in something that's all about us, right? Something that's going to affect us at that moment in time. And as salespeople, we should be employing whatever we can to have a message that's going to resonate with our prospect. Here's my approach.

My Two Main Objectives

I have two objectives in my mind for the first 10 seconds of a sales call. Objective #1 is to put my prospect in a positive, receptive state of mind. Objective #2 is to get them talking from that positive, receptive state of mind.

Then, in the next 30 seconds, you need to keep earning the right to stay on the phone until that person's invested in the conversation.

My 5-Step Smart Call Process

My process includes the following five steps:

1) **Introduce yourself and your company**

2) **Use smart calling intelligence to make a connection**

3) **Deliver a possible value statement**

4) **Add credibility using social proof**

5) **Transition to the question**

Now let's break down the steps and I'll share some examples:

Introduce Yourself and Your Company

This first part is pretty straight-forward. Let's say, for example, I sell a service to book publishers that's pretty unique in that it can help them get mass distribution and get them to the top of the best-seller list pretty quickly. See the example below for my simple introduction.

Example:

"Hey (prospect name), I'm Art with Books Are Us."

Use Smart Calling Intelligence To Make the Connection

Next, smart calling intelligence is information you gather about prospects that ties them to your product or service through something they value. Now you can't know what is of value to a person for sure but you can make an educated hypothesis based on what they post, what you find about their company, what you see about trends in the industry, questions you ask someone in their company, etc.

Sticking with the above example, if I was a good sales guy, my radar would constantly be out there looking for people who are planning to publish books.

I would probably partner with companies that teach people how to become a self-published author, perform research on prospects, study the social media profiles of prospects, and figure out how far along in the process they are. If my prospects worked at a company, I would do this thing called social engineering (I didn't invent the term, computer hackers did). It's just simply calling an organization and asking questions of someone other than the decision-maker.

So I might call in and talk to an assistant or someone in the marketing department. I'd introduce myself and say, "Hey, I'm with Books are Us, and I'm going to be speaking with your CEO on his new book project and how we may be able to help him. I imagine you probably work closely with him, don't you?" If they do, I'd say, "Well let me ask you a couple of questions. What do you know about his marketing strategy, and what are his plans to make a big impact?"

You take all the information you gather to craft a statement that will help you connect with the prospect. It shows them that you're not just smiling and dialing. On a psychological level, that person will think, this salesperson is different. They have actually done some research and know something about me.

Example:

"I understand that you're in the process of coming out with this killer book, (book name)" and I also understand that you're looking to make a big splash when you release that book and that you're self-publishing."

Deliver the Possible Value Statement

The possible value statement shows that you specialize in delivering a result that can benefit the prospect. It is what your product or service can provide them. However, don't reveal what your service is.

Example:

"Well, what we have a track record of is doing exactly that with self-publishers."

Add Credibility Using Social Proof

Then, use social proof to add the credibility piece where you give an example of what you've done for someone else.

Example:

"Matter of fact, with one of our most recent clients, we helped them reach number one on Amazon, and they had a relatively small list."

Transition to the Question

The last part is the transition to the question. Don't ask for a decision or even hint at the fact that you want to do business with the person. Instead, ask one of the easiest questions in the world, which is, "Can I ask you some questions?" You want to make it very easy for them to answer. All you are really trying to do is to use the first 10 seconds to earn the next 30 seconds. At the end of the opening, you want them saying, "Oh yeah, sure, what do you want to know?"

Example:

"Basically what I'd like to do is ask you a couple of questions right now to see if we might have the basis for further conversation."

And that's it!

It's not complicated. The real key is just trying to find out something. And again it doesn't need to be earth-shattering stuff. The level of this will be dependent on the sophistication of your call. If you are doing something a little bit more transactional, you probably won't spend as much time as you won't need to go into as much detail. But still, the more you can make the conversation about them, the better your chances of them leaning in and saying, "Okay, sure, yeah. What do you have?"

Want to learn more from Art Sobczak? Follow him on:
Blog: smartcalling.com
LinkedIn: linkedin.com/in/artsob/

#11 Why Stories Sell (Just Ask the Swimming Pigs...)

PAUL SMITH

"Tell stories. Don't just make sales pitches."

ABOUT PAUL SMITH:

Paul Smith is one of the world's leading experts on business storytelling. He's a keynote speaker, storytelling coach, and bestselling author of the books Lead with a Story, Parenting with a Story, and Sell with a Story.

His research on the effectiveness of storytelling has been featured in publications including the Wall Street Journal, Ink Magazine, Time, Forbes, Fast Company, The Washington Post.

He is also the Principal of thoughtLEADERS, a firm that offers consulting, coaching, and instruction on communications, strategy, operations, and leadership.

Before starting his career, Paul earned a BA in economics and accounting from Hendrix College and an MBA from the Wharton School at the University of Pennsylvania. After graduating, he joined Proctor & Gamble where he worked for 20 years. During that time, he held leadership positions in both research and finance functions and most recently served as director of consumer and communications research. In 2012, he joined both thought-LEADERS and Story Makers, where he is today. Paul's lessons and principles are said to be must-haves. Clients say he gives businesses the tools to write better storylines and improve the quality of client deliverables. Further, he builds instant rapport with teams and inspires them to engage in the importance of communications and structured thinking.

A few years ago, my wife and I were at an art fair looking for decor for our kid's bathroom. We came to the booth of an underwater photographer named Chris Gug who takes mesmerizing pictures. My wife got attached to a picture that looked as out-of-place as a pig in the ocean. The reason was that it was literally a picture of a pig in the ocean. I had to ask him, "I don't get it. This is just crazy. Pigs don't swim. What's the deal?"

He explained that a few years earlier, a local entrepreneur decided to start a pig farm for bacon. He found this island, Big Major Cay, which was uninhabited and where he could keep the pigs for free. He says to me, "Look in the picture, back behind the pig up on the beach. What kind of vegetation do you see?" I kind of squinted and looked up and said, "I don't see anything but cactus up there."

He says, "Yeah. That's the problem. Pigs don't eat cactus." These pigs had nothing to eat. Fortunately, what happened was a local restaurant owner from a neighboring island was boating his kitchen refuse over each night and dumping it overboard a few dozen yards offshore. "Even though pigs don't normally swim, one little pig paddled his way out there to get the food. Then two little piggies, and three little piggies ...here it is, three generations later, and all the pigs on Big Major Cay can swim."

I bought that picture for whatever he was willing to charge. If he hadn't told me that story, it was just some stupid picture of a pig in the ocean. But now, I was not just buying a picture, I was buying a story that had a picture with it. Stories like that actually make the product or service you're selling more valuable and that's my number one sales secret. Tell stories instead of just making sales pitches.

What Do I Mean By a Story?

Today, people mean all sorts of things by the words 'story' and 'storytelling'. When I say story, I actually mean a real story. A narrative about something that happened to someone. There's a time, a place, and the main character who faces some kind of opportunity or challenge. Events happen and the problem or challenge is resolved with either a success or a failure.

HOW TO SELL WITH STORIES

How can you incorporate stories into your sales process? After interviewing professional sales and procurement managers at over 50 companies (including Costco, Abercrombie & Fitch, Xerox, and many more), I found that storytelling is being used throughout the sales process. Successful sales professionals are using storytelling from the introduction,through the pitch, and even after the sale. Below, I've outlined the top 25 most useful sales stories you can tell, broken down by the part of the sales process they fall under.

Introducing Yourself

"Explaining What You Do Simply:" The first story should explain what you do in a simple way that prospects will understand. It should also drive them to want to know you more.

"Who I've Helped and How I've Helped Them:" The next story is also for prospects and should illustrate a real person who you have helped and how you helped them. For example, if you install windows and doors, you might say, "Last month I went to our client Bob's house because he had a window that broke during a storm. I showed up within two hours of the call and fixed it so his home would be secure by nightfall."

Preparing for the Sales Call

"Personal Motivation:" This story is one that you create for yourself that is inspirational and gives you a boost of motivation. It can be a story about someone else that inspires you or a story from your past.

"Relax and Take the Stress out of Sales:" Here's another one for yourself which is used to ease anxiety or stress before a sales interaction. It should be a story that makes you feel calm and happy.

Rapport Building

"Why I Do What I Do:" This is a story you tell your prospects to explain why you care so much about the thing you do for a living. It's kind of the Simon Sinek thing, nobody cares about what you do until they know why you do it.

"I'll Tell You When I Can't Help You:" Next, is a story that shows prospects that if you're not the best solution for what they need, you will tell them so they can go somewhere else. Then, when you tell them you are the best solution, they believe you because you are the kind of person who will tell them if you're not.

"I'll Tell You When I Made a Mistake:" Share a story with your prospect about a time when you made a mistake. This shows them that they can trust that if you screw up, you're going to admit it openly.

"I'll Go To Bat For You:" This is a story to prove that if you have to go fight some battles back at your company headquarters to do right by the customer, you will. You can't just promise people you'll do that. You have to tell them a story about a time you did that for somebody else, so they'll believe you.

"Who You Think I Am:" In general, salespeople have a bad reputation. If you know you're going to pitch a new prospect and they already have preconceived notions about you, this is a story you tell to diffuse that notion right off the bat so they don't think that you're the bad guy they're expecting. "Your Company's Founding:" Did your company start in the basement of your founders, was it a family business, or something else? Whatever is it, everybody needs to be able to tell the founding story of their company.

"How We're Different From Our Competitors:" This is basically a marketing story about how your company does something for a customer, versus how your competitors do it. This is meant to lead your prospects to think, "Oh, yeah. I like the way that you do it better. I want to go with you."

Sales Pitch

"Your Product's Invention or Discovery:" If your company only sells one product or service, then this is the same story as your founding story. However, most companies have lots of products or services. If applicable, tell the founding story of the particular product or service that you're pitching.

"Explaining the Problem:" This is the quintessential story of somebody who has a problem that your product or service solves. Tell the story about the pain that they might be experiencing to help identify problems they may not know they had.

"The Solution:" Share a customer success story with your prospect where a customer used your product or service and it solved their problem.

"Combine the Problem and Solution:" When you put a problem and solution together, it's really powerful. Present the problem and a story about how to solve it. It's like a before and after story.

"Value-Adding:" This is the kind of story that, literally, makes the product or service you're selling more valuable to a customer. Take, for example, the story in the opening about the swimming pigs.

Resolving Objections

"Objection Response:" This is just a story to resolve whatever objection your buyer presents. Instead of a fact or a figure, tell them a story that will help them realize, "Oh, that's not going to be a problem for me after all."

"Price Objection:" This is a story that overcomes an objection based on price by showing a situation where a customer from the past hesitated on price but then decided to buy and it was a good solution in the end.

"Resolving Objections Before They're Brought Up:" These are stories that disarm the prospect's common objections before they are mentioned.

Closing the Sale

"Creating a Sense of Urgency:" This is a story about the bad things that will happen if a prospect waits to buy. It is useful when you've made the sale and the response is, "Hey, that all sounds great. I know I need it. I can afford it. But now's not the right time. Come back in six months. It will be a better time for me." You need to tell a story right then about somebody else who waited and regretted it. "Arming Your Sponsor:" This is a story for situations when you're not going to be in the room when the decision is finally made, which happens a lot for salespeople. You need a good, short, memorable story to tell your sponsor so they can go in and repeat that story in front of the decision-maker(s).

"Coaching the Break-Up:" If you get your buyer to buy from you, it means they have to stop buying from somebody else. In a lot of industries, customers have been buying from the same supplier for years. How are they going to fire the old company?.

The "Coaching the Break-Up" story is about how some of your other clients have easy ways to break up with their existing suppliers without creating an enemy.

Managing Customer Relationships

"Service the Sale:" This is a story for new clients about your best existing customers and how they're using your product or service successfully. Pick your best customers who love your product or service. This way your newest clients learn how they can become your next best clients.

"Build Loyalty:" Loyalty-building stories are next. Whatever your best customer service stories are, tell them to your newest clients. Not your newest prospects, but the ones you just closed. This story encourages them to think, "Oh, yeah. I want me some of that."

"Summarize the Call:" Lastly, summarize your calls. This is a story that you tell your co-workers about the awesome sales call you just had, or the phenomenal failure you just suffered. It helps to ensure that they will not repeat the bad mistake you made, or they can follow the successful path that you just set. It's basically teaching your peers about your best and worst sales experiences.

Stories are powerful because they draw people in, get their attention, and subtly deliver messages and beliefs. By incorporating stories into your sales process, you can improve your interactions with prospects, customers, peers, and yourself to become a more effective salesperson. Take some time to craft the types of stories listed above and then take note of the impact they have on your sales interactions.

Want to learn more from Paul Smith? Check him out on:
Website: leadwithastory.com
LinkedIn: linkedin.com/in/smithpa9

#12 Tune Into Your Buyer's Station

STAN ROBINSON JR.

"Everyone listens to the same radio station, and that radio station is called WIIFM (What's In It For Me). I ask people, "Have you heard of it?" People's eyes go up and they think and they say, "Nah, not really." But everyone listens to it."

ABOUT STAN ROBINSON JR:

Stan Robinson, Jr., Director of Training and Associate Partner at Vengreso, is a sales expert with over 30 years of sales experience. He is passionate about helping B2B leaders succeed through coaching and implementation programs.

Stan earned a BA in Psychology from Harvard and a Masters in Public Affairs and International Relations from Princeton. During his college years, he picked up a door-to-door sales job to pay for school.

After college, Stan stayed on the path of sales and marketing, holding a variety of roles at several companies including J.D. Edwards, Dun & Bradstreet, and Cybershift. A turning point was between 2006 and 2011, while Stan worked at Minicom Digital Signage as an inside sales representative. It was during this time that he discovered the power of LinkedIn for prospecting and building brand recognition.

In 2011, Stan left Minicom and joined The Efficiency Xperts as a marketing consultant. After three years, he stepped out on his own, founding SHR Marketing as an Independent LinkedIn Consultant and Social Media Strategist. After seven successful years, Stan left SHR Marketing to join forces with Vengreso in his current role.

Stan's wide range of work experience has helped him acquire a great deal of knowledge and wisdom. His clients say he is professional, knowledgeable, patient, and creative. Further, his keen intellect and business acumen have helped him earn the reputation of being a high-caliber professional who can help companies utilize LinkedIn and social media to effectively grow their businesses.

WIIFM: The Radio Station Everyone Is On

There's a radio station we all listen to, everyone in the world. You may think, "No way. I surely don't." But trust me, you do. It's called W-I-I-F-M and it stands for 'What's In It For Me?'

My number one sales secret is this: You need to understand your buyers and decision- makers enough that you're able to have a conversation around what's in it for them. The truth is, that's all they care about.

You may be a nice person. I think I'm a nice person, but I understand that people don't care about Stan Robinson Jr. They only care about what Stan Robinson Jr, and Vengreso, in my case, can do for them. They care about how we can help them solve a problem, look better at their job, make more money, save money, reduce risk; whatever their objective may be.

To close sales, you need to tune into your prospect's radio station so you can understand what's in it for them.

HOW-TO TUNE INTO YOUR BUYER'S STATION

How do you tune into your buyers and understand what they want and need most? Here are a few strategies that have been highly effective for my clients and myself.

Understand Common Buyer Concerns

As you get into your sales role and learn about your buyers, you will be able to identify the common concerns of decision-makers. Doing so will help you to predict what your buyers care about.

For example, in the B2B world, if someone is Head of Sales, nine times out of 10, they want their sales teams to get better at creating more sales conversations with qualified buyers. So a great starting point with a Head of Sales would be talking about creating more sales conversations.

If you are targeting the VP of Marketing, they tend to be interested in branding as a general issue. Now, if they've just undergone a massive, multi-million dollar rebranding campaign for the company, I'm not going to lead with that in the conversation. But, in many cases, marketers are concerned about growing their brand so I start with that in mind.

Once you have identified the common concerns of your potential buyer, it's time to research them on an individual level so you can hone in on their needs.

Research Decision Makers

You don't want to rely entirely on common buyer concerns because, as in the example above, they don't always apply. To learn more about the buyer, research them on a personal level.

Thanks to technology, prospect research has become much easier. You can gain a great deal of insight by looking at someone's Linkedin profile and other social media accounts, their annual reports, their industry, what the president talked about last in terms of their corporate goals, press releases, interviews, etc. Try to find their objectives and what is holding them back.

The more you know, the better you can effectively address the buyer's WIIFM.

Learn Their Communication Preferences

After the first two steps, you know the buyer and what matters to them. The next important piece is communicating with them in the way that they prefer. Consider the channel, the time, and the communication style.

Channel

By figuring out what channel a person prefers to communicate on, you increase your odds of connecting with them. For example, if you are messaging someone on LinkedIn but they primarily use Twitter, you are missing an opportunity. Browse a person's social profiles to find where they are most active. Additionally, you can check their website(s) to see which contact details they share and list most prominently.

Time

The second piece is figuring out the best time to contact someone. Some decision-makers get into the office early and you can reach them before the day takes off and gets busy. Others may be more accessible in the afternoons. If you have conversed with the person before, check the timestamps on when they call or message you. If not, check their status on social media or call their office.

One little tip for LinkedIn is to look for the 'active status' green light. You can see if someone is actually on. If they are, you can send a quick message asking "Hey, is this a good time to talk?" Different people will have different communication preferences. Some may respond to a Linkedin direct message, others may say, "Hey, just text me."

Communication Style

Lastly, pay attention to how a person communicates so you can adapt your messaging to their preferred style. A tool like Crystal Nose can give you a sense of the buyer's personality and whether you need to get right down to business in an email, or whether you can lead with something like, "Hey, Happy New Year to you."

Communicating according to the preferences of your buyer is an important piece to the puzzle because if you can't reach them, you can't show them that you can solve their problem.

Get on the Buyer's Radar

Next, a challenge for salespeople, in general, is earning your buyer's trust. If you are reaching out to a prospect through a cold call or message not only do you need to address their WIIFM but you also have to let them know why they should listen to you. However, you can remove that obstacle by getting on your prospect's radar before reaching out to them.

How? Become visible to them on social media. For example, on LinkedIn, you can add them and post regularly, comment on something that they've shared, tag or mention them in something that's relevant. Or if it's a discussion they could contribute to, say, "Hey, I'd love to get your input on this idea because I know this is an area of your expertise."

Getting on a prospect's radar turns a cold call or message into a warm lead.

Address the Pain Points

Last but not least, once you have done all the pre-work above and are ready to reach out to the buyer, you need to speak to their pain points and show them what's in it for them.

As far as the content, the subject line needs to read like an advertising headline. Capture their attention by talking about something that's either very personal for them or a problem that you know they are trying to solve. It may be a generic problem, like more sales conversations, or it could be something specific like, "Hey, I noticed that your CEO was talking about X, Y, Z. I have some ideas to help you in those areas."

As for the message, explain that you can help and include a call to action. You don't want to go into too much detail here but you should direct them to contact you to learn more.

Here's an example:

"A lot of clients that we talk to have no unified Linkedin strategy. We found that barely 50% of sales professionals make quota. Your team may or may not be facing that, but I'd love to share some ideas with you on how our clients have been able to generate more sales conversations, which of course

means that more of their sales team is making quota, and everyone's happy. Are you available next Monday at 9:00, the following Monday at 12:00, or the following Monday at 4:00? Or if it's easier, here's the link to my calendar, pick a time that's convenient for you."

This message is short, addresses the main pain point, and drives the desired action.

Give Your Buyers What They Want

There you have it. Above all else, to be successful in sales you have to tune into the radio station everyone is on; WIIFM. Answer what is in it for your customers. It's not about you, a product, or a service. It's about how your solution, whatever it is, will solve a problem your buyer is currently facing. You can discover your buyer's WIIFM by understanding the problems people in their position commonly face and by researching their specific company and role. Next, to effectively reach them, figure out their communication preferences, get on their radar, and craft an effective message that drives action. In doing so, you can optimize your sales process and offer high value solutions your buyers truly appreciate.

Want to learn more from Stan Robinson Jr.? Follow him on:
LinkedIn: linkedin.com/in/stanrobinson
Twitter: @stanrobinson

#13 The Silver Bullet Is Talk Time

LAUREN BAILEY

"You listen to sales calls and it's all about the rep and what they want. What I want to say to those people is, 'Good for you buddy but call your grandma because I don't give a damn.'"

ABOUT LAUREN BAILEY:

As the Founder and President of Factor 8, the Founder of #GirlsClub, and an official contributor on Sales Hacker, Inc., Lauren Bailey is on a mission to help people feel more successful at work.

Lauren spent almost 20 years launching and leading inside sales organizations around the world. During that time, she recognized that sales reps and managers were often unprepared to sell over the phone. She learned that by properly preparing people for their roles, they became more confident which transformed careers, departments, companies, and lives. As a result, Factor 8 was born in July of 2008.

Now, the company has grown into an award-winning front-line sales digital training program that specializes in phone, inside and digital sales. It's built by sales leaders, 100% results-focused, and has a client base including industry-leading companies like GoDaddy, ADP, ZipRecruiter, and Staples.

#GirlsClub is Lauren's second business and a passion project which offers a 9-month training and mentoring program for women. She knows first-hand what it's like to feel unprepared and isolated in front-line management, so she offers a support system to help. The aim is to change the face of sales leadership by helping women gain the skills, confidence, and encouragement they need to advance.

Voted one of the "Top 25 Most Influential Leaders in Inside Sales," "Top 25 Sales Coaches." and "Top 35 Most Influential Women in Sales," Lauren is known as a true leader and a pioneer. She is a professional who has gained the admiration of the entire inside sales community and is said to have energy, smarts, presence, original thought, and repeated success.

Back in my single days, I was calling a guy I had a crush on who was in one of my classes. I looked down and to my horror, I had been talking for three minutes into his voicemail. I hung up and asked myself, "Did I really just tell Steve that I was single over a voicemail. Did that actually just happen?" It was a horrible voicemail and I cringe to this day. I didn't have a plan and was just winging it. Unfortunately, many sales reps today are doing the equivalent in their sales calls. They go in without the knowledge they need to be successful and without understanding that the game has changed.

Coffee's Not For Closers Anymore

Coffee can't be for closers anymore because, in digital sales, 90% of your calls are going to go to voicemail. It's hard to get people on the phone, it's hard to keep them on the phone, and it's nearly impossible to get them to call you back. But nothing really happens until you have a conversation. We can play the sales versus marketing game all day long and, sure, marketing is going to brand you but nobody is going to buy something until you actually talk with them. So if you want to get better results, you need to focus on getting into more conversations. You need more talk time.

HOW DO YOU GET MORE TALK TIME?

Here are three ways you can increase your talk time.

Leave Better Voicemails

First, your voicemails need to be on point. No three-minute babble fests. Leaving an effective voicemail is the simplest skill but half of the reps today aren't even leaving them at all. You can make a few small tweaks and drastically improve your results. I had a client the other week go from getting no callbacks to getting 27 after my online voicemail course.

The number one trick? Never sell over a voice message. Why the hell would they call you back? People don't want to be sold to. Instead, the purpose of your voicemail is to leave a brand impression and to get a callback. If it takes seven brand touches to get someone to buy something, each voicemail should be a brand touch. That's it.

Now, I've left my share of bad voicemails. I think we all have. The truth is, if you don't think about it, take a good training, and work really hard to craft a fantastic voicemail, you're going to leave a shitty one. So take the time to develop an effective voicemail and don't stop until you start getting more callbacks.

Optimize Your Introduction

Second, you need to optimize your introduction when you get a prospect on the phone. 95% of the intros out there suck and, no, your intro should not be your value prop. All that does is scream sales call. Instead, you want to lead with value to get them to lean-in to you and talk right away.

What is value?

Think about what is in it for them. People care about the same things all the time. They want more time, more money, less risk, more happiness, less stress, etc. Speak to something they will care about right off the bat that your product or service will give them. Then, you need to ask them a question tailored specifically to them and that value.

For example, "Hi this is Lauren from (company name) and my goal is to see if I can help you get a little bit more return on your investment from your leads. Are you buying leads today?"

They won't really be listening anyway but you need to tell them something that perks their ear enough so that they stop answering their email, tune in, and answer your question. The goal is to get them talking.

Overcome the Brush Off

The third and final tip is to get really good at overcoming the brush off. The brush off is not an objection. An objection you can actually refute, it comes later in the sales process, and it's informed. A brush off is basically "Piss off I'm busy." It is not "I don't like your product." They don't even know who you are but want you to go away because they are busy. You need to overcome that and not take that personally.

Now to ace these, I recommend you write your own script and continue to fine-tune it over time. Don't take anyone else's. Additionally, focus completely on your prospect, it's not about you. Remember, SWIFT (So, What's In It For Them?). Further, keep your voicemails and intros short, less than 10 seconds. And always, always, deliver your messages with personality. Be you!

These three super simple skills can double or triple your talk time leading to more conversations and more sales. That is the challenge in today's world where people don't like to be on the phone. The silver bullet is to become an expert on getting people to talk to you.

Want to learn more from Lauren Bailey? Follow her on:
Website: factor8.com/our-services/sales-bar
FREE ONLINE TRAINING
LinkedIn: linkedin.com/in/insidesalesadvisor

#14 Every Good Product Needs to Solve a Real Problem

GARRETT GRELLER

"No one can replicate a story that's authentic and true."

ABOUT GARRETT GRELLER:

Garrett Greller is the Co-Founder of Uncle Bud's Hemp. The company offers a collection of pain relief, skincare, sun care, personal care, and pet care products. He attended Indiana University from 2014 to 2016 and earned his Bachelor's degree in Creative Advertising and New Media Marketing.

The founding of Uncle Bud's Hemp originated with a problem Garrett faced as a teen—at just 16 he was diagnosed with arthritis. He tried a variety of medicines to relieve his pain, but nothing worked. Eventually, he experimented with hemp oil from a dispensary and found that it greatly reduced his pain without any negative side effects. However, shortly after finding this helpful solution, he moved to Indiana for college where the oil was illegal. Garrett and his Dad decided they wanted to make their own legal hemp product for pain relief. They knew a manufacturer and began getting samples. Garrett tested everything on himself and found one that worked great. After experiencing relief from his chronic pain, he wanted to share his solution with others. It was then that Uncle Bud's Hemp was born. While it was not smooth sailing to get Uncle Bud's off the ground, it is now sold in every Wal-Mart nationwide and has been picked up by GNC, Amazon, Urban Outfitters, Kroger, Target, Ace Hardware, Big 5, and Vitacost. Through this roller-coaster journey, Garrett has learned a lifetime of business secrets in just a few short years.

I'm relatively new to the business scene. My father and I started this business when I was halfway through college. I always say it has been a great learning experience, like going to graduate school but times 10. I am hands-on and I love what I'm doing so it does not even feel like work.

The mission of Uncle Bud's as a company is very personal to me because it was also my mission. I believe that the core reason the company is so successful is because it has a quality product that solves a real problem many people face. The only reason I took the product to market was because it worked so well for me, which leads me to my sales secret...

My top sales secret is that you have to have a product that works and an authentic story to show how it solves a real problem.

A Good Product and a True Story

There is a lot of BS in the market these days. Consumers are bombarded with sales messages and products. However, Uncle Bud's has been able to stand out from its competition and fly off the shelves. But why?

Well, in the beginning, I was desperate to find a solution to my pain. I was a teenager at the time so I didn't want to be taking pain meds that would knock me out or cause other health problems. However, I was in so much pain that I couldn't bear day-to-day life without a remedy.

The hemp oil my Dad and I had manufactured was a miracle solution for me and I honestly wanted it to help as many people as possible with it. To get the word out, I shared my story. When other people heard my story and could try the product without a huge investment, many did. When they did, it worked for them too which resulted in referrals and repeat customers.

I see many companies with stories but the products don't live up to them so they lose customers after the first purchase. The key is identifying a problem, finding a true solution, and sharing a story that illustrates the realistic results people can expect. The better your product is at solving the problem, the better you will position yourself.

HOW TO CREATE A GOOD PRODUCT WITH AN AUTHENTIC STORY

So what can you do to create a good product with an authentic story? Here's my advice.

Identify a Problem

The world is full of problems, which is usually a bad thing, but those problems create opportunities for people to step in and solve. As an entrepreneur or salesperson, before you can sell anything, you need to know what problem your product or service is solving. In my case, many people were suffering from chronic pain and couldn't find a natural, chemical-free remedy that worked.

If you are wanting to start a business venture, look for a real problem you can solve for people. If you are in sales, understand the pain points of your customers. Do whatever you can to deeply understand their position whether it is interviews, site visits, or research. The primary focus shouldn't be on money but providing true value and relief in some way.

Create a True Solution

When I had to move to Indiana and couldn't bring the hemp oil, I was in a state of panic. I didn't want to go back to living in pain or taking expensive injectables or anti-inflammatory pills. I experienced the problem first-hand and needed a solution. In my case, the solution was a legal product that had the healing powers of hemp.

We didn't cut corners and we weren't doing it for profitability. We were in search of a true solution to the problem. I believe by making this the primary focus, you will be on a path to success. In sales, you need to focus on how the product or service solves the problem for your customers. Illustrate the benefits emotionally, physically, economically, etc. The key takeaway is that it has to be a true solution.

Tell an Authentic Story

The great thing about having a real solution to a real problem is that the testimonials roll in. People get excited when something works and relieves them from the stress or pain of a previous problem. I was ecstatic when we made a product that worked and felt bad not sharing it.

As Uncle Bud's grew and made it into Wal-Mart, we approached Toni Braxton with the product. She had been suffering from Lupus so we sent her our products and let them speak for themselves. After using them, she agreed to come on board as a brand ambassador to share her story.

Toni's testimonial and presence have been a powerful backing of our brand. The thing is, she had never worked with brands before and wasn't interested in a sponsorship or anything but she believed in the product.

When you have a good product that solves a real problem, you get an authentic story by default, and often many of them. Use those stories to strengthen your brand.

Don't Give Up

The last thing I'll add to my secret is not to give up. When you know your solution is good and can help people—keep at it. We had several obstacles along the way which were very discouraging. First, when Indiegogo shut down our campaign after racking up about $14,000 in pre- orders, we were extremely deflated. Second, when we were bringing in consistent sales to pay the bills but not making much of a profit, I was ready to let Uncle Bud's be a side gig while I pursued something else. But when you have a good product and story, not only do people want to buy it, use it, and share it, people higher up in the food chain want to invest in it and become a part of it. So if you know you have something good, be persistent, find workarounds when you hit obstacles, and network to find out who may be able to help you get to the next level.

Want to learn more from Garrett Greller? Follow him on: LinkedIn: linkedin.com/in/garrett-greller-a3929310a/

#15 Leave It in the Bag

BOB PERKINS

"All the tech that can help us is really good,
but people still buy from people."

ABOUT BOB PERKINS:

Bob is the Founder & Chairman of AA-ISP (American Association of Inside Sales Professionals).

He is a nationally-recognized Inside Sales Innovator with extensive executive experience building and leading highly successful inside sales organizations.

His 25 years of Inside Sales experience includes leading sales teams at Unisys, Silicon Graphics, Grid Systems, UnitedHealth Group, and Merrill Corporation.

Bob is now a popular keynote speaker nationwide and also has a widely popular video channel called Inside Sales Studio where he discusses trends and tactics relevant to Inside Sales Leaders and today's digital transformation.

Bob sees a tremendous opportunity, both in and outside the US, to bring respect and attention to the beautiful and wonderful profession we call inside sales, and he is on a mission to do so with AA-ISP.

Those who know Bob say that he is leading the way in elevating the role of what inside sales professionals do for businesses. He is known as a class act, an effective and efficient leader, an asset wherever he goes, and a great example to follow.

I worked with a lady named Patty while selling computers at Grid Systems and she won a $1.5 million deal with Aetna. She tells the story of going into the office of the Senior VP of field sales who was considering outfitting Aetna's salesforce with laptops. She had a bag, like a large briefcase, and she kept the laptop in it. Throughout the meeting, the VP kept peaking over the desk and looking at her bag. They were talking about his team's needs and software and all but he was getting antsy. He finally said, "Well are you going to show it to me?" And she goes, "Well I can, sure." The rest is history.

Leave It in the Bag

The moral of Patty's story and my top sales secret is to discover, build rapport, and find the pain points before you pitch. Leave it all in the bag. How many sales reps do you know that would lead with the shiny new laptop and its specs? To this day, if I'm talking to a sponsor or prospect of some sort, I literally have to say in my head, don't pitch. Hold off. Find out as much as you possibly can through questioning. Let the anticipation build to the point where they are asking you to see your solution.

Why Leave It in the Bag?

Why should you leave it in the bag? Because you can't properly present a solution without fully understanding the problem you're going to solve. At Merril Corp., we would do demos and everyone would sound the same. We had a checklist of things to talk about. I say throw the checklist away and talk about what is most important to the person in front of you. Spend the time digging into the discovery, build rapport, and get your prospect talking. Doing so will help them feel understood and will empower you to offer a personalized solution that they won't want to refuse.

How-to Leave It in the Bag

When Patty walked into that VP's office, she had a plan. Although the laptop she had was flashy and impressive on its own, she wasn't going to use that. She smartly put the business's needs first. She opened up a conversation to fully understand why the field sales reps needed the computers and how they would generate value for the business. She created a value proposition that ran much deeper than a good-looking computer.

You can do the same by setting the right intentions before your conversations. Further, here are some tips and practices that can help you during your interactions.

Ask Open-Ended Questions

First, you have to get the person talking and the best way to do that is by naturally asking open-ended questions. For example, questions like:

Can you describe...?

Can you walk me through what a typical...?

Can you paint me a picture of...?

How do your clients react to...? You don't want to be rapid firing question after question but should use open-ended questions to inspire conversations. Don't stress sticking to a script. One way you can practice open-ended questions is to sit in a circle with six or seven other reps and do a role play. Let's say you've released a product recently, you would pretend you're talking to the VP and each rep has to ask open-ended questions to discover their needs. If a rep asks a closed-ended question, they get buzzed and get kicked out. The last person standing wins.

The purpose of this drill is to uncover questions and topics you may have never thought about, to strengthen your ability to ask open-ended questions and to remind you that when you think you have covered everything, there is always one more question you could ask.

Track Buzzwords

When listening to or researching your prospects, take notes on how they talk about their problems. Write down the words they use, which I call buzzwords. So if you're a sales trainer and someone says, "Hey, we really need to train our people on discovery because when they discover they find out that most prospects are not compliant with regulations and our product helps them become compliant."

You would write down regulations and compliance, and would mention these words when eventually 'opening the bag." Why? They are most important to the prospect and are going to resonate deeply with them. It helps you speak their language and ties your product directly to their needs.

Be Authentic

Finally, good sales is based on mutual respect and trust. Honesty and authenticity always. I had a salesperson come into my home recently because we wanted tile in a couple of rooms and he asked us, "Are you sure you want tile?" We said, "We think so." And he said, "Well, let me tell you a few reasons you might not." He was honest, despite the benefits in it for him if we went with the tile, and he earned our trust and loyalty. During the discovery process, it's important to make a real connection, be honest, and truly work on understanding how you can provide value to the person in front of you.

And a note for sales managers—trust is the glue that keeps people motivated and engaged. Without trust, your reps are going to tighten up and won't perform. To build a trusting relationship, talk about something unrelated to work with each rep each day. Take them to lunch. Be vulnerable. Admit when you make a mistake. Lead by example. And if you're going to ask someone to do something, be willing to do it yourself.

Being successful in sales is all about the individual. It's the person. It takes empathy, guts, passion, perseverance, follow-through, follow-up, finding the pain, and finally meeting the needs. All the tech that can help us is really good, but people still buy from people. In your next sales pitch, remember sales discovery is key. Deliver world-class service and win the deal by asking open-ended questions, keeping track of buzz words, staying true to yourself, and leaving it in the bag.

**Want to learn more from Bob Perkins? Follow him on:
LinkedIn: linkedin.com/in/perkinsbob
AISP Website: aa-isp.org**

#16 The Magic of Selling

DAVE KURLAN

"You don't have to demo anything. You don't have to present anything, and you don't have to show anything or propose anything or quote anything. You just have to make people want to buy from you."

ABOUT DAVE KURLAN:

Dave Kurlan is a sales performance expert, writer of an award-winning blog, top-rated keynote speaker, best-selling author, radio show host, successful entrepreneur, and sales development industry pioneer.

He's the founder and CEO of Objective Management Group (OMG), which is an industry leader in sales assessments and sales force evaluations. OMG was named the top sales assessment tool for the past decade. Dave is also the CEO of Kurlan & Associates, a leading sales leadership development and training firm. His two companies have appeared several times on the Inc. 5000.

In the authorship realm, Dave has written Mindless Selling, Understanding the Sales Force, and the best-seller, *Baseline Selling: How to Become a Sales Superstar by Using What You Already Know About the Game of Baseball.*

He has received countless honors and awards throughout his career including being inducted into the Sales and Marketing Hall of Fame. He's also been named a "Top 50 Influencer" by Top Sales World five times and a "Top 10 Trainer" by The National Sales Training Association.

Dave is known to be a thought-leader and true sales pioneer. His tools and analytics from the Objective Management Group are said to create value and deliver insights that profoundly impact how companies hire and onboard new salespeople. Clients say he is brilliant and always at the forefront of the sales profession.

After I graduated high school, I was failing college and needed to find something else to do. The only job I had had up until that point was doing tennis court maintenance. So I went on a job interview, which ended up being a recruiting class to sell Cutco knives. At that point in my life, I was antisocial and petrified of people. I mean, if I were ever at an event with people, I'd be in the corner hoping nobody came up and spoke to me. I walked out of the room at the end of the little recruiting event, positive that I was the worst possible fit for that job. However, as I headed down the stairs, there was a voice inside of me telling me to go back. I made myself turn around and forced myself to take the job selling knives.

I started the job and managed to hang in there for three years. In fact, I was so good at selling knives that I was a sales manager within three months. That's when I thought, "Maybe I can make a career out of something like this."

I set a goal when I was 18 that by the time I was 30, I would be in some kind of sales consulting business. Sure enough, I made the goal come true. Now, with over five decades of sales experience, I'm here to share my top sales secret.

Make Magic Happen
With Strategic Summaries

Many salespeople can listen and ask questions to identify the problems, consequences, costs, and compelling reasons why someone would buy. However, hardly anyone can summarize what they heard in a way that differentiates them from every other salesperson. Few can create the kind of urgency that causes prospects to want to do business on the spot.

My secret is the ability to succinctly summarize what I hear and tie it up in a bow so that that other person goes, "Yes. That's it. You get it. Can you help me?" That is the magic of selling.

HOW TO USE STRATEGIC
SUMMARIES TO CLOSE SALES

Here's how you can use strategic summaries in a way that moves your prospects to buy from you more often.

Listen and Ask Questions

To sell something, you have to uncover a compelling reason a prospect should buy. But to find that out, you have to talk with them and get to know them. You need to get them to open up and share things about themselves that they don't share with everyone. This requires listening carefully, being likable, and asking good, timely questions.

Don't skip ahead, don't get distracted. Stay focused on the client and learn about them. Keep listening and asking questions until you discover why they need your product or service. Without uncovering a compelling reason to buy, you can't create urgency, and if you don't create urgency, you can only get a prospect as far as, "This is nice to have," and not to, "I must have this, and I must get it from you."

1) Summarize Your Findings

Once you uncover the person's reason to buy now, it's time to summarize your findings to them. Your summary should include four parts:

2) Identify the Prospect's Problem/Goal

Use the personal details you have gathered from your prospect to summarize their goal or problem. It should reveal to them that you understand their situation and should serve as an external confirmation of their needs.

3) Address the Urgency To Solve/Reach It Soon

Identify why it is important that the person takes action now.

4) Share the Emotional Consequence of Not Doing So

Include an emotional reason that the person needs to buy now and why it is important to do so. This is often the consequence of not being able to do something, how it impacts them personally, how bothersome it might be, and what they need to do about it.

6) Use the Inoffensive Close

The close of the summary shouldn't be a hard sell. I call it the 'Inoffensive' close.' You create a strong case so the prospect wants your help to solve their problem and you can simply ask, "Can I help you?"

Let's look at an example. If a business development company called me trying to gain me as a client, a good salesperson would uncover that my company has analyzed 1.8 million salespeople but I aim to reach 14 million. They might find that I am retiring soon and want to achieve this before I do. In that case, the summary would sound like this:

"So you're at 1.8, Dave. Your goal is to go to 14 million, and you're running out of time. There are only seven more years before you want to retire. If you don't hit that 14 million in seven years, the legacy you want to have left will evaporate. Do you want my help?"

It can be as simple as that.

Practice

Delivering effective sales summaries, overcoming objections, and closing sales take practice. I recommend investing in personal development and using role-playing regularly.

Personal development: You can read books. You can read blogs. You can watch videos. You can listen to audios, but it's all knowledge. You've got to get engaged in actual training and get coached to improve. If your company isn't willing to pay for that, dig into your pockets and do what every other professional does and invest in professional development.

Role-play: Only through properly guided role-play do salespeople get a constant diet of what their conversations need to sound like. I encourage salespeople to role-play with a colleague for 30 minutes per day.

In summary, while the key to being successful in sales can be broken down into 21 sales competencies, I think a major factor is a strategic and carefully planned summary. First, you have to listen and ask good questions to get the information you need. Then, you craft your summary by identifying the person's goal/problem, addressing the urgency, sharing emotional consequences of inaction, and using the inoffensive close. Lastly, fine-tune your summary pitch with lots of ongoing practice and personal development.

Want to learn more from Dave Kurlan? Follow him on:
Blog: omghub.com
Email: DKurlan@kurlanassociates.com
if you're interested in sales development,
or DKurlan@objectivemanagement.com
if you're interested in assessments or selling assessments.
LinkedIn: linkedin.com/in/davekurlan

#17 Don't Overcome Objections, Block Them

VICTOR ANTONIO

"If you can use storytelling, present your product, and block objections at the same time, that is the trifecta of the ultimate presentation."

ABOUT VICTOR ANTONIO:

Author, speaker, and business consultant, Victor Antonio has built a 20-year career as a top sales executive and CEO of the high-tech company, Force, Inc.

He has delivered sales motivation keynotes and conducted sales workshops in Europe, Asia, Latin America, UAE, Australia, South Africa, and the Middle East. Victor has shared the big stage with some of the top business speakers in the nation including Rudy Giuliani, Paul Otellini (CEO of Intel), John May (CEO of FedEx Kinkos), Daymond John (Shark Tank), and many other top business speakers.

He has also published three books on Amazon including Sales Ex Machina: *How Artificial Intelligence (AI) is Changing the World of Selling, Sales Models: 50 Models for Effective Selling*, and *The Greatest Gift*. Those who know Victor say he is the quintessential sales teacher. No matter what industry you're in, he will give you the formula to increase your bottom line. His keynotes are known for being "eye-openers," providing new insights and tactics attendees can implement when they return home.

I believe if you understand how people buy, or why they don't buy, you can sell to them more effectively. And I have a strategy for it. If you learn this one strategy, you'll get a 10% close rate increase—easy.

I Don't Need to Overcome Objections, I Need to Block Them

Let me tell you the story of how it came about. A few years ago, a company calls me up and says, "Hey Victor, we sell a software product with $3,000 and $6,000 tiers. We have six trainers and we are looking for a seventh trainer."

I said, "Okay cool. How much do your trainers make?" The guy tells me the number and I couldn't believe it. It was that high. I was skeptical so I said I'd think about it and call him back. A week later he followed up and said he'd fly me down to Orlando to come to a conference, see the training, go to dinner, and decide if I was interested. I agreed and flew down.

I sat in the back and watched as the trainer was doing his whole presentation. At the end of the day, he closed half the room on the $6,000 product. I asked the guy, "How much money did he make?" Once he told me, I was in.

After about a month of studying, they sent me down to Mississippi. They figured I couldn't do a lot of damage down there if you know what I mean. So at the end of the day, I closed about 17% of the room and I walked out of there with about $5,000. I was thinking it wasn't bad for my first time but they were like, "No that is bad. We closed 17% of the room and our minimum is 33%." After that, I was like "Oh Crap!" So for the next few months, I was struggling. I'd get to 24%, then go back down to 20%, then back down to 17%. I just wasn't getting it.

Finally, we were doing an event in California with 300 or 400 people and they said, "We're going to send out the big gun. His name is Clint. He's the guy that knows how to do this. He's going to watch and provide the necessary feedback." So he watches me and after the first session, he comes up to me and says, "I know what you're doing wrong. You've got to understand that people in the audience have objections in their heads that they aren't going to voice and you've got to take those objections and tie them down." I asked, "How?" And he just said, "Just tie them down, Victor." Well, I didn't know how to do that but was going to find out.

After that, I was reading a book on how people buy and it hit me, and it has become my number one sales secret. I don't need to overcome objections, I need to block them before they even come out.

HOW TO BLOCK OBJECTIONS

Here's how you block objections with my response block system.

Step 1: Raise the Objection

If someone raises an objection, they've taken a position they are likely not going to change. But if you raise it first, you still control it.

For example, if a common objection in my audience is, "This looks a little complicated, Victor." I need to raise that before anyone says it. If they say it first, I'm screwed. So I'll say something like this from the front of the room, "Now, some of you might be thinking this is really hard to use. And you might be a technophobe, you're just afraid of technology. And if that's you, I want you to pay attention."

So what did I just do? I raised the objection about being a technophobe. Never raise an objection that isn't there but figure out what the most common objections are, and plan how you can raise them in your presentation.

Step 2: Offer to Resolve It

The next step is for you to offer to resolve the objection. For example, after raising the objection about being a technophobe, I could say, "If I could show you how to use this technology, with a couple of simple moves here and there, would you be open to that?" After this, most people will be nodding their heads yes.

Step 3: Demo Something

Third, you demo something.

In this stage, continuing with the example above, I could do the demo and say, "Let me just show you something, how easy this is to use. Point-click. Drag-drop." Whatever I show, that's the demo. I'm showing how simple it is.

Step 4: Tie-Down the Objection

Lastly, here's the tie-down. Remember, I am tying down, not the sale, but the objection. What's the objection? In this case, the product is too difficult to use. After the demo, I would say something like, "Based on what I've shown you, do you think with a little practice and our support that you can do it?" And I would wait for the verbal yes. Once they say yes, they have verbally committed to overcoming that objection and it's successfully blocked.

Here is what is powerful about that. Most people have five to seven objections about why they don't want to buy. But if you can block the objections consistently, let's say, during the 30 to 40 minutes you're talking, you can feel the resistance going down. So I went from an average close rate of 20%—30% to 50%—60% and sometimes it went even higher. That made me more money than I care to admit.

I wrote a book on this tactic called Response Block Selling. The book has 22 scripts for 22 common objections. If you can sequence those throughout your presentation because you know what the objections are and know how to block them, I'm telling you, you will feel the resistance go down and you will close more deals. And if you can use storytelling, present your product, and block objections at the same time, that is the trifecta of the ultimate presentation.

Want to learn more from Victor Antonio? Follow him on:
Website: victorantonio.com
LinkedIn: linkedin.com/in/victorantonio
Courses: salesvelocityacademy.com

#18 Keep It Real

TAMI MCQUEEN

"Ask questions and listen with the intent to understand, not with the intent to respond."

ABOUT TAMI MCQUEEN:

Tami is the Co-Founder of 31south, a full-service marketing and advertising agency that offers creative solutions for its customers.

Prior to starting her own agency, Tami was part of the SalesLoft team, one of the fastest- growing B2B SaaS Startups in the U.S. She became the Director of Marketing in 2014 and was the FIRST marketing hire. By the time she left the company in 2017, it was valued at over $50 million.

Tami is a former NCAA Division 1 collegiate tennis player and all-Intercollegiate Tennis Association Scholar-Athlete. She earned her B.S. in Advertising and M.S. in Mass Communication from Murray State University.

She serves on the executive board for the Kula Project and the Global Conservation Corps, which is an advocate for rhino conservation in Southern Africa and drives the empowerment of women-led, business initiatives through mentorship programs. Further, Tami led the Global Social Strategy at Women Who Code—the largest and most active community for technical women in the world.

Colleagues of Tami say she is a high-energy, creative problem-solver with a unique outlook. Her personable spirit is said to evoke confidence and trust and she is said to be a "dream come true in the marketing world."

When I was growing up, I would set up a little plastic table on my parent's driveway with my boombox and would hit tennis balls against the garage door. When I was tired of tennis, I'd sit at the table and talk with people as they walked by my driveway. I had one cassette tape at the time and it was Michael Jackson's 'Bad' album. I'd say, "Hey, you've got to listen to a song. I'll charge you 50 cents to listen to a song and play one round of tennis." My upsell was if they wanted to dance, that would be an extra fee. That was the beginning of my sales career right there on that driveway.

Now, many years later, with over a decade of strategic experience in B2B and B2C markets, I've learned a lot. However, I would say the secret to my success in sales and marketing starts with a very basic approach that is simple, yet often missed. The thing is, you have to keep it real, treat prospects like people, and put yourself in their shoes.

Be Human and Have Empathy in Your Interactions

If you look at most B2C brands, they have completely humanized communications. They're genuine and transparent. However, most B2B brands are still very formal. They follow a playbook to check off the boxes that need to be checked. This approach creates distance between companies and their clients.

My success has been largely due to humanizing my communications in B2B and B2C but also having empathy. By putting those two together you get the ultimate recipe for success whether you are in a business transaction or building rapport in a new industry.

HOW TO HUMANIZE YOUR COMMUNICATION TO MAXIMIZE SALES

How can you humanize your communications and show true empathy? Here are six of my best practices.

Get Personal

The first step is to get to know prospects and customers like they are regular people in your life. Instead of sending an email based on, "Day 1 email," and a call based on "Day 2 call," etc., really try to understand what it is that makes them tick. What is their dog's name? When is their kid's birthday? What do they support? How do your past experiences resonate with them? You need to understand what their issues and problems are and who they are as a person.

Listen to Understand, Not to Respond

Next, when having conversations, listen to understand the message that the other person is conveying instead of thinking about your follow-up questions. Be open to the conversation going in an unpredicted direction based on the reality of your prospect's situation.

Approaching conversations with this intention enables you to work collaboratively with your prospects or clients. It allows you to understand what it is that they're looking to accomplish and achieve, and what their visions are. This is much more effective than just selling what your product does or what it can do. Listen and learn how you can help the prospect truly solve their problem or challenge.

Follow-Up Conversations With Key Takeaways

After conversations, it's important to follow-up to confirm your key takeaways. A lot of times, assumptions get us into trouble. We think we heard one thing or assume the direction of the conversation and it's really another. I recommend reaching out with a message such as, "This is what I understood from our conversation. Is that what you took away as well?" This confirms you are both on the same page.

Be Transparent About Your Goals

Many people feel they can't put their intentions out there in sales. I say be honest and open about your goals from square one. You need to know exactly why you are communicating with a person and lay it all out for them. There doesn't need to be any hidden agenda. For example, you can say, "Look, this is what I want to accomplish. This is what I'm here to accomplish. Does that align with some of your objectives and what your vision is? If not, let's try and level those and bring us back into the middle of where we are both on the same path to success."

If an opportunity does not work out, it's okay to say, "Okay this is not an opportunity we're going to be working together on, but I'd love to stay in touch and work with you in the future." You never know when your goals will align or who they know that might need your help.

Own Your Shortcomings, You're Human Too!

No human knows everything and it shows your authenticity and humanity when you own your shortcomings. I've learned to own my mistakes instead of trying to work around them. If something goes awry, just say, "Look, I messed up. I'm sorry. I forgot about the meeting. I didn't send the right thing. I'm sorry, that was my mistake entirely." Don't be afraid to say, "Look, I'm really not an expert in that but I know someone on the team who is. Let me talk with them and, either, I'll bring them into the conversation or we can follow up on that at a later stage."

Be real about who you are, including your flaws and your strengths. This will help to establish trust and credibility.

Take an Omnichannel Approach

Next, real human interactions aren't restricted to one channel. You connect with family and friends in person, at events, over the phone, through text, on social media, via email, etc. The same goes for prospects and customers. You shouldn't only be visible in their email inbox. Make a more impactful impression by using the many channels available to us all, including online and offline options.

For example, when I'm going to an industry event, I start by identifying who is attending that I want to connect with from potential investors to prospects to hires. Then I think about what kind of periphery event I can host to capitalize on the event. A happy hour? An exclusive dinner with a tiny curated group of people. I aim to create an experience that people are going to be moved to share and they're not going to easily forget. Additionally, I'll reach out to set up meetings with other attendees who I'd like to speak with. It's also really important to understand what the key sessions are that you want to attend. Reach out to them ahead of time on social and say, "Hey, I'm really looking forward to attending your presentation at the event. I want to know about 'X, Y, Z,'" whatever it is that you're talking about. Then, go to the session, sit in the front row, take a photo, and tweet about it.

After the session, go up and say something to them. For example, "Hey, I really appreciated that," and ask any follow-up questions you have. Then, when you get back into the office, write an article about why it was impactful for you, share it on LinkedIn, and tag that person. Thank them for being willing to share such valuable insights with you.

This kind of omnichannel approach makes a memorable impact, puts a face to a name, and facilitates a real human connection. Plus, it helps you to gain authority and recognition in your industry.

Support Others in Your Industry

Lastly, be a valuable member of your industry who helps to move the whole forward. Give a lot of your time for free. Sit on panels for free. Create helpful free content. Talk in the early days for free, and just be willing to help people.

Over the years, I've sat down for coffee with many different folks that were, either, in an early stage in their career, looking to grow, or in different industries. I not only shared a lot of the insight about the company or what I was doing but listened to where they were at too.

I attribute a lot of the success that we've had at 31South to being present, helping other people, and doing what we can to be helpful. Today, many of the folks who I met years ago are doing incredible things in the world and I'm able to reach out to them now and learn from their successes.

In summary, above all else, in all sales and marketing, you have to humanize your communications and be truly empathetic. Get personal, ask questions with the intent to understand, follow up to ensure your understanding is correct, own who you are, use multiple channels to connect with people, and give back. These can help you to maximize your success in your career.

Want to learn more from Tami McQueen? Follow her on:
LinkedIn: linkedin.com/in/tamimcqueen
Twitter: @localatlast

#19 Certainty Sells

JORDAN BELFORT

"Everything changes when you are in control."

ABOUT JORDAN BELFORT:

Jordan Belfort is a world-renowned sales trainer, a best-selling author, an entrepreneur, and a motivational speaker whose life today represents the ultimate redemption story.

After barely surviving his rise and fall as an American entrepreneurial icon, he is now thirteen years-sober and assisting individuals and organizations in breaking through whatever barriers hold them back from achieving success. Whether speaking to a room full of hard-charging salespeople or to a jam-packed convention center filled with 'everyday people,' Belfort's teachings captivate and inspire his audiences.

In the 1990s, Jordan built one of the most dynamic and successful sales organizations in Wall Street history. To this day, his proprietary sales-training techniques and daily motivational speeches are the 'stuff of legend'— earning him a reputation as a 'motivator without peer.'

He's acted as a consultant to more than 50 public companies and has been written about in virtually every major newspaper and magazine in the world, including The New York Times, The Wall Street Journal, the Los Angeles Times, the Herald Tribune, Forbes, BusinessWeek, Paris Match, and Rolling Stone. Further, his life story was turned into a major motion picture by Warner Brothers, directed by Martin Scorsese with Leonardo DiCaprio playing the role of Belfort.

Jordan Belfort's two best-selling books have been published in 22 countries and translated into 18 different languages. Additionally, he is a frequent guest-commentator on CNN, CNBC, Headlines News, and the BBC.

People who have attended Jordan's training say his Straight Line selling techniques are quite simply the best out there— a surefire way to increase your sales, grow your business, and influence others. He is known as someone who genuinely believes in sharing his knowledge to help others, and using it to make the world better.

Really good salespeople sell the same fucking way every time. It's no different than a professional safecracker who walks up to a safe and goes to pick a three-number lock. Does he go for the third number first? No, that won't work. He goes for the first number first, click. Then the second number second, the third number third, and pulls down the handle.

If it opens, he closes the deal. If it doesn't open, he goes back and does the first number again, the second number, and the third number. If it still doesn't work, it may be one of those fancy safes that have five numbers. Human beings also have up to five numbers in their combinations. Once you understand that there are these distinctive elements that must line up in every sale, you'll see every sale is the same and there is a system to closing them all. An Epiphany Catapults Stratton Oakmont.

Towards the beginning of my career, I discovered the untapped niche of selling $5 to $10 stocks to the richest 1%, something no one had tried at the time. I tested it myself with my partner Danny Porush and we were killing it, so I decided to bring on some other kids and teach them. I was giving regular training, teaching them how to overcome objections, and had a whole system in place, but none of them were closing. We were calling the same people, selling the same stocks, and using the same scripts, but we were closing and they weren't. I went on a quest to figure out why. I started reading every book I could find and went to training events and seminars across the country.

After my 30-day quest, I came back and the guys were all depressed. They weren't making any money and wanted to go back to the penny market which was more painful than I could bear. I called a meeting, stood up in front of them and said, "What's so hard? I'm doing it, Danny's doing it, I know you can do it. What's the problem?" They were like, "There are so many objections. Thousands of them." I said, "Well, let's write them all out."

Everyone spouted off all the objections they could think of and there weren't 1,000. There weren't even 100. It turned out to be 14 fucking objections! And half of those were repeats. I got so angry and said, "Don't you guys get it? Every sale is the same. It's a straight line and I drew a long thin line with an "x" on either end. This is the beginning, your opening, and this is the end when you close."

There was something about the visual of this straight line that caused a window of clarity to open up within me. I felt like I had accessed information I never had before. I knew and could explain what I did and why it worked. Everything made sense at this moment and over the next three hours, I taught them an entirely different way of thinking about and executing the sale. It was very regimented, using this idea that you are moving in a certain direction throughout the entire process, on a straight line.

The next morning, at 9:30, my team picked up the phones and started dialing. Mind you, none of them had opened an account in a month. And what happened that morning was so incredible. These 12 former Forrest Gump-ites were opening accounts like mad, you wouldn't believe it. Within a few weeks, they were on pace to make a million dollars. They started telling their friends and people were coming from everywhere. It went fucking wild.

I took these kids that could barely walk and chew gum at the same time and had them sounding like Wall Street wizards that could go toe-to-toe with the toughest, meanest, most sophisticated investors in the world.

The Straight Line System: Every Sale Is the Same

The premise of the straight-line system is that sales is about the transference of emotion and the primary emotion that you're transferring is certainty. However, there are three parts you must line up.

PART 1: THE CERTAINTY SCALE

First, when someone buys something, they are certain it will provide them with something. And there is a line of certainty from one to 10. At one, they think the product sucks, at 10, they think it's awesome. You want to get prospects to a 10 before you ask them to buy.

Whatever you're selling, the second someone enters into the encounter and knows they are being offered to buy something, they size up everything they know to get somewhere on the line. They have preconceived ideas about what they are buying.

No matter where they are, you, the salesperson, better be at a 10 and you have to know your product is the best. You take the certainty that you feel and transfer it through your passion and tonality to the prospect. By the end, they should be like, "Damn! I'm certain."

That's what selling is.

Part 2: The Trust Scale

So let's say someone walks in at a five and by the end, they are at a 10 on the certainty scale. You then ask them to buy. Will they?

Most people say yes they will. But what about if in the process of getting to a 10, you did or said something that made them distrust you? Will they still buy?

No way. People don't buy from people they don't trust, like, or connect with. You have to get them to a 10 on the trust scale in addition to the certainty scale. A one is the most snake-like horrible person and a 10 is someone you trust and would let watch your children. It's not enough to get a 10 about the product, they need to be a 10 about you.

If you do that, then will they buy? Maybe.

Part 3: The Company Scale

The third part is, what if they don't trust the company? They could love the salesperson and the product, but they also have to trust the company at a 10. Those are the three elements.

They must love the product, trust and connect with you, and trust the company. Get them to a 10,10,10 in a single moment in time and then ask for the sale. Every natural salesperson does that automatically. That's the 'x' at the end of the line.

Script Out Your Sale

The key to the whole thing is to really script out your process. Script out your sale before it happens. If you don't do that, you are selling yourself short and making your life so much more complicated than it has to be. I think the reason people don't use a script is that they think it's useless.

They wonder, "How could you possibly script out a sales conversation? There are too many things they could say and too many ways it could go." That's true if they are in control. But what if you are in control? Everything changes when you are in control. Take Control Immediately.

I've always had this innate ability from literally the first second I open my mouth, prospects are like "Woah, this is an expert," and they defer. Danny was the same way. If you're an expert, people will usually let you guide them through the encounter and won't interrupt you.

A key moment that opened up my strategy to myself and my team was when, in that breakthrough meeting, the guys said they weren't able to get their pitches off. I was like, "Wait, that's not happening to me. I'm getting the objections at the end but I'm getting the pitch out." And I realized it was because I was presenting myself as an expert and they weren't. I was earning the right to guide the encounter and they weren't even getting the offer out.

So one of the most fundamental parts of the straight-line system is you must take immediate control of the sale. You need to establish yourself as an expert within the first couple seconds to overcome that initial automatic negative reaction that says, "Oh, damn, another salesperson is calling." Then, the whole universe of possibility opens up.

HOW TO TAKE CONTROL IN THE FIRST FOUR SECONDS

Within the first four seconds, you can use tonality, certain words, and body language to make prospects see you as a sharp and enthusiastic expert in your field.

Tonality

The biggest lesson I learned at Rothschild (prior to Stratton) was the power of the telephone. I learned you could make millions from phone calls. I also heard the difference between the people who sounded good versus those that didn't. Some brokers would get bogged down in the facts while others would focus on bigger concepts and the future. You have to be the guy that sounds fucking good. Paint the picture and transfer your certainty from the second they answer the phone.

Certain Words

You have to know what to say. Some people have the natural gift of language where they know just what to say, how to say it, and when to say it. For those that don't, it's even more important to script out your calls. It will give you confidence that you know what to say and have the roadmap in front of you that shows where you're going (to the x at the end of the line).

Body Language

Lastly, body language is in how you make eye contact, how you shake hands, how you dress, and how you hold your body. You must exude confidence and certainty. You can hear a smile, charisma, and confidence over the phone in a split second and so can your prospects. The Straight Line is About Improving Communication.

Not knowing how to sell is a huge problem for many companies and many people. And the sad thing is it's really easy to learn. I go into companies for corporate training, and many are using a circle system. They are going in fucking circles. The scripts are so toxic I can't believe they are making sales. Most people struggle and don't feel comfortable, and they do far less than they could because they are not able to communicate effectively.

The visual of the straight line gives context to those who are not natural-born sellers. It's a very simple concept that is about turning you into your best self. It removes the possibility that you will fail from bad communication. You may fail for other reasons but it won't be communication. And the first step, that stops many salespeople before they start, is you have to take control of the situation immediately. Use certainty, confidence, tone, body language, and words to take control and you can make every sale the same. Then your sales will become like that safe, unlocked by lining up a series of elements following a simple, repeatable process.

Want to learn more from Jordan Belfort? Follow him on:
Website: jordanbelfort.com
Instagram: @wolfofwallst

#20 Lead With Truth and Offer Value

MARK METRY

"Lead with your truth and then go in with the potential value proposition."

ABOUT MARK METRY:

Mark Metry is the 22-year-old best-selling author of Screw Being Shy, host of the global top 100 podcast, "Humans 2.0," and a Forbes featured TEDx keynote speaker.

He is a first-generation immigrant who was born in Massachusetts to his Egyptian parents. Growing up, Mark faced racism and bullying and developed severe social anxiety as a result. He also suffered from autoimmune health conditions, which further contributed to his anxiety.

As an outlet, Mark became interested in online gaming and learned how to code online games. In 2010, he started a YouTube channel which gained 35,000 subscribers, and in 2013, he founded the world's first Minecraft server which turned into a six-figure business.

A few years later, Mark attended college and things took a turn for the worse. He faced severe depression, obesity, and social isolation. However, he began to work toward becoming a new, better version of himself and started the "Humans 2.0" podcast in 2017.

On "Humans 2.0," Mark frequently converses with billionaires, neuroscientists, professional athletes, Pulitzer Prize-winning journalists, and New York Times best-selling authors, exploring today's dynamic of the human experience and mental health. By 2018, "Humans 2.0" was ranked one of the top 100 podcasts in the world, alongside big names like Gary Vaynerchuk.

In 2019, Mark was invited by Forbes to do a two-hour interview, he gave a TEDx talk, and appeared on the Amazon Prime TV docuseries, The Social Movement.

Mark's been featured on over 100 radio and podcast shows and his work has been featured in Forbes, Influencive, Inc. Huffington Post, and Fearless Motivation. He is known for having tremendous insight about optimal living and has a genuine realness that is warm and welcoming. Mark's integrity, drive, and authenticity are said to be second-to-none.

When I was 20, I had just overcome a huge personal struggle and I didn't see anyone like me trying to have down-to-earth conversations on a podcast so I went for it. I launched "Humans 2.0."

As I began working on booking guests, I discovered tiers. A random person on the street that has a LinkedIn account but doesn't really use it is in tier 10. People like Will Smith, Barack Obama, and Donald Trump are tier 1. I saw myself at the very bottom tier and I started working my way up.

As I worked my way up the food chain, I uncovered several key secrets to prospect and book guests. These keys to success are what helped me grow into a global top 100 podcast within one year!

Up the Frequency

It definitely took me a while to pick up steam but what changed it for me was looking around the podcast industry and seeing that people were only posting one time per week. I thought to myself, I can definitely invest more time into this, why not 10x it? And it's a card I borrowed from John Lee Dumas, host of "Entrepreneurs On Fire" because he posted every day. So I said, what if I can interview three people per week while everyone else is only interviewing one? That's 12 people per month versus the four most other shows were doing. And it worked. The more people I interviewed, the more quickly I was able to go up the guest hierarchy.

Start With Your Top 10 Connections

Who did I interview first? Well, I didn't have a very big LinkedIn following but did have a few connections from the business that I was running. I reached out to the top 10 people that I already had in my network for an interview and got started. Nobody really knew the first 10 guests I had on my podcast. I mean, maybe some people did as I had some pretty cool people on there but they weren't well-known figures.

The Networking Effect

Once I landed those first 10 to 15 guests, I reached out to people who were outside of my network. They were not big fish but were similar in the number of followers, or maybe they had a bit more, but nothing crazy.

At this stage, I began to get the network effect. I'd have these great conversations and guests would ask who I was and what I was doing. Then, they would start introducing me to their awesome friends, some of them became guests, and we helped each other out in various ways.

Analyze Social Media Activity

The first big guest I ever had on was Jay Samit, and that happened after about 40 episodes. Jay is a business tycoon who was involved with the founding of LinkedIn and eBay. I saw he was totally dominating in some circles online, like Instagram. However, I realized he wasn't that popular on LinkedIn so I sent him a personalized message there and that's how I ended up getting him on the podcast.

After that, I have always looked into a prospect's social media presence. My best advice is to look at all the places a prospect is active and reach out to them on the channel where they are least popular but still active. This way, your message will be way more visible.

Interview Friends of Prospects

Another thing I've done that's helped me book a ton of guests is I'll poke around on social media in a target guest's personal life to find out who they hang out with in real life. Then, I'll interview the ideal guest's friends. Once I have, I'll send my main prospect an email to invite them on and tell them I've already interviewed their friends. I've landed several big guests that way, as it helps to build your credibility.

Create a Mutually-Beneficial Offer

Next, a lot of people won't randomly talk to you for 45 minutes or an hour but if you can create a mutually-beneficial system or platform where you can say, "Hey, I'd love to talk to you, pick your brain, and you can share what you're working on whether it's a book coming out a business, or some kind of a program." That creates an exchange of value. They share their time and get something out of it, and that's how I've got so many different guests on the show. I don't just email them about what I want.

Keep the Pitch Authentic and Relevant

I think another big lesson is to take whoever you're trying to message and do it in a really human way. Provide them the most relevant information possible.

For example, when I messaged Jay, my message was along the lines of, "Hey Jay, I'm a 20-year-old in Boston. I loved reading your book, Disrupt You. I host a podcast and I talk to really interesting people, and my audience primarily consists of younger people and younger entrepreneurs. I'd really like to interview you and you can share what you're working on."

That's all I said. He responded and said, "Yeah, message me after Christmas break."

And I've had success so many times when I send a massive person some kind of an email or message that seems pretty informal, not beginning with, "I have been featured in Forbes, NASDAQ, etc."

To get information about your prospects, you can go to their LinkedIn or other social profiles and see what they've posted about recently. See if they've shared anything actually relevant to what you're doing and mention it to make a genuine connection.

Lead with your truth and then go in with the potential value proposition. I've used this to book people on LinkedIn who have like 2 million followers.

Use Systematic Follow-Up

Lastly, follow-up is also key. Very rarely is it one and done. Prospects are usually a moving target. Sometimes people will see my IG direct message but won't respond so I'll follow up and DM them again a week later. And the same for email. But there are other people who I will message every two weeks or every month for a year.

The hardest guest that I have ever had to get on was Dave Asprey, Founder of Bulletproof. I had been messaging him every week for months and never heard anything. I saw that he was working with a PR company so I started following his CEO on IG and commenting on his stories. Eventually, the conversation happened and it coincided with the launch of Dave's book. And that's another thing, a lot of times you're going to have to be patient because people want to wait to do interviews until it's the most opportune time for them.

But I have a whole system for follow-ups where I set reminders about who to contact when to contact them, and what to say. It's an ongoing game you have to play.

All of these approaches and strategies together have helped me to go from booking tier 10 guests to more tier 1 guests. As a result, I've been able to grow my podcast which enables me to reach, impact, and influence more people with my mission of sharing self-development knowledge.

Want to learn more from Mark Metry? Follow him on:
Podcast:
markmetry.com/humans-2-0-podcast
LinkedIn:
linkedin.com/in/mark-metry
Instagram:
@markmetry

#21 It's Not About You

VERNON BROKKE

"It's not about you. It's about the client, the company, and providing the solution."

ABOUT VERNON BROKKE:

Vernon Brokke is an established professional with over 35 years of experience in sales, management, marketing, and business ownership. His primary focus is to help business owners, managers, and sales personnel learn what to do and how to think to win large, complex accounts.

Vernon has owned several franchises including Jackson Hewitt Tax Service, City Publications, and The Growth Coach. He also founded his own business strategy firm, The Brokke Group, where he leverages experience gained from working relationships with IBM, Cisco, Juniper Networks, and Riverbed Technology, and emerging companies Rolm Corporation, StrataCom, Redline Networks, and Calient Networks.

Apart from the Brokke Group, Vernon shares his knowledge through other avenues. He is a M'ain Stage Speaker at The Survive and Thrive or Crash and Burn Small Business Success Summit, where he's helping business owners learn how to reduce their uncertainty in economic downturns.

Additionally, he published the book, Mastering Large Sales Opportunities, where he reveals the 10 blind spots every sales leader must know to ensure they capture and win high-value accounts.

Vernon is known as someone who has devoted himself to helping organizations understand how to turn their opportunities into results. His strong commercial background allows him to go where others — who base their approaches on theory — simply cannot. He has developed innovative tools and techniques to help others gain clarity and unlock the potential in their companies. While most business development teams "chase" complex deals, Vernon is known for making those deals materialize into profitable results, without having to chase them.

When I was in outside sales I would make cold calls all day, and I almost never got turned down by a receptionist to get a meeting. There was one time I was turned down by a guy who was known for hating everyone. Besides that, I got every meeting.

My approach was to treat people with kindness. I would call the operator and say, "I know you're busy. If someone calls put me on hold, I'll wait." And I realized the receptionist is the most important person to talk to. No one talks to them much but they run the telephone system.

So I would talk to the receptionist, be really nice, and they would tell me who to talk to, who the decision-maker is, how to get to them, and then they would help me.

I focused on them and that mindset leads me to my #1 top sales secret.

Be the Liaison Between Your Client and Your Company

My top sales secret is to always remember it's not about you. Think about that wherever you are focused on yourself.

I look at myself as being the conductor in an organization. I am the liaison from the client to the company and the company to the client. I don't have the responsibility or authority to lose a deal. I've gone to management and said, "Look, this is the situation. This is what the client is saying." So I am the liaison to them. It's not about me. It's about my client and my company.

I have to build that balance between working with the client and working with the company to find the best interests for both. So you have to represent that on both sides. Go to the client and say, "Here's what the company is willing to offer, are you willing to accept it?" And then you bring in the different components of the organization to understand, this is what we need to do to get this business, do we want it?

Always remember, it's not about you. It's about the client, the company, and providing the solution.

HOW TO STOP MAKING IT ABOUT YOU

To make your sales transactions less about you, your quota, or your sales tactics, you need to start to reach out to other folks. The more that you ask questions and make it about them, the more they will actually tell you how to sell to them. If you try to sell to them and be the best salesperson, they will turn off. But if you ask them what they are trying to accomplish, and just be real in trying to understand what their situation is, then you will understand how to sell to them.

I have a great example of an interaction with a client.

One month, I was already over quota, and I had earned my trip to Hawaii for the year. I had closed six deals in one week which was unheard of. I was just pumping them out and they were closing left and right. But I had this one deal that was on the fence.

I called the prospect to see if we were going to do the deal or not. The guy answered and said, "I don't know, I can't make a decision." He shared with me that he had a heart condition and this was really stressing him out. He was working himself up.

One of the benefits of a full pipeline is you don't have that pressure to push when you don't feel it's right, and in this situation, I didn't. I felt bad and didn't want to make his health problem worse so after listening, I said, "I am going to make your job easy, I am pulling my proposal." I took it off the table. I wasn't going to call him anymore, I wasn't going to take him to lunch.

I didn't do this as a sales tactic, I did it out of sincerity. It wasn't about me. I was ready to let him go even though I knew we had a better solution for him, although it was more expensive. In the long run, he ended up coming around.

It's important to strike the right balance of drive and motivation matched with empathy. The best salespeople have a perfect balance. If you're too driven, you'll piss people off. If you're not driven enough, you won't make your deals. If you get that balance right, you'll make that seven-figure income you're looking for. But you have to know it's not about you. It's about the client and the solution and providing the knowledge, skills, and trust.

Want to learn more from Vernon Brokke? Follow him on:
LinkedIn: linkedin.com/in/vernonbrokke/
Website: Brokke.com

SALES SECRETS:

PROCESS & STRATEGY

#22 Rockstar Rebel Turns Copier Sales Warrior

DALE DUPREE

"You need to be the rebellious salesperson that's looking to make a difference for the buyer, not yourself."

ABOUT DALE DUPREE:

Dale Dupree, also known as the Copier Warrior and the Founder of the Sales Rebellion, is the Sales Manager at Zeno Office Solutions, a Xerox Company. His career in the business systems industry began in 2004 when he joined his father to work in the family copier business. Dale was the Vice President of Connectivity Business Systems for eight years when the company was acquired by North American Office Solutions. He worked with North American as a Sales Executive for five years and then took on the role of Vice President of Sales.

A stark change from his previous six-year career as singer/songwriter for his band Imperial, Dale has been incredibly successful at channeling his creative energy into sales. Dale's associates and clients speak of him fondly, saying he shows them what it looks like to give 100% all of the time.

As an avid content creator, online audiences across the Web follow Dale for his unique and engaging content that he shares across LinkedIn, YouTube, and his "Selling Local" podcast.

Dale aspires to follow in his father's footsteps who Dale says was truly a man of integrity and an incredible salesman. He has established his own tricks of the trade and they have garnered him success both individually and as a sales leader. Now, he is stepping into the role of a sales influencer and authority, with several books on the horizon and his offering of sales mentoring services.

When you think of a copy machine, you may not find it the most exhilarating product in the world. Most people don't find anything too intriguing about business equipment. But that's where the opportunity lies. Where many see mundane or boring, I see an opportunity to completely turn the rulebook on its head to make an impact. My secret to success lies in reading between the lines and being a rebel. An attitude that has served me in both the music and business systems industries. Here, I will reveal exactly how I have been able to cut through the noise and become the sales legend I aspired to be.

Rockstar Musician to Rockstar Sales Warrior

Growing up, I loved to write and play music. I wanted to be a rockstar and at the ripe age of 17, I became one. I managed tours across the U.S. while singing and songwriting for my metalcore band, Imperial. We were signed by Pluto records and I had the whole package, including the long hair and plugs.

After about six years, I moved home and started working part-time with my father. I was amazed and inspired by him and how he operated. He was driven by strong intentions and made a profound impact on every person he helped. I started gaining traction, my passion grew, and I decided to give copier sales 100% of my attention.

To excel, I had to do my homework. I dissected the anatomy of sales and the role human psychology plays in it. As a result, I developed an understanding of the nature of sales and developed game-changing tactics that blow the majority of conversion rates out of the water.

Authentically Serve Your Community

The thing is, I didn't want to buy into the grind and constant rejection that is so common in the sales world. I wanted to bring truth, authenticity, and value into every step of mycareer and every interaction.

Serve Them, Not You

As I dove into human psychology and evaluated the current landscape of sales professionals in my industry, I realized a cold, hard truth. People don't like salespeople and there is an obvious reason. Sales reps are known to be focused on themselves and their own agendas. They have quotas to meet, conversion rates to shoot for, a number of years to work before retirement, and on and on. Most don't REALLY care about their clients beyond what's in it for them.

I took a different approach. I switched from serving myself to 100% serving my clients. I treated people like people and got creative in the way that I communicated. Further, I focused on building relationships with clients that went beyond business. It wasn't about closing a deal today. It was about building long-lasting real relationships with people who I could really help. I may not sell to them now, in the next year, or ever. But, I may sell to their brother, cousin, or friend because of our relationship. I believe when your entire mindset is truly focused on your customers, you will be able to be effective and money will be a natural byproduct.

R.E.A.S.O.N.: How to Become a Sales Warrior for Your Community

So how can you change the game and become a sales warrior for your community as soon as today? Above all else, you need to establish your foundation and get your mindset right. Who are you? What matters to you? Why are you in sales? What drives you? How can you truly help people? Why do you want to help your community?

Set your intentions for your sales career. For me, I was going to be a legend and the greatest sales rep in my industry. I was going to truly serve my community by offering them the best service they ever had.

Once you have your foundation, I use a system called REASON as a guide. REASON isan acronym for radically educate, attention, story, outline, nuances. Here are the basics:

Radically Educate: When creating your first-touch marketing material, do something off the wall that is going to break through a person's everyday mental pattern. An example is the old crumpled up paper trick. If you aren't familiar, here's how it works. A brand sends a marketing piece in the mail. If they don't get a response, they send a second piece that has been crumpled up and then flattened out. The piece says, "Hey! You threw away our last message but we found it and sent it again. Give us a call!" This and other tactics following the same concept are intriguing and entertaining to people, and as a result, are highly effective at getting them to take action. I'll put a newsletter in a box the size of your living room if you are ignoring my marketing. You need your buyer to understand you will go all-in for them.

Captivate Full Attention: Once you have connected with a customer, the next step is to keep them fully engaged. You have to truly understand who they are and how you can be of service to them. Keep them engaged in the adventure that started with the first touch. Stay consistent, be creative, and make it fun.

Share a Story: Lose the old robotic sales script. Rip it up and throw it in the trash. Nobody cares if you tell them, "Hi I am with XYZ company and I want to sell x to the decision-maker." They will keep their walls up and hope you go away as soon as possible. But if you share a compelling story, you can connect with the person and get their brain activity going. Then, the walls come down and they start to like you. You can even make them feel like the decision-maker is missing out if they don't introduce you to them. So share your life, your story, be vulnerable, and it will allow them to do the same.

Outline: Once you have connected with the client and understand their needs, outline the agenda you would like your relationship to follow. It should cover what they can get from your business. Often salespeople focus on the product's solution and never want to talk about what could go wrong. I do it a bit differently. People can buy the copiers I sell online from Amazon so I have nothing to gain by rattling off product specs. Instead, the reason they should buy from me is because of my service. When something goes wrong, I will be there so they don't have to stress. This is the key value. So I sell the copier but primarily, I sell myself. I am the value they can not get anywhere else. I am the one they can count on.

Nuances: Lastly, picking up on nuances is key to success in sales. It can help you break the pattern and stand out. Pay attention to the fine details that often get overlooked. How is the person's body language? Did they mention their favorite color? What can you learn about them from their appearance? Picking up on these little details and using them to show your clients you care and pay attention is absolutely game-changing.

These tips make up my REASON system which I use to disrupt the pattern and connect with people. By following these steps and approaching sales to truly help and serve your community, you can become a badass sales warrior. Don't be afraid to step out and be different. In today's sales environment the competition is tough. You have to go all in, be the rebel, connect, and serve!

Want to learn more from Dale Dupree? Follow him on:
Website: copierwarrior.com
LinkedIn: linkedin.com/in/copierwarrior
Instagram: @copierwarrior
YouTube: youtube.com/channel/
UC-BqyrLcd1uRE9zjAZuFDeg

#23 Lead With the Business Case

TONY J. HUGHES

"Selling is about making a positive difference for the customer, professionally and personally. If that's not what we're doing then I don't think sales is ethical."

ABOUT TONY J. HUGHES:

Tony is an international keynote speaker, best-selling author, leading professional selling educator, award-winning blogger, and the most-read LinkedIn Author on Sales leadership.

He is ranked by Top Sales Magazine as the "Most Influential Person in Professional Selling in Asia-Pacific" and has also been named a Top 50 Keynote Speaker, a Top 25 Global Sales Expert and Influencer, and one of the Top 25 Voices on Linkedin, amongst other honors and awards.

Now an experienced CEO and company director with 35 years of sales and business leadership experience, Tony has held roles at a variety of companies including RSVPselling, Sugar CRM, Fujitsu, and Link Telecommunications. To the benefit of salespeople worldwide, he has also shared golden nuggets of his sales wisdom and insights through two best-selling books: The Joshua Principle: Leadership Secrets of Selling and Combo Prospecting.

Those who know Tony say his teachings can help you increase deal size, better understand your customers, improve forecasting accuracy, win more key accounts, and get to the next level in your career. He is known as a true professional who is approachable and knowledgeable.

One of the biggest struggles I had to overcome as a salesman was realizing that I was my own biggest problem. It wasn't external factors, it was my attitude. When I would go to parties on the weekends and people would ask me what I did for a living, I couldn't bring myself to say I worked in sales. I was embarrassed because I thought it was unethical and all about manipulating people.

I needed to fix that and become a true believer in what I was doing or find another profession. What I realized was that selling can be a noble profession if it is about genuinely helping to make a positive difference for customers both professionally and personally. It couldn't be about me.

Selling Is all About the Customer

My top sales secret is that selling is not about you, your product, your solution, or making a sale. It's really about the other person, the customer, and helping them achieve the outcomes that they care about. You are actually more of a consultant, a subject-matter expert, and an educator, helping people to solve problems. A friend of mine put it well saying, a benefit is only a benefit if it solves a customer's specific problem. Someone can tell you how they have the greatest tasting coffee creamer in the world all day but you won't care if you don't drink coffee. So, first, you need to find out who your prospects are, what problems they have, and how you can solve them. Then, you can lead with a hyper-relevant business case that shares how you can provide the value they care about. Customers Now Want Industry Experts.

Why is it so important to approach a sale from the perspective that it's all about the customer? Well, aside from being the right thing to do, and protecting your job in the future against AI and automation, it's what customers expect.

Research in 2011 and 2012 for The Challenger Sale books, found that the way an organization engaged with customers accounted for more than half of the influencing factors on why customers go with one supplier over another, beating out factors such as the offering and price (price was less than 10%).

Salespeople are the biggest point of difference and buyers expect three things from us:

1) **To truly know them**

2) **To tailor the information based on knowing them**

3) **And to anticipate their needs and what's important to them**

To engage customers and influence them to buy, you have to contact them with a personalized pitch that is meaningful to them in their role, at their company, in their industry. And, you need to have unique insights to share based on your knowledge as a sales professional in the industry.

HOW-TO LEAD WITH A PERSONALIZED BUSINESS CASE

How exactly do you build a personalized business case for your prospects?

Research Prospects to Define Buyer Personas

Figure out who you need to talk to at an organization and what matters to them. I suggest mapping out the people in the organization and figuring out "the power grid". Who makes the decisions and how does power trickle through the ranks? Identify the key people you should talk to and then figure out what matters to them. You'll need to consider the industry, company, role, and person.

For example, if you're selling to a CFO, you may find every CFO across every industry cares about seven things and, in this particular industry, they are focused on these other three, and at this company, they are focused on these two. Then, you research the CFO and find out who it is, what their personality is like, and what they care about most.

I suggest trying to reach the highest-ranking person who has a problem you can solve.

Then, have them sponsor you to talk to others in the business of inferior ranks. When you go in at the middle-management level, you often get into a situation where they try and carry the business case and fail which blocks the sale. If you can't get in with a high- ranking individual, start super low. Low-ranking individuals are often easier to get to, more free with information and have more time. Gain what you need to try and go in again with someone high. Build a Baseline Hypothesis of Value for the Buyer Personas.

Next, it's time to craft your opening pitch. No prospect likes to be qualified by a stranger which begs the question, on what basis will a person give you their time? They are sure as hell not interested in another vendor coming to pitch to them. For this reason, opening, not closing, is the most important part of the sale. You have to come in with a message that speaks to how you can help them with what they care about. I call it generating a hypothesis of value.

To do that, use what you learned researching your buyer along with your unique insights into the industry. You need to choose an angle to approach them with an offer that is hard to refuse.

Here is a real-world example.

I'm part of a global sales academy for one of the biggest business travel management companies in the world and there are three key personas in that industry:

- The CFO/CEO, head of a business that cares about numbers
- The Executive Assistant who does all of the travel bookings in the organization
- The Key Travelers who are highly valuable employees that easily get burnt out; if travelers are not run well then they aren't productive so you want to get their input

If you call them all up and say, "Hey, we're the global leader in travel management, can I come and tell you about the joys and wonders of our solutions?" They'll likely say, "No thanks. I've got no time. I'm not interested"

Instead, the business case for each of these audiences should be different and tailored to the individual. Here's how to lead with the business case:

The Key Traveler (Low-level)

For the key traveler, I would run a narrative like, "Hey Tony, I'm looking at working with your organization to improve the way that it's running travel for you. From what I can figure out, you are one of the key travelers inside the organization. I'd like to get your perspective on how you think things could be done better for you in travel. If we can just set aside 20 minutes for the conversation, I've got some ideas on how you can get more personal value out of the company's travel spend. How's your calendar next week?"The EAIf you're calling the EA, you could say something like, "Hey Mary, the reason I want to get together is, I work for travel bookers all the time and I've got some ideas for how you can get back 6-10 hours per week of your time and stop travel from invading your personal life. If we could just get 20 minutes, I'll share how you can elevate the value of what you are doing inside your business so your team will value you even more. How's your calendar for next week?"

The CFO/CEO (High-level)

And for the CFO/CEO, it could sound like, "Hey Wendy, travel is typically the third biggest expense on your P&L and I'm seeing organizations drive 8% to 12% of costs out of it as a line item in a way that reduces risk for the organization. We could cover the basics in a 20-minute conversation. How's your calendar for next week?"

These are three very different conversations, each personally tailored to the buyer persona. I show each person in a quick opening that I understand their role, pain points, and business in-depth. I also share unique insights that can benefit them and ask for a low-commitment, 20-minute call.

Lead With the Business Case

Let's face it, it's easier to talk about your product or company because you know it inside and out. But that's no longer what people need or want. Further, in the age of growing automation and AI, that approach will make you a commodity that can be easily replaced.

Leading with a personalized business case requires more work because it's different for each client. It also requires courage because you often have to step outside of your comfort zone and speak to things that may not necessarily be in your area of expertise. However, it makes you a unique and valuable asset for every person you contact. Plus, in the end, you will secure your future career, maximize your income by truly helping others, and be able to sleep at night knowing you are a noble salesman.

Want to learn more from Tony Hughes? Follow him on:
Website: tonyhughes.com.au
Sales Advice: rsvpselling.com
LinkedIn: linkedin.com/today/author/hughestony
YouTube: youtube.com/channel/UC2J5-BEjFztyt-i6fiKrQ

#24 What Does It Mean to Be a Sales 'Expert' Anyway?

ANTHONY IANNARINO

"I learned I was a much better salesperson before somebody told me I was a salesperson."

ABOUT ANTHONY IANNARINO:

Anthony Iannarino is a best-selling author and internationally recognized speaker. His three privately held staffing firms generate annual revenues of over $50M. These firms serve some of the most recognized brands in the U.S.

Anthony is also the author of three best-selling books, Eat Their Lunch, The Lost Art of Closing and The Only Sales Guide You'll Ever Need.

He delivers keynote speeches and training sessions that provide transformational advice to sales organizations across the globe. His blog (www.thesalesblog.com) is read by some 60,000 people every month, making it a go-to resource for sales professionals.

Anthony has continually been named one of the 25 most influential people in the world in sales and marketing. His contributions to the industry are second to none.

Continue reading to discover Anthony's expert sales secret and how you can apply it to your own sales career.

When I first started in sales, I was 15 and absolutely hated it. I worked for the Muscular Dystrophy Association and my job was to cold call community organizations across America. The goal was to have them host a bike-a-thon to raise money for the Muscular Dystrophy Association. I spent maybe a month there making phone calls and nothing happened. I mean nothing. Even at 15, it was clear to me that there was no leadership, no coaching, and absolutely no help. So I quit and took a job at the local skating rink as a floor guard. Quite the change in jobs, but at 15 I was more interested in being rejected by teenage girls than being rejected while making cold calls.

Fast forward a few years, and I began working for the family business—a temporary staffing agency. My job was to interview candidates and place them. At one point they said, "Listen, when you don't have anybody to interview and there's nothing to do, call some of these companies and see if you can help them." They did not describe that as a sales job. Had they, I would have said no immediately. So in between interviews, I would call on companies and ended up winning some business. Even as I closed deals, I still did not think of myself as a salesperson; I was simply finding ways to help people who needed help.

A few years later, I decided to move to L.A. and was playing in a band while still working for a branch of the staffing agency. A new manager came in to transform our failing branch and he quickly recognized that I was winning accounts while his three legitimate salespeople were not. My manager came to me and said, "I want you to go into full-time outside sales." I turned him down without hesitation declaring boldly that "I wasn't hired for that. I hate salespeople. They're smarmy, manipulative, selfish, pushy people that try to make people buy things they don't even need." Despite my objections, my manager told me to cut my hair and wear a suit because I was going to be a salesperson. If I refused, I would be fired. And so began my official sales career.

What Sales Is Really All About: Listening

I was a terrible salesperson during my first few months on the job. I walked around with this huge binder that we used to give our sales presentation and I literally read it page by page. It was horrible. It wasn't until my manager told me that no one cared about what was in the binder that things began to turn around. He told me that I needed to figure out the two or three things that mattered most to my customers. To do that, I soon learned that I needed to be quiet and listen. I needed to let people finish their thoughts. By listening, I learned what really mattered to my customers and was able to identify ways I could help them. Much like my initial approach when calling on companies at my family's business, I became more focused on helping than selling.

For anyone in sales, I encourage you to not think about doing sales in the traditional sense, but rather look at it as an opportunity to help people. That subtle change in approach makes a world of difference.

By listening and focusing on the two or three things that really mattered, I was able to land the largest account in the western half of the U.S. for a $4 billion company—it was a $10-million-a-year deal, for five years. I would have received a $450,000 commission check but life had other plans in store for me...

I had a grand mal seizure and ended up having brain surgery. Unable to drive for two years, I moved back home to Columbus, Ohio where I rejoined the family business. While others may have called it quits, I came back more determined than ever to produce better results and become the best sales leader I could be.

BECOMING AN EXPERT

To become the best, I became an avid reader and a student of sales, and business in general. So, in thinking about my sales secret and want advice I can offer emerging sales leaders, it is this—become an expert. And by that I mean you need to develop a business acumen that enables you to command a room, control the process, resolve concerns and provide value in every meeting you attend. You have to be what I call a "level four," or the highest level of value creation. You need to become an expert at the intersection of your business and your customer's business.

While becoming an expert in anything takes time, below are some tips on how to go about making the shift.

Think Strategic:

Becoming a consultative expert for your customers means starting first with the strategic outcome they want to achieve then working down to the solution. That's one of the main differences between coming in at level one, which is all about the product or solution and coming in at level four, which is strategic. I'll use the analogy of someone buying a drill. People don't buy drills. They buy holes. They want the hole. So you start with the hole and explain to them, "To get that hole, you're gonna need a drill, and you're gonna need a really good drill bit. Once you get your drill, I can get you the hole that you're looking for."

When thinking strategically, it's about working backward. Start with what your customer wants to achieve and then have a discussion about how to get those results.

Have a Theory:

To be an expert for your customers, you should do enough research to develop a theory. Based on their current situation, develop a working assumption of what they are likely concerned about or what they should be concerned about. As you develop and present your theory, you will be able to state what you think should be changed and how that change can positively impact them. Practically every business has systemic challenges so use those standard challenges to develop your theory.

Manage Concerns, Not Objections:

Being an expert means driving the conversation and managing concerns that may interfere with your progress. Instead of worrying about closing the deal, focus on getting to the next milestone. Doing this requires you to uncover your customer's concerns, even if they aren't explicit in explaining them.

For example, when someone says, "We don't have time right now," what they are really saying is, "I don't hear enough value in what you're saying to trade my time for that." So, you have to look for the real concern and address it head-on. Don't just respond to the initial objection; look to understand the reason behind the objection.

As you grow your expertise, you'll see that what you're doing is really less about sales and more about helping your customers achieve results. Sales will naturally come as you provide value and become a consultative leader that others depend on for guidance. To be successful, I challenge you to think first about helping your customers and not solely about closing the deal.

Want to learn more from Anthony Iannarino?
Follow him on:
Website: thesalesblog.com
LinkedIn: linkedin.com/in/iannarino
Twitter: @iannarino
YouTube: youtube.com/user/iannarino
Facebook: facebook.com/thesalesblog

#25 'No' Doesn't Mean No Forever

JAMES 'SAY WHAT SALES' BUCKLEY

"I think my clients can hear me smile over the phone."

ABOUT JAMES BUCKLEY:

James Buckley is a SaaS Sales Professional specializing in Business Development and Personal Branding. He is currently the Director of Sales Execution & Evolution at JBarrows Sales Training.

James is also the creator of the well-known #Saywhatsales where he distributes sales tips, advice, and general value to the rising number of sales professionals present on social media. With over 15K followers, James' life goal is to change the way salespeople view their role.

Graduating from Maryville College, one of James' first sales jobs was selling door-to- door. He has also worked in various sales roles at companies such as Cirrus Insight and RingLead.

James says that he is the type of person who finds the silver lining in everything and always wants to make people laugh. Co-workers of James say that he is the definition of passion and hustle and a great resource on what it takes to be successful. They refer to him as one of the most persistent people they have ever met and someone who does whatever it takes to get the job done. He is also known for having a great sense of humor, a happy and charming personality that is infectious, and the ability to convert conversations into business.

When I first started using social media, all I did was repost content that I thought was funny with a 'thumbs up' or 'laughing face' emoji. I just wanted to make people laugh. I had Facebook and would share stuff every day. It was interesting because people started to gravitate towards me and say how much they loved my content but it wasn't even mine, it was other people's.

I'd attract friends, followers, others in my industry, and even clients. Because I was providing content that people found valuable, they were sending me messages and interacting with me. Eventually, many would ask me what I actually sold. Is there a better question that someone can ask you in sales? I don't think so. I quickly learned that social media and content could be used to connect with people and build value, and most importantly, for sales, it could be a gateway from a hard 'no' to a 'yes.'

"No" and "Never Talk to Me Again" Don't Mean the Same Thing

When sales reps hear the word "No" from prospects, they often remove them from their pipeline but that is a HUGE mistake.

The truth is when people say 'no' initially, it doesn't mean no forever. They may have had a flat tire that morning, had a fight with their spouse the night before, or had a rough month with their business which put them in the mood to say no. Or, it could be they just don't know who you are so they don't care what you have to say. No matter the reason, there are times when people are just not open to opportunities regardless of whether something can actually help them or not.

So when someone says no to me, I put them on a follow-up list. If someone says, "Stop emailing me", I stop emailing them. But that doesn't mean I don't call them, shake their hand at a show, or send them a box of chocolates on Valentine's Day.

Hearing no is okay, it just means the prospect isn't ready to take a step yet. I repeat it's okay.

WHAT TO DO WHEN SOMEONE TELLS YOU NO

So what should you do when someone tells you no?

The Follow Up

When I hear no, I set a task for about a week later to reach out to the prospect via social media. I find the platform they are most active on and I send them a friend request. In many cases, I get comments, likes, or shares from that very same person who wasn't interested in talking to me. By connecting with them, it makes them aware of who I am and what I do. And it helps that I put out a great deal of positive content to engage people.

Three to four months down the line, I will call that same "no" client again and say, "Hey I'm doing this positive thing where I call people and thank them for interacting with my content and you were on my list today so thank you!" I tell them that the last time we talked, they weren't interested in my product, and I check to see if their interest level has grown.

By this point, the prospect knows me and often wants to hear more about what I have to say. This is only because I helped them to get to know and like me on social media. But why social media, you may ask.

The Power of Positive Association and Familiarity

Social media rewards the pleasure centers in the brain in the same way that drinking or gambling does. When we see new likes and other notifications, it makes us feel good and keeps us coming back. So when you connect via social media, you can help to associate yourself with those positive feelings in the mind of your prospect.

Social media is also helpful because it allows you to build value outside of what directly results in monetary compensation. You can engage and entertain people so much that they come to you asking you what you sell. When they feel familiarity, it is the doorway to interest. True story, I get people that say "Fuck off, leave me alone!" and then they like my content and come to me. It's funny to say to them after the fact, "Remember when you told me to fuck off?! Now, look at us!"

When to Cut Your Losses

Now, there is a point when you should cut your losses. If after you have connected and engaged with someone, they are still not open to change or growth and want to stick to the same old way, that's probably a prospect you don't want. However, they might know someone who is interested and it never hurts to ask. Further, they might be a valuable conversationalist or something else. No is hardly ever a completely closed door but know when to stop pursuing them for the sale.

The Six-Step Universal Sales Cycle

I like to break down my process into something I call the six-step universal sales cycle. It applies to all types of sales. Here's how it works:

Content. Post content online regularly on social media platforms. Content is the way to put yourself out there and draw people in. For me, I like to make people laugh and spread positivity and sales knowledge. People dig it and want to engage with it.

Connection: Content leads to connections. People engage with your content, like your posts, comment on posts, share posts, download content, open emails, etc. When they do that, you establish a connection with them.

Conversation: Connections lead to conversations. You should start a conversation with any person who interacts with your content and establishes a connection. Say, "Hey, I saw you liked this, what do you think about XYZ?"

Develop a relationship/trust: As you chat with someone, you begin to build a relationship and may even establish trust with them. They become aware of who you are and what you're about.

Ask for an opportunity: Once you have established a relationship, it can lead you to the point of opportunity, where you can potentially offer them a solution. For me, it's when I make the follow-up call three to four months out.

Make the sale: From the opportunity, you can make the sale and close the deal.

Even if someone says no initially, use this six-step sales cycle to engage them, connect with them, and move them down the funnel towards the sale. Yeah, it may take three months, six months, or even a year but if you are constantly working this cycle at all different stages with a continuous flow of prospects, you are going to be successful.

THE SUCCESS EQUATION

My other key to success is to follow this equation in all your interactions:

C+P(3)= Success

What does that mean?

Be courteous, professional, persistent, and patient.

The truth is no one will like you if you're not courteous. You have to be professional to gain trust and respect. You can't give up if you want to close the sale, and people will buy on their own time so you have to be patient.

Set your ego aside and don't give up when you hear no. No means you are about to get to know that person a little better. Marketing yourself as a valuable expert in your field is the key to having consistent conversations. Further, personally branding yourself (on social media platforms) as someone who can solve problems ensures that people look to you for answers when it comes to needed change. Isn't that what we're all selling anyway? Change!!

Want to learn more from James "Say What Sales" Buckley?
Follow him on:
LinkedIn: linkedin.com/in/jamessaywhatsalesbuckley
Website: saywhatsales.com

#26 Your Customers Don't Care About You...Now What?

STEVE HALL

"The terrifying truth about your customers is that they're just like you. They care about themselves and don't give a damn about you. You have to put yourself in their shoes."

ABOUT STEVE HALL:

Steve Hall is known as Australia's leading C-Level Sales Authority, an executive sales coach, a managing director, and a storyteller. With a career spanning over 50 years, he has a wealth of knowledge to share on the topics of business, leadership, marketing, and sales.

Steve's career began back in 1968 while he was still attending the University of Bristol. He began dabbling in a wide range of industries and held various positions. His colorful and varied work history has enabled him to become highly skilled at understanding others and putting himself in their shoes.

After climbing the ranks at Unisys for 14 years, Steve left and joined Tailor Made Systems as the Sales and Marketing Manager. Again, he stayed with the company for 14 years (through an acquisition where TMS became IBS AB) and worked his way up to International Sales Manager. Next, Steve changed directions a bit. He took on a few 6-month consulting jobs for clients and, in 2010, began consulting through Moss and Hopper. After that, he worked for himself while partnering with different organizations and businesses.

In 2016, he became one of the founding members of Sales Masterminds APAC (SMA). All members of SMA are keynote speakers and writers on the topics of sales, marketing, and related topics. Further, each member has a global following of marketing professionals and senior executives.

Most recently, in 2018, Steve co-founded the Executive Sales Forum International which offers executives a peer advisory forum, access to some of the biggest names in sales, and world-class executive sales coaching services. He has been published in many publications such as the *Australian Financial Review*, BRW, and Salesforce's Quotable blog. Additionally, he has been a guest on webinars and sales podcasts around the world, is a regular contributor to *Top Sales Magazine*, and is a member of the Sales Experts Channel.

Known for playing the devil's advocate, Steve asks the hard questions that get results.

I have had a very long career which has granted me the opportunity to work in many industries, roles, countries, and businesses. The skill that has been the most instrumental to my success in every business and role is the ability to see things from the point of view of others. Your prospects don't give a damn about you, your sales pitch, or your product specs. Here's how I use that fact to my advantage.

Understand Your Customer's True Want and Work Hard to Help Them Get It.

As salespeople, we all have our interests. For example, when you have a sales meeting, you typically talk about customers, pipelines, prospects, products, competitors, and targets. Your "stuff." In your sales pitch, you may cover the features and benefits of your product or service. However, what do you think executives talk about? They are consumed with their "stuff"—customers, regulations, industry changes, risk, and more.

My secret is to forget about yourself, your quota, and all "your stuff" when working with a prospect. Focus on them. To quote Simon Sinek, "Why do your customers want what they want? What's the core objective that they're trying to achieve? And how can you help them achieve that core objective? If you can truly help to solve a problem the company and person are facing, they are going to listen to you. But how can you uncover the true objectives of your customers?

HOW TO UNDERSTAND THE CORE OBJECTIVES OF YOUR CUSTOMERS

How do you understand what your customers really want? Here are four actionable steps you can put into practice today:

1. Build Relationships With Potential Clients

The easiest way to understand your prospects and what they want is to get to know them. Continuously nurture relationships with people in your target market. Build your personal brand and reputation. Network.

You can't just persuade everyone that they need to buy from you right now because the truth is they don't. However, what you can do is build

167

relationships with people, learn about their needs, and provide helpful information. If you build your relationships effectively, they will come right to you when they are ready.

John Bedwany used to say, "When a company in my area is ready to go to market, they will know me, and I will know them." I always thought that was brilliant.

I had one client who I talked to for three years without making a sale. I went down to talk to them about their issues, I gave them the occasional demonstration, but they were never ready to buy. However, the day finally came when they were ready and I had no competition. They just said, "Okay, we're ready. How much is it?"

I'd been regularly talking to them, so they already trusted me. They knew who our customers were. They knew we could do what they wanted. So you need to plant seeds and water them. Eventually, a good portion of them will sprout. Plus, if prospects already decide on their solution independently, it's harder to sell them. Instead, try to reach them early in the buying cycle and help them find the solution.

2. Answer These Four Questions

When it's time to pursue a prospect, you have to do your research. First, who is the person you need to talk to? Once you identify who it is, answer these four questions:

1) **What do people in their industry care about?**

2) **What do people in their company care about?**

3) **What do people in that position care about?**

4) **What do they themselves care about?**

For instance, if you need to talk to the CEO of a particular company, you should look at their industry and understand what is going on at the current time. In Australia, we're having a Royal Commission into Misconduct in the banking industry. When you're talking to individuals in banking, they are obsessing about it. If you try and talk to them about anything else, you have a slim chance of it resonating. But if you can say, "Hey, I can make this go away," or, "I can help you restore your battered reputation," you've got a much better chance of getting through to them.

Next, you need to look at what the CEO's company is focused on. Is it customer relationships, growth, reducing churn? Find out but consider it from the CEO's perspective. Why is that focus important to the CEO and how does it impact them?

Lastly, on an individual level, what interests does the CEO have? What is their perspective within their company and role in the issue at hand?

By considering all four of these perspectives, you can equip yourself to effectively understand your target and have a meaningful conversation with them. The ability to see your prospect's perspective strengthens with experience and working in different industries. However, you can also research sources like reports, industry magazines, and LinkedIn. The higher you go, the easier it is because they are featured more in the press, reports, etc..

3. Call Out Your Biggest Competition: Doing Nothing

Third, when speaking to your potential customers, it's important to understand what many salespeople forget. Your biggest competition isn't anyone else. It is the prospect opting to do nothing. I advise calling out the elephant in the room. Risk cuts both ways. There is a risk of doing something but there is also the risk of not doing something.

Prepare by looking into your client's future. What will happen if they don't opt for your solution in the next 12 months? 24 months? Longer? What risks will they face? Your predictions have to be well-researched and realistic. The goal is to get the target to associate with the pain of not doing anything and how it builds up into something unbearable.

Why put off that toothache, when you could have the tooth extracted tomorrow?

4. Speak the Language of Your Audience—No Jargon!

My last tip is to be aware of the language you use when speaking to potential clients. While it depends on what you're selling, we all tend to over complicate things. Also, it's a natural phenomenon to think that other people understand what we understand. As a result, we often tend to talk to people as if they understand the things that we understand. But they don't.

Remember your customers are NOT thinking about your "stuff," they are thinking about their "stuff." They don't want to put effort into understanding your offering. It is your job to make it the simplest, easiest, least risk, fastest way to get what they want.

It's easy to use our own terminology but you should avoid jargon at all costs unless it's the customer's jargon. When I was selling ERP to publishers, I could talk about publishing, ISBNs, first print runs, new title releases, book production, and pub dates because that was their language. If I talked about computer language, I'd have lost them. So always remember, even though you may be speaking to highly educated, intelligent people, keep it simple!

These four tips can help you to understand your customer's core objectives so you can provide them with a pain-alleviating solution. The bottom line to my secret and philosophy is that it is all about them. Without being able to solve their problem at the right time, you won't be able to truly fulfill the role and duty of a salesperson.

Want to learn more from Steve Hall?
Connect with him on:
LinkedIn: linkedin.com/in/stevehallsydney
Website: thesalesexpertschannel.com

#27 The Beauty of Imperfection

TODD CAPONI

"I ended up taking everything I owned and I bought a sales training company. It was a giant risk. I did that for three years, and it changed the trajectory of my entire career dramatically."

ABOUT TODD CAPONI:

Todd Caponi is the author of the award-winning book, *The Transparency Sale*. He is also a keynote speaker, workshop leader, and trainer as Principal and Founder of Sales Melon LLC.

Up until 2018, he spent nearly four years building the revenue capacity of Chicago's PowerReviews from the ground up as their Chief Revenue Officer. Through his efforts, he turned the company into Illinois' fastest-growing tech company.

Prior to that, he held sales leadership roles with three other tech companies, including ExactTarget, where he helped drive the organization to a successful IPO and a $2.7B exit through the acquisition by Salesforce.com.

Todd is a former American Business "Stevie" Award winner. He has also owned and operated his own sales training company. His vast sales experience and knowledge have made him a true icon in the industry.

As an Indiana University grad, my first sales job was actually selling ads for the Indiana Daily Student Newspaper. I knew early on that I wanted to go into sales—probably because my dad worked in sales for 40+ years. So while many sales leaders take an unorthodox journey into sales, mine was a fairly straightforward path.

My first real sales role after graduating from college was selling overnight shipping. We were expected to make 500 cold calls a week and at the end of each week, we had to show at least one sale. I lived in Southern California at the time so my territory extended from Pasadena to the San Gabriel Mountains—it was a massive territory! They literally gave each of us a phone book and that was our "list." It was a definite learning experience, to say the least.

Culture Matters

I eventually got into the technology space where I continued to do more cold calling. Back then, companies were relentless (and I'm sure many still are). For salespeople, in particular, there was an overwhelming culture of fear where if you didn't perform, you would be fired. While it was a challenging environment to work in, I got to a point where I wasn't bothered by the constant rejection. Every "no" got me one step closer to an eventual "yes." That was the way I looked at it. I didn't allow myself to get swallowed up by all the negativity.

As I continued to climb the ranks, I eventually accepted a role with SAP. I spent three years there and they were three of the most fun years of my entire career. Unlike everywhere else I had worked until that point, SAP created a fantastic culture. It was at that time that I realized how important having a positive work environment is for an organization. Everyone I worked with would literally run through a brick wall to help one another. That type of commitment and togetherness is indispensable. It helps motivate you like nothing else.

Taking Risks and Learning From Mistakes

While I loved my time at SAP, in 2000 I decided to join the barge of million-aires that had headed to the coast for what we eventually would call the "Internet Bubble." With billion- dollar valuations, the allure of running an internet startup just seemed too good—until the bubble burst. By the time I left in 2000, the barge had gotten far enough away that I ended up running straight into the water. For a couple of years, I ran a series of startups—and by "ran," I mean I ran them straight into the ground. It was a disaster.

At that point, I was lucky to get whatever job I could so I started working for a company that did financial consolidation and data warehousing. I hated it. Through that process, though, I learned two valuable lessons about myself:

I have to be passionate about what I'm selling if I'm going to be successful.

While I'm pretty good at sales, I'm really good at teaching and coaching.

These two realizations led me to my next career move, which was life-changing. I ended up taking everything I owned and bought a sales training company. It was a giant risk but I knew even if it wasn't successful, it would help me grow and develop in my career. In my mind, I had two options—either start this company or go and get my MBA. I'll never regret choosing the former.

While the first six months were rough (I think I only made $12,000 in sales), things eventually turned around. Even though it was terrifying, the experience changed my entire career trajectory dramatically. I ran that business for three years, which ultimately led to several future opportunities and granted me more first-hand knowledge than any MBA program ever could.

I went on to work for companies like Right Hemisphere, ExactTarget, and PowerReviews. In these roles, I was able to leverage the knowledge I had gained while running my training business. While it's definitely been a wild ride, I wouldn't change a thing.

Transparency Always Wins

For anyone who knows me, my sales secret won't come as any surprise. My secret is that transparency wins—I even wrote a book on it!

You're probably asking, what do I really mean by transparency wins and how can I apply that concept when selling? Let me share a brief story. As the Chief Revenue Officer of a fast-growing company, we commissioned a study with Northwestern University on the impact of ratings and reviews. On a retail site like Vineyard Vines, or something like that, the website functions as the salesperson in many respects. Interestingly enough, the study found that on a site like Vineyard Vines, products rated between 4.2 and 4.5 on a five-point scale actually sold better than products rated as perfect 5's. The study confirmed that imperfection actually sells better than perfection.

While I had already been tossing this concept around in my head, the study got me thinking, "Are we teaching our reps to sell as though we're perfect? What happens if we start embracing this imperfection and lead with it just like a website would do in a self- guided type of sale?"

More often than not, companies and salespeople present their products and services as if they are perfect. When we do that, though, we slow down the sales process because now we're forcing our buyers to find out on their own why we *aren't* perfect.

Benefits of Leading With Our Imperfections

While it may seem counter-intuitive, I believe that every organization should embrace what they aren't good at and lead with their imperfections. Here are three reasons why leading with your imperfections is actually to your advantage in the long run:

Speeds Up the Sales Cycle: The Corporate Executive Board (CEB) released a study that found in a typical sales cycle, buyers in the evaluation phase spend 61% of their time doing research beyond what a prospective vendor provides them with; imagine how much time you could save if you just gave your prospects the information they are actually seeking? By being transparent from the beginning, you will save your prospect countless hours of homework and ultimately speed up the sales cycle.

Increases Win Rates + Qualifies Deals Faster: When you lead with your imperfections, you're going to qualify deals much faster. You're also going to spend less time pursuing a deal that is bound for failure. After all, if you're going to lose, wouldn't you rather know it was a bust deal from the onset? If you approach your prospects with nothing to hide, you're ultimately going to win a higher percentage of deals and weed out the ones that were never a good fit from the start.

Makes it Difficult for Your Competitors: By highlighting your known weaknesses, you are able to control the narrative and not your competitors. Leading with your imperfections puts you in the driver's seat and makes it really difficult for your competitors to compete against you because you have stolen their ammunition.

HOW TO APPLY "TRANSPARENCY" TO YOUR SALES PROCESS:

Do Your Homework: I think the number one thing you need to do when applying this idea of transparency to your sales process is to make sure you know what kind of information a potential customer is going to find when researching your company. The last thing you want is to be blindsided in a meeting. So do your homework and embrace the information that you find. In doing this, it may be helpful to work with your marketing team to create content that speaks to your weaknesses—this goes back to the idea of owning the conversation and controlling the narrative.

Personalization is Key: Too often, salespeople have a tendency to talk about themselves, their companies, their products, etc. Remember, the sales process is not about you; it's about your customer. Instead of thinking about how great you are, think about how great your prospects can be.

Don't Complicate Negotiations: In negotiations, it's not Texas Hold 'em. You don't need to hide your tells. I think there is an opportunity to go in and be perfectly open and honest about what you need to get a deal done. When you do that, it's amazing the trust you can build.

I like to think that being 100% transparent is the same as being "flawsome" (to borrow a term coined by Tyra Banks). It's embracing your flaws, but knowing that you're awesome anyway. So, this is not a matter of teaching your reps to go out and say, "Hey customers, this is why we suck." It's the idea that we should be presenting ourselves as a "4.2" instead of a perfect "5." When we do that, we're being authentic and transparent and actually disarming the part of the brain that doesn't want to be sold to.

Despite what you may have learned in school, people don't buy perfection, they buy authenticity. Use that to your advantage.

Want to learn more from Todd Caponi? Follow him on:
Website: transparencysale.com
LinkedIn: linkedin.com/in/toddcaponi
Twitter: @tcaponi

#28 Master the Process

WES SCHAEFFER

"Rookies practice until they get it right, professionals practice until they can't get it wrong."

ABOUT WES SCHAEFFER:

Wes Schaeffer is an avid storyteller, author, sales keynote speaker, podcast host, marketing expert, and CEO of The Sales Whisperer. He and his team help businesses close B2B sales faster, easier, and at a predictably scaleable margin.

A proven inbound marketer, CRM and sales guru, Wes has never earned less than $100,000 since 1998 but continuously strives to achieve increasingly impactful goals. He drove sales in management positions for NetTest, ClearCube Technology, and Egenera. He then took on the role of Director of Inbound Sales and CRM Marketing Automation at X2 Technologies followed by the Territory Sales Manager role at EXFO. In 2006, Wes launched The Sales Whisperer.

Wes is also the author of five books, *The Definitive Guide to InfusionSoft*, *It Takes More Than a Big Smile, a Good Idea, and a Twitter Account to Build a Business that Lasts*, *The Sales Whisperer Way*, *Qualified Leads Have PAIN*, and *Lead Nurturing Best Practices*.

Outside of work, Wes practices jiu-jitsu, is the father of seven children, and is a veteran of the U.S. Air Force.

Those who have worked with Wes say that he comes from the heart and truly cares about making a positive difference in the lives of others. He does so by cutting through the clutter and helping companies get laser-focused to produce outcomes. When it comes to leveraging the right strategies to drive revenue, Wes is known as a true expert.

When I started in sales, I was young, aggressive, and had a can-do attitude. I would study sales books, learn concepts, and apply them, but I was just pulling in bits and pieces. I was like a short-order cook saying, "Hey I learned you can do stuff with celery. Let's chop some up and throw it in." There was no larger strategy — just micro tactics.

After nine years, I hired my first sales coach who I worked with exclusively for two years. He introduced me to a system that was a game-changer for me. It was a comprehensive sales system that applied to everything. By year 11, I had mastered sales.

You Have to Master the Process

So many people wing sales or do it "their way" thinking they have a natural gift or enough hustle to bring them to the level of mastery. The truth is, you may be naturally gifted and may hustle hard but to be a master, you need to first learn a sales system. Once you do, you will have the wisdom and knowledge to adapt the system to how you see fit but you have to earn that right. If you wing it out of the gate, you'll lack the understanding of the framework you need to operate successfully on a sustainable level. People have gone before you and figured out a lot of this stuff, so it's in your best interest to take advantage of it.

I'm still a newbie in jiu-jitsu, I've still got eight years to go before I can reach the mastery level because the techniques take time. You've gotta learn what to do in every scenario — just like in sales. My instructor in Brazilian Jiu-Jitsu is 53 years old and has done it since he was 19. When I first started, I thought he was a magician or a Wiccan, he was so good. But he said, "Look, man, I've just failed more than you've tried." Now two years into it, I see it. There is a system and the mastery of that system is a process.

HOW TO MASTER THE PROCESS

How can you master the art of sales? There are four stages you have to go through:

Unconscious Incompetence

You start and you get destroyed and you don't know why you're getting destroyed.

In this stage, you don't know what you don't know, which is the most dangerous place to be. Many people never make it out of this phase. They might get lucky and close some sales but they can't repeat their success because they don't understand what makes them succeed and what makes them fail.

Conscious Incompetence

You get destroyed and you recognize why you're getting destroyed.

In this stage, you begin to learn what you don't know. You analyze your performance in a systematic way which allows you to see what drives success and what doesn't. While you may be overwhelmed and your ego might take a hit, you are ahead of those in stage one because now you know what you need to do.

Competence

You stop getting destroyed.

In this stage, you take actions to systematically improve. You begin to implement strategies for success and see consistent positive results. You continue to practice, drill and rehearse. Rookies practice until they get it right, professionals practice until they can't get it wrong.

Unconscious Competence

You start to destroy others.

This is the stage of mastery. I don't care if you're a bricklayer, a musician, a coder, or a salesperson—the question is, can you do it successfully without thinking about it? If you can, you've become a master. It's here that you earn the right to make tweaks to optimize a system because you are above it.

To become a master of sales, you have to go through that progression.

Hopefully, you work with a company with a good system that can nurture you through and teach you the fundamentals.

What if Your Company Has a Bad System?

Unfortunately, most companies today don't have a good infrastructure to help you become a master of sales. But even if your employer has a system you perceive as bad, you can't complain about it until you legitimately try it and fail. Once you do, you can say, "Look, boss, I followed your recommended procedure to the letter and it didn't work, maybe we should change the process."

That's going to be a difficult conversation to have. If you have a good boss, they'll work on changing the process. If you have a bad one, they won't and you'll know you're in a bad place and it's time to move. But you can leave with a good conscience knowing you did everything they said but it was a bad system. Unless the company changes it, it will fail eventually.

You can also seek out a sales coach to help you find a good system that you can implement wherever your career takes you.

What About the People That Don't Follow Systems?

The rebels. There are always those that don't like to follow the rules. Those who think they know better. They are often in stage 1. I know for every story, secret, and rule, there is a story, secret, or rule that goes against it. But the thing is, you have to know the rules of the system to know which parts to break and challenge, otherwise it's not a meaningful or intelligent adaptation. Look at Eddie Bravo, the big jiu-jitsu guy. He brought a whole new game to martial arts but he didn't invent it from scratch. He mastered the fundamentals and then modified them.

So you have to learn the system before you can beat the system. Then it's just a gut- feeling, intuition, doing it long enough-thing where you'll know when it's time to challenge the status quo.

Want to learn more from Wes Schaeffer? Follow him on:
Website: thesaleswhisperer.com
LinkedIn: linkedin.com/in/thesaleswhisperer
YouTube: youtube.com/channel/UC2qIIZ-
VvIuLGVZ9PMB9bfg
Instagram: @saleswhisperer

#29 The Psychology of Sales

SHARI LEVITIN

"Until you take responsibility for everything in your life, not just sales—how you feel, how you look, how optimistic you are—you will never get to the next level in your career."

ABOUT SHARI LEVITIN:

"Shari Levitin is an energetic, wickedly funny sales guru, who helps sales teams bridge the gap between beating quota and selling with an authentic heartfelt approach". She is the founder of the Shari Levitin Group where she has helped create more than $1 billion in increased revenue for her client companies.

Shari is the best-selling author of *Heart and Sell: 10 Universal Truths Every Salesperson Needs to Know*. She has also been a contributor to *Forbes*, *CEO Magazine*, and *Huffington Post*.

Additionally, Shari was chosen as the first adjunct professor at the University of Utah David Eccles School of Business to teach a course in sales. She's an Advisory Board member of the Sundance Institute, a designated Women's

Sales Pro, and was featured as an expert in the new Salesforce documentary film "The Story of Sales."

"Shari, her husband, and son live in Park City, Utah. When she's not creating killer content and presenting at sales kickoffs, Shari enjoys skiing, rock climbing, reading and standing on her head".

Growing up, my parents placed a huge emphasis on personal development and learning. On vacations, we literally would have a seminar hour every day at 9:00 a.m. where my parents, brother and I would present on a topic of our choosing. Sounds crazy to some but that is just an example of how intense and driven my family was; it also helps explain a lot about why I am the way I am today.

At the age of four, my mother escaped from Nazi Germany with her parents and moved to Los Angeles. With little money, one of my mother's favorite things was to go to the library and read. She would get ten books at a time, then ten more, then ten more. So while I'm not from a family of salespeople per se, I'm from a family where learning and growing meant life or death. This type of thinking has shaped me and my entire career.

The Importance of Owning Your Fate

As an avid reader myself, like my mother, one of my favorite books is called a *Man's Search for Meaning* by Viktor Frankl. The book chronicles Frankl's real-life experience as a prisoner in Nazi concentration camps during World War II. Frankl's book helped me understand that no matter who you are, you can't change what happens to you but you can change how you deal with it. This is true in sales, in business, and in life.

When I first started in sales, I was tasked with helping sell timeshares by standing outside supermarkets and inviting people to take tours. To cover more ground, I sold on roller skates and actually had a great deal of early success. I even became the top salesperson. With no formal sales training, though, I was selling on pure excitement and enthusiasm. Like many young sales professionals, I soon ran out of steam and hit a wall (not literally, even though roller skates were my sales tool of choice)! So what do you do when you hit the inevitable sales wall?

I eventually learned that I needed to understand the psychology of selling. I needed to know why I did what I did. My mentor helped me through this journey.

Some 25 or 30 years ago, my mentor and I were sitting out on a balcony and he asked me, "Shari, what's your goal for the new year?" I said, "Oh, I'm going to make $100,000." And he says, "Really, what did you make last year?" I said, "I made $40,000." And that's when he told me something I'll never forget. He said, "If you want to hit a higher goal than you've ever hit, you have to not only look at what you want to achieve but what you're willing to give up." Before he said that, I had never realized all of the habits, ideas, and attitudes I had to give up in order to get to the next level in my career. His advice has stuck with me ever since.

So what bad habits did I need to give up? I needed to let go of what I call "bad ego." I often tell people that there is good ego and bad ego. Good ego gives you the ability to claim greatness. It allows you to be confident in your abilities. Conversely, bad ego is what allows us to make excuses and say, "It's not my fault." It's when we say, "My SDRs gave me terrible leads" or "It's not the right economy." With bad ego, the pronoun is always, "they," "she" or "he." I learned really quickly you can't take the glory for being great if you won't take the responsibility when you're not.

We are extremely powerful beings but when we blame, we lose our power. If you're not getting good leads—or if you're not happy at your company—or whatever the situation may be—stop blaming others for your shortcomings. Regain your power and find a way to make the situation better. When I find myself blaming other people about everything that's wrong in my life, I think of Viktor Frankl who persevered through tremendous hardships and found a way to deal with the hand life had dealt him. Instead of wallowing in self-pity, look at what *you* can do to change your situation.

The Two Most Important Attributes You Must Have for Influence in Sales

Before starting my own company, I spent several years at some of the world's largest hotel brands, including Marriott, Four Seasons and Hilton. Sticking to my roots of selling timeshares, I became the top, top salesperson, because I did something few at the time were doing: I listened.

As I became a good listener, I soon learned that there are two essential skills that all salespeople must have: empathy and competency. If you've been reading along and patiently waiting for my sales secret, here it is—if you really want to influence people, you have to be empathetic and competent when selling. Plain and simple.

Why Empathy and Competency Matter:

Here's a sales tip that I hope you will remember—when it comes to empathy and competency, the order matters. Empathy gets you in the door, competency, reliability, and integrity keep you there.

Empathy: What does it mean to be empathetic in sales? It means you need to know your customers and what makes them tick. You must lead with what is important to your customer and not what is important to you. This is true of all relationships when you think about it. The best relationships—in business and in your personal life—are built on trust. When we meet someone for the first time, we try to establish a rapport with them so they don't feel intimidated. If someone is intimidated, they immediately go into fear mode, which is hard to recover from in sales. This is what happens when you immediately make your sales pitch without building a relationship with your prospect. In order to become successful in sales, you must first learn to be empathetic.

Competency: Once you have established a relationship, now you must show that you know your product and market. Your customer needs to know you're competent before they can fully trust you. This is where doing your homework comes into play. You want to become your customer's trusted advisor. And this means you must be reliable and continuously demonstrate your integrity. Follow through on what you say you are going to do and always have your customer's best interest in mind.

As you continue to grow as a salesperson, I encourage you to think about the psychology behind why and what you do. Not only will it help your sales performance, but it will also inform all aspects of your life.

Want to learn more from Shari Levitin? Follow her on:
Website: sharilevitin.com
LinkedIn: linkedin.com/in/sharilevitin
Twitter: @sharilevitin
YouTube: youtube.com/user/LevitinGroup
Facebook: facebook.com/ShariLevitinGroup

#30 Get The "F" Up

CHAD BURMEISTER

"You're not going to have a high competency on day one. That's going to take time. So what do you need to do? Get the F (frequency) up."

ABOUT CHAD BURMEISTER:

Chad is the Founder and CEO of ScaleX.ai, a company focused on helping funded startups bring their products to market faster than ever before.

Voted as one of the "Top 25 Most Influential Inside Sales Leaders" by the AA-ISP for 10 years in a row (2009—2019), Chad has no doubt made his mark on the industry. Before founding ScaleX.ai, Chad built several high-performing inside sales teams at companies including Cisco-WebEx, Riverbed Technology, ON24, and RingCentral.

He also served as the President of the Colorado Chapter of the American Association of Inside Sales Professionals for over six years. And, he hosted a weekly webinar for seven years which helped to advance inside sales to the next level of professionalism and performance.

Those who know Chad say that he is high-energy and personifies a great leader. He is said to be one of the most deeply connected and widely respected people in the sales enablement industry. Further, with over a decade working in SaaS, he has proven he has an impressive ability to drive revenue results.

Although I'm an introvert, I always wanted to be in sales. I was originally inspired by my cousin and uncle who were in pharmaceutical sales at Pfizer. I remember my cousin bought a Porsche at a very young age and put "1st Mil" on the license plate. I asked him how I could get started and he told me to decide where I wanted to go, study people's resumes who were there, and plot a map to get there.

I didn't know how to sell out of the gate but I landed my first sales job at a company called Olsen Staffing Services. We sold a product where we would staff temporary workers. I struggled there. I didn't know what questions to ask and wasn't catching on. They gave me a chance and I ended up getting fired. I was lacking the competency and guidance I needed.

My second sales job was at Airborne Express where I was surrounded by good salespeople and supported by a formal sales training program. Within eight months, I was the number one salesperson. So to the people who are sitting in a sales role today and not reaching their full potential, there is hope. Even if you're not supported by formal training or helpful mentors, I've figured out an equation that can help you succeed anyway.

The Equation to Sales Success R=FxC

My top secret to maximizing sales success is to use the equation that revenue equals frequency multiplied by competency. We all know what revenue is so let's take a closer look at the other two parts of the equation.

What Is Frequency?

Frequency is the amount of sales activity you perform. Activities can include a phone call, an email, a social outreach, a video, a physical letter, etc.

What Is Competency?

Competency is your proficiency in your role. It is the result of a combination of skills, personal traits, knowledge, and abilities. The development of competency is an ongoing process that happens over time. In most cases, when you start a new job, you will not be high on the competency scale.

HOW TO COMBINE FREQUENCY AND COMPETENCY FOR SUCCESS

Imagine a new student in an archery class. How many arrows are they going to need to shoot to hit the bullseye three times? 50? 100? However, over time, as that student practices, they will be able to hit the bullseye with far fewer arrows. They will become more efficient. The same goes for sales.

The way my sales success equation works is if your competency level is low, you should up the frequency of your sales activities to make up for it (shoot more arrows). As your competency develops, you can slow down your frequency because you won't need as much activity to hit your targets.

Whenever I have new people that join my company, I always teach them this equation. To me, the frequency piece is **so, so, so** important, especially early in a sales career.

HOW TO INCREASE YOUR SALES ACTIVITY FREQUENCY

How do you adjust your frequency according to your competency level to improve your revenue production?

Set A Goal

The first thing you should do is look at the sales activities you are currently completing each day. For example, let's say you are using SalesLoft and are supposed to load 25 prospects per day and make 25 calls.

Next, figure out how you can level that up. How many sales activities can you realistically do each day to up your frequency? Figure out what makes sense and take note of the number.

Talk To Your Manager

Next, set aside a time to meet with your manager. In the meeting, explain the theory about increasing the frequency of your sales activity to boost your revenue production while you work on improving your competency. Present your plan to increase your frequency by the number you decide is realistic. It's also a good idea to ask for some support to help in the process of improving your competency such as asking your manager to listen in on calls and provide feedback and/or partake in some role-playing.

The conversation can sound something like this,

"Hey, this company has been great. I've been here for a month. I'm doing okay, right? I've sold a couple of deals. But, I want to 5x it. If it's okay with you, instead of just two or three phone calls, I want to make it eight phone calls in my sequence. I promise you I won't let any slip. Then instead of the three emails, I want to make it four. And I want to send a physical letter to at least a hundred CEOs and CFOs because I've heard physical content can get as much as 10% to 15% reply rates. So if it's cool with you, I just want to crank the knob and show you, as my leader, what that can do for you, the company, and for me on my commission check."

What leader is going to say no? Not any good leaders that I know.

Crank the F Up

Once you get the go-ahead, it's time to crank the F (frequency) up. How? All you have to do is clone the existing sequence, cadence, and playbook and double or triple everything in it.

HOW TO IMPROVE YOUR SALES COMPETENCY

Next, competency comes down to being able to identify your prospect's problem and effectively position yourself to solve it. It is developed over time through experience. However, my template workflow for a good sales conversation can help. I call it APPCOM which is an acronym for Acceptance, Purpose, Probing, Consultation, Objections, and Motivate to Close. Here's a closer look at each of the steps.

Acceptance

With most people, especially introverts like myself, our general knee jerk reaction is to get straight to business during a sales interaction. That's the wrong approach. Instead, you need to gain acceptance. By that I mean connect with the prospect about something besides business (skiing, weather, etc.) and get them feeling good about talking to you.

If you are on a video call, you could say, "Hey, (prospect name), you know, I see that's a cool office there. Where on planet earth are you today?" Once they answer, you can reply, "Oh, (city name)? Wow, cool. Isn't that where the Hall of Fame is?" Or something relevant to that area.

Have a friendly chat about something that establishes a positive connection and gains acceptance. A little research before-hand won't hurt.

Purpose

After gaining acceptance, state your purpose for the conversation. As the rep, it's your job to take the reigns. If you let the customer control it, it's going to go down the wrong path.

Say something that defines the purpose such as, "So by the end of the conversation, we're going to see if it makes sense to have another conversation. Are we on the same page? Is there anything else you'd like to achieve today?"

Then, the customer has the chance to say what they'd like to see. Once they've shared their goals, summarize and say something like, "Okay, great, I'll make sure we cover those points."

Probing

Probing is the third step. This is where you go through question after question, collecting as much information as you can to discover the customer's problem and the impact of their problem. It helps to plan questions out, such as:

Can you tell me about your company at a high level?

Will you tell me about your department and its areas of opportunity?

Can you tell me about you personally?

You want to get the client talking and giving you a lot of information. Eventually, they will get a bit tired of talking. Over time, you'll learn to sense the moment coming. At this point, you have to give them some value.

You should say something like," Thank you for sharing all that with me. It's been really helpful. The reason I am asking you all of this is because…"

And explain how it helps you to solve their problem. I like to throw in a story about a past customer I've helped at this point for reinforcement.

After you've given them value and a reminder of the purpose of the call, briefly return to discovery. You can say something like, "So real quick before we get into showing you anything today, I have a couple more quick questions." Then, collect any other information you may need to fully understand the prospect and their problem.

Consulting

Step four is where you become the consultant based on all of the things you've learned about the customer and their problem. Summarize the problem first and then, within the first five minutes, address the points that the customer cares about. You can go into other ancillary things later.

Overcome Objections

Next, be ready to overcome objections. You should create a list of the top 10 objections your customers have and your responses to them. Often, as salespeople, we hear the same types of objections over and over so we need to get good at overcoming them.

For example, a common objection is on price. If a prospect says, "Well, you know, $40,000 is a lot of money for your product." You have to have a comeback to that.

You could say, "Hmm...interesting. So you said that the problem you're having is that your current team of SDRs isn't delivering enough meetings. The reason for that is that they didn't do enough activities. You came to us because you're going to see 30,000 activities in three months instead of 30,000 activities in a year, right? So, hang on, what did we say earlier you spend for three BDRs for one year, like $250,000? I'm confused, $40,000 compared to $250,000, I don't get it. How is $40k expensive? Am I missing it?" Then you make them talk their way out of it, handle their own objection.

Having these objections and responses well-versed can help you get to the close.

Motivate to Act:

The last piece of the puzzle is motivating your prospects to act. You have to ask for the sale or conversion action when it comes time.

There are two parts to this; the best action commitment (BAC) and a minimum acceptable action (MAA). The BAC is the best possible outcome of the conversation while the MAA is the minimum outcome you find acceptable.

I recommend starting with the BAC and then if it sounds like too much for them you can work back to the MAA. If you start with the MAA and they say no, you have nowhere good left to go.

And that's it. No matter where you are in your sales career, you can work on driving more revenue and becoming a better salesperson. If you are new and have a lot to learn, start by cranking the F up. Work hard and learn as you go. You can also use my APPCOM template as a guide in sales conversations to help you improve your competency and close more deals.

Want to learn more from Chad Burmeister? Follow him on: LinkedIn: linkedin.com/in/chadburmeister

#31 Influence the Sales Process by Finding the Gap

JIM KEENAN

"Our job as salespeople is not to be order-takers but to be influencers, and understanding the gap enables us to influence the sale."

ABOUT JIM KEENAN:

Keenan is the CEO and president of the sales consulting and recruiting firm, A Sales Guy Inc. and is the celebrated author of *Not Taught: What It Takes to be Successful in the 21st Century That Nobody's Teaching* You along with his most recent book, *Gap Selling: Getting the Customer to Yes.*

With over 20 years of sales experience, Keenan was named one of the Top 30 Social Sellers in the world by *Forbes.* He was also named one of the Top 50 Most Influential Sales and Marketing People by *Top Sales World Magazine* every year running since 2012.

In addition, he has been featured in *Harvard Business Journal, Huffington Post, Entrepreneur Magazine, Inc.*, and *Forbes.*

While Keenan remembers selling all the way back in elementary school, he entered the sales world professionally after graduating from the University of Colorado at Boulder with a BA in Political Science. He started out as a sales manager at Born Information Services, then became the VP of National Sales at ICG Communications, followed by VP of Wireline Sales at Intrado.

During his time at Intrado, Keenan founded his first start-up, cr8Buzz.com, a social network to help the little guy gain exposure. In the following years, he was the VP of Avaya and 2 Wire before founding his second start-up, Socially Booked. Soon after, he founded A Sales Guy Inc., which, for the last 8+ years, has been helping B2B companies around the world to generate more revenue.

Keenan is also a mentor at TechStars, where he helps up-and-coming start-up founders get the ball rolling, and a Ski Instructor at Vail Resorts.

Those who know Keenan say he is a fun, refreshing, and likable person who brings order to the chaos and simplicity to the sales process. He speaks from experience and has no- nonsense ideas that work. His extensive knowledge of social selling, sales best practices, sales talent acquisition, and personal branding are said to be equally matched by his positive, infectious personality.

When people buy something or make a choice, there are two things that drive them; pleasure and pain. We all make decisions to move toward pleasure or away from pain.

However, research has shown that people are more inclined to move away from pain rather than toward pleasure so why do most sales strategies focus only on moving toward pleasure?

Find the Gap

My top sales secret is to find the gap. When people buy something, they are looking to change. Whether they know it and come to you saying, "Help me," or you get a hold of them and give them enough information for them to realize it.

When someone is trying to change, their natural decision process is comparative, although most of us don't sell or think about it this way. People ask, "Where am I today? What's going on? What's the impact? Do I like it? How is it affecting me?" Then, they think about the future and ask, "What could I have tomorrow? What could be different tomorrow? What would be the impact?"

The space between what they have today and where they could be tomorrow is the gap. That gap dictates the value to them, the sense of urgency, the intrinsic motivation, and the desire to move; all of it!

So if you don't know your prospect's gap then you don't know how they are going to make a decision. If you don't know how they are going to make a decision, then you can't influence the sale. Our job as salespeople is not to be order-takers but to be influencers, and understanding the gap enables us to influence the sale.

HOW-TO EXECUTE GAP SELLING

Gap selling is more than just asking questions. There are certain types of information you need to gather.

Perform Discovery Around the Current State

The first step is to perform discovery around the current state. You need to understand all of the current state information that is relevant to the sale. How are they doing things? How are their systems set up? How big is the organization?

I break the current state down into five sections:

Physical facts: Non Judgemental stuff like the size of the organization, where they are located, the number of employees, etc.

Problems: What are the current problems they are struggling with that cause issues?

Impact of problems (Most important): How are the problems impacting their organization?

The emotional impact of problems: How do they feel as a result of the problems? Do they feel angry, frustrated, scared, etc.?

The root cause of the problems: What is causing the problems to exist in the first place?

Once you are clear on the current state and you can articulate it, you need to flip it and discover the future state.

Discover the Future State

The future state is where a prospect wants to go and what they are trying to accomplish.

I also break this part down into five sections:

Physical facts: What do you want the physical facts to be in the future?

Problems: What problems don't you want to have tomorrow?

Impact of solving problems: What will the impact of solving those problems look like?

The emotional impact of solving the problems: How will you feel once the problems are solved?

What is the solution that will address the root cause?

Once you have all that in place, you'll understand the gap and will know if it's big or small. Based on the size of the gap, you'll know the probability of them buying and how much time and effort they will put in to make it work. A lot of times, customers have never looked at their decision this way so when you go through the whole process, you help them see it better than they did before.

Most sales methods spend all the time in the future state. What do you need? What do you want? What benefits will you get? Instead, we anchor the prospect in the current state, addressing the pain and then we compare it to the pleasure of the future state. To my knowledge, the way gap selling is structured, makes it one of the only sales methodologies that use both pain and pleasure in the process. We put both on the table, creating a powerful view of the decision at hand.

Use this gap selling strategy to leverage both pain and pleasure motivators and effectively influence your prospects throughout the sales process.

Want to learn more from Jim Keenan? Follow him on:
LinkedIn: linkedin.com/in/jimkeenan
About Keenan: asalesguy.com/about-keenan
Company Website: asalesguy.com
Twitter: @keenan

#32 'Selling' Is the Wrong Way to Think About Sales

JASON JORDAN

"If the benefit your prospect sees is big enough, then the cost becomes irrelevant. If you start with the cost, you're digging out of a hole the entire time."

ABOUT JASON JORDAN:

Jason is a recognized thought-leader in B2B Selling and Management, a popular speaker and writer for the *Harvard Business Review*, *Forbes*, *Entrepreneur*, Salesforce.com, and more. He is also the best-selling author of *Cracking the Sales Management Code* and *Sales Insanity*.

He conducts ongoing research to advance the discipline of sales management and specializes in: sales management best practices, sales metrics, pipeline management, forecasting, CRM, change management, leadership development, and coaching.

Jason is also a Leading Partner and Co-Founder of Vantage Point Performance, a board member of the Sales Education Foundation, and an Independent Consultant who has coached clients including General Electric (GE), FedEx, Samsung, and HP.

Jason's professional career began after graduating from Duke University with a BA in economics and the University of Virginia's Darden Graduate School of Business Administration with an MBA.

Before co-founding Vantage Point Performance, he spent 20 years working in various roles such as the Business Transformation Leader at Renaissance Worldwide, Director of Business Development at Hitachi Data Systems, and Principal of Sales Effectiveness at Mercer. He developed and fine-tuned his skillset, which brought him to where he is today.

Jason is known as a masterful keynote speaker and author who shares insights that carry the power to transform most any organization.

One of my early jobs was at Circuit City. Customers would come in and I would do what any bad salesperson does. I'd say, "Oh, hey, let me show you some VCRs. This is the price range. These are features." Basically, I was just a talking brochure. But one day I was standing around and I heard one of my peers doing something different.

A couple walked up and said, "Hey, we're looking for a VCR."

He replied, "Oh, that's interesting. Let's talk about this for a second. How big is your television?" And they said, "Well, my television's so and so." He says, "Oh, really, that's kind of small. How far do you sit away from it?" And they said, "Well, I think the couch is probably 10 feet away." He replied, "Wow, that's a really small television for that use." And they agreed, saying, "Yeah, it is kind of hard to see sometimes with the captions and things."

He went through this whole thing, putting himself in their shoes, and ended up selling them not only a VCR but a big-ass television! I was like, "Why don't we all ask people about their needs?"

It's All About the Buying (Not the Selling) Process

From that experience and many that were to follow, I learned that selling is really the wrong way to think about what we do as salespeople. It's not about the sales process but the buying process.

If you think about it in the most simple possible terms, a salesperson is there to facilitate buying. We often get so caught up on sales activities, processes, and tools that we think our job is to execute from the sales perspective. However, in reality, all we're supposed to do is just hold the buyer's hand through each step of the process and make sure that they have what they need to go to the next step. Salespeople need to be asking questions like, "If I'm the buyer right now, what is it that I need? Do I need information? Do I need comfort? Do I need negotiation?

I had a client one time, he was a brilliant guy, he said, "I don't even train my salespeople how to sell." He said, "I train my salespeople how their customers buy. If they understand how their customers buy, they're smart enough to figure out the selling part."

So I think sales is about making sure that you continue to move through the buying process, holding the buyer's hand.

HOW-TO GUIDE YOUR CUSTOMER'S THROUGH THE BUYING PROCESS

How do you make that shift? It's not that complex. You could hire a company to come in and do customer services and segmentation, and that's useful. That's how marketing strategies come about, but as a salesperson, you just need to talk to your customers.

Interview New Customers and "Would-Be" Customers

When you lose a sale, people often think, "Oh, we lost a sale. We should go back and do a post mortem and see what happened." And you should, but my company has learned just as much from asking customers after we won a deal about why we won it.

So I would say interview your customers and the people that you lose, and ask them:

- How the process went on their side
- What things were they considering as they looked at you versus your competitors?
- At what point did they decide to go with you or a competitor?
- Who were the buyers that really made the decision?
- If you lost, ask what did the competitor do to outperform us in this buying cycle of yours?

Customers will often tell you, especially after you sell them something. You have this honeymoon period before you actually have a chance to screw it up. You'd be surprised what comes out of customers' mouths when you just ask them a simple question.

Keep Tabs on Existing Customers

Next, you shouldn't stop with new customers and would-be customers. Also, keep the lines of communication open with existing customers.

I'll give you a quick little story to illustrate why.

I was working with a company one time, an insulation distributor, who worked with contractors. They'd sell insulation tiles and construction materials. We did some analysis and discovered that many of the bigger customers weren't really profitable because they were negotiating thin margins, demanding a lot of deliveries, and not paying.

We put together an account management process and said, "Here's what you have to do. Go out and talk to all of your top 10 big customers, and ask them what you can do to get more of their business." One of the guys said he wasn't going to do it and we said, "Well, your CEO says you're going to do it, but tell me why you don't want to."

He said, "Look, this guy right here, for instance, we go to church together. I've been calling him for 10 years. If I go up to him and ask him what I can do to get more of his business, it's going to be a joke. He's going to laugh at me. And I've probably got 80% of his business as it is."

We said, "Okay. Well, I see your point but you still need to go talk to him." The guy comes back and says, "I can't believe the conversation I just had. I thought I had 80% of their business. I have like 30%. I asked him why he was giving so much business to competitors, and he said because they would deliver it on a palette. As it is, we have to break it down off of a palette, put it on a truck, and take it to him which is more work for us."

He was getting out-sold in a way that he'd prefer to sell because he was making assumptions and not actually talking to his customers.

Just like I learned that day while on the sales floor of Circuit City, if we are only focused on selling the VCRs by rattling off prices and features, we might as well be a brochure.

We are going to miss a lot of sales opportunities. Instead, focus all of your efforts on the buyer. Who are they? What are the common problems they face which they may not have even identified yet? How can you resonate with those needs and help them with a solution? Open up the lines of communication!

Find out why customers do and don't buy from you and use that information in future interactions. Additionally, don't assume your current customers are fully satisfied. Keep tabs on them to find out if there is any way to improve and earn more of their business. Because at the end of the day, the selling process only moves forward if the buying process does.

Want to learn more from Jason Jordan? Follow him on:
LinkedIn: linkedin.com/in/jasonjordansalesmanagement
Company Website: vantagepointperformance.com

#33 A Winning Equation

RYAN REISERT

"We can never fail by trying—we only fail by repeating the same mistakes over and over again."

ABOUT RYAN REISERT:

Ryan is the Director of Sales at ConnectAndSell, Inc., a mentor for Plug and Play Tech Center and Co-Author of *Outbound Sales, No Fluff*. Ryan has also co-founded three companies throughout his career.

His book *Outbound Sales, No Fluff* was recognized on SalesHacker's "Best Sales Books: 30 Elite Picks to Step Up Your Sales Game" list and on BookAuthority's "92 Best Sales Books of All Time" ranking.

A well-established entrepreneur and leader in the sales development space, Ryan comes from humble beginnings in Hillard, Washington. Both of his parents were janitors and his two siblings are felons. However, from a young age, he had the will to succeed.

Ryan always did well in school, participated in many school activities, was a three-sport varsity four-year letter winner, and was the first in his family to go to college. Having a knack for numbers, Ryan earned his B.S. in Mathematics from Washington State University. He aimed to teach high school math and help guide kids like him who had a rough start in life.

However, one trip to San Francisco in 2008 changed everything for Ryan. He knew he had to live there so he packed up all his things and made the move with no money and no job. Being a difficult time for the country due to the economic collapse, Ryan struggled to catch a break and ended up working at Starbucks.

Finally, he was brought on by Rex & Company which was backed by AIG. He gained experience with Salesforce, had his first quota, and crushed it. Although the company laid off everyone shortly after, Ryan had earned the experience he needed to break into the sales industry.

In the following years, Ryan built his resume and experience working for companies including eSearchVision, Uversity, Sellpoints, Booshaka, Sprinklr, and ZenProspect. He quickly climbed the ranks from sales executive to VP of sales.

Ryan is known as a true mentor and leader in the sales development realm. He is said to bring an exceptional level of sales intelligence, experience, and humility to the table. Direct reports say he inspires hard work, leads by example, knows how to relate to customers, and creates vibrant teams that feel like family.

In 2008, when the world was burning and I had just got laid off from my first sales job at Rex & Company, I was introduced to a recruiting firm. Within a week, I had three job offers. The next job I took was at eSearchVision, a Pay-Per-Click advertising platform. All of a sudden, during my time in that job, it clicked for me. This is math. Underneath sales, there was a process just like any equation. And that's when I realized sales was for me.

Sales Is a Process You Continuously Improve

Now over ten years later, I always go back to the fact that sales is a process. It has a beginning, middle, and end, and each part should be broken down, analyzed, and optimized. Everything you do should be documented and followed to a "T" as much as possible. And as you learn what's working and what's not, you can make adjustments to your process.

I believe you're doing sales wrong if you're:

- Out there just kind of shooting from your hip
- Guessing and not preparing
- Not putting together a script
- Not gaining a consistent understanding of why you get certain results
- Not asking that question 'why' ahead of each of the things that you're doing
- Not creating an "if this, then that"-type flowchart

When someone comes to me and asks me a sales question as a leader, I ask them what's the process? If the process is not documented, I tell them they've got to document it first—otherwise, we don't know what we're talking about. Once you have a simple process, things become easy. You can analyze, make tweaks, and track the results.

Without a well-defined process in place, even if you do have success by luck, you won't know how to repeat it. Further, when you fail, you won't know how to avoid failure again in the future. You should always be asking, "What is the process?"

HOW CAN I CREATE A SALES PROCESS?

If you aren't sure where to start with creating a sales process, you can break it down into four parts: Target, Message, Channel, and Timing.

Part One: Target

The first thing you want to ask is who are you targeting? That is the most important. If you don't know who you are talking to, you have nothing. Identify your target audience(s) and get into the fine details of who they are.

Part Two: Message

Once you know who you should be talking to, you need to define what you are going to say. The more personalized and relevant, the better.

Part Three: Channel

Third, where does your audience want to receive the message (email, direct mail, Facebook, etc.)? Be sure it's not where you want to deliver it, but where they want to receive it.

Part Four: Timing

And finally, timing. When is the best time to reach your prospect? You can't always know for sure what time is best but you can use data and past interactions to get a better idea. Additionally, if you contact a prospect at a bad time, you have the opportunity to find out when a better time will be for a follow-up.

So, that's it—identify the target, message, channel, and timing. And you know what? You may find out that you were wrong initially about one of the parts, and that is okay. Then you identify the mistake, try something else, and document the result. You will likely also find new ways to improve upon what you have over time.

When I was working at the first company I co-founded, TheLions, we were introduced to new technology at the time called Yesware. I started to realize how much it could impact sales by improving the messaging part of our sales process. It was the first time I could find out who had opened my emails and respond in real-time. I could also start to put a new process behind my messaging so I wasn't repeating the same emails over and over again.

Using Yesware's templates and open analytics completely changed the game and our company's ability to grow fast. In less than a year, we went from having no clients, to representing 40 of the fastest-growing companies in San Francisco. Our growth was really on the back of Yesware and our improved process. That's when I got super excited about how you can create a sales process and use ongoing analysis, tools, and data to accelerate it.

The Bottom Line

Everything you do needs to be tested, documented. and turned into a standard operating procedure that is stored in each department's operating manual. If you don't know what to do in any situation, connect with leadership or your peers and ask the question, "What is the process and how can we improve it?" You can never fail by trying—you only fail by repeating the same mistakes over and over again.

Want to learn more from Ryan Reisert? Follow him on: LinkedIn: linkedin.com/in/salesdevelopmentrepresentative

#34 Shifting to an Outcome-Oriented Sales Mentality

MARK HUNTER

"Sales is about influence and impact. When we influence and impact people positively, it's amazing what we can accomplish."

ABOUT MARK HUNTER:

Mark Hunter, aka the "Sales Hunter," is a world-renowned sales consultant, speaker, and coach. He has written two best-selling books, *High-Profit Selling: Win the Sale Without Compromising on Price* and *High-Profit Prospecting.*

Mark has received several distinguished honors including being named one of the top "30 Sales Gurus" by Global Guru in 2018; he was also named a "Leading Sales Consultant" in 2018 by Selling Power. His blog has been cited as one of the top sales blogs on multiple occasions and is viewed as a go-to resource for sales professionals across the globe.

Mark spent the first 15+ years of his career working for three Fortune 200 companies where he held both sales leadership and marketing positions.

He quickly rose through the ranks at each company he worked at and was tasked with leading hundreds of salespeople.

Through these corporate positions, Mark began to see the shortcomings of salespeople, which led him to become a sales consultant, speaker, and coach. For the past 20 years, Mark has been able to work with thousands of salespeople and leaders through his consulting business and remains committed to developing world-class sales leaders.

I always tell people that I owe my entire sales career to the Seattle Police Department. Sounds crazy I know, but it's true. During my last semester of college, I got four speeding tickets within about a six-week timespan. A few months after getting my fourth ticket, I received a notice in the mail that pretty much made it impossible for me to afford car insurance. With few options, I needed a job that supplied a car and sales was one of the few professions that provided such a luxury. So, that is how I got started in sales—by virtue of my own stupidity.

My first job consisted of selling sides of beef. No joke. I'll be the first to admit that I was not the most mature during my early days and actually got fired from my first sales gig within about 10 months. Over time, I wised up and was fortunate to work for some major food companies like Pillsbury and General Foods. It was at General Foods that I began to listen to people and stopped focusing on my own needs. I started playing the "long game" and shifted my focus from making money to what I now call "legacy leadership."

Legacy leadership is a concept I talk about a lot today and refers to the legacy you leave behind. Instead of thinking solely about how much you earn, try asking yourself, "What will people say about me in 20 or 30 years and how can I truly influence and impact people?" When I asked myself those questions, I experienced a transformation that continues to this day.

Why focus on influence and impact you ask? Because it will help you stay motivated. Salespeople that are really into influence and impact are excited to make sales calls because they *want* to have that next conversation. They *want* to see their prospects and clients succeed. If you're only focused on closing deals and putting more money in your pocket, prospecting will drain you and become a laborious chore. If you can make sales about more than yourself, you'll be rewarded in the long run.

Leveraging Your Three Greatest Assets

Throughout my career, I've discovered that I have three tremendous assets: *my time, my mind and my network.* To be successful in sales, I offer the following advice that is part one of my sales secret:

Protect Your Time: While everyone is busy, not everyone is productive. To be successful, you need to maximize your time and decide how to best allocate each hour of your day. This might sound crazy, but I never put together a to-do list. To-do lists are major time sucks that help track a series of activities that may or may not be important. Instead of creating a list, think about what outcome you want to achieve. Once you have established your desired outcome, allocate your time to achieve that objective. To do this effectively, never let others decide your time for you.

Grow Your Mind: Every great salesperson, no matter where they are in their career, is focused on learning more and getting better at their craft. At no point in time should a salesperson ever stop learning. I challenge myself to learn something new every day. Having that kind of discipline has helped me get to where I am today.

Nurture Your Network: A person's network is truly priceless and something that should be respected. Your network includes clients, prospects, colleagues, employees and so on but no matter how you characterize them, they are all people. Everything you do in sales should be about the people in your network and how you can make *them* successful. When you have a sales mentality that is people-centric, you'll not only find it easier to stay motivated but you'll likely experience greater success.

Creating an Outcome-Focused Sales Strategy

As you leverage your time, mind and network, you'll naturally find yourself shifting to an outcome-focused sales mentality, which is part two of my sales secret! As I've already alluded to, the most successful salespeople are focused on the big picture and don't get caught up in the drama of the moment. While it might be hard, I always tell people, "Don't sweat the small deals."

To help make the shift to an outcome-oriented mindset, below are a couple of tips.

Qualify Fast: In order to make the greatest impact and protect your time, you'll want to qualify potential prospects fast. This isn't intended to be a way to brush people off without caring; rather, it is a way to help you both meet your desired outcomes. If you discover early on that your product or service isn't a good fit for a customer, why would you waste your prospect's time selling something that won't help them succeed? This is what I mean by qualifying fast. The faster you focus on the desired outcome, the easier it will be to see the bigger picture and what role you should or shouldn't play.

Play the Long Game: Extending on my point above, you need to be ready to play the long game. Even if a prospect is not a good fit now, building and nurturing those relationships is still important for future opportunities. If you can take a step back and see where you might plugin at a later time, you'll lay a foundation for future success.

While I got into sales, in many ways, out of necessity, I couldn't be happier with the career I've had. Through my many failures and successes, I've learned that I love influencing and impacting people's lives. I firmly believe if you approach sales as a way of helping people achieve their desired outcomes, you'll find great success and satisfaction.

Want to learn more from Mark Hunter? Follow him on:
Website: thesaleshunter.com
LinkedIn: linkedin.com/company/the-sales-hunter/about
Twitter: @thesaleshunter
YouTube: youtube.com/user/TheSalesHunter
Facebook: facebook.com/TheSalesHunter

#35 Win Every Deal in Your Industry

LEE BARTLETT

"If you sell with authenticity and integrity, sales becomes an incredible profession with a long-term compounding effect."

ABOUT LEE BARTLETT:

Lee Bartlett is the co-founder of Bartlett Schenk & Company and has enjoyed a highly successful sales career working for a variety of tier-one institutions. He has held roles in large US, UK, and European-based corporations including Merrill Corp, Intralinks, and Imprima.

With extensive experience selling to the financial sector and C-Suite executives, Lee has built multi-national sales teams, co-founded a tech start-up, recently authored his first publication *The No.1 Best Seller*, and launched his own consulting firm.

He shares his personal sales methodology and experiences in his book and blog, both of which discuss the mindset, strategies, and processes of top salespeople.

Those who know Lee say he has a razor-sharp client focus and an incredible depth of product knowledge, which enables him to solidify huge amounts of new business.

He is said to have a natural ability to forge strong client relationships and build a level of trust that often renders the competitive pitch process a formality.

Throughout my sales career in the finance industry, I became extremely good friends with the largest financial institutions in the world and earned their business. But they didn't buy from me because I was their friend, that came as a side effect. They bought from me because I was the person who ALWAYS overcame the challenges they were facing.

In any type of sales, there are always these internal barriers that you must get through to justify the spending of resources. I managed those barriers and took responsibility for them. As a result, my clients trusted me and still do. I never let them down which created a compounding effect. Once you get to that point, people say, "I want that person on my team." That's the stage you want to get to.

"I Want it All" Mentality

It was when I got to Merrill, that it became clear to me that I wasn't just a company employee who did binary deals. Instead, I functioned as an intermediary who sat between my customer and my employer. I felt an equal responsibility to deliver revenue to my employer and to serve my customers.

I was the senior pitcher and would present at board level meetings all over Europe, Asia, the US, and wherever these large transactions were happening.

I won the majority of business in my industry to the point where my job became mostly account management. There was nothing more to do and nowhere to grow. It was at that point, I decided to start again from the bottom with Imprima, which was launching a competing product early in the adoptive cycle. I took a year off and then set out to win all the business in the market again.

It is in this approach that my top sales secret lies. Salespeople should, but often don't, ask themselves this one simple question:

"How do I win **ALL** of the business in my industry?"

As your brain seeks to answer the question, it will reframe your entire sales approach and strategy which will require you to redefine your ideal persona, how you converse, and how you act.

HOW DO YOU WIN EVERY DEAL?

If you are going to play in this game of sales, these are the things you want to do.

Map Out Your Success

Once you are thinking about winning every deal, you have to map out the territory. Plan out what success looks like by answering questions like:

- How do you gain more business in your territory?
- Who do you need to partner with to earn more business?
- Who can you add value to that will then add value back?
- Who are the industry influencers that you can align yourself with?
- How can you multiply your efforts?
- How can you leverage up?
- How can you train your team to be your eyes and ears?
- Which customers do you need to win to leverage the rest of the market?
- Who will be your ideal case studies?

These answers will create the cornerstones of your plan.

Become a Trusted Partner

As I already touched on, you need to be the person people want on their team. This requires a genuine intent and desire to care for your customers.

Imagine you built a company and want to sell it so a corporate advisor and law firm can come in and dispose of it. Would you want the people who are best at disposing companies? Or, would you want someone who understands and cares about what you've spent the last 10 years building? Someone who wants to make sure they get the right value for you and who will do whatever it takes to deliver?

You need to be the latter for your customers, caring about them, standing up for their needs, and never compromising on what you promise. The compound effect of this is enormous.

Find Your Knowledge Threshold

Next, you need to speak industry-specific language to your target audience and have a deep understanding of how your product or service benefits them. However, there also has to be a point where you say, this is enough and you bring in an expert. If you don't have a defined point, it's easy to find yourself in a board meeting like a deer in the headlights.

On the other side, you don't want to hand off the sale too early without fully qualifying the lead. So you need to identify where that knowledge threshold is for you and conduct yourself and your sales process around it. As a result, you'll conserve your company's resources and will end up being able to converse up to the point where you are comfortable.

Build a Network in Your Industry

I stayed in my lane, the finance industry, throughout my career because the compound effect of a long term sales career is powerful. Your network is everything and you have to work to build and grow it over time.

Choosing the right place for your skills and personality is also important. The goals of the company you choose have to align with what you want. The product or service has to align with your personality. The offering has to align with what you see as beneficial in the industry and it has to align with what your customers want and need.

Once all the stars align, it gets kind of easy. It's just execution.

Build a Team

At Merrill, we were doing fast-paced high-revenue deals worth six to seven figures. I was the senior pitch person but taking all the credit is not something I can do. You can only close that many big deals with a solid team behind you. They need to keep you informed in an efficient way that allows you to continually update the customer.

It's essential to train your team to make sure they:

- Can spot opportunities
- Are in touch with you all the time
- Tell you about everything

Then, you translate the insights you receive into opportunities or simply use it to delight the customers.

Optimize Your Sales Process

Lastly, when I would walk into a board room to make a pitch on these extremely high- value transactions, I often wouldn't have time to do discovery. I had systems in place that allowed me to understand the customer before I went in so I could tailor the entire pitch to them. Then when I'd walk in, read the energy of the meeting, and be ready for anything. You have to know the ins and outs of your sales interactions and build the systems to prepare you for whatever may happen.

Once you reach the level of a sales professional who is dominating your market, or even when you begin to feel the compounding effects that help accelerate your business, it becomes a force that's near impossible to stop. You'll understand what's going across the industry and can then relay a lot of what you are doing on other deals without breaching confidentiality. This enables you to streamline processes for your customers based on best practices, exponentially increasing the level and value of service you can offer. As a result, everyone will want you on their team.

Want to learn more from Lee Bartlett?
Follow him on:
Website: leebartlett.com
LinkedIn: linkedin.com/in/leebartlettuk

#36 Provide Value That Prospects Actually Value

NOAH GOLDMAN

"Sales is a service. At the end of the day, realize that what you're up against is that "BUY" button."

ABOUT NOAH GOLDMAN:

Noah Goldman is a well-known sales leader, sales coach, the host of The Enterprise Podcast, and a startup advisor. He has led sales at a series of startups, including Martin Lang, has consulted with some of the fastest-growing startups in the world, and has been featured in the *San Francisco Chronicle*, the *Wall Street Journal*, and *Condé Nas*.

Where did Noah's journey start? He attended business school and then got into the tech industry working on finance mergers and acquisitions. It was there he realized how important sales is in moving the needle for companies. He quotes Mark Cuban saying, "Sales Cures All."

This realization inspired Noah to join the sales operations teams of several companies in the following years where he became a proponent of proper sales processes and having the right people within an organization. This led him to his entrepreneurial efforts which involved consulting on the topics of sales, coaching, and HR.

While Noah has helped startups at the corporate level, today, he's spending a lot of time helping entrepreneurs, sales leaders, and individual contributors to run a proper sales process with an effective sales mindset. He is also working on a book, *What it Means to be a Salesperson in the Age of A.I.,* which will be coming out in the near future.

Noah is a leader and mover in the sales world who is passionate about helping others to optimize their sales results. Read on to learn what he recommends as his top-secret to sales success.

Ten to fifteen years ago, there were those squeegee guys in New York that would just come up to your car, start squeegeeing your windshield, and then demand payment. You'd feel like "No, go away, I didn't ask you to clean my window or say it was okay."

Just how many salespeople today are like those squeegee guys? How many go to prospects, start giving their spiel, and then expect prospects to buy? Push them to buy? I'll tell you there are far too many who approach sales with just a selling mindset, rather than one of service. The self-serving approach is already causing salespeople to fail and, in the years to come, it will cost them their jobs.

Give Prospects Value
They Can't Get Elsewhere

While there are many secrets to sales, I'd say one of the most important things in our current time is for salespeople to add value that the prospect sees as valuable; something that they can't get elsewhere.

I think a lot of salespeople think, "Oh, well selling's about relationships and my customers like me," and blah, blah. blah. They might love you, but if they can buy from a "BUY" button without having to talk to you for 15 to 20 minutes, without having to travel to a place to buy from you, and without having to go through a demo to get a price from you, they're gonna do it.

To come out ahead, you have to ask yourself, "What is the net positive benefit that you offer to your prospect in their eyes, not yours?" You might say, "Well, I'm all about quality and I'm all about giving value." That might be true, but the question is, does your prospect think that? And here's one way I like to illustrate the value misconception.

Let's say there's a person wanting to buy a Mercedes Benz and it's that person who can open up the hood and tell how much horsepower it has and all that jazz. That buyer really hates car salespeople because they know more than most of them. In fact, dealing with the rep is usually a nuisance because they are not being given something that they can't otherwise get on their own. The salesperson may think they are the most helpful rep in the world because they dish out all the specs but the customer is rolling their eyes and wishing they could just press the buy button.

You have to give each customer value that is valuable to them which is going to be unique to each interaction.

HOW TO PROVIDE TRUE VALUE TO EACH OF YOUR PROSPECTS

How do you avoid being that squeegee guy or a nuisance? How do you make yourself invaluable to and irreplaceable in the sales process?

You need to ask yourself, what is it the prospect values that they cannot get on their own? Not something that is quote "valuable," meaning that you think it has value or someone has thought it had value before. What is something that he or she wants that they cannot get? Ask that question to your prospects. "What do you want that you're having trouble getting?" That is the way you can be a salesperson that serves. And when the robots come for your job, and they will come for your job, you'll be irreplaceable. But they are going to come for the people who will tell you endlessly that they are adding value when their prospects don't give a crap.

I'll leave that point with this. I was talking to a CEO six months ago and he had bought some sales automation technology. I said, "What was the sales process like?" He said, "Well, I had to talk to this guy and I had to do this and do that." I said, "Could you have figured it out on your own if they would only let you buy it with a button?" And he's like, "Yeah." So that salesperson was extraneous and a negative value in the sales process. Make yourself irreplaceable!

As a salesperson looking for a job, or as an organization looking to bring on salespeople, understand where salespeople are necessary in the sales process. Where is it that this person will be seen as valuable by the prospect and where can the person be seen as serving them?

If I was thrown in the role of being a sales guy now for Mercedes Benz, the first thing I would want to do is talk to every person who ever bought a car from the dealership and ask why they did. I'd say, "Tell me why you bought this car. Tell me what you appreciate about this car. Tell me what you didn't know before you got into this dealership." If you look at the guy, Ali Reda, who recently broke the world record for the number of cars sold in a year, he says, "People come in and I'm more here to help them and solve problems. It's a lot easier when you're not selling things. We're zero pressure."

Ask "How do I serve?," not "How do I sell?" You figure that out and you've figured out the sales game.

Want to learn more from Noah Goldman? Follow him on:
Podcast: www.enterprisesalespodcast.com
Twitter: @noahgee

#37 It's Time To Think Strategically

MARIO M. MARTINEZ JR.

"Know your stuff. Know your competition. Know the strategy."

ABOUT MARIO M. MARTINEZ JR:

Mario M. Martinez Jr. is the CEO & Founder of Vengreso. He spent 82 consecutive quarters in B2B sales and leadership roles growing hundreds of millions of dollars in revenue annually. Mario is also the host of the popular "Selling With Social" podcast.

Mario is one of only 20 sales influencers invited to appear in the Salesforce documentary film, "The Story of Sales." He is recognized as the Number 1 Top Sales Performance Guru in the world and in 2018 was named a Top 10 Sales Influencer by *Modern Sales Magazine* as well as one of the Top 25 Most Influential Inside Sales Professionals. In 2017, Mario was listed as the 6th Most Influential Social Selling Leader across the globe.

Mario previously worked at companies like PGi, Sprint, E|Solutions, and Premenos.

As a world-renowned sales leader, Mario is a trusted source for sales insights and advice. His unique background and experience make him a true sales guru.

Oddly enough, I actually owe my sales career to the Ritz Camera chain. To help pay for college, I started working for a Ritz Camera store in Concord, California when I was 16 as a "photo finisher." I would take customers' 35-millimeter rolls of film and put them through our system—printing the film and making slight touch-ups along the way—a little magenta here, a tad of cyan here, etc. Because we were a small store, I also supported sales and ran the cash register.

One day, when I was about 17 or 18, our regional manager (a guy by the name of Hunter with a horrendous toupee) comes up to me and says, "I need to talk to you about some of the numbers." He opens up the books and says, "Do you realize that you are one of the top sales producers in our region?" I was stunned. In my mind, all I was doing was giving helpful advice to customers. I didn't even think of what I was doing as sales!

Fast forward a few months and I'm now enrolled at UC Berkeley. I go to Hunter, the regional manager, and ask for a transfer to the Berkley store so I can be closer to campus. Hunter comes to me and says, "Mario, I'd like to talk to you about your transfer. I have to deny it. I can't transfer you as a photo finisher. Berkeley is our second-highest-grossing revenue store in the whole region. I need you to go into sales."

And that's what I did—under the condition that I continued doing exactly what I had been doing at the Concord store.

The Importance of Having a Customer First-Mentality

While I didn't realize it at the time, my success at Ritz Camera was tied to my desire to simply help people. I would point out ways to improve customer's pictures and when they would ask how, I would make suggestions—buy this particular kind of film or this piece of equipment. My main objective was to help customers take better pictures, which ultimately helped me produce sales for the region.

This type of customer-first mentality laid the foundation for my entire sales career. If you remain focused on adding value to your customers, you're more likely to find success.

While my time at Ritz Camera was invaluable, I went on to land this great B2B internship that eventually got me an opportunity at a consulting company as a sales and marketing manager. That then led to an opportunity where I became the youngest hire for a company called E|Solutions, which was owned by Sprint. I was one of the first 35 technology salespeople hired, at the mere age of 21. That was quite the ride as you can imagine! Through it all, and to this day, I remain focused on adding value and simply helping my customers.

THE PVC METHOD

Throughout my career, I've perfected something I refer to as the PVC Method, which builds on the idea of adding value to your customer as noted above. The PVC method encompasses three things—personalization, value and a call to action. Let me break it down for you...

Personalization:

Like with any relationship, before someone opens up to you, you have to make a connection with them. You want to understand them on a personal level that enables them to trust you. When you first meet someone, you have to "look for the fish on the wall." What I mean by that is be on the lookout for something that allows you to start a conversation. Do they have a picture of themselves reeling in a giant marlin? Ask about it. The more you can learn about your customers on a personal level, the more you will understand what motivates them. Ultimately, this will enable you to customize your content and your approach.

Value:

As I've noted above, adding value is the most important thing you can do. In every sales position I've ever held, I've always gone back to the same two steps: find the problem, educate on the solution. After you've established a more personal relationship with your buyer, you should have an easier time getting at the heart of their problem. Once you understand what the problem is, add value by offering solutions. It's that simple.

Call to Action:

The third element that should never get overlooked is the call to action. Having a clear call to action means never leaving a meeting, a phone call or an email without driving to something else. You always need to clearly outline the next step you want your customer to take; if you leave it open-ended, they probably won't do anything.

The more I brought the PVC method into every type of outreach—a cold call, an email, or even a LinkedIn message—the more success I had. To any salesperson out there, I highly encourage you to bring the PVC method into every aspect of your sales process as well.

Being a Strategist:

At its core, the PVC method is all about strategy, which leads me to my sales secret...to be successful you need to be a strategist. When I'm working an account or opportunity, I know exactly who all the players are, a plan to make them my friends, and a plan to ask them the right questions.

Many salespeople, especially in big companies, make the mistake of getting upset when the deal doesn't go their way. But they often don't have the data behind why their deal fell through in the first place. They don't understand the financials. They don't understand the mechanics of what it's going to take. They haven't thought about their deal strategically enough.

To be a true strategic thinker, I challenge you to answer the below questions about all the deals you are working:

1) **Who are your competitors?**

2) **What is the pricing of your competitors?**

3) **Who are your key relationships inside of an account?**

4) **What is your unique value proposition as it relates to the opportunity you're working on?**

Answering these kinds of questions is the first step in understanding the entire strategy. Being a sales all-star is about knowing your stuff—your competition and all the reasons why someone is going to say no, both internally and externally. When you can answer all these things, then you're truly ready to sell.

While there are many factors that drive success, being a comprehensive strategist is at the top of the list.

Want to learn more from Mario M. Martinez Jr? Follow him on:
Website: vengreso.com
LinkedIn: linkedin.com/in/mthreejr
Twitter: @M_3jr

#38 Close More Deals With a Treasure Map

KURT SHAVER

"The principle still applies. Different tools, but old rules."

ABOUT KURT SHAVER:

Kurt Shaver is the Co-founder and Chief Sales Officer of Vengreso, a digital selling solutions company. Kurt is an expert when it comes to motivating sales teams to adopt new tools and techniques, a skill he has developed over a 33-year career in sales.

Interestingly, Kurt didn't study business in college. He graduated from the Georgia Institute of Technology with his Masters in electrical engineering. However, he realized before graduating that his future was in the sales world. His career began by performing sales management roles for various software startups. Then, he became the VP of business development at the Monticello Corporation. After three years, he transitioned into the Director of Sales at Websense and four years later he became the VP of Sales for GFI Software, Inc.

A key turning point in Kurt's career came when he was working as the VP of Sales for GFI Software and was the executive sponsor for the rollout of Salesforce.com. The experience inspired him to launch his own Salesforce consulting business in 2008, now known as SalesFoundry. When LinkedIn went public, Kurt saw a bright future for the platform as a sales generation tool. He shifted his focus and began training corporate sales teams on LinkedIn and ended up helping thousands of salespeople across the globe to improve their sales skills. Six years later, he partnered with five other founders and converted The Sales Foundry into what it is today—Vengreso.

Kurt is known as a seasoned sales pro with an exceptional grasp on digital selling methodologies. Further, business associates describe him as someone who is genuinely interested in guiding others to success.

I am no newbie to the sales game. My career began back before anyone even had cell phones. We would use the old corded phones to call our clients. For a long time, I believed that in order to close a sale, you had to wine and dine clients, treating them to a steak dinner to build a true relationship. My how that view has changed.

Over the years, I have fully adopted technology, utilized it to empower my sales, and taught others how to do the same. While much has changed over the past 33 years, I have learned principles that are every bit as relevant today as they were 20-30 years ago. However, they do take different forms today. The modern buyer requires a modern seller so you have to join the movement. But that doesn't mean forgetting lessons from the past. One of the most important secrets to my success has been gaining 100% buy-in from everyone on a buying committee to close a deal. Here's how I do it.

Without 100% Buy-In, The Deal Won't Go Down!

Throughout my career, I have learned many tricks of the sales trade. However, there is one secret that has helped me to land sale after sale. It is a primary foundational step that many people in sales overlook and it costs them.

Here's the premise. Research has been performed on an ongoing basis to uncover how many people are involved in B2B buying decisions. The most recent number I saw was 6.8 people. While it has always been important to identify who the decision-makers are, it's even more important now because the number of people involved is growing. So, whether it's 6, 7, 8, or more, they all need to give the thumbs up to what you're selling.

If even one person says no, the deal will not go down. To get all of the people on board, you have to know who the people are, what influences them, what pain points they experience, etc.

You Have to Draw Your Treasure Map

My way of identifying and organizing the decision-makers is to build an org chart. I include how a business is organized, who is in charge, and the role each person plays. For me to navigate it, I like to lay it out like a treasure map. Then, you go person to person, figuring out how to sell them on the product or service.

When I was managing sales reps, I would ask them about the progress of their deals. They would often tell me that a deal was on track and give me an estimated close date, like three weeks. I would always say, show me the org chart. If they couldn't show me who the decision-makers were, what they knew about them, and where they were in the process of selling them on the deal, the deal wasn't on track as far as I was concerned. The org chart is the underlying key to success.

HOW TO BUILD YOUR ORG CHART AND USE IT TO CLOSE MORE DEALS

In modern times, you can use data from LinkedIn or tools like Seamless or Salesforce to scrape all the information you need to piece together an org chart. It's much easier nowadays with all of the tools and technology available. However, you can also go straight to the source.

The Old "Flip It on Them" Trick

Back in my early days, when I was selling big deals for AT&T, I'd be sitting with my prospect, face-to-face, and I'd be totally transparent. I'd say, "It's important for me to understand your organization." I'd start drawing an org chart and would pretend like I was getting kind of stuck. Then, I'd take the piece of paper, turn it around, lay the pen on it, and say, "I'm not really following all this. It's probably faster if you just drew it out."

Often, they would pick up the pen and say, "Oh, the director of IT is this. The director of security is this. The VP of network structure is this. The CIO is this." They'd work on it for like five minutes and then hand me my treasure map! I'd say, 45 out of 50 prospects would pick up the pen and do it for me.

If you are meeting prospects face-to-face, or even virtually, you can use the same tactic to flip it onto them and have them draw the org chart for you.

The Two Questions You Need to Answer

Once you know the people who are on the buying committee, you need to figure out the answers to two questions for each person.

1) **The first question is if that person was to implement your solution, what would it mean for the business?**

2) **The second question is if they were to implement your solution, what would it mean for them personally?**

3) **The intention is to get the person thinking forward, psychologically putting themselves in**

the mindset of having acquired your solution. Further, you want them to start sharing some positive things that you can use later on to close the deal. For example, for the personal question, they might say that your solution will help to position them for advancement or help them to go home at 5 o'clock each night. On the business question, they might say, I could reduce one person from my team or reassign them into another position.

You want to understand what it means to the business and what it's going to mean to the person when they buy your solution. Once you know what those benefits are, you can circle back to them in the closing stage and appeal to each of the decision-makers. The key is to understand who you are selling to and to appeal to every person involved in the decision. In doing so, you can make the entire sales process much smoother, reducing objections and naysayers. While there are many secrets, this is one that everyone in B2B sales should know!

Want to learn more from Kurt Shaver?
Connect with him on:
LinkedIn: linkedin.com/in/kurtshaver
Twitter: @kurtshaver
Website: vengreso.com/our-team/kurt-shaver

#39 Harnessing Your Sales Superpowers

SCOTT LEESE

"You can let this ruin and hold you back your whole life or you can turn this into a superpower."

ABOUT SCOTT LEESE:

Scott Leese is one of the top sales leaders and trainers in the nation. As the Founder of Scott Leese Consulting, LLC, Scott has trained thousands upon thousands of salespeople across the world.

In addition to his consulting business, Scott also serves as the Senior Vice President of Sales for Qualia Labs, Inc., which is based in San Francisco, CA. As a highly sought-after consultant, advisor, leader, and trainer, Scott has a proven track record of building sales teams from the ground up.

Prior to starting his own consulting firm and heading up the sales team at Qualia, Scott worked in sales for several major companies such as Main Street Hub, Democrasoft, DotNext Inc, LeapFish and Reply, Inc.

Scott has twice been named a "Top 25 AA-ISP Inside Sales Leader" and is the author of *Addicted to Process*, a top-selling book on Amazon.

I went into sales for one major reason—to make up for lost time.

From battling colon cancer to my addiction with opioids, I spent my 20's unlike any typical college grad—battling for my life and working to get it back.

Little did I know, I would use my journey to help others recover in sales.

As an athlete growing up, I went to a small Division II school called Dominican where I played soccer and tennis. I studied religion and psychology as an undergrad and I was content having a good time playing sports. After graduating, I went on to grad school at Arizona State and at age 23, my life took a very crazy turn. I got extremely sick and spent the next four years in the hospital fighting for my life. I had more surgeries than I care to count. I was diagnosed with all kinds of autoimmune diseases and ended up with severe ulcerative colitis and eventually colon cancer. It was an absolute nightmare.

At age 27 when I was finally healthy enough to enter the workforce, I had yet another hurdle to overcome—I had become addicted to opioids. To say that the odds were stacked against me is quite an understatement. Despite these tremendous hardships, my competitive spirit never died.

So at 27, I took an entry-level sales job where I made 100 calls a day. Having no real work experience to speak of, I knew sales was a profession where I could use my competitive spirit to make money. And I needed money. With little training, I remember driving home my first day and telling my wife, "I am not going back. I don't know how to sell. I'm terrified of the phone. I suck at this." And she essentially punched me in the gut and said, "What else are you going to do?" Her statement hit me like a ton of bricks and awoke something in me. She made me realize that while sales was not going to be easy, I'd already been through and overcome so much that cold calling should be no big deal.

From that point forward, I attacked sales with a different type of fervor that has helped propel me to where I am today. I emerged at 27 more

241

motivated than you could imagine and just dying for any opportunity. While I could have let my medical issues hold me back and become my excuse for not achieving greatness, I turned my hardships in life into my superpower. All the challenges I had faced in my early 20's became my ultimate motivator.

If It Ain't Broke, Don't Fix It

As a big sports guy, I brought my love of sports to sales. In fact, I approached sales like I approached baseball. That's how I was able to find success early in my career. I developed a process and didn't tinker with it—I did the same process over and over again. Just like I used the same batting stance when stepping up to the plate, I leveraged the same logic in sales. I didn't worry if 25 calls in a row went south; I trusted that my approach was the right one. I didn't get caught in the trap of over-correcting and changing up my process for fear of striking out.

Throughout my career, I've worked in a variety of sales roles at several great companies but have always stayed true to my sales process. Sure, I've looked for ways to push myself and my teams but the core of my process has remained constant. For anyone just getting started, or for those that have been at it for years, I highly encourage you to create your own sales process for optimal success.

Time Is of the Essence

While there are lots of tips I could offer I have two sales secrets to share. My first one is this: don't wait. Having not gotten started in sales until I was 27, I always wish I would have started sooner. Of course, that wasn't entirely my fault so for me, it's partially bad luck and partially my own stupidity. So for anyone reading this, if you're not taking yourself seriously—in sales or in life in general—start now. Don't wait until you're 30 or later to finally take your career seriously. I regret not getting started sooner and often wonder where I would be if I had started my sales career at 18 and not 27. So that's one piece of advice, but that's the bonus.

The Addiction Method of Selling

Here's my real sales secret: it's four words and they have to go in this particular order.

- **Pain**
- **Value**
- **Urgency**
- **Solution**

Find the pain, build value, create urgency and discuss solutions (PVUS).

That's what I refer to as my addiction method of selling. Get somebody to admit they have a problem, help them understand that fixing that problem is important, get them to a place where they realize they need to act, and then get them into rehab, so-to-speak. If you can find the pain and deliver value, you can create urgency and then share your solution. I'll warn you that the biggest challenge is always finding the pain and then delivering your value.

So how do you get someone to admit they have a problem? You can't just accuse them straight away of needing help. It's a delicate process that requires asking caring questions. Once you start digging and asking the questions that get to the core of their problem, you'll gain their trust and discover how you can provide value. The more open your prospect becomes, the easier it will be to get at the heart of their issues. As you get better at asking the questions that matter, you'll find it easier and easier to create urgency and offer solutions.

While I may have had a late start to the sales game, I strive to make up for lost time every day. If I could offer one last piece of advice it would be to stop making excuses and start living. We've all dealt with some kind of hardship that has set us back; instead of using that as a reason to stop trying, turn it into your personal motivator—your personal superpower.

Want to learn more from Scott Leese? Follow him on:
Website: scottleeseconsulting.com
LinkedIn: linkedin.com/in/scottleese
Twitter: @thescottleese

#40 Evolve from Salesperson to Consultative Sales Coach

KEITH ROSEN

"Salespeople don't need more fancy ways of closing a deal, they need to learn how to become coaches for their clients."

ABOUT KEITH ROSEN:

As the CEO of Profit Builders and a leading pioneer of management coach training, Keith Rosen is transforming sales teams through a unique philosophy and innovative approach which begins with creating world-class executive sales coaches.

Over the past 30 years, he has impacted hundreds of thousands of salespeople and managers in practically every industry imaginable. As a result, he has become globally recognized as an authority on sales and leadership and highly sought after by global brands.

In addition to speaking, Keith has also shared his insights through several award-winning books, including *Coaching Salespeople into Sales Champions*, *Own Your Day*, and *Sales Leadership*.

He has also been recognized for his work on many occasions. Keith was one of the first to be inducted into the Top Sales Hall of Fame and was named the "Sales Education Leader of the Year." He also received high praise from some of the world's most elite media outlets—*Inc.* and *Fast Company*—which both named him one of the five most influential executive coaches. Further, he has been featured in *Entrepreneur, Fortune, The New York Times, Selling Power,* CBSNews.com and *The Wall Street Journal.*

Those who know Keith say he is brilliant at teaching effective communication and hugely talented in the realm of sales education and development. He is known for his ability to shine a light on new ideas and re-energize leaders to connect and coach their teams.

In many ways, sales has always been in my DNA. My first exposure to sales began after college when I worked selling door-to-door. I sold everything from steak knives to home remodeling services. I then moved into inside sales, working the phones and setting up appointments for our outside sales team. After these early stints of canvassing neighborhoods and cold calling, I worked for a few Fortune 500 companies, like E & J Gallo Winery. It was at Gallo where I was promoted to a management role and saw first-hand the importance of great leadership.

While these early experiences helped develop my sales and leadership skills, they also led me to my life's true calling—coaching. Through my first sales roles, I saw that there was a need for salespeople and managers to be supported at a much deeper level. When I first started selling door-to-door, I was handed a pitch book and told to go sell. That was the extent of my training. Experiences like these made me realize that traditional sales training was just not cutting it anymore and a new approach was needed.

It was during this time 30 years ago that I read an article about life coaching. I read the piece and then looked up and said, "Thank you. This is my dharma. This is my purpose. This is my reason for being on this planet." And that is when I decided to start my coaching practice.

Thirty years, three million managers and salespeople, 75 countries and five continents later, here I am, doing my best to make an impact — one person at a time. Of course, I've had my ups and downs but through it all, I've stayed true to my primary purpose, which centers on making a positive impact on people.

The Path to Sales Success Is Through Consultative Coaching

While people often come to me asking for a sales training program, my first reaction is always, "Sorry, I don't have one." As you can imagine, this often baffles people. I say this because the future of sales does not require more training; it requires a change in mindset around what it means to be a professional salesperson.

So, my sales secret is this—if you want to become the top 1%, shift your thinking and strategy and strive to be what I term *"a consultative sales coach"*—someone who coaches their client on how to succeed. That is what will give you and your organization a competitive edge. Salespeople don't need more fancy ways of closing a deal, they need to learn how to become coaches for their clients.

While becoming a sales coach for your client may not always jive with the culture of the organization you represent, it is worth investing the time and effort to make the change. If you have a coaching culture, you are going to experience anywhere from a 2X to a 4X minimum increase in sales and revenue. You're going to cut your sales cycle in half and you will be able to turn around underperformers in 30 days or less. I've witnessed this first-hand throughout my entire career.

HOW TO BECOME A CONSULTATIVE SALES COACH FOR YOUR CLIENTS

Based on my own experiences, below are a few ways to get started with becoming a consultative sales coach for your clients:

Ask Great Questions

Being a good sales coach starts by asking great questions. The greatest salespeople I know sell with questions, not answers. They don't get on the phone and blindly pitch their products, concerned only with their sales quota. They seek to understand their prospect's point-of-view. That is why professional selling and coaching are so synonymous. They both encapsulate not only the skillset but the mindset of what it means to be a true sales leader—this applies to both salespeople and managers.

Pick the Right Clients

In sales, it's really hard to turn down business but sometimes, turning down a client is the best decision for your long term success. For me personally, if I don't think I can move the needle and drive results for a client, I graciously bow out. Why? Because I only want to invest in the clients I believe in—the ones where I can have the greatest impact. If you're working with a prospect that you know is not a good fit, be honest with them and yourself. Finding success ultimately starts with working with the right customers. If you are working with the wrong customer, you are doomed to fail.

Stay Authentic

Staying authentic is one of the greatest challenges salespeople have, and it's something I have struggled with throughout my career on several occasions. Perhaps the greatest piece of advice I can offer any salesperson out there is to never surrender your core values and individuality for anyone. Too often, we feel like we can't disagree with a prospect or client because we're so afraid of losing the sale. If you approach your clients like a coach and not a salesperson, it will be much easier to speak your mind, even if it's not what your customer wants to hear. In some ways, coaching your clients is like parenting—just like kids, clients don't always know what's best for them so they need you to guide them. While it won't be easy, stay true to what you know will add value.

Remember, It's Not About You

Lastly, just like coaches do with athletes, you need to build trust with your customers. This starts by focusing on them and *NOT* you. It's essential that you seek to understand their challenges and point-of-view and let go of what you feel and need. When you're having a conversation with a prospect or customer, make sure you are fully present in the moment. As a consultative sales coach, you need to be unconditionally supportive—even if that means they don't buy your product or service. By coaching them on what they actually need, you'll build greater trust and create a lasting relationship that will likely result in future business and opportunities.

Making a Meaningful Impact Through Client Coaching

As you become a coach for your clients, you'll see that the true reward is not simply about closing deals and getting more business; the real gift is seeing the impact you are having on your customers. I love hearing how my coaching has positively impacted those around me and I firmly believe that the best salespeople should share this same mentality.

Want to learn more from Keith Rosen? Follow him on:
Facebook: facebook.com/keitharosen
LinkedIn: linkedin.com/in/keithrosen/
YouTube: youtube.com/user/KeithRosenTV
Twitter: @KeithRosen

#41 Why a Cookie-Cutter Salesperson Won't Cut It

LEE SALZ

"If it's important to the people you sell to, it should be important to you."

ABOUT LEE SALZ:

Lee B. Salz is a leading sales management strategist, speaker, and columnist. He is the founder of Sales Architects and The Revenue Accelerator.

He has authored five best-selling books including *Sales Differentiation—19 Powerful Strategies to Win More Deals at the Prices You Want*; *Hire Right, Higher Profits, Soar Despite Your Dodo Sales Manager*; *Stop Speaking for Free! The Ultimate Guide to Making Money with Webinars*; and *The Business Expert Guide to Small Business Success*.

Lee also serves on the Editorial Advisory Board of Sales and Marketing Management magazine and is the Program Advisor to Kansas State University's Strategic Selling Institute. He has built a LinkedIn sales management group that boasts more than 300,000 executive members, the largest of its kind.

Lee has been featured in the *Wall Street Journal*, CNN, *New York Times*, Dallas Morning News, Selling Power, Sales and Marketing Management, ABC News, MSNBC and many more leading publications.

Lee is said to be a visionary, an innovator, and a captivating speaker. Clients say he strikes the perfect balance of humor, practical ideas, and experience which motivates salespeople to think and act differently when selling.

Imagine you sell copiers for a living. Today is a very exciting day for you because, after several years of work, your R&D team has finally produced the first copier in the world that can print 50 shades of gray. Tomorrow, you have a meeting with a CFO to pitch the copier. Will you be focusing on the 50 shades of gray?

I hope not.

How you explain what you sell should depend on what matters most to your prospect and CFO's don't care about color shades and hues. You shouldn't have one pitch that you stick to no matter what and shouldn't necessarily share what excites you most about your product or service. When it comes to what you sell and how you sell it, you need to be different and tailor your conversation to your audience.

Sell Differently

What do I mean when I say sell differently?

Continuing with the example above, the CFO cares about the financial impact that the copier has on their business so you would want to emphasize the cost/value benefits. If later in the afternoon you meet with the VP of Marketing, they will be less concerned about the financial impact but will want to know about color shades, hues, and other functions around the copier.

Further, if you're meeting with an IT manager, they won't care about the financial impact or the color shades and hues but will care about reliability, security, and integration. So although you're selling the same copier to all three people, you need to have three completely different conversations.

Not everybody cares about every differentiator you have, so think about what's most important to the person you are targeting and make sure the information you share is hyper-relevant to them. You want your conversations to be so on-point that prospects say, "You know, no one's ever talked to me about this before".

HOW TO DIFFERENTIATE WHAT AND HOW YOU SELL

So how do you sell differently? You need to differentiate yourself from all of the other salespeople your competing against. Here are three ways to get started.

Never Stop Learning and Evolving

Whether you're new in sales or have been in it for three decades, never stop learning. There is no endpoint or destination in sales where you can just kick your feet up and do the same thing over and over. Every industry and company changes. Further, how, when, and why people buy is evolutionary. If you're not constantly seeking to learn more about your industry and buyers, you're destined to become dated.

Become an Expert on What Your Prospects Care About

Next, whatever is important to the people you are selling to, should also be very important to you. You should become an expert on what your targets care about.

For example, when I built the sales team in the technology training industry, I never learned the courses from a technical perspective. I learned what was important to the IT buyers and the people who took the classes. That's how I helped the sales team fit the product to the buyer.

It was the same story when I built a sales team in the employment screening industry which is drug testing and background screening, I was never a scientist in the laboratory but I did know the process of how a drug test was to be administered. I knew the consideration points for companies that didn't have a drug-testing program, and you bet I knew how to take the program to the next level.

So ask, who are your clients? What are their pain points? How will your products or services help them on a day-to-day, real-life basis? What matters to them in regard to their company, their position in the company, and their personal perspective? Knowing these answers is key to being able to differentiate your pitch. The more they feel understood, the more likely they are to buy from you.

Cultivate Drive or Move On

Lastly, you need to be driven. When you look at what makes someone successful, one of the keys is having passion. People can sense when you are all-in and believe in what you are selling and when you aren't.

One of the things I've told every employer I've ever worked for is that it doesn't matter how much money I make. If I wake up every day dreading having to go to work, I am going to hand over the keys and say, "Thank you very much but I'm out." There has to be something to get me fired up.

But what if you don't feel driven in your role? You have three options:

Find Your Drive

Explore the different aspects of the job, industry, and customers and look for an aspect that inspires you. When I first got recruited into the drug testing industry to build a sales team, I thought, "Really? Drug testing?" It looked boring and I wasn't excited about it.

However, I put it on myself to try and find that passion or I wouldn't be able to stay there. Once I started getting into the industry, I learned about opportunities we had to help Fortune 1000 companies protect themselves, their workplaces, and their employees. All of a sudden I got really fired up about it.

I found something that I cared about and it drove me to success. So investigate your role to see if there is any part of it that gets you excited.

Find a Driven Manager

If you can't find the drive from the company, another option is to find a manager and team that inspires you and lights a fire in your belly. Passion can be contagious.

Move On

Lastly, if you just can't get excited about the role you're in or the people you're working with, do yourself, the company, and the customers a favor and move on! You will be much more effective and happy somewhere where you can be passionate about what you are doing.

So all in all, selling differently is the key to success in sales. You can't be the same as everyone else. What you sell and how you sell it should not be a cookie-cutter elevator pitch but a unique conversation specific to the particular buyer. You can start on the path to differentiate yourself by continuously learning and evolving as a salesperson, becoming an expert on each of your customers, and ensuring you are somewhere where you have a drive to succeed.

Want to learn more from Lee Salz? Follow him on:
Website: salesdifferentiation.com
LinkedIn: linkedin.com/in/leesalz

#42 How To Go All-In and Win

JASON MCELHONE

"I have faith after almost 30 years of massive amounts of rejection but also an incredible amount of success, that if I'm in it, I'm going to win it."

ABOUT JASON MCELHONE:

Jason McElhone is the CEO and Founder of Remote Sales, Inc. which aims to be the #1 remote job work website in the world.

Jason's career began in 1992 after earning his Bachelor's degree in Economics from St. Lawrence University. He got his Series 7 license and moved from New York to Fort Lauderdale at the ripe young age of 22. In Florida, he was hired as an entry-level stockbroker at a firm that was a sister company to the one from the Wolf of Wall Street movie.

After about six weeks, Jason figured that he was in the wrong place to establish his career and moved on, having five-year stints at two other firms. Eventually, in 2000, he went into business for himself, trading his own money alongside the money of his clients.

During the 2008 recession, like many, Jason lost everything and had to start over from square one. He worked in a factory for $9 per hour for six months before landing a position at MarketSource, Inc. At MarketSource, he worked his way up to Director of Inside Sales over a period of almost 12 years, during which time he built the Lead Generation Program from the ground up and helped to almost quadruple the business. He played an important role in helping MarketSource deliver $7B of revenue growth in 2018 alone.

Now, Jason is venturing out on his own again, this time having over 25 years of inside sales and lead generation experience and over 1M cold calls under his belt.

If I had to boil sales success down to one thing it is this... you've got to be in it to win it.

Whether you're going to make a million cold calls over a 27-year period or you're going to send out thousands of emails and social touches on LinkedIn, you cannot get around the fact that most of your time in the sales business is going to be a grind. There's going to be massive amounts of rejection and failure. With this being the case, you have to go "all- in" with the mindset that you are going to win in the long run if you want to be successful.

HOW DO YOU GO ALL-IN?

I find that the desire to win is very hard to find these days.

When I was at MarketSource, we hired about 500 people each week for our programs. We would conduct thousands of interviews every month looking for people who were willing to show up every day, work their asses off, be coached, and commit to doing their best. Unfortunately, we would only see that all-in attitude in maybe one out of every 10 candidates, if that. The all-in, hustling, winning mindset is one that is essential for sales success.

If you are looking to improve your sales performance, here are four ways I recommend going all-in to win.

THE FOUR-STEP MULTI-CHANNEL APPROACH

Sales is a numbers game so you have to be out there making contact. I don't make 300 to 400 dials per day now as I did back in my early stockbroker days. But, I come really close to that when you factor in what I do on all my channels.

I send thousands of emails every week, do hundreds of social touches including InMail via Navigator, make thousands of calls, and even send some text messages. Here's my standard four-step approach to generating leads and meetings:

Step 1: Email

I like to send an email first. I think the email helps warm your list, so to speak. But it also starts to develop your brand.

Step 2: Phone Call

Within 24 hours of sending an email, I follow-up with a phone call. Why? Because nobody does it. Everyone's spamming prospects with email but they're not following up with a cold call shortly thereafter.

Step 3: LinkedIn

Next, I'll reach out in the next day or two on LinkedIn and send a connection request or a short two or three sentence InMail via Navigator.

Step 4: Event Meeting

Lastly, if I'm going to show (like CES) I might send a text like, "Hey, are you going to CES? I would love to connect. Jason at Market Source."

Over the last three years, I was able to generate 250 to 300 meetings a year with key personas at Fortune 1000 accounts by using the above steps and then 'rinsing and repeating' over the course of a one-two-month period. I was all-in. I figured out this system, and I worked it every single day.

Embrace Rejection

The next important thing to note is all the rejection that comes with sales. I still am not able to get around the fact that 85% to 90% of people are not going to answer the phone. Response rates on email, no matter how good your subject line and message are, are around 2% to 4%. So, I'm still not getting a response from 97% of the emails that I send.

However, when you take the multi-channel approach, people will say, "Yeah, didn't I see your video on LinkedIn?" or "Didn't I read one of the blogs that you wrote?" Everything, including cold calling, is going to become more effective.

Still, sales is a numbers game that is mostly rejection. You've got to show up every day. You have to make the phone calls. You have to send the emails. You've got to do the social touches. You've got to create your own content, build your own brand. and then you've got to rinse and repeat. Amidst the rejection, if you're in there putting in the work, it's going to come back around for you.

Cultivate Long-Term Vision

Third, I find there's a level of entitlement that has festered since the social era has evolved which says, "I'm just going to show up. I'm going to be here for 12 to 18 months and then I'm on my way. Oh, by the way, if I don't have full benefits and if you're not going to give me at least two weeks of vacation off I'm out of here."

In my experience, in both the brokerage business and the almost 12 years that I was at MarketSource, it takes at least three to five years to get past the initial ramp-up and build momentum. After that point, you start to generate a significant number of referrals and that's when you see the 'hockey stick growth.' You can't generate a significant amount of momentum for yourself if every 12 to 24 months you're moving on to the next gig. I think you've got to be around a little longer than a year or two to make a major impact and become successful.

I understand if you're an SDR and you want to get yourself up to a director level and eventually a VP—but otherwise, in my opinion, sticking with a company for at least four to five years is what's going to separate the real winners from the rest who lack that long-term vision.

Find People You Like to Work With

Lastly, there's an old saying that the most important thing is that you get the right people on the bus. Once you've got the right people, you can figure out the twists and turns. My advice to a young SDR or somebody looking for a sales job is to find people you like to work with.

If I'm an SDR coming to interview or I'm sitting down and I want to be on someone's team, the first thing that should be on my mind is, "Do I like them? Do I think that we can work our asses off together and build something special?" If the answer is "No" or I'm not sure," I'm in the wrong place.

You've got to get the right people on the bus because no business or sales venture is going to be easy. There's going to be plenty of downs to go with the ups. But if you enjoy working with the people, as I did way back in the day when I was in the boiler room with 200 or 300 kids my age, you're going to figure it out. I think the love of what you do comes over time.

Cultivate the Winning Mindset

The bottom line is that 90% of sales is rejection, on a good day. We weren't driving $7 billion of revenue as an entire organization at MarketSource without falling on our faces thousands of times per month. If you want to be successful, you need to decide you're in it and be willing to work, learn, stick with it, align with good people, and survive the grind. If you do, I believe you will win.

Want to learn more from Jason McElhone? Follow him on: LinkedIn: linkedin.com/in/jasonmcelhone

#43 Multiplying Your Sales Productivity

BRYAN NAAS

"Everyone is subject to failure but that is not a bad thing. It's a part of the learning process. We have to think about the improvement that we gain from failure."

ABOUT BRYAN NAAS:

Bryan Naas is the Director of Sales Enablement at Lessonly. His areas of expertise include training, software sales, account management, implementation, and support.

His career began as 6th-grade social studies and computer technology teacher. After a few years of teaching, Bryan transitioned into a customer relationship manager role at DyKnow, a classroom management software company. He stayed with DyKnow for just over five years, advancing to a sales rep and then a customer success manager.

Next, Bryan became the learning architect at ExactTarget, a global sales enablement company. This role utilized both his teaching and sales experience. After about 11 months, ExactTarget was acquired by CRM-giant Salesforce.

Bryan joined the Salesforce team and took on various roles including sales enablement manager, senior manager, and director of product enablement.

Feeling the itch to return to the fast-paced start-up world, Bryan joined Lessonly as the director of sales enablement. He is also currently a mentor for VentureSCALE, a venture capital and private equity firm that helps early-stage technology companies build effective sales and revenue strategies.

Colleagues of Bryan say he is a very driven individual with great insight in the areas of technology, education, and instruction. He is known for bringing invigorating energy to the workplace. Further, he quickly gains respect from customers and colleagues due to his helpful spirit and creative problem-solving skills.

When you look at how professional athletes, musicians, and artists spend their time, most of it is practicing. In the NFL, teams practice five days per week and only perform one day. However, in sales, we do the opposite. Most reps spend the majority of their time performing and hardly any time practicing. The reality is, if you don't put in the practice time, you can't expect yourself to improve. That's why my number one sales secret is that you have to make practice part of your daily routine.

Build Sales Practice Into Your Daily Routine

If you take time to learn and practice, at least a little bit every day, you are going to be a much better sales rep one year from now than you are today. However, if you keep doing the same thing, a year from now you will be in the same place.

In general, I think we do a poor job of practicing in the business/sales world. For example. if we have a new product that comes out, we'll often put together a cheat sheet, PDF, or one-pager, send it to the sales team and think they are good to go.

If a musician gets a new piece of music, they aren't going to try it for the first time on- stage. If Bill Belichick handed Tom Brady a new play on game day and said, "All right we're gonna run this today" the players would scoff and think that was ridiculous. It should be the same for sales. We should be practicing our pitch when new products come out, when we face new objections, and even when nothing changes.

If you make practice a part of your daily routine, whether it's just five minutes in a meeting, a one-on-one, or a quick role play, it's going to make you a better salesperson. With that practice under your belt, when you get in front of a customer or prospect, you will be better equipped to perform and close it.

HOW-TO INTEGRATE PRACTICE INTO YOUR DAY

How do you incorporate practice into your everyday routine?

Unfortunately, when you talk about sales training it can cue eye rolls. I think the reason so many sales managers and leaders look down on it is because they see time spent training as a trade-off to time spent selling. When in reality, it can be a multiplier.

But we have to get rid of this idea that sales training is a full eight-hour day in a room where someone's telling us about a new sales skill with a PowerPoint. That is terrible and we shouldn't do that.

Enablement and training are much different now. With the right strategies and tools, you can spend a quick five minutes learning something, ten minutes practicing, and get on the sales floor.

What kind of practice do I recommend?

Role-Playing Is Key

My number one go-to recommendation is role-playing.

Yes, it's hard and many reps shy away from it but it's a very effective way to fine-tune your selling skills. I believe the reason many don't like to role play is that it makes you vulnerable. You have to put yourself directly in front of your peers and be willing to fail in front of them. And, let's be honest, you're going to fail a lot because that's a part of the learning process.

To overcome that fear and awkwardness, it's important to view role-playing as what it really is, a way to get feedback and improve. It's okay to fail, it's okay to get laughed at, and it's good to laugh at yourself because you are learning. Better to do it during a role- play than when you're speaking with a prospect, right?

Of course, the company culture and approach often come from the top down. If you are in a leadership role, I encourage you to accept and expect failure with the understanding that it is an opportunity for learning and growth.

When you can create a culture where failure and vulnerability are okay and the focus is on everyone getting better to excel and maximize returns, then you see some amazing things happen.

Types of Role-Playing

Role-playing with regular consistency, both formally and informally, is important. Here's a closer look at both types.

Informal Role-Playing

Informal role-playing is when you role-play casually in day-to-day life. It's not scheduled or graded but spontaneous and 100% about the feedback. Here are some examples:

Practice micro role-plays which are quick exercises that last five minutes or less. You can do them before hitting the sales floor or phones, in between meetings, or during lunch.

A quick role-play during a one-on-one conversation to show a new technique, practice a skill, overcome an objection, etc.

Peer role-playing where you grab a peer, jump in a conference room and practice something that you're getting ready to do with a prospect. Even if a peer is of the same tenure at your company and in the same position, you each have different experiences and can offer helpful tips to each other.

Practice something that you just tried and failed at with a prospect.

These in-the-moment role-plays should be normal, everyday events.

Formal Role-Playing

Formal role-playing is scheduled and structured and enables you to receive formal feedback.

When you get into the more formal role-playing situations, there should be feedback criteria (or scoring rubric as we would call it in the industry). It should lay out a more formal set of criteria such as how well are you crafting your discovery questions.

The scoring mechanism is there as a guide to help you know where your focus needs to be the next time you get in the ring. The feedback is really about the specific things that you can do to improve.

No matter which type of role-playing you're doing, formal or informal, it should always be about getting feedback to improve your skillset. A regular habit of practice ensures consistent feedback so that you can continue to hone your skills.

The Bottom Line

Success and advancement in sales require practice and learning on an ongoing basis. All your time shouldn't be spent in the game. Put in the practice to fine-tune and develop your skills so you can make increasingly better use of your game time.

Want to learn more from Bryan Naas? Follow him on: LinkedIn: linkedin.com/in/bryannaas

#44 SAM I Am

MATT MILLEN

"Who are you? I am a winner. I want to win.
I didn't come here to hang out. I know one speed.
Put the pedal down and go fast."

ABOUT MATT MILLEN:

With over three decades of experience, Matt Millen has been considered one of the top sales leaders in the industry by his peers and is currently the Chief Growth Officer for Sapper Consulting. He oversees the sales development, business development, and client success teams and is responsible for driving business growth initiatives and revenue rainmaking opportunities.

Matt has extensive experience in customer experience design, strategic planning, and sales innovation. Prior to joining the team at Sapper, Matt was the Chief Revenue Officer at FLEXE and held Vice President roles at Outreach.io, T-Mobile, Robbins Research International (a Tony Robbins company), Government Acquisitions, and Gateway Computers. In his earlier years, he was also the Director of Sales at Tech Data Corporation and a Regional Sales Manager at Zenith Data Systems.

Those who have worked with Matt say that his drive, determination and will to win are unprecedented and that there is a reason why everywhere he goes—records get broken. While the goals he sets may feel somewhat "challenging or unrealistic" to obtain, Matt has been known to demonstrate that there is no goal he can't reach by properly influencing his team to equally support and collectively work hard to achieve the goal at hand. He not only has a visionary approach but also the drive to bring his vision to life.

Early in my career, I learned to appreciate two things in life that had a massive impact on my career...

The first was getting a mentor. I had a great mentor that saw my potential but recognized how rough I was. I was way too confident and cocky and thought I knew too much. I think many of us salespeople start this way. The truth was, I wasn't that good and needed someone to invest in me and chisel off my corners. A lady named Terry really took the time to invest in me as a person, leader, and contributor so I am very grateful for her.

The second thing I picked up was the power of peer groups. I was surrounded by tremendously sharp people at Tech Data, and I identified five other directors who I wanted to learn from. We met every single month to develop and encourage each other. We all had different challenges, opportunities, and strengths and were there to help each other grow.

These were the makings of my foundation that helped me to get where I am today. Now, after 30 years in sales leading various businesses, I've developed a system for sales success in the teams I lead. I believe each salesperson needs to have three key pieces fine-tuned to be successful.

Execute SAM to Drive Sales Success

The methodology I bring is called SAM: Story, Activity, and Mindset. What does that mean?

Story: The story part involves the words that come out of your mouth — the conversations that you have all day, every day. You need to know your story and it needs to be compelling, confident, and relevant. Further, sales is the transfer of energy so you need to deliver it with energy, passion, and conviction. If you only get five objections, time, money, interest, or whatever it is, you've got to know how to handle them in a great way. If you don't know your story and know it well, you can't sell.

Activity: Next, the activity part involves how you spend your time. It matters. Take your story to the street and do it as many times as you possibly can. You want to get better and better. Figure out how to do it at-scale if possible.

Mindset: Lastly, the mindset part involves your attitude toward the business. As a coach, I can teach you the story, I can coach you through the activity, but you have to come in with the right attitude and mindset. Are you someone who complains about something and slows down, or someone who says "Screw it!" and doesn't let obstacles stop you or get in your way? Mindset matters.

SAM I am. Master all three parts of SAM to rise to the top.

HOW TO EXECUTE SAM

How can you start executing SAM today?

Fine-tune Your Story

The first part is your story. Work with your team and your leaders to craft your story. Identify all of the objections to your offering and prepare to overcome them with ease. Practice and practice until you know it like the back of your hand and can do it in your sleep. Understand the value you are bringing to your customers, and share the story of the value with confidence and charisma. How you come to the table and tell your story is going to determine if you are successful or not. And if you don't believe in the story, the people you're talking to won't either.

If you have trouble with confidence and get nervous when you speak to clients, I encourage you to implement a little trick I use to get myself into a state of gratitude. When you are in a state of gratitude, you cannot also be in a state of fear or anxiety. It is not possible. So the trick is getting yourself into that gracious state. I used to get very nervous speaking in front of people so I'd listen to a particular song that got me pumped up and excited. Then I'd look at a funny picture of my daughter that I kept on my smartphone. It warmed my heart and made me smile. After that, I felt invincible.

If you continue to struggle, another very helpful resource is a mentor. Seek out someone who has mastered their story and been a success, and ask them for help and coaching.

Overall, you need to be able to craft your story, practice it, and deliver it with passion, confidence, and energy.

Optimize Activity

The second part is your activity. Frequency is key. Practicing and practicing and practicing. Your leadership team should be helping with setting goals so that you are consistently making calls and sharpening your skills. Additionally, I greatly encourage accountability partners. Find a colleague who is fired up like you and make them your first and last call. Set goals at the beginning of the day and encourage each other, and then follow-up at the end of the day. Another thing I like to do above and beyond is to make five calls after 5 PM. Most people are leaving the office or checking out of work and it creates an opportunity to differentiate your sales call from the rest. Your activity level has to be high and strategic for your results to be among the best.

Cultivate an Unstoppable Mindset

The third is your mindset. To illustrate the type of mindset you need, I'd like to share my experience working as the VP of Sales with Tony Robbins. What I took away from Tony, above all else, was a mindset. My attitude toward everything (experiences, self, career, etc.). Tony redefined what was possible, how I should think about it, and how things should be structured. Time is not a measure in Tony's world, the outcome is. Time was irrelevant when something had to get done. It was not about resources, it was about being resourceful.

For example, I lived in San Diego at the time and one of the folks at the Robbins organization from Denver was coming to run meetings with me in LA. He called me Friday at about 6 PM and said that his Monday morning meeting canceled. Now, most people would say, "Okay, now I have a little more free time Monday morning for whatever." But no. He said, "Matt, I am telling you right now, the next call you get from me will be letting you know that I filled my 9 AM meeting on Monday." Keep in mind, it was the weekend. I got a call Saturday afternoon saying he filled his Monday 9 AM slot. Like who else does that? These were the kind of folks we had, everyone was so committed to the mission.

The necessary mindset is beyond what is convenient—what most people do. If you want the greatest rewards, convenience has to go away and you have to do whatever it takes to the best of your ability. And I don't think I'm giving you a secret. Everybody knows what to do but not everybody does what they know. You have to do what you know to be the best you can possibly be.

In summary, SAM I am—story, activity, mindset. You have to know your story, you have to execute the activity, and you have to have the right growth mindset to do whatever needs to be done to be successful.

Want to learn more from Matt Millen? Follow him on:
LinkedIn: linkedin.com/in/mmillen

#45 Calculated Persistence: The 23/52 Touch Process

MATT WHEELER

"If you don't hear back, you don't know a thing.
You make an assumption."

ABOUT MATT WHEELER:

Matt Wheeler is the CEO and Co-Founder of qualifiedMEETINGS, a proven sales process, and full-service sales development program. The company predictably grows pipelines while simultaneously providing data intelligence to improve conversion strategies.

He is also currently on the board of directors for Synapse, the guide for Florida's innovation community and the Pyle Foundation, a corporation that raises money for local charities.

Before starting qualifiedMEETINGS, Matt worked in many positions across various industries starting out as the President and CEO of Wholesale Seafood and then spending time as the Sr. Corporate Sales Executive for Netcordia (acquired by Infoblox), the Sales Development Manager for AccelOps, and the Business Development Manager at SevOne. In the following years, he was the Senior Manager at ForeScout Technologies

Inc. and the Director of High Velocity Sales and Business Development at CollabNet.

With over two decades of sales experience, Matt has personally made over 250,000 outbound calls and has managed over 10 million sales activities via his SDR teams. Further, he has contributed over 250 million dollars in new customer sales as an SDR and through his inside sales programs over the last 10 years. Everything he's done he credits to the proven methodology known as qualified MEETINGS "23-52 Touch Process" which he will share in this chapter.

Undoubtedly a veteran in the sales world, Matt's meeting generation programs are said to be second-to-none. He is known as a phenomenal, hands-on inside sales leader who thinks strategically, motivates teams to execute, and can scale out an organization.

If you're not just trying to shove that square peg in a round hole, the basics of sales is about truly understanding your buyer, their buying process, and the most effective way to engage them about your solution.

Most people don't spend enough time figuring these out. They get a little bit of data and start making assumptions. I've seen sales reps and sales leaders that will disqualify a buyer persona if they fail to close a few deals with just five or six touches each. In reality, getting in touch with a C-level person in an enterprise environment takes about 32 touchpoints, on average, and those touches have to be done within a limited timeframe to get a response.

So you need to invest time understanding the buyer, persona, and vertical, and building a repeatable process long enough to consistently get in touch with them.

Prospect Smart Using a Calculated Touch Process

When you are talking about sales activity, it all comes down to the pipeline. It's a simple, traditional perspective that holds true today. Guide people through the process and educate them effectively and professionally.

I have a 23/52 sales methodology that prevents you from pursuing a lead too long or too short. I'm a firm believer in "If you don't hear back, you don't know a thing." If someone isn't responding, you don't know if it's because they are too busy, the timing is off, they aren't interested, or they aren't receiving your messages. So I contact prospects either 23 or 52 times, respectively for inbound or outbound leads, to get a definitive answer.

Why 23?

The 23-step process for inbound leads requires that an inbound lead is touched 23 times within 60 days. The touches happen through the pillars of communication I mentioned above and each touch is done in an educational manner. Over time, I've found that most inbound leads convert at the 15th touchpoint.

It's important to note that just because a lead comes in and doesn't respond right away, that doesn't mean anything definitively. Don't assume they aren't interested. Keep peppering them with educational information.

We had a security company client with a massive amount of inbound leads. They would pick the low-hanging fruit off the tree and the rest got the classic four to five touches (call, email, voicemail, LinkedIn request, etc.) With this 23-step process, they were able to increase their conversions by 156% within 90 days.

If it's not an enterprise prospect, say it's midmarket or SMB, you may not need 23. It may only take 12 or 14. The important thing is to put a process in place and perform enough touches (thousands!) to find out where the magic number lies for your business.

The 52-Step Outbound Process

Next, the 52-step process is designed to reach and educate outbound leads through the same six pillars of communication within a 90-day period. My strategy involves understanding your target profile so you can replicate their story. I solve a very specific problem for a specific customer and share the story with people just like them in similar verticals.

Identify Your Target Profile and Learn Their Story

Not sure who your buyers are exactly? First, pick 25 to 50 companies and two to three verticals. Then, go out and create the messaging based on that persona and vertical and try it down multiple channels of communication (calls, video messages, voicemails, emails, direct mail, social media, and possibly SMS). Run an educated test and truly look at what the responses are and where the best place to spend your time is.

Once you identify the personas and verticals you should be working with, build those profiles out so you can identify what the educational cycle should look like. Then, you can reach out for a very specific reason and it's no longer a cold call. It's true education.

Why 52 Touchpoints?

In a C-level enterprise environment, it typically takes 32 touchpoints to make contact. However, if you haven't got a lead on the phone after the 32 touchpoints, there's a dead spot from 33 to 40-something and then it spikes back up again until you hit 52, so I go until 52.

One of the things I've seen from the persistent interaction with our lead database is that people sometimes come back and say "Okay, you've really come after me for the past 90 days, what is it that you want?" This is where the educational side needs to be dialed in and you need to be trained. You better have your story together and be ready.

Why did you call that person so many times? It's not to be annoying. It's because you've identified that organizations like theirs and people in their position typically benefit from the solution that you offer. At that point, you need to go in and have a drilled down business conversation.

There is a whole different chapter I could write around latent vs. active buyers. Latent buyers aren't really looking, they're responding to some of the messages and you don't want to start bullet point selling them. They don't care yet! You've gotta go in and do a business case, continuing to talk about the problems you solve and the people you solve them for. It can't be a high-level sales thing. You have to understand their business so you can speak to them and have that dynamic interaction.

The Responsibility of the Organization

From my perspective, the infrastructure around the sales development role should be defined and managed by the organization, including the messaging, the verticals, the personas, and the best places to go sell. If you leave that all up to the sales reps, the messaging will be all over the place. However, if an organization can align all its reps in one unified direction around who the buyers are, the efforts will be much more focused and effective.

So dig in to learn about your buyers and the education they can benefit from. Then, build the process to get in touch. Remember, it takes more touches than most people think and you need a system to track how many you've done. By studying your data over time, you will learn the average touches for your business and can continuously optimize your pipeline for higher conversion rates.

Want to learn more from Matt Wheeler? Follow him on:
Website: qualifiedmeetings.com
LinkedIn: linkedin.com/in/jmattwheeler

#46 All Sales Start With a Problem

JOSH BRAUN

"If you're talking about your solution and how great it is without the prospect telling you all about their problems and why they matter, you are doing it wrong."

ABOUT JOSH BRAUN:

Josh Braun is the Founder of Sales DNA. With more than 20 years of sales experience, he is a teacher turned sales expert. Josh has worked in a variety of sales positions and has spent time with companies such as ChildU, CompassLearning, Jellyvision, and Basecamp. In each of his roles, Josh was able to make significant contributions that led him to where he is today.

He now helps inside sales teams increase cold outreach response rates and get more meetings. Josh also runs the Inside Selling Podcast where he teaches listeners how to sell through simple acts of caring, being curious, and making people smile.

Josh's clients say he is a master at breaking things down into the simplest terms in order to get results. Further, they say his ideas on how to communicate with prospects are exactly what sales reps need to know to maximize efficiency. He is known as a true sales genius and the type of person you quote your entire career.

My first sales job was selling language, writing, and reading to five-year-olds, which was a tough gig. When I stepped into the classroom, despite my best efforts, I had blank faces staring at me. But, over time, I learned how to explain and "sell things" in ways that actually got my "prospects" to care. So while my background really is in teaching, it turns out that selling and teaching have a tremendous amount in common. And my roots in teaching have been instrumental to my success in sales.

Now 20-some years later, I have worked in various companies and positions. I've helped facilitate millions of dollars in growth, exceeded my quotas, gone through an acquisition, managed and coached sales development teams, created sales playbooks and strategies, and more. The biggest lesson I have learned—which I now teach to CEOs and VPs of sales looking to increase conversions—is this…

Solutions have no inherent value without problems.

If You're Selling, You Should be Focused on the Customer's Problem

Focus on the problem? You may think that sounds backward. Everyone is always preaching how important it is to be solution-focused. However, when it comes to sales, the key is in the customer's problem. If you're talking with the prospect about your product or service and how great it is—without the prospect telling you all about their problems and why they matter—you're doing it wrong. I don't care how great your offering is, it doesn't matter if you don't connect it to the buyer. How do you do that? Here are a few tips.

Identify or Uncover the Buyer's Reason to Change

When people are presented with a proposition to buy something, they have a couple of questions in their heads. The first and most important is, "Why should I change?" They think, "I'm doing fine, I'm making progress, why do I need to change?" So, as the salesperson, you need to identify or uncover that reason for the buyer.

I'll give you a great example of how to do that. One day I was at the mall waiting for my wife. I had recently bought a new pair of running shoes for an upcoming marathon but thought I'd kill some time in the running store. As I walked in, the store associate approached me. She didn't ask how I was doing because I would have said fine. She didn't ask what brought me into the store because I would have said I was just browsing. Instead, she asked a really smart question, she said, "Have you ever had your gait checked?" I said, "My what? What are you talking about?" Moments later, I was on a treadmill with a camera. She showed me the tape and it turns out my feet are pronated. She said, "You know if you run that marathon with pronated feet and those sneakers, you're gonna hurt yourself." The last thing I want to do is hurt myself so I bought a $150 pair of sneakers.

She showed me why I needed to make a change.

When I walked in I had no reason to buy anything because I already had a brand new pair of sneakers. But, she uncovered a problem I wasn't aware of, educated me on the impact, and I made the decision to buy to avoid that problem. Great salespeople don't just ask about problems, they help you find problems that you didn't know about. So you need to understand your product or service and the problems it solves—not the list of benefits written in marketing lingo but the real problems.

How do you do that?

Find the Real Problems Your Prospects are Facing

How do you find the real problems that give prospects a legitimate reason to change? You have to get inside the world of your customers. The company from the running store example above came up with the genius idea to get into the science of the foot, which is important to any quasi-serious runner (whether they realize it or not). By analyzing a person's manner of walking, a whole set of doors can be opened. It's a brilliant lead generator.

With that in mind, what matters to your prospects? What will give them a reason to change? To truly figure this out you need to take the time to learn about your prospect's life, including:

- What they bump into on a daily basis
- What kinds of problems they face
- What they enjoy about their job
- What they don't enjoy about their job
- What their long-term and short-term goals are
- Why they do what they do
- What magazines they read
- What podcasts they listen to
- What conferences they go to
- What blogs they follow.

You can figure this out by researching prospects online, reading what they post about on social media and online, following their blogs, and listening to their podcasts. If your manager says it's okay, I also recommend calling a couple of real customers and requesting an interview to discover the above.

When interviewing existing customers, I recommend the 'jobs-to-be-done' technique. If you haven't heard of it, Google it. It's the only method that I know that gets to the cause or the reason why someone bought your product or service. If you're selling a weight loss product, you can't just ask someone why they bought your product because they'll say, "I just wanted to lose weight." But that's not the truth. They bought your weight loss product because they just got divorced and they wanted to go on Tinder and meet someone more attractive. Or, they were going to a wedding and wanted to look better for the opposite sex. The jobs-to-be-done interview technique uncovers those truths of why eventually enough dominoes tipped over and caused a customer to buy and you can use those reasons to resonate with future prospects.

You need to become a complete expert on your prospects so you can truly solve their problems. So do your homework, dive deep, and keep all of your findings in a central document like a Google Doc, and update it periodically to keep it fresh and relevant.

Speak Your Prospect's Happiness Lingo

Once you crack the true problem code, you can actually speak the lingo of your customer and begin a meaningful conversation. What does that sound like? When I worked at Jellyvision, we started off saying, "We help HR professionals save time and money." Well, that might be true, but that's not how people talk and it didn't resonate.

When you actually talk to customers and ask them why they buy, they say things like: "We bought Jellyvision because we wanted to feel less frazzled during open enrollment," and "We wanted people to stop knocking on our doors, asking us the same questions about benefits over and over again." That's very different language. It's their lingo, and it's what you need to use to speak to your prospects because it will resonate with them on a deeper level.

Bonus Secret: Accept That You Can't Make Everyone Happier and Move On

Lastly, I think a fundamental flaw in sales is assuming that you can make everyone happier. That's just not true. Not everyone will have a problem you can solve at that moment and that is okay.

Take my grandma, for example. She had a crappy toaster. Only one side worked, it only might light toast, and it took forever. Despite that, every time I tried to sell her on a new toaster, she would never let me get her one. I would say this one can make two pieces of toast, it can make them dark brown, and it's fast. Although those were the benefits, they weren't benefits to her. Why? She wasn't in a rush, she only wanted one slice, and she liked light toast.

So although a solution has clear benefits, if it doesn't increase the happiness of your particular prospect, the benefits won't matter to them. If that's the case, I suggest you move on. The world is a big place and there are many other people who you can make legitimately happier.

Connect Your Prospects With Truly Beneficial Solutions

In summary, sales solutions have no inherent value without problems. It's very important that you get close to your customers, uncover their problems (or educate them on problems they didn't know they had), understand how you can increase their happiness by solving that problem and use the customer's lingo in your marketing and sales conversations. As a result, you can get inside the world of your prospects and truly help them improve their quality of life with your solution.

Want to learn more from Josh Braun? Follow him on:
LinkedIn: linkedin.com/in/josh-braun
Website: joshbraun.com

#47 Stop Looking for Interested Buyers

DAVID WALTER

"When you innovate and educate, you can help prospects realize their needs."

ABOUT DAVID WALTER:

David Walter is a #1 Best-Selling Author and the Marketing Director at MSP SEO Factory— a company providing IT marketing to businesses in the United States. He also ran a telemarketing firm for 13 years and successfully helped businesses make millions with his unique cold calling strategies.

David's claim to fame came from setting a record 15 appointments each and every day for six months while cold calling for a PEO company. He unpacks how he was able to achieve this tremendous feat in his book, *The Million Dollar Rebuttal*. David often speaks at trade shows and other industry events and is a telemarketing and sales trainer for major companies.

Those who know David say that he is an incredible speaker that keeps everyone on the edge of their seats. His presentations are said to be strong, positive, and worthwhile experiences.

While I don't think you should try to sell ice to an Eskimo, I do know you can sell a lot more to people who don't know they have needs.

When Procter & Gamble first launched Febreze, they positioned it to people who wanted to get rid of bad smells in their homes. It was a great odor eliminator and could even get the skunk smell out of clothes. But when the product launched, it failed massively.

P & G went on a mission to figure out why — visiting customers and asking why they weren't buying Febreze. A pivotal discovery happened when they went to one particular customer's house.

A lady opened the door and a pungent, horrible cat smell poured out. Still, they went in and began to discuss her experience with the product. She explained that she used the product once or twice but didn't really need it. A bit perplexed, they asked her if she could smell the odor at that moment. She said no.

The customer didn't think she had a bad odor in her home and therefore, didn't need an odor eliminator. With this insight, P & G repositioned Febreze as a "final touch" to the existing cleaning process and it took off.

Sell to People Who Don't Know Their Needs

Just like people get used to their homes and don't detect foul smells, people and businesses get accustomed to problems and inconveniences and no longer notice them or think about them. It could be an old copier or a clunky software program that does the job, albeit poorly. If they haven't self-identified their need, they'll usually say they aren't interested in a solution, so your pool of interested buyers will always be small.

To be more effective in sales, the focus should be on helping your prospects realize they have a need. When I worked in a call center selling a worker's compensation program, I became notorious for booking 15 appointments per day when everyone around me was booking just two. My secret was that I wasn't just selling workers comp programs. I blew my prospect's minds with a whole new concept they'd never heard of.

I took the old idea that people had— which was slow and inefficient— and put a new exciting thing right next to it. That's how you get people to realize that old thing is not good anymore. Then the customer decides they want the new thing and essentially sells themselves. When you begin educating people on your product or service in this way, rather than looking for interested buyers, your success rate will grow.

How To Help Customers Discover Their Needs

You just need to focus on educating. Your offering needs a unique selling proposition (USP) that is different from everything else. It needs to set your offering apart in a definitive way. Then, you teach prospects about that difference.

Tell your prospects you're not trying to compete against their current provider and don't say their current provider is bad. Just explain that you're trying to show what else is out there (that just so happens to be newer and better).

You can say, "Look, you're not looking to change right now, but things are changing in the future and you want to be prepared for that."

About 20 years ago, I remember I made a call for an IT service and we were offering a flat fee model for unlimited support which was way different than the pay-per-service model everyone else was offering. So I was talking to a lady at a law firm and she said, "I'm happy with what I have, we're happy, we're happy, we're happy."

I said, "Okay but have you heard of this new unlimited concept with a flat fee."

She didn't believe me! She said, "I never thought anything like that would exist in the IT world in a million years but I'm happy with what I have."

I said, "I get it. You're not going to change right now. But I just want to do one thing. I want to have Tony come out there and just show you that a real company will stand behind this unlimited guarantee that exists. Because you don't believe it and once you see it, it might change the way you think about IT in the future."

She agreed and said, "Okay but tell Tony I'm completely happy and don't want to change." So Tony went out and did the whole presentation.

I followed up two weeks later and she switched!

Many people think you're wasting your time if you set appointments with people who don't have an immediate need. And if you don't have a new, exciting, and better offering, you are. But if you have an innovative, stand out USP, and you focus on education, you can close them all!

**Want to learn more from David Walter? Follow him on:
LinkedIn: linkedin.com/in/david-walter-7940a468**

#48 A Watched Pot Never Boils

RYAN SERHANT

"People hate being sold but they love shopping with friends."

ABOUT RYAN SERHANT:

Ryan Serhant is a former actor turned American real estate mogul, producer, business founder, author, and TV personality. He is best known as the star of Bravo's two-time Emmy-nominated "Million Dollar Listing New York" and as the founder of The Serhant Team.

Named the #1 sales team in New York and the #3 sales team in the U.S. by the *Wall Street Journal*, Ryan's team at NestSeekers International consists of more than 60 experienced agents and marketing support staff who consistently sell over one billion dollars per year in real estate. They maintain a diverse inventory of exclusive listings and have built relationships with thousands of agents around the world. Combining these tools with an intimate knowledge of the market has enabled them to earn a lifetime list-to-sale ratio of 94.5%.

In September of 2018, Ryan shared insights into his sales tactics in his first book, *Sell It Like Serhant: How to Sell More, Earn More, and Become the*

Ultimate Sales Machine. It became a best-seller on the *New York Times*, *Wall Street Journal*, and *Los Angeles Times* book lists.

As a real estate expert, he is also a frequent contributor to 20/20, CNN, CNBC, The Today Show, and Bloomberg TV, and is often quoted in *The New York Times*, *Forbes*, *Wall Street Journal*, and *Wall Street Journal China*.

Ryan's clients say his expertise is crucial when determining when to buy and which neighborhood to buy into, and his guidance is the key factor in maximizing their profitability and satisfaction in the homebuying process.

The worst salespeople — who make the least amount of money — are the ones out there selling every single day. It's just like dating. If you walk into the bar, sit down, and try to close it early by talking about how good you are going to be that night, the date is over. But if you ask questions, focus on the relationship, and make a friend, you have a chance at a future.

Stop Focusing on Selling

While everything is about sales at the end of the day, my focus is 100% on relationships. I'm never asking, "How can I sell more?" Instead, I ask, "How can I improve and grow my relationships? And how can I make them better?"

Human beings like people who ask them questions because they like to hear themselves talk. It soothes them. There are studies that show this. When you ask other people questions about their lives, and you shut up and don't give them too many facts, they begin to trust you and like you. You become a friend. And as a friend, you will sell 10x more than you are selling now.

HOW TO STOP HARD SELLING AND START BUILDING PROFITABLE RELATIONSHIPS

How do you stop hard selling and build profitable relationships?

Know Who You are as a Person

You can't be a salesperson without knowing who you are. If you ever watch "Sell It Like Serhant" on Bravo, that's the first thing I teach every single person. I ask, "Who are you? What makes you tick? What do you like? What are your interests? How are you going to connect to people on the street and those that walk into your store?"

Almost everyone can't answer those questions at the beginning. They're like, "Umm...I'm Sam, I sell, and I like football." That's no good. You need to have a clear understanding of who you are, why you do what you do, what you're passionate about, and what you're not passionate about. Figure out why anyone should have an interest in what you have to say.

Become an Expert

Next, it's all about what you know. Everything is on the internet nowadays so people can find out just about anything on their own. So why do they need you? People will hire you and pay you if you know more than what the internet is telling them.

If you're lucky and you have a good smile and a great handshake then great, you'll do some deals. But people don't hire me because I'm nice or because I'm on TV. They hire me because when we sit in a room, I look them in the eye and I tell them exactly what we are going to do, how we are going to do it, and facts about things they didn't know. I just do my homework, it's not brain surgery.

If you don't take the time to research and know your shit, why should anyone hire you? You need to know your stuff so that when you go into those meetings and meet new people, they're like, "I could learn this online myself but it seems like you know more and can offer additional expertise."

You build a relationship and trust by sharing your knowledge.

Create Friendly Shopping Experiences

Lastly, people need to feel like their decisions are their own. Like in the movie Inception, they introduced the idea that you can plant an idea in someone's head. That is really what sales is about.

You can't drag a horse to water but you can create an experience that sets things in motion so that someone makes the decision you wanted them to make all along. You want it to become their idea and their decision, although you planted the seeds along the way.

For example, say you have four pairs of shoes to show someone and they say their budget is $100. You don't show them the best pair first. You show them exactly what they want to see, the $100 pair. Then, afterward, you show them something that they can't afford, say a $250 pair. But you don't just show them, you're upfront and tell them they can't afford them.

You could say something like, "Listen since you're in the store anyway, we just got this new pair of Jordan's in. Don't buy these, they are way too expensive but check them out for fun. They feel like walking on clouds— it's insane! I'm not supposed to do this but do you want to try them on? You're size 12, right?"

They'll be hard-pressed not try them on. Especially because, as a salesperson, you tell them not to buy them. You've become a friend helping them try cool shit on. After that, you take the person back to the shoes they wanted for $100. Now, all of a sudden, they look at the same wall of shoes and point to the one that is $125, $150, and say, "Do you have those in my size?"

All you have to do is set up the experience.

Become a Shopping Companion

In summary, people hate being sold but they love shopping with friends. They like to try stuff on and say, "Does this look good? Do you love this? Do you hate that?" If you can make as many friends as you can to "go shopping with," then you're never selling anyone. It becomes like, "Hey, let's go shopping for apartments," versus, "Hey, I've got some apartments that I think would be really great for you to buy." It's the same action but two totally different conversations.

Want to learn more from Ryan Serhant? Follow him on:
Youtube: youtube.com/user/OfficialRyanSerhant
Instagram: @RyanSerhant
Facebook: facebook.com/RyanSerhant
Twitter: @RyanSerhant
Website: ryanserhant.com

#49 Plant the Seeds You Know Will Grow

AMIR REITER

"...find the path of least resistance and focus on it."

ABOUT AMIR REITER:

Amir Reiter is the Founder and CEO at CloudTask, which is a managed workforce provider that helps grow companies through repeatable sales, customer success, and customer support activities. He is also on the Chairman Advisory Board for Upcision and is a member of Modern Sales Pros.

Amir spent over a decade working in sales before beginning his own entrepreneurial journey. He hasn't looked back since.

Prior to entering the workforce, Amir earned a BS in Physiological Science and Chemistry from the University of Arizona's College of Medicine in Tucson. He has earned several certifications through global industry leaders including HubSpot, Google, AA-ISP, NetSuite, Wrike, and many more.

Those who know Amir say that his commitment and work ethic are second-to-none. He's always looking for ways to improve himself and everyone around him. Further, he's known for talking a big game and then turning that talk into revenue.

My first sales job was selling copiers door-to-door at the age of 21. Next, I sold $3,000 vacuums through 3-hour-long, in-house demos. After that was B2B water products. I've just always been selling. And I'm one of those guys that when I first started, I was more comfortable actually walking into buildings versus calling.

But when I finally got on the phones, I was like "Oh my god, I did all of that walking for nothing!" I realized I could probably get a lot more done on the phones. Then, channels kept opening up and I kept learning. All of a sudden, it got to the point where I was uncomfortable if people weren't saying no to me.

To help you accelerate your sales career and drive results, here are three micro sales secrets I've learned throughout my career and my number one top sales secret.

Micro Sales Secret #1:
Don't Take Rejection Personally

I learned this secret when I was working for the water service company. I would find people who had five-gallon bottle water coolers and would sell them on replacing them with filtration machines. But I would get straight up rejected regularly. I'd walk into a building and they'd immediately be like "Get out!" or "We're not interested!" And I would feel an emotional reaction to that.

My VP of Sales told me something that stuck with me. He said, "When you get rejected, it's not personal. They just don't want to do business with the company you are representing." I needed to take the emotional side out of it.

To do that, I just started brainwashing myself to ignore the rejection and focus on the fact that I was lucky to even have the opportunity to get rejected. In some places, like in Syria, you, unfortunately, might not have the option to actually sell something to somebody or even ask for something. So learn to be grateful to have a job and realize that "no" is not a no to you—it's to the company. Don't let it slow you down or demoralize you. Just keep pushing on.

Micro Sales Secret #2: Get All the Stakeholders Involved

I discovered my next micro secret when I was selling multimillion-dollar robotic equipment to big committees in the medical industry. Selling to one person wasn't enough. I had to know and engage all of the committee stakeholders who had a say in the decision.

To do this, you need to have a bigger vision, understand there may be more stakeholders involved, and learn how to ask who they are in a polite way. If I'm talking to the CEO, I might say, "Hey, I know that you probably care about support and it's top of mind but you're probably really busy making your product better. Can I get an introduction to the person in charge of support?" This will garner more respect than, "Hi can I speak to the person in charge of your support."

Micro Sales Secret #3: The Company You Work for Can Dictate Your Future

Next, going to work at NetSuite, I learned micro secret number three. The company you work for can dictate your future. Everybody knew who NetSuite was and they bought it so I was jumping on a fast-moving train.

If you're working at a company that's not really known— not a Google, Salesforce, or IBM — I would say learn as much as you can and fight as hard as you can. However, also know that you have a career and the organization has an opportunity to match your ambition or not. Right?

Be aware of what they're doing and talk to them about your needs and aspirations. For example, if I worked for you, I could be like, "Hey, this is an amazing journey. I'm working, I'm giving you 100% but you know I need some support with Google Ads and I need some bigger deals." Make your desires known and set timelines for yourself. If you don't reach the milestones you want with a company, move on.

That's the beautiful part about having a job and not owning the company, you can move on whenever you want.

Top Sales Secret: Your Seeds are Everything

Okay, now we are to the number one secret I wish I had known at the start of my career — understand that your seeds are everything. Before you know your cold call pitch or your product, make sure that you're targeting the right people. At our organization, CloudTask, for instance, we've grown 150% this year and I still don't think we're targeting the right people.

How do I do my targeting?

With Sales Navigator, you can really target your audience and with Seamless you can get the lead information.

I search by position — say, VP of Sales, location — say, San Francisco, companies size — Series B, and keywords — hiring. From that point on, I would do an omnichannel approach; following, liking, commenting, messaging — on every channel.

I'm like glue. I archive any conversation that has no value so every conversation I have open is an opportunity that I need to push until I get a "no."

But you want to increase your odds by ensuring you're planting the best possible seeds.

My biggest advice is to find the path of least resistance and focus on it. Find that one thing, that one person, that you can help and scale that. It's not easy because you're tempted to load up sequences in your SalesLoft or Outreach.io but those days are going to start dying very soon. One person, one niche.

Want to learn more from Amir Reiter? Follow him on:
LinkedIn: linkedin.com/in/amirreiter
Instagram: @amirreiter
Facebook: facebook.com/amir.reiter

#50 3 Secrets to Earning Trust in 60 Seconds

JEREMY HAYNES

"When you want to make a lot of money and scale a big business, you have to take responsibility for creating customers in your market."

ABOUT JEREMY HAYNES:

Jeremy Haynes is the CEO and Founder at Megalodon Marketing, an industry-leading personality branding digital agency. He is also a coach and mentor to thousands of digital agency owners through his training program the Digital Marketing Manuscript (DMM).

Further, with the help of the 25+ person team of Megalodon Marketing, Jeremy acts as a marketing/advertising consultant to celebrity personalities, New York Times best-selling authors, speakers, businesses, e-commerce companies, and entrepreneurs.

Before launching the DMM, Jeremy launched three training programs in collaboration with Tai Lopez including The SMMA program, The Entrepreneur Start Kit, and How To Be A Traveling CEO.

Additionally, prior to launching Megalodon Marketing, Jeremy worked as a digital marketing specialist for Cardone Training Technologies, Inc. where he marketed Grant Cardone's products, services, and properties.

Jeremy has earned an incredible reputation in the information product and marketing industries. Those who know him say he is an unbelievably talented digital marketer and coach who helps businesses and individuals to drive revenue where they didn't even know it was available.

Humans only give their time, energy, and resources to things that they expect to give them a return. If you give me time and energy and I don't return it to you somehow, you're going to be pissed and aren't likely to do it again. It's just how we operate.

Now, let's apply that to digital marketing.

To get someone to pay attention and care about you and your brand, they need to think that you'll offer them something in return. They need to trust you and think you are a safe investment.

Humans make these kinds of decisions and judgments on a subconscious level in milliseconds. There is no thinking about it. No conscious process of, "Is that person soft as shit or strong and healthy?" or "Is that someone I can trust?"

To make people immediately trust you and see you as a safe investment, you need to integrate three cognitive biases into your marketing efforts.

Three Cognitive Biases For Building Trust

The conscious mind fires off 20 to 40 neurons per second while the subconscious mind fires off 20 to 40 million. You should not give a shit about the conscious mindset. By focusing on the subconscious, you can establish the biases you need to get the human to care, trust, and understand that other people are already caring, trusting, and understanding you. These biases are authority, social proof, and curiosity.

Why is this so important?

There is only a small portion of the population that are first movers—people that will do things, take action and believe new thoughts that aren't already proven by other people. Everybody else on the planet requires that other people have already done something for them to trust it themselves. So that's what we are trying to do.

For example, let's say you're walking through the mall and you see a long line wrapping from the Apple store all the way around the block. Are you going to stop to see what's going on? Will you feel curious? As humans, groups of other humans giving their attention to something piques our interest. The curiosity takes us over and we want to figure out what's going on. Social proof breeds curiosity.

Authority also plays into the equation. If I look somewhere and see a bunch of people huddled outside a store that I don't care about, I am going to look but as soon as I see it's not an authority, I'm not going to give it more attention. But if it's the Apple store and I have Apple products, there's a pretty high probability that I will consider Apple as an authority in my mind. So in that case, it will likely get my attention.

So authority, social proof, and curiosity need to align in your marketing content for people to care about you.

HOW TO ESTABLISH AUTHORITY, SOCIAL PROOF, AND CURIOSITY

You can establish these three biases through a piece of content. I recommend a 60-second video that can be pushed out on Instagram and Facebook through paid advertising.

Here are some tips on what to do.

Create Authoritative Video Content

The content should show groups of people looking at you or the subject for which you are trying to build authority, curiosity, and social proof. Speaking on a stage or in a group in front of an audience is perfect as it gives you the perception of authority. Additionally, the average attention span in the newsfeed is 1.8 seconds so your clips should rotate every two seconds or so.

You don't have to wear a suit, you don't have to go over the top, and you don't have to have jets or crazy cars. But people know what those things cost so if you incorporate some of those materials, it helps through the law of association.

What if you're not on stage?

If you don't have any content where you're positioned as an authority, you need to put skin in the game and go legitimately get the footage. You don't fake it. You actually go out, speak on stages, and burn money to build these assets. It is a revenue-driven action and it takes time.

I went to an event with just 20 to 40 people in the room, but I don't give a shit. I know 400,000 people are going to see that video and it's going to make a much bigger impact. So, yeah, you take actions like that because you see how they play into getting you a result in this larger sales cycle.

Use the Power of a Referral

Next, what's the most powerful way to get introduced to somebody?

Through a trusted source.

If you have a friend that introduces you to somebody, that person will likely transfer the trust they have in your friend to you.

Over your 60-second video of montage shots, have audio or audio and video of somebody introducing you. It could be on a stage, on a podcast, in a meeting, etc. In mine, it's one of my clients introducing me to a group and he says, "Ladies and gentleman, let me introduce you to the man who I met through Grant Cardone, who helps me make millions of dollars as my digital marketer. He's since helped Dan Lok gross over $x amount and he's helped Tai Lopez. Without further adieu, here's Jeremy Haynes."

A referral is an extremely powerful way to gain trust as it provides additional social proof.

Push Out This Intro Video First

When the video is ready, you'll want to share it with your target audience through Facebook and Instagram. Do not pitch them first. Your goal is to get people to watch 10 seconds so you can establish the three biases. Then, you're going to retarget the people who watch with more content to shift their beliefs.

Build Social Proof Online

You should also build social proof on your online video content. You use two types of ads to push the content out. One with the objective of engagement and another for video views. You're telling Facebook, go find me people who are actually going to interact with my post.

Then, when this piece of content goes in front of people who are just getting to know you and it's framing their beliefs, there should already be dozens of people in the comments like, "Dude this is the shit!" And with people tagging their friends, like, "Watch this video!"

Keep in mind, if any of that social proof isn't there, your audience is going to feel like a first mover, which will lower the probability they will watch it.

Once a human has seen this content and you've established the right biases, they actually have a higher probability to give a shit about you. You make them subconsciously know that you can be trusted, you're safe, and you're someone they can invest time and energy into. And they will know that other people are already getting a return on the time and energy they are putting into you.

Then, with that premise, you can proceed with your content to shift their beliefs, break limiting perspectives, and prepare them for conversion. No, this is not common knowledge and it's not from books. It's from thinking through how to respect the digitized sales process and take actions that motivate people to respond.

Want to learn more from Jeremy Haynes? Follow him on:
Instagram: @Jeremy
Email: ceo@jeremy.expert

#51 Be a World-Class Listener

DAVID DONLAN

"In sales, you're trying to get to some outcome beyond the signature and you will only get there by asking good questions and listening."

ABOUT DAVID DONLAN:

David Donlan is a businessman, public speaker, advisor, and lecturer. He is currently the CRO of Zoovu in Boston where he develops conversational marketing strategies for enterprise and mid-market companies looking to increase their top-line revenue growth and sales.

Before joining Zoovu, David was CRO of Crayon.co. As a sales leader, he was responsible for developing the go-to sales and marketing strategies for mid-market enterprise companies globally. And prior to Crayon, he was an early employee at Hubspot where he helped to grow the company from 100 customers to more than 15,000—ultimately, leading to a massive IPO.

David's also held sales leadership positions at prominent marketing and media firms from startup to acquisition including The Aberdeen Group that was acquired by Harte-Hanks, The Boston Herald, and BitPipe (acquired by Tech Target).

He has demonstrated exemplary sales leadership abilities which have enabled him to exceed every benchmark set in front of him. Those who know David say he has a deep understanding of marketing, selling fundamentals, and plain human nature. He is known as a true leader who has the confidence to know he can win and the humility to ask for advice and learn from anyone within an organization.

When I started at Hubspot, I was one of seven or eight salespeople on the team. During the first year, our approach was to generate leads, hire people, train them, and sell, sell, sell— as much as we could. However, after some time, we noticed the churn numbers were really high. Because we wanted to be a big company that created tremendous value for our customers, we decided we needed to change our sales process.

Rather than trying to close as many sales as we could, we would get people on the phone and ask them questions. Questions about their business, marketing, sales, lead generation, and how happy they were. Every call became a discovery call and the top reps would never demo the platform until they went through a very thoughtful, deep discovery process. However, the reps that still made quota but who were struggling were the ones that would show-up-and-throw-up the demo.

So if you were a rep who was hitting 200% of your number and you were making it look easy, it was because you were putting in thoughtful effort in the discovery calls.

The Best Salespeople are World-Class Listeners

I learned my top sales secret and Hubspot and have continued to see the importance across many roles— you have to listen.

If you are not a world-class listener, you are not going to make it in sales. In fact, some of the best sales hires I've had were folks who had never been in sales before but were really good at listening. But in order to be a good listener, you have to be extremely inquisitive, very curious, and unafraid to ask questions.

You will feel the sales process going a lot smoother if you listen 100% of the time and ask the right questions to get your customers talking 70% to 80% of the time. It's always hard, it's always a grind, but I can't hammer enough on the concept of listening as it makes it much easier.

HOW TO BECOME A WORLD-CLASS LISTENER

If you want to improve your listening skills, here are my top three tips.

Ask Simple Questions

I've always started by asking easy questions that my prospects know how to answer. Where are you located? How many employees do you have? How many people in sales? How many people in marketing? What's your background? Ask questions they know the answers to so they can warm up.

Once you get them talking, start asking deeper questions to get to the why behind their decisions. Don't be afraid to say, "Okay, can you tell me more about that?" Depending on the size of the company, you might ask, "Okay, how does that make you feel?" I've found that the simpler the questions you ask, the better the experience will go for both parties.

And something I always tell everyone is if you want to get really good at asking questions, go watch, Columbo. It's a detective TV series where the main character just asks very simple questions. Because he asks so many of the right questions, he builds his case and always catches the guy at the end of the show.

Read Regularly

Next, you need to do things that help you develop the muscle memory to be a good listener. One of my buddies, Todd Speicher, is an unbelievable world-class salesperson who was always really good at asking questions and listening. One day, a long time ago, I asked him how he does it and he said that he reads for two hours every day. I then asked him how he finds the time with three kids and this and that going on and he said, "I make time."

So I took that tip and applied it, not right away but a bit down the road and it really has helped. It doesn't have to be a business book, it could be fiction or non-fiction. Some people enjoy reading the New York Times every morning on their tablet or phone. I personally like to read books.

I actually just started a new book about comedy movies in the 1980s and how John Belushi, Eddie Murphy, and Chevy Chase changed the way that we watch movies today. I love it, it's great, and there are some aspects that I'm learning about how these artists do things a certain way and I see how I can apply some of that to how I run a business.

In summary, I find the more that I'm working on exercising my brain by reading, the more it really helps me to stay inquisitive and curious. It can get complicated with kids and a busy schedule but if you make time to do it, it pays off very well.

Call Back to Dig Deeper

Lastly, if you don't get past the surface level on a discovery call, take your notes, sit down with your manager, and go through them. When you identify where you could have dug deeper, call the prospect back on the phone and say, "Hey, do you have one quick second here? I'm sorry to get you back on the phone but I forgot to ask you a question."

It's like anything else, if you miss something at the gym, you can go back the next day and do it. Don't be afraid to go back, recognize you made a mistake, and fix it. Doing this shows that you truly were listening to your prospect and thinking about what they said. And while it may seem counterintuitive, the follow-up often builds the prospect's confidence in you.

Sales is really about asking questions leading up to an outcome and the outcome is not always just the sale. Sometimes the sale is just the beginning. The outcome could be watching your customers grow or building a long-term relationship. Whatever it is, you're trying to get to some outcome beyond the signature and you will only get there by asking good questions and listening.

Want to learn more from David Donlan? Follow him on:
Twitter:@ddonlan
LinkedIn: linkedin.com/in/daviddonlan/

#52 Stay Curious

BRIAN POTTER

"I'm big on knowing your numbers but even more than that, I would say you need to know your customer."

ABOUT BRIAN POTTER:

Brian Potter is a salesman, mentor, and advisor. He is currently the Field Learning Consultant at SAP Concur where he helps to connect the dots between sales leadership, revenue operations, and enablement. Prior to Brian's consultant role, he was a Senior Sales Executive for about a year and a half, followed by a Regional Sales Executive for three years.

Brian also spent about five years at American Express as the Business Development Manager where he helped middle-market businesses implement payment solutions to drive savings, reduce liability, and streamline expense management. Before joining AmEx, Brian worked with FedEx for eight years in various sales roles. In his last three years, he handled a territory with an $18 million annual revenue goal.

With over 15 years in sales roles across various brands, Brian has become highly skilled in the areas of business development, selling, and sales operations. Those who know him say that he is a natural mentor and high performer. He is someone who continuously drives success and will not hesitate to take time out of his busy day to share his best practices.

When I first started at Concur, it didn't seem like it was going to be hard to get ramped up. I figured, "I know Concur, I use it, it should be pretty easy to sell." But my numbers will tell you otherwise. I bombed and after the first year, I had to do some self-reflection to identify how I could improve.

In year two, I was able to turn the ship around and qualified for President's Club but I had to fix a big mistake I was making— I wasn't effectively tying the product and benefits to the prospect.

I would say, "We do this and that, here's my demo, we're awesome." But I wasn't adding, "Here's why it is important to you and why it's important to thousands of our other customers like you."

However, to give the "why" beyond the product or benefit, you first have to discover what it is.

Be Curious

I'm big on knowing your numbers but even more than that, I would say you need to know your customer.

I talk to salespeople all the time and ask, "Who do you sell to?" And they say, " Everyone." So I ask, "What was the last big deal you sold, and what does the customer do?" And they reply, " Oh, ABC company and I don't really know what they do but they bought my product!"

Sure, it's great to close a sale but my number one secret would be to become super curious, get to know your customer, know what their business does, and know what the personas within that business do.

Most products today are not necessary but they are nice to have so a sale depends on showing your target the business case for why your product will provide ROI as well as laying out how it will personally benefit them.

If you're selling to CFOs, find out what's important to them. Do they really care about XYZ? Or, do they actually care about going into a board meeting next week and having to answer why their earnings aren't where they're supposed to be?

It's not always easy but if you can figure out how you can help that CFO not sweat during the board meeting, or offering a solution to whatever their real concern is, your job is going to be a whole lot easier.

HOW TO KNOW YOUR CUSTOMERS

Where should you start to be curious and get to know your customers?

Call your existing clients

Let's say you come into a new job at a new company and you have three main personas. You need to figure out what they do and what is important to each of them. An easy way to find out is to call them up, ask them questions, and listen.

Say, "Hey, you're using my product today and I'd love to get a coffee or have five minutes to pick your brain on why you bought it." In the meeting, ask them:

- What do you do?
- Why did you buy the product?
- What were the struggles you had before?
- How did the product solve the problem?
- What does that solution mean for you in your position?

Go straight to the source to investigate how you are already providing value.

Research target personas

Next, I'd also say try and get involved with some local organizations composed of your target personas. You're not always going to have an open door, for example, you can't exactly join a CFO Alliance if you sell to CFOs.

However, more than likely, you can find some free content on their website that can give you a sense of what topics are important to them (e.g. a webinar or article on a particular topic). And, there are definitely online resources available through Google, social media platforms, websites, etc.

Identify 3 key points for messaging

Once you do all that research, you're going to find a lot of information. For example, if you ask a CFO what they do throughout the month, they are probably going to come back with literally 37 different responsibilities. Narrow it down to two or three key points that you can focus on in your custom messaging.

For example, you want to say something like, "Hey (target's name), as an award-winning CFO locally, more than likely you are likely running into problems with these three things. Do any of those resonate with you? Is that something we could schedule 10 minutes to talk about?"

By narrowing it down, you are able to customize the message, probably hit home with something that is important to them, and not feel overwhelmed with analysis paralysis from having 37 talking points. Keep it simple, concise, and clear.

Practice

Lastly, practice your message. Ask successful salespeople around you to listen to your pitch and your messaging and to give you feedback. Roleplay. Ask your manager to hop on a call to practice and be a sounding board. This support can help you fine-tune what you are saying to prospects and make it as effective as possible.

Today, most of what is sold is not a must-have. It is nice but not necessary. So becoming curious to understand what your target personas care about is the key to an effective customized pitch that will help you close more sales.

**Want to learn more from Brian Potter? Follow him on:
LinkedIn: linkedin.com/in/brianpotter**

#53 What's Your "One Thing?"

DAVID KREIGER

"If you try to chase two rabbits at once, you catch none."

ABOUT DAVID KREIGER:

David Kreiger is an amazing leader and a true B2B lead generation pioneer. He is currently the President of SalesRoads where he helps companies increase their revenue, lower their fixed costs, and gain market share by outsourcing their inside sales functionality.

David has been named one of the 50 Most Influential in Sales Lead Management twice and has been a finalist for Best Contact Center and Best Contact Center Executive/Director. His sales efforts have helped establish and drive growth for countless companies from startups to Fortune 500s.

Prior to joining SalesRoads, David was a Brand Management Manager for The Beanstalk Group and a Sales Operations and Marketing Manager for TradeOut. He also earned his BA in Political Science and Economics and his MBA in Marketing and Management from the University of Pennsylvania.

Those who know David say he is a detail-oriented, dynamic leader who has the tenacity and multi-track focus to drive success. His company SalesRoads is said to be a "true gem" in the industry, providing companies with effective and strategic outsourcing partners that not only help companies improve their client relationships but also drive profitability.

When you try to focus on too many things, you can't do any of them well, and I learned this lesson the hard way in my career.

A few years back at SalesRoads, we were helping a client with a big appointment-setting campaign. Meanwhile, they were also moving their inbound tech support from the Philippines to Dallas. They asked us, "Hey, you're a call center, can you do our inbound tech support during this transition?" We thought "Sure!" and literally added about 16 inbound seats for tech support overnight. We ended up doing a great job so I decided we should add tech support to our services.

Now, tech support and sales are very different so I wanted to build out the website, create support roads, and basically have a new company branch for tech support. But it's hard enough to do appointment setting and lead generation really well. To start thinking I was going to do tech support too (when there are many competitors who are doing it pretty cost-effectively) was over-ambitious.

My initiative ended up being a waste of six months. We lost the focus on our primary offering, we weren't doing our core business well, we weren't going after as many new clients, and weren't iterating. We scrapped it and went back to focusing on our primary offering.

Focus on One Thing

From that experience and others, I've learned that focus equals growth. And a book I read from Gary Keller, The One Thing, really helped me further formulate my top sales secret which is to focus on one thing at a time.

For those who aren't familiar, Gary Keller started Keller Williams Realty, the largest real estate franchise company by agent count in the world. He built an amazing training for real estate agents and has done a fantastic job of building that brand and organization.

After growing that business, he wrote the book based on the concept that you can boil almost anything you need to do in life down to one thing. Whether it's the one thing you need to do this year, this week, or today.

A lot of times we get so lost in the details of all the things we need to do that we forget to prioritize. This can let the most important things slip through the cracks. I'm the type of person that likes to try and get everything done so this learning was very transformative for me.

It relates to sales success for me when coaching. In the past, I would identify many behaviors that a sales rep needed to improve upon. For example, they need to ask more questions, they need to listen better, they should slow down, etc. The problem is, the rep comes out of the coaching session overwhelmed because they have to change too many behaviors.

It's much more effective to work with them, ask them questions, and identify the one thing they can change to get the biggest positive benefit. Then, we write it down and memorialize it. It's easier for me as the coach to approach it that way and it's also easier for the sales rep to execute it.

Whichever role you are in from business owner to sales manager to sales rep, identifying the most important step and remaining focused on that will require discipline. However, if you can do it on an ongoing basis, it will completely propel your success in whatever you want to do.

HOW DO YOU FIND THE "ONE THING?"

The hardest part is distilling priorities down to the single most important thing. Here are some tips on how you can find yours.

Priority Planning

What I do every quarter is I sit down with my team for a full day and we think through our top priorities. We ask, "What are our biggest issues and our biggest opportunities?" And we spend literally an entire day trying to find the one thing that can have the biggest positive impact on the company for the quarter.

So take the time on a regular basis to assess where you're at, where you can improve, and what actions you can take to make that improvement. Then, narrow your potential changes down to the one that will likely make the biggest difference.

Daily Reminders

Once you identify your one thing, you need to look at it every day. I have a journal that I use every day to make notes about things I'm learning. In it, I write down my targets each day and they are always based on the priority I've identified. You have to stay disciplined and keep your priority top of mind.

Utilize a Coach

Lastly, a business coach can help too. Hiring one has been transformative for me. Even though I went to business school and learned about entrepreneurship, there is no book that can teach you everything. You have to do it and learn through experience. The same is true with sales. And it's better to learn with someone on your side, over your shoulder. Someone talking with you about the issues, coaching you, pointing out your blind spots, and giving you a framework. They can also help you stay focused on the one thing you need to do to be the most successful. If you are in sales, you have a built-in coach in your manager. Share your focus point with them so they can help to hold you accountable.

I know life happens, and business happens, and things get busy. However, if you put aside a small amount of time for prioritization, even just four full days per year and five minutes per day, you can propel yourself toward success at a much faster, more efficient rate.

Want to learn more from David Kreiger? Follow him on:
LinkedIn: linkedin.com/in/davidkreiger/

#54 Go and Smell the Money

NICOLAS VANDENBERGHE

"You have to pay attention to where the money is and how you're going to get it."

ABOUT NICOLAS VANDENBERGHE:

Nicholas Vandenberghe is an expert in sales, leadership, and entrepreneurship, with over three decades of experience.

He went from selling newspapers on the streets of Paris in high school and studying business at Stanford to selling three tech companies with over $11 million in revenue and running sales for a $2B telecom company.

Now, Nicholas is the CEO and Co-founder of Chili Piper, where he is re-inventing inbox, calendar, and scheduling for sales professionals.

In his spare time, Nicholas re-reads the 27 chapters of Neuroeconomics, Decision Science & The Brain by NYU star professor Paul Glimcher, in the hope of bringing its findings to the science of sales and marketing.

Those who know him say he is a forward-thinking executive and highly effective agent of change. Among his qualities are a sharp focus on client success, innovation, and efficient management.

He has been endorsed as a backable tech entrepreneur and has the unique ability to quickly grasp a new environment and develop game-changing insights.

Sales has always been a passion of mine and a natural inclination. I started selling newspapers on the streets of Paris while in high school and outsold everybody about seven-to-one.

Later on, I got a job at the Boston Consulting Group where we were doing these big strategy projects. We did one for Lloyds Bank, the third-largest bank in the UK at the time. Very quickly, I found myself selling again. I convinced the bank executive that he needed to be much more scientific about how he did his headcount forecast and that we could help.

I then went back to my team and said, "How do you write a proposal?" They said, "What do you mean?" I said, "I want to write a proposal because these guys are interested in buying from our firm." I figured out the proposal and we got the business— 450,000 British pounds!

Go and Smell the Money

After many years in sales, my top sales secret is this: you need to go out and smell the money.

What does that mean?

One, go.

You have to show up and be present. I sold so many newspapers back in the day because I showed up and went to talk to the people who were walking in the streets. If they were serious, I'd tell them about data, if they were funny, I'd crack a joke. I'd engage them lightly. But just being there was 99% of the sale. And this is true in transactional sales. If you're making calls and sending emails, you have to show up. It's as simple as that.

Second, you have to pay attention to who has the money and who is going to spend it.

In time, I could spot the people on the streets who were going to buy my newspapers. And later, when I was selling to a UK bank, I could figure out which executive was going to buy.

You have to develop the ability to know where to find the money and then to know how to get it. You need to be able to distinguish between people who have money and are ready to spend it from those that don't have it or aren't ready to spend.

If you don't, you can be a very talented salesperson but will waste a lot of time trying to sell to the wrong people.

HOW CAN I SMELL THE MONEY?

Going and smelling the money comes down to showing up and being able to qualify leads— identifying who is going to move and who isn't.

Read Prospects

There are many old models to qualify leads by budget, authority, needs, etc. But I don't believe those are fully effective.

Every situation is different and people often don't tell you the truth. Sometimes they say they have no budget, but then they buy the next day.

You need to learn how to read behind what's being said to understand what's really happening.

This requires time in the field, recognizing patterns, and learning about your target prospects in-depth. Who is involved in decision making and what are their personal agendas? What pain points do they have and how can you solve them?

Personal-Based Value Propositions for Stakeholders

Once you can smell the money, you need to craft value propositions for the people who have it. Plan how to communicate to them that you have their personal interests in mind as well as solving the problem for their company at large.

A key component in understanding your prospects can be found in the "Theory of Mind," practiced by Steve Jobs. It involves being able to read, act on, and motivate people's emotions without being personally affected by them. It's a way of empathizing without feeling other's emotions yourself.

For example, you could understand that a particular person in their position is interested in making more money and earning more clout. In response, you could use a value proposition that shows how this move will grow the company's revenue and give them a measurable result to claim. Also, keep in mind, you may have to appeal to multiple stakeholders. Missing just one could create an obstacle in the way of your deal.

For example, at Chili Piper, when we talk about an account, we have segmented messaging for the Head of Demand Generation, the Sales Operation Manager, the Head of Sales, etc.

Screen Sharing

Lastly, one of my favorite qualification methods at Chili Piper is screen sharing. You ask your prospect to show you their current process by sharing their screen with you.

Say, "Hey I understand you have a problem, can you share your screen to show me?" You can learn a lot more from seeing the problem than from them explaining it.

You see all the shit they are dealing with and people feel that. Then, you can provide a meaningful solution that applies directly to their pain points.

In summary, before you sell, go and smell the money. Work on being able to see who has it and who will spend it. Then, work on understanding your customers and their motivators and craft personal value propositions to drive their decisions.

Want to learn more from Nicolas Vandenberghe?
Follow him on:
LinkedIn: linkedin.com/in/nvandenberghe
Company Website: chilipiper.com

#55 What Overcoming Adversity Can Teach You About Sales

DANIEL DEFILIPPO

"You can't beat someone who never stops."

ABOUT DANIEL DEFILIPPO:

Daniel DeFilippo is currently the Director of US Sales Development at Mimeo, where he brings his customer's content to life through print and digital formats via their enterprise app and global print facilities.

A sales veteran with over eight years in the field, Daniel has played significant roles as a Vice President of Sales and Sales Consultant where he has 12X'd and 30X'd pipeline for his clients, revolutionized Salesforce tracking, built his own playbook for ongoing training and mentoring, and everything else you can imagine for sales development.

He knows what it takes to build a successful sales team from the ground up, and will break down your current system, dissect it, and build a well-oiled selling machine for your business.

Those who know Daniel say he is an extremely passionate, hardworking sales professional who has a strong desire to not only succeed but ensure the people around him are also successful. He is known for motivating others, encouraging them, and keeping a sharp eye on the important numbers that make sales teams successful.

About 16 years ago, I was in a bad car accident and I lost my four best friends and my Dad. I was on life support for a month or two after the accident and was told I'd never walk or talk again. I didn't want to spend the rest of my life in my house on disability so I started trying to overcome this the only way I could— trying to lift my leg under the comforter of my hospital bed. One day, the nurse saw it and said, "Maybe he will walk again." Six months later I was jogging.

The determination required for me to overcome that incredible challenge is something I use to drive my success in sales and to make a positive impact on the world.

With that in mind, here are my top secrets to sales success.

Do What You Love

First, it's important to believe in what you are doing. You never know when your time is up. I got a second chance and I'm doing my best to positively impact people on the SDR teams, IDR teams, and leadership teams every single day. That's what gets me out of bed. I love molding, coaching, and growing sales teams—it's all about the people for me.

Bring a Positive Attitude

People often ask me how I come to the office positive and energetic every day when I went through such hell? And I say we gotta be here and make cold calls whether we like it or not. Let's have fun with it and enjoy it. I believe you're only as happy as you allow yourself to be. Being positive takes practice but it allows you to bring that energy and productivity.

To become more positive, I recommend reading The Power of Now by Eckhart Tolle. It changed my life with its lessons about living in the moment. It also helps to understand the subconscious mind. I used to tell myself in the mirror, "I'm going to break sales records, I'm going to make sales today," and I might not have believed it but my subconscious mind didn't know that. It hears the messages and will help you achieve them.

Fake It 'Til You Make It

Next, if you're new or green, the other person on the phone doesn't have to know it. Until you are an expert in your field, you can at least look and sound like one. What I do is give my team a vertical expertise doc. It has the customers we work with, common pain points for those customers, buzzwords, publications they read, and case studies so they can be an expert on any vertical on their first day. Find out the key pieces of information you need to know from the best salespeople on your team and keep them in front of you until you know them by heart.

No Excuses

Next, I learned how to write great emails from a hospital bed because I couldn't talk. I was mute for two years but nothing would stop me. I could email, I could read, I could research, so I got really good at writing cadences. It was taking a horrible situation and finding the good in it to come out better.

Now, when I hear people say they can't close a deal because they are using a competitor or something, I'm like, "Dude, I was closing deals when I couldn't walk or talk." So it really puts it into perspective what is possible. Always look for a way to achieve your goal and don't give up.

Work Smart

To be the best you also have to work smart. Think things through. In my situation after my accident, we had to decide what we were going to fix first. The heart, then the legs, then the voice. One step at a time by importance.

In sales, you also need to be strategic and think through the smartest way to work. I always loved the magic hours, 8 to 9 in the morning, 12 to 1 during lunch, 5 to 6 after work (local time). During those times, you have a 5x connect rate. Why would you not call during that time!? And when you direct dial, you get a connection 98% of the time, while a non-direct dial gets a 51% connection rate.

Research the stats, learn your craft, and optimize to make the best use of your time.

Be a Master Multi-Tasker

Lastly, to be a 10xer, you have to be a master multitasker. What made me the 10x person, was focusing on my work 100%. I'd be on my Seamless, Outreach, and LinkedIn while making calls. Not a second would be wasted. While the phone is ringing, I'm researching. You'd never find me sidetracked on Facebook or some non-relevant website during work hours.

You have to put all your concentration into working as effectively as possible. Ask yourself how are you using the time while the phone is ringing? Are you twiddling your fingers or doing something productive? That one extra email, one extra blast can be the difference in your quarter. If you do 10x the work, you can put 10x in your pockets.

I don't think recovering was too incredible because I didn't see it as having a choice. I was determined to live, determined to walk, determined to tell my story, determined to regain my voice. Find what you love, set your goals, prioritize, take it one step at a time, and don't give up. Take the time to work smart and focus on work when it's time to work. And remember that those willing to put in the extra effort will be the ones that come out on top.

Want to learn more from Daniel DeFillippo? Follow him on: LinkedIn: linkedin.com/in/daniel-defilippo-0691b97/

#56 Be Crystal Clear About What You Want

JEREMY MCGILVREY

"The only way to gain your success is to be crystal clear and have massive confidence in what you sell."

ABOUT JEREMY MCGILVREY:

Jeremy is a Harvard-educated Click Funnels landing page expert, number-one-best-selling author, and a two-comma-club winner for his online marketing strategies which catapult entrepreneurs through online marketing and sales.

He is widely known as one of the most influential entrepreneurs in the Internet Marketing industry for the uncommon results he's been able to create for himself and his clients utilizing sales funnels, behavioral-based email marketing, and innovative traffic strategies.

Jeremy is also the author of Instagram Secrets: The Underground Playbook for Growing Your Audience Fast, Driving Massive Traffic, and Generating Predictable Profits where he shares his insights into Instagram marketing.

Jeremy has an insane journey of ups and downs and everything in between. He is known as a down-to-earth-guy who is open, honest, and shares his knowledge freely. His clients say his encouragement and motivation helps to turn their dreams into reality.

Six years ago, I had no place to live, I was given a $300 check, and I was told good luck. I parlayed that into going to Harvard, becoming a #1 best-selling author, and earning the two-comma-club award with Clickfunnels by generating a million dollars. And it all comes back to the habits, the way you live your life, and more important than anything else, knowing what you want.

You Have to Get Crystal Clear

Want to move into a different home? Increase your income? Drive a nicer car? Hit 200% to quota? First, you've got to get crystal clear about where you want to go and how you're going to get there. Too many people, if I were to sit down with them and ask, "Where are you going and what do you want?" don't know and wonder why they don't get there. It's kind of silly.

So the number one sales secret is to know what are you trying to sell, what are you trying to accomplish, what are your goals, and how are you going to get there.

HOW TO GET WHAT YOU WANT

How do you bring what you want into focus and achieve it?

Set Your Reference Point

Everyone's life would change this moment if they just changed the standards they believe they deserve.

When I was down and out and had nothing, I was pissed off— I wasn't happy. All of my family was like, "Why are you mad all the time?" I was like, "Well, I'm eating what I don't want to eat, I'm living where I don't want to live, I'm driving what I don't want to drive, and I'm wearing what I don't want to wear." I was outrageously angry.

The rest of the world wants to conform and say, "This is my lot in life, this is the way things are going to be." That's major bullshit. Your lot in life is what you make it. Set your reference point where you want to be. How much do you want to make? What do you want to drive? What kind of lifestyle do you want? Then, reverse engineer your plan to get there.

Reverse Engineer the Process

When it comes to goals, figure out where the endpoint is and where you are now, and reverse engineer the process of what you want to do.

A problem of goal setting with people is that they don't want to admit where they are now because their situation isn't great. I don't care if you're trying to map a path on your GPS in your car or phone or in your head to a goal. You can't put in the endpoint without adding in the starting point. You've got to figure out where you are right now. What are your bad habits right now? What are the unconscious bad habits that are producing the results that you don't want? What is all that? And then you figure out how to get to the results you want.

I got into the two-comma club very quickly because I understood what it was going to take. I understood that progress was in the process and I repeated it until I got results.

But how do you figure out the process?

Learn From the Best

I learned how to do what I want to do by talking to the biggest names out there who are actually doing it. I can guarantee you that whatever you want to do, someone else has achieved it. And then they've documented the journey in outrageous detail about how they did it. If somebody lays out a 600-page book telling what the process is, it's probably a good idea to read the book, read their blogs, watch their YouTube videos, and do what they do.

A myth is that uber-successful people hide their secrets and don't give away the best information. We just give you a piece of it so we can sell you other things. Nothing could be further from the truth.

However, beware, you must learn from people who are their own best customer. Do not take advice from people you wouldn't trade places with. There are so many people out there trying to teach people how to do stuff and that's their business. They teach people how to do stuff instead of actually doing it. You've got to do your due diligence to see that these people are producing results themselves.

And you don't have to try like hell to get into Harvard. You can watch Harvard lectures on YouTube for free. Almost all the information that you need is free on YouTube. It's insane—the internet leveled the playing field for all of us.

Minimize Distractions

Next, I believe a lot of people are struggling with spending major time on minor stuff. To become the best, you have to focus on your goal and minimize distractions.

I talk extensively in my new book about social media being a weapon of mass distraction. Everyone wants to have these notifications for all kinds of garbage out there. There's no way in hell you can spend your time looking for the bottom of your Facebook or Instagram feed if you know you are trying to achieve a lofty goal. You just can't. You don't have time for that stuff. You just have to shut that off and focus on work.

But it can be easier said than done. Habits work on a loop. You have a cue, that makes you engage in the habit, you have a routine where you're doing the habit, and a reward for having the habit. And the reward 99% of the time is dopamine that hits the neurotransmitters in your brain. After that happens from a particular activity repetitively, it creates a neural signature. This can look like checking social media multiple times throughout the day or watching Netflix every night.

The only way to get out is to consciously be aware of what you're doing. If you are aware of, "I probably shouldn't be on Facebook right now, I probably should be reading xyz blog about this." Or "I probably shouldn't be watching Netflix right now, I should be watching a video on YouTube about how to do this." You become aware and then begin to shift your behavior to orient it toward achieving your goal.

When you're a student of the business, and you're obsessed and hungry with figuring out what the solutions are, you don't want to watch Netflix, you don't give a shit about what people are doing on Facebook and Instagram. It's about what can I do to grow myself and make myself so incredibly valuable that people can't resist buying from and working with me?

Become a Master of Your Craft

The number one thing everyone is looking for is an absolute certainty that you can provide what you say you're going to provide.

I closed a deal today at a decent price. There were no negotiations whatsoever. I told them, "Here's my price, here's what I can do for you, I'm the best in the world at this, take it or maybe try your luck with someone else."

And I emphatically believe, you can put a lie detector on me, I believe I'm 100% the best in the world at developing tightly-engineered sales funnels that will convert cold traffic into warm fires that will repeat buy.

But I wasn't born the best. What made me the best was my ability to not own a television, my ability to not get addicted to distractions, was my ability to not spend major time on minor stuff and to really dive deep and become a master of my craft.

It's so crucial to have outrageous confidence in your ability to what you're selling and what you're doing. And the only way you are going to have that confidence is to become a student of that business that is constantly carving out time each and every day to read the books, watch the videos, listen to the audios.

If you look at any speaker or salesman, the number one contagious thing that they have is their confidence and their certainty in what they are selling. You'll get that when you do the work and figure out how to master your craft. And then you present that in a very simplistic form to your prospects.

Want to learn more from Jeremy McGilvrey?
Follow him on:
LinkedIn: linkedin.com/in/jeremymcgilvrey
Book Website: CEObook.com

#57 Sell With Your Ears

MICKELI BEDORE

"I close more deals when my offer is all about them."

ABOUT MICKELI BEDORE:

Mickeli Bedore is a Salesman above all other titles and host of the podcast, Coffee & Closers. He has successfully built flourishing profit streams over the last two decades, spending 15 of those years in Manhattan, Philly, LA, and Denver turning underperforming product lines/territories into high-performers at some of tech's biggest names (IBM, Oracle, Concur, Verizon).

In 2014, Mickeli turned his attention to the Twin Cities tech startup scene. Since then, he has launched four startups, helped lead two companies to acquisition as a revenue growth advisor, and spent every free second in between helping empower fellow startup founders by teaching them how to confidently "sell" themselves and their visions.

Mickeli's devotion to the art and science of startup sales has gained national (Men's Journal, Touch of Modern, Uncrate, etc.) and local (WCCO, Pioneer Press, Finance & Commerce, Twin Cities Business Journal) exposure.

Those who know him say that he is an inspiration, helping them to be better, work harder, and fine-tune the craft of sales over time. His numbers are said to be nothing short of remarkable which many identify as the result of his outstanding ability to nurture relationships.

When you go to the doctor's office and the doctor walks in the room, the first thing they always say is, "So, what brought you in today?" I don't know if they are too busy to look at the notes or ask the receptionist but they always ask you that. What happens next is, you start unloading the trunk of problems that you've been experiencing, "I have a cough but my foot kinda hurts, and let's also check my cholesterol." You give your doctor all the information they need to solve all your problems and get you back to full health.

Now, if you can take that same approach and apply it to your sales process, getting your prospects to begin opening up and unloading, you can offer them a customized solution that they'll have a hard time refusing.

SELL WITH YOUR EARS

My number one sales secret that I would use to rebuild if I were to lose it all and start over is to sell with your ears. What does that mean? Selling with your ears means getting your prospects to open up and talk, listening, and then making your offer all about them.

What does that look like? Engage and immediately ask them about their business. What would they change right now if they could change anything? Then, as your prospect tells you whatever is going on, listen, and categorize the things you can and can't offer them. Then, at the end of that, position yourself and equally position other people in your network that can solve other things, and bring it home as a community.

THE ART OF THE ASK

How exactly do you go about selling with your ears? It is all about the art of the ask.

Collect Information

The goal is to get your prospects talking openly with you. To do that, I take the approach of the doctor mentioned above. I ask them about their business in general through questions like: How is business going? What would you change if you could change anything? What stresses you out and keeps you from being present with your family and friends?

Maybe they say, "Well, revenue is down." Then you say, "Has it always been down?" And they say," No, just this past year. We have a toxic person on the team and they are slowing things down, and we haven't been doing the right activities, etc."

Dig in to get the details of what is holding their business back, even if it isn't directly related to what you sell. Listen and take notes about all their pain points.

Create a Complete Solution

Will you be able to solve all of your prospect's problems? Most likely not. But what you can do is identify the things you can solve along with the things you can't. And although you can't solve everything, you probably know (or can get to know) people that can. So once I know a prospect's pain points, I come up with a complete solution that includes what I can solve and who can solve the other problems, and we come together as a community to offer a complete solution.

Follow-up Call

After a call, I always follow up with three tangible to-dos for me, three to-dos for them, and, in addition, I'll make connections to three people who can help with the other stuff. I'll also send them a joint execution plan of how the sales process is going to go. Then, I'll put a follow-up call on their calendar and circle back in a few days while everything is fresh in our minds.

Using the art of the ask to sell with your ears can help you get a job, make new friends that will get you a job, find a business partner, or close a prospect. While you don't sell the world, you can find out what problems you can sell. Ask open-ended questions to find out what all is going on, solve what you can, and refer them to partners that can help to solve the other problems.

**Want to learn more from Mickeli Bedore? Follow him on:
Podcast: bedorebusinessgroup.com/coffee-and-closers
LinkedIn: linkedin.com/in/mickelibedore**

#58 Scale Unscalable Behavior

GARY VAYNERCHUK

"My jabbing and right hooking are predicated on the fight. Some fights are easier than others."

ABOUT GARY VAYNERCHUK:

Gary Vaynerchuk is a serial entrepreneur, an angel investor, a five-time New York Times best-selling author, chairman of VaynerX, the subject of the online documentary series, "DailyVee," and CEO of VaynerMedia. He is also one of the most sought-after public speakers alive today, VaynerMedia is a full-service digital agency servicing Fortune 500 clients across the company's four locations. Additionally, VaynerX includes various brands including lifestyle brands ONE37pm and PureWow. Gary is also a partner in VaynerSports, Green Street, and the reservation app, Resy.

Gary considers himself a "purebred entrepreneur" who successfully started his first franchise selling lemonade at the age of seven. He went on to sell toys and baseball cards in high school and earned tens of thousands of dollars. In the late 90's he identified the internet as a growth opportunity for his dad's local liquor business and turned it into one of the first alcohol e-commerce platforms in the U.S. (Wine Library), growing it from $3MM to $60 MM.

While growing Wine Library, Gary began a YouTube channel where he posted daily long-form episodes. They caught on, landing him appearances on national TV with Conan O'Brien and Ellen DeGeneres. These appearances helped propel his career forward, leading to hundreds of keynote speaking opportunities and a book deal that would become an international best-seller.

Gary's career and presence have continued to grow and evolve over the last several decades. He is very active across all social channels, sharing his advice openly and honestly. Because of this, Gary is considered a go-to source on a variety of topics from entrepreneurship to digital marketing, and everything in between.

In my wine business, I recently decided to produce 30,000 cases of wine instead of 10,000. We've sold the 10,000 cases but the other 20,000 is a lot to move. I've been pushing it and there is work to be done. But because I want to bring as much value to my audience as possible, I'm willing to give up my biggest asset which is my time in order to scale the unscalable.

Scale Unscalable Behavior

Salespeople are at their best when they are the most knowledgeable about what the consumer wants. When you are on the front lines communicating with your audience, you gain context that is the gateway to understanding what to say.

But people think you can't scale personal interactions. Most are automating or delegating emails, social media posts, social interactions, phone calls, etc. to focus on other areas. I say call everyone and have a conversation with them to find out what value you can bring. Scaling the unscalable is the way to mass awareness at the top of the funnel.

HOW TO SCALE THE UNSCALABLE

How do you scale the unscalable?

Put in the Work

Reply to every comment you get on social media.

Email people back when they email you.

Call them.

Do the stuff that no one else wants to do because that means it has a chance. When everyone is doing the same thing, nobody is going to win because it all becomes noise.

Focus on Value

I focus completely on bringing as much value as possible and then I hope that whatever I'm trying to sell, I can naturally do without me having to ask more. But I'm not scared to ask if I have to.

Don't Spam

Advice to B2B people out there, don't spam. Think about what your audience needs and make that content to bring macro value and then use that as a halo effect for yourself.

Think about it. Why do you like me? I bring value. Adding value helps build your brand, it builds the relationship, and it makes you want to support it.

Stay in the Middle

Next, as you get out there, you're going to get love and hate. I don't get too high on myself, I don't go into a private room and not talk to anyone. Too many people love the accolades but don't want to deal with the hate. They keep buying into the accolades and they think they are somebody so the hate drives them down.

The more you are driven down by hate, the more you have been reading into the press clippings and the good shit you've been told. I just keep it right down the fucking middle.

Don't Expect Reciprocation

Lastly, even with all of the value I offer, not everyone buys from me. That's something you have to sign up for when giving actual value for free. Not everyone's going to buy and you can't give with the intent to get something.

It can't be like, "Hey, I'm going to take you golfing at the best club," but what I'm really saying is, "I'm going to take you golfing so I can get the account and if I don't get the account, I'm going to feel angry about it."

That's the wrong framework and it leads to a lot of disappointment and a lot of negativity. So for me, I'm completely and utterly focused on bringing value. How much value?

The boxing analogy is a good one. My jabbing and right hooking are predicated on the fight. Some fights are easier than others. The harder the fight, the harder I have to lay my jabs, and the harder I have to hit my right hook. It's completely predicated on the fight.

And then there are moments when I need something and however those chips fall, they fall, and I adjust to whatever the reality is.

Want to learn more from Gary Vaynerchuk? Follow him on:
Website: garyvaynerchuk.com
Facebook: facebook.com/gary
Twitter: @garyvee
Instagram: @garyvee
YouTube: youtube.com/user/garyvaynerchuk
Snapchat: snapchat.com/add/garyvee
LinkedIn: linkedin.com/in/garyvaynerchuk

#59 Drive the Activation Metric

NATHAN LATKA

"The people at the top understand the activation metric and they drive near-automatic upsells.

ABOUT NATHAN LATKA:

Nathan Latka is the host and executive producer of "The Top Entrepreneurs" Podcast, founder of a database ranking software, GetLatka.com, a best-selling author, and, most recently, founder of Founderpath.com—a place where SaaS companies can get funding without selling equity.

At the young age of 19, Nathan founded the software company, Heyo. com, with just $119 in his bank account. Five years later, it received a $10.5 million valuation and he sold it.

The following year, Nathan started his "Top Entrepreneurs" Podcast where he interviews the world's top SaaS entrepreneurs to uncover how they go from being a startup to a real business. The show has been going on for almost four years now with more than 11 million downloads, and over 3,000 guests.

Meanwhile, Nathan also wrote a #3 WSJ instant national best-seller, *How to Be a Capitalist Without Any Capital*, where he shares his belief that you don't have to be university-educated, have money, be creative, or even have an idea to get rich. You just have to be willing to break the rules he outlines.

Nathan is known, and most loved but sometimes hated, for his unorthodox give-me-the-numbers interview style. He is said to get right to the heart of business with his rapid-fire interview-style. Further, those who have worked with Nathan say he has a genuine desire to support both small businesses and enterprises with tools to help them succeed.

When you're selling SaaS, you have to focus on the price point. The biggest mistake I see a lot of early founders make, let's say those with less than a million in annual recurring revenue, is they try to put too much emphasis on a $30 sale and the economics don't work. But once you get the price right, you then have to shift your attention to focus on what the biggest companies at the top are doing to kill it.

The Activation Metric

What the top 1% are focusing on is the activation metric.

And by at the top and killing it, I mean folks like Manny Medina at Outreach who added $10 million in net new bookings last quarter and just passed $60 million in ARR.

But what is the activation metric?

The activation metric is what a company has to get their new customers to do in their software to increase their pricing plan.

Let's say, for example, you're an email marketing company like Mailchimp. Your base plan supports 1,000 contacts, and you're company's pricing plans increase based on the number of contacts a client needs. In this case, you would have to get your users to 1,000 contacts in 20 days to drastically increase your ability to upsell. That's the activation metric you measure.

The people at the top are seeing high net revenue retention rates because they understand the activation metric and drive near-automatic upsells. What that means is if a year ago, you had customers that were paying you $10,000 per month, you could churn $1,000 off that, but you upsell that same customer base up to $20,000 so your net revenue goes from $10 grand to $19 grand.

HOW TO FIND YOUR ACTIVATION METRIC AND DRIVE UPSELLS

How do you figure out your company's activation metric?

Do the Math

First things first. What I encourage every new founder to do when you're launching your company, whether it's a software company or anything else, is you have to do the math.

Look at the price points you're going to launch with, and then multiply them by the number of customers you think you can get to buy your product. When you multiply those two together, if the revenue is not there, you have to change something.

You either invent a product that goes to more customers or increase your price point—4x it, 10x it, and focus on fewer customers. But you want to make sure that you get your customer count and your price point right.

Find Your Top Customers

With that squared away, the best way to figure out your actual activation metric is to guess for a year and at the end of the year, go into your payment processor and export your customer list.

Sort it by who paid you the most to who paid you the least. Your top interest is going to be your top paying customers because those are the ones you want to replicate.

Customer Interview

Once you have your top priority customer list, you want to reach out and ask why they use your service and pay you so much.

Perform customer interviews.

For example, you can email the top ten customers that paid you the most.

The email subject line can read: "We're canceling your account…"

And then the body of the message reads: "We're canceling your account unless you tell us why you're paying us so much."

Then, they'll write you back saying, "OMG don't cancel our account. We need it so much because of…boom"

And that "boom" is your activation metric.

Implementation

Next, you have to align your entire development team, your entire sales team, to get people to hit that activation metric in the first (#) days, across (#) team members, in (#) use cases.

That's how you figure it out.

It's not tracking historic behavior pre-purchase. It's about finding out what makes the top-payers pay and then using that information to upsell other customers.

Brainstorm Upsell Strategies

We're in planning for next year and something else I encourage everyone to do is ask your team in a strategy session what they would do if something catastrophic happened and they couldn't add any new customers. How would they grow the business with the current customers? Then, brainstorm around that. It's another effective way to figure out how to drive upsell revenue.

Lastly, charm, charm, charm. Charm like you've never charmed before. Whether it's doing webinar sales, appearing on cable shows, or telling your publisher you're not putting this book out without your face on the cover. You've got to charm.

Want to learn more from Nathan Latka? Follow him on:
Twitter: @NathanLatka
LinkedIn: linkedin.com/in/nathanlatka

SALES SECRETS:

PERSONAL DEVELOPMENT

#60 Throw Your Limits Out the Window

CYNTHIA BARNES

"If it is to be, it is up to me."

ABOUT CYNTHIA BARNES:

Cynthia Barnes, Founder of the National Association of Women Sales Professionals (NAWSP), is on a mission to help women in sales reach the Top 1% and Dance on the Glass Ceiling™. She has built a community of over 14,000 women in sales from around the world who come together for support and professional development that only another woman can provide.

Cynthia is also the Founder and CEO of Barnes Sales Institute, a Top 35 #WomeninSales Influencer, a Sales Trainer, a Keynote Speaker and an overall boss in sales. Her top goal has always been to empower women sales professionals through unparalleled support, advocacy, and professional development.

Cynthia earned her Bachelor of Science degree from the University of Phoenix in Business Administration and her Master of Science degree in Leadership and Organizational Dynamics from the University of Michigan. Further, she gained over 15 years of sales experience prior to starting the NAWSP and her sales institute by working at companies such as the University of Phoenix, Searle Pharmaceuticals, Mary Kay, and Total Quality Logistics.

Those who know Cynthia say she is a natural leader with a phenomenal drive, commitment, and attention to detail. Wherever she goes, success soon follows. She is recommended for any role that values a great work ethic, management, and organization. And her intuitive grasp of other people's purpose and significance is said to make the impossible possible.

My father, who is African American, grew up in the segregated South, Jim Crow. He sat me down when I saw six-years-old and said, "I've got to tell you something and this is important," so I knew he was serious.

He said, "You have two strikes against you, you're black and you're a girl." I said, "What does that mean?"

And he said, "That means that you are going to have to work twice as hard for half of the credit."

He also told me that there are three types of people in the world, those who make things happen, those who wait for things to happen, and those who wonder what the hell happened. So he said, "Mark my words. In order to be successful, you will have to make things happen and work very, very hard."

That started me on the path to put in the work and try to be the best. As a result, I've been at the top of the leaderboard in sales ever since, even back to my Girl Scout days.

Take The Limits Off Whatever You Think You Can Achieve

My number one sales secret for those of you who are looking to get to the top and be the best is this... take the limits off of whatever it is that you think you are capable of. Dream bigger than you ever have.

355

The entire world around you was made from people just like you and there is no one more special than you so why not?

If the commission is uncapped at your company and the top person is making $250,000 per year, don't limit yourself to what they have achieved. Don't only aspire to be where they are. Set your goals higher. If it's possible to make $250,000 it's possible to make $500,000.

WHERE DO YOU START?

So where do you start if you want to dream bigger and set limitless goals? Here are five actionable tips:

Reverse Engineer Limitless Goals

First, ask yourself, if time, money, and resources were not factors, what would you have, who would you be, and what would you do?

Write your answers down.

Then, ask yourself, what does it take to get those things?

Regardless of where you are now and who you have access to, reverse engineer what it takes to get what you want and write it down. Identify what you don't have, and cultivate a plan to get it. Break it down to the most minute and minuscule activity you can measure.

If you don't break it down into actionable items that you do daily, you will never get there.

I know that in five years, I want to be on Oprah's couch when you tune into Super Soul Sunday so I have to reverse engineer it. I have to ask, "What do I need to do today, to be on at that 11 a.m. hour?"

I need to position myself as an influencer, I need to do speaking engagements, and I need to create content every day. Content is what people can see when they don't see me. In order to make valuable content, I need to be a subject matter expert on women in sales. I need to read everything about what it takes to succeed and what is going on in the industry. It's a daily quest and that's what I do.

Remove Limiting Beliefs

Next, you have to remove the underlying belief that you aren't worthy of achieving higher goals. There are two types of motivators in humans; push and pull.

Push motivators are attached to Maslow's hierarchy of needs and include things like making sure you have enough money for rent, food, bills, insurance, your car payment, etc.

Once those needs are met, you need to shift and aim for more or you will get stuck. Let's say you are a $50,000 employee. If you drop down 10%, your mind will scramble to get back up to the $50k. And the reverse is true, if you go up 10%, your mind will self- sabotage because you're not comfortable at 10% either way.

You need to come up with pull motivators to bring you to a higher level. What will get you to $100,000? Then, you develop the mindset to go after it. But it's a mind shift. You can't go to a $50,000 employee and say you are a $100,000 employee because he's thinking, "I'm eating tuna and Ramen, smiling and dialing every day. I can't even conceive getting to $100,000."

You have to have goals so big they scare you but you also have to have the self-concept that you are worth it. You're worth the $250,000 per year, or whatever your target is.

Your competition is working hard so why shouldn't you? The U.S. mint prints money every day, why shouldn't you get yours?

Be You!

As you pursue your goals, it's always important to stay true to you. I'll never forget a lady named Cecilia who came up to me when I started at Total Quality Logistics (TQL) and said, "Cynthia, you are too nice. You are dealing with a male-dominated industry and you have got to stop being so nice." And I said, "But I am nice. I believe that you get more bees with honey than you do with vinegar."

She said, "Try this. Try this." But it wasn't me. I am respectful, kind, and firm but to say I should sell a different way because I am in a different industry doesn't make sense. I believe that if you sell authentically and stay true to yourself, you will go further. So I took my personality and what I knew, and I crushed it.

Always be authentic to who you are.

Pick a Niche to Get Rich

Next, when you market to everybody, you miss everybody. You have to drill it down. When I was at MaryKay, I didn't have an ideal customer persona who I was going after at first. I thought that if women washed their faces, they were a good candidate for me. But that wasn't true. When I got granular and specific on who I was going after, I was able to be more effective. My persona ended up having three main characteristics: She had to believe in anti-aging skincare, she had to be of a certain socio-economic level to afford high-level skincare, and she had to have a network of people who she could go out and refer to me. When I identified that, I was able to spot "her" more easily.

At TQL, taking my Mary Kay learnings, I asked, "What if I could get granular and specific so instead of calling a blueberry company on Monday morning and then a window walls company in the afternoon, I concentrated on one industry and got really good at it?" So I specialized in window walls. I learned how to haul them, what kind of straps you need, what kind of truck you need, weight limits, etc. I was able to converse with my prospects in their language with confidence.

You have to pick your niche so you can become knowledgeable enough to be a trusted advisor to your prospects. I took this everywhere I went. It was about knowing the industry and knowing how to best solve what keeps them up at night.

Study the Behavior of the Best

Lastly, pattern your behavior after those who are most successful. Don't let them dictate your ceiling but study their success. There was a guy on my team at TQL named Rob. He was amazing, he was a million-dollar broker. I went and I sat behind him and I watched what he did all day. He had two monitors and never got off task. His screen was all about business. No Facebook, no Instagram, no web browsing, nothing. So I said, you know what, for the next 30 days, I was going to be all about the business too. I deleted the apps off my phone and deactivated my Facebook account.

Then I asked Rob what his secret to success was and he said, "Every Monday, I walk in ready to work." He said, "I do my prospecting on Sunday during the Reds games." I said, "What do you mean? There's nobody in the office Sundays." And he said, "I create my list so that I am ready to go on Monday." So I walked in the door with my list on Monday that had 500 cross-referenced possible prospects and I was ready to smile and dial. And it worked!

When you remove your limits and raise the bar, everything changes and you can really chase your dreams. Identify your limitless goals, remove limiting beliefs, stay true to you, pick your niche, pattern yourself after success, and go for it. Other people have so why not you? Dance on that glass ceiling!

Want to learn more from Cynthia Barnes? Follow her on:
LinkedIn: linkedin.com/in/cynthiabarnes
NAWSP Website: nawsp.org

#61 Put Your Sales Career In Overdrive

SALLY DUBY

"I believe helping people find their passion and becoming great at whatever they do is a key ingredient to success in inside sales."

ABOUT SALLY DUBY:

Voted one of "The Most Influential Inside Sales Experts" by the AA-ISP, Sally Duby is the Chief Sales Officer at The Bridge Group, Inc. and has built a reputation as an EXPERT in skyrocketing revenue growth through the transformation of inside sales and sales development teams.

In addition to her role at The Brigde Group, Inc., Sally frequently conducts workshops on inside sales best practices for Sales Hacker, venture capital firms, and leading executive management organizations. She is also the co-founder of VP of Sales Forum, an organization that provides a trusted networking and education platform to sales executives.

Sally is a veteran of technology inside sales and sales development, with over three decades of experience working with well-known companies such as Oracle, Skype, Ustream, and Phone Works. Throughout her career, she has helped lead transformations to reflect the latest industry developments, trends, and technology.

Those who know Sally say she's incredibly brilliant and very skilled at what she does. Further, she has helped hundreds of technology companies build high-performing sales organizations. She is known to bring the highest level of professionalism, smarts, and a "can-do" attitude to the projects she works on.

Do you know the saying that hindsight is 20/20? Looking back, things become more clear and you can identify the lessons and patterns of situations. Moreover, you can see what the best course of action was. In every company that I worked for, there have been lessons and growth.

At Network General, I learned the method of madness to inside sales and how important it was to have a centralized team for sales development, inside sales, and renewals. At Ingres, I learned no matter how much you want to scale, it's not going to be a success without the product market. Even with the best product out there, you have to have the best sales and marketing to create demand. And, at Skype, I learned the value of literally using the product to sell the product.

All of this is clear now but wasn't from the beginning. My realization is that I could have learned a lot faster every time I entered a new company and role if I would have had an inside expert to guide the way. To show me the company's strengths and weaknesses along with the tip and tricks. So for all those sales reps, or really anyone, entering new territory, my top sales secret is to look for someone who is among the best to accelerate your onboarding.

Find a Sales Mentor

A sales mentor can accelerate your sales success. Bottom line.

When I started at Oracle, I didn't have a mentor and I had to learn the hard way what would be successful and what wouldn't. Through trial and error, I figured out, "Oh, hey that worked! I'll do that." If I would have had someone to model myself after early in my career, I could have greatly sped up the learning curve and accelerated my sales success sooner. Later in life, I did find mentors that I would sit with, shadow, ask questions, and they helped me frame what I was doing. It made all the difference.

After over a decade of inside sales management at Oracle, Network General, and Ingres, I joined an inside sales consulting company, Phone Works, with someone who I had met at Oracle. The biggest lesson I learned in the 14 to15 years I spent there is, as much as we like to think that all of our companies are unique when it comes to sales and marketing, there's a science to it. If you don't understand it or try to bypass it, you will always fail. You have to have the framework and process there. You can put your twist on it once you know the framework, but you have to have the right people, with the right process, and the right messaging.

So if you are entering a new space and don't know the fundamentals, seek out someone who does and who is successful, and learn from them. There is a method to the madness.

HOW DO YOU FIND A SALES MENTOR?

So how you find a sales mentor to help you step up your game?

Internal mentors

Preferably, you find a mentor within the company you work at who has mastered exactly what you want to do. Look around at the top of the leaderboard. Maybe not the very top because those people often use a style that won't work for everyone. Instead, look for someone who is consistently hitting their numbers, hitting that 100-120%.

When you get the opportunity, ask them, "Hey, I noticed you are killing it and I want to learn from you. Can I ask you some questions and shadow you to learn more about what you do to be so successful?" If you can, listen in on their calls and pitches, find out how they structure their day, ask what their messaging and cadences look like. If a tough situation comes up, ask them how they would handle it. You want to crack the code to find out what breeds success in your role.

External mentors

You may wonder, "Does it have to be someone inside the company?" Well, there are benefits to an external mentor or consultant as well. When you are in a company for a few months and start drinking the Kool-Aid, you can lose perspective. An outside view can help you to look at something in a new way or approach it from a different angle. Both internal and external mentors can be beneficial in different stages but in the beginning, I recommend starting with an internal mentor. Once you have your feet wet and a firm understanding of the fundamentals, you can further accelerate your growth with the help of an external mentor.

Want to learn more from Sally Duby? Follow her on:
LinkedIn: linkedin.com/in/sallyduby
Twitter: @sallyduby
Website: bridgegroupinc.com

#62 A Journey from Food Stamps to Millionaire Sales Expert

MICHAEL PEDONE

"I was never jealous of the 'haves' as a 'have-not.'
I viewed it as something that is out there that
I could get, too."

ABOUT MICHAEL PEDONE:

Michael Pedone is the Virtual Sales Training Expert who founded SalesBuzz. com to help B2B inside sales teams discover better strategies. He also founded eTrafficJams in 2002, an SEO company that he sold in a seven-figure cash deal after five years.

Michael had a series of sales jobs in which he learned many important lessons. His work experience includes inside sales positions for ForeFront Direct/SmartCertify, Hydrogen Media, and DuPont Publishing. After pitching his revenue-generating ideas to companies he worked for and getting turned down, Michael struck out on his own.

Now, SalesBuzz is a passion project for Michael. He fulfills his desire to show people exactly how to rid themselves of call reluctance and improve their sales. His company offers live online workshops to show outbound sales teams how to craft messages that pique interest and start conversations.

Those who know Michael say he is a great trainer with the heart of a teacher, a person who is very "real world," and someone who offers straight-for-ward no-nonsense advice. He has lived phone sales from the bottom to the top and relishes in something that makes most people want to hide under their desks.

My story is one with humble beginnings and a happy ending. I grew up very poor with a single mom and two brothers. I remember all of us sharing a can of Chef Boyardee and living off of food stamps. Nonetheless, my mom always told me, "You can be anything you want to be but you are going to have to work for it." I didn't like living as a "have-not" but used that dislike as fuel to motivate me to build a better life.

A Rough and Unconventional Path to My Big Break

I realized early on that school was not my thing when I had four Fs and one A on my high school report card (the A was in guitar class). After high school, I joined a band and toured around Ohio. In the meantime, I also worked the midnight shift at Denny's washing dishes. I remember feeling like a loser when my friends would come in after nights of partying with pretty girls and I would have to wash their dishes. Again, this was fuel for me to make changes.

Soon after, I landed my first sales job at a car dealership. But after a bad car accident, a failed relationship, and a call from a person from my past, I soon set on a new path to Florida...

Things didn't exactly go as planned at first, however. I ended up homeless and it was at this point that I found a sales job at Glamour Shots. I walked in and told the manager, "I'm looking for a job and I can sell." He hired me on the spot. I worked eight days straight and earned enough to buy a new truck.

Soon I found roommates, had a place of my own and was on a path of learning. Following this job, I had a series of sales jobs, and at each of them, I used the same secret to level up and become a top performer. I also used my secret to learn what I needed to know to build and sell my first company for over a million dollars.

But what is it? What's the secret?

It's as simple as this: *Find the people who are the best of the best at what they do and who have already achieved the level of success you are after and learn from them. Oh, and ignore everything else.*

HOW TO LEVEL UP BY STUDYING FROM AND LEARNING FROM THE BEST

How exactly do you put this secret into action?

First, you are going to meet a lot of pretenders. You need to look at any expert with a critical eye and ask, "Is what they are saying true or are they just telling me what I want to hear?"

An all too common scenario is one where they had a job at their dad's location. They did really well at sales, and now they've started writing a bunch of books and they think they're some guru. But if they had to go out in the real world and work for somebody else, all of a sudden they wouldn't know what to do.

Now that you've read the fake guru disclaimer, here's how to start on the right path.

Shadow and Role Play With the Top Dogs

For me, there were a couple of people who I shadowed at every place I worked. I would look at the board to see who the top person was, and not just for the week or the day, I would look for who was consistently up there. Next, I would set out to learn from them. I would beg them if need be, asking, "Can I come in early and role play with you?" I would even pay them if I had to.

Now, listen, the only thing salespeople hate more than cold calling is role-playing. I know. But iron sharpens iron and if you start role-playing with some of the top people you will get better. The key is, you can't role play with other people that suck or who are at the same level as you. You have to get the people who know what they're doing.

Record and Audit Your Calls With a Mentor

Next, I recommend you record your sales calls and review them with a trusted mentor. Someone who has proven sales results and whose success you would like to replicate. You need to ask them for critiques, not criticism, but you also need to turn down your sensitivity meter so you can get honest feedback and use it.

Feeling hesitant? The truth is, most salespeople don't want their calls recorded because the ego gets too bruised. But think about it this way. If you push through the call audit and you make yourself better, you're gonna be at the top soon. If you don't, you're going to stay where you are forever.

To be successful, you first have to know what the steps of the sales call process are and any good salesperson understands them. Too many novice salespeople just go all the way to the end of a script no matter what. They ask questions but don't listen to the answers because they don't know what to do with them anyway. So use call audits to fine-tune your sales process.

Go to the Bookstore

Last but not least, I'm big on books. I have this outlook that whatever problem I'm facing, somebody else had that problem and they found a way to solve it, and they probably wrote a book about it.

There have been a few times in my life where I felt like I should be doing something else but I just didn't know what it was. When I felt like this, I would go to the bookstore. Most people don't even know what a bookstore is, because they just download something on their iPad now, but I would go to the bookstore, go to the self-help section, and look for help.

Success Is a Habit

One day, I didn't know what my problem was, I just knew I was unsettled. I walked into the bookstore and it just so happened there was a book being advertised called, *7 Habits of Highly Effective People*. And man, that thing hit me so hard, because I was like, "Wait a minute. I want to be highly successful. And if it's a habit, that means I can do it so I need to learn from that book." I bought that damn thing right away and read it from cover to cover. It had a huge impact on me and became one of the cornerstones for me and my foundation.

My Brian Tracy Story

Another time, I was at work and a rep came in from Brian Tracy and did a pitch about his upcoming seminar. I was really interested so I went to my boss and asked if he would invest in me going to the course. He said no and when I scrounged up the money to buy my own ticket, he refused to give me the day off. I went anyway and faced a real scolding upon my return. It was at that moment, I realized this company didn't have my best interest at heart and I quit. It was the scariest thing ever because I had just put money down on a house with my wife, I had a two-year-old at home, and I had no college education.

After walking out, I was going through rapid waves of panic and relief. I would feel like I couldn't breathe and then in another 15 minutes, I felt like the weight of the world was off my chest. So you know what I did? I went to the bookstore.

When I did, there just so happened to be this book called *Who Moved My Cheese* on the stand right in front of me. It's a short book about how to deal with change and I read the whole thing in about 15 minutes. To my surprise, my panic attacks went away. I realized there was something bigger and better for me on the other side of this and I was letting a company that did not have my best interest at heart, hold me back.

But with that being said, I had to take ownership. I knew that I didn't have a college education and I was horrible at answering interview questions. At the time, Monster.com had just become popular and I went there to look for a job. I noticed they had a resource section on how to answer interview questions so I studied it like crazy, applied, and had a job waiting for me three days later. Not only did I get a base salary of $45K, but they also gave me time off, plus commission on top of that, so I was gonna be able to make $80-$90 grand a year.

Long story short, books have been instrumental to me on my path. You can tap into the knowledge and wisdom of those who have shared their learnings through publishing. There are so many books out there, it's just finding the right thing at the right time. For me, that simply took walking into the bookstore's self-help section and being open to what I found.

Why Stay at the Bottom and Hide?

Wouldn't you rather go through a little bit of embarrassment or pain and level up than stay in the same place forever? Yeah, I sounded stupid in my recorded calls. I've made some really dumb sales calls in my time but I can laugh at it now and that's how I learned not to do it again. And, yeah, I was scared out of my mind to walk out of a job even though it was not right for me but I learned to overcome the fear of change. You have to check your ego at the door and do everything you can to learn from those who are where you want to be. As my mom told me when I was young, you can be anything you want and can learn to achieve the same success as those who you admire, but you will have to put in the work.

Want to learn more from Michael Pedone? Follow him on:
LinkedIn: linkedin.com/in/michaelpedone
YouTube: youtube.com/user/SalesBuzz
Website: salesbuzz.com

#63 Working on Your Core

LARRY LEVINE

"The whole key to selling from the heart is being vulnerable and knowing when to ask for help."

ABOUT LARRY LEVINE:

Larry Levine has more than 27 years' experience in B2B sales and is the author of the best-selling book, *Selling from the Heart*. He successfully sold office technology, document management solutions, and managed services to customers ranging from up-and-down the street accounts to Fortune 500 companies.

In the fall of 2013, Larry accepted a new challenge as a major account rep for a Japanese OEM in Los Angeles, one of the most competitive markets in the world. He walked into a zero base territory with no MIF to flip. Using his LinkedIn sales strategies, he booked $1.3 million in hardware sales in 2014 and left behind a $1.6 million pipeline for the next rep to develop.

Today, Larry coaches B2B sales professionals to do what he did. Since 2015, Larry has coached both quota-busting tenured reps and green millennials just beginning their careers. Both appreciate the practical nature of his coaching.

Early on, I knew that I excelled at building relationships. Despite my dad being a rocket scientist for the U.S. Air Force, I didn't possess his same genius brainpower and struggled in school. I barely graduated high school and only went to college to appease my parents. Where my dad was book smart, I was street smart.

So after graduating high school in 1982, I went to college and double majored in health science and marketing. As a massive extrovert, I knew I wanted to get into sales—pharmaceutical sales to be precise. After graduating from college in December 1987, I immediately started looking for a pharmaceutical sales job but was not having much success. During my search, my dad told me about a guy he had met on an airplane who worked for a big copier manufacturer. According to my dad, this guy said, "Tell your son that if he can sell copy machines for a year and last, then he's worth his weight in gold out there in the sales world because people like to hire copier reps."

After hearing my dad's story, I opened up the Yellow Pages and found the biggest ad I could for a copy machine company. I called up the owner of the company, got an interview, and a week later was hired. That was my first sales job and it was the worst experience I ever had. I only made $18,000 in my first year selling copiers. Despite my misgivings, I stuck through it and dedicated myself to learning my craft.

Understanding What Drives Sales Success

After making the commitment to learn my craft, I started interviewing anyone and everyone that could help me develop my skills. I interviewed salespeople; I interviewed my customers. I even started interviewing executives and office managers.

The main question I asked everyone was this: "What is it that you like and don't like about salespeople?"

As most would guess, common responses included things like, "I don't like broken promises" or "I don't like being lied to." And people absolutely hated when salespeople only came around when they wanted something.

On the flip side, when I asked people what they liked and respected about good salespeople, the response was always the same—people liked salespeople that showed interest and genuinely cared. That was a big aha moment for me. As a people person, I knew one of my greatest strengths was my genuine desire to help people. While there are all kinds of sales techniques and tactics, at the end of the day, I learned that the most successful salespeople are the ones that are willing to help. If you're not willing to help, then why are you really in sales?

From that point forward, I did what came naturally to me—I put people first and my sales career flourished because of it. I showed my customers that I was authentic and that I truly cared. I sold from my heart, which leads me to my sales secret.

Selling from the Heart

Anyone who knows me at all will not be surprised by my sales secret. My sales secret is simple—you have to sell from the heart. What do I mean when I say you have to sell from the heart? I mean you have to care. Your primary concern when selling from the heart is not your commission check but whether or not you can actually bring value to someone. If you can do that, the rest will come with time.

How to Sell from the Heart?

Okay, so you've bought into this notion that you have to sell from the heart, but how do you actually put that into action? My response is this: you have to work on your core.

Here is an example. Not too long ago, my back was extremely out of whack from all the flying I had been doing. After seeing an orthopedic specialist, I started doing physical therapy three times a week. On my second visit to my physical therapist, he asks, "Larry, what do you want to accomplish at the end of this?" I replied that I wanted to get back to lifting some light weights without having back pain all of the time. My therapist then says, "Okay. You need to start working on your core."

So I started working on my core and all of a sudden, I was having great workouts. During this process, something clicked in my brain—when my back was hurting, I was in a horrible mood. I didn't eat right, I wasn't sleeping well, and things were just off. My entire core was off, which affected everything. The same is true in sales.

If your core is out of whack as a salesperson, nothing else matters. If you have a bad personal life, if you're not eating right, if things are just off, you're never going to succeed in sales. In sales, the emphasis is always placed on things like product knowledge, handling objections, assessing clients, and so on. In doing this, we often forget to work on ourselves, which is paramount to everything else.

For me, working on my core means allocating the time to self-reflect and mentally prepare for each day. I get up at 3:30 a.m. every morning and from 3:30 to 4:00, I sit in my office in complete silence. I use the time to think about everything I need to do. I reflect on what I did the day before and what I can improve upon in the day ahead. And then at 4:00 a.m., I head out for the gym. It may not sound like much, but that kind of routine allows me to work on my core and mentally prepare for whatever may come my way.

Working on your core may look completely different for you, but it's vital that you get into the habit of working on yourself—whatever form that may take. As you work on your core, you'll see your entire world start to transform, which will help position you for success—personally and professionally. It will also make selling from the heart that much easier.

Want to learn more from Larry Levine? Follow him on:
Website: sellingfromtheheart.net
LinkedIn: linkedin.com/in/larrylevine1992
Twitter: @Larry1Levine

#64 Roll Up Your Sleeves and Get to Work

CHRISTOPHER FAGO

"Proactively doing what nobody wants to do shows that you are committed and are willing to do whatever it takes. It sets you apart from the rest."

ABOUT CHRISTOPHER FAGO:

Christopher Fago is currently the Technical Sales Manager at Palo Alto Networks. Prior to his current role, he was the SDR Team Founder of RedLock. Christopher was the third sales hire at RedLock where he spent 17 months creating the go-to-market strategy for the company's SDR team.

Interestingly enough, Christopher's childhood dream was to be in the music industry but when the industry began downsizing, he got a job selling high-end furniture in a mall.

After about a year selling furniture, Christopher got a job at a SaaS data intelligence company, Billian's HealthDATA. He spent five years there as an Account Manager, supporting some of the largest companies in the healthcare industry.

Christopher later pivoted to the tech industry and joined Mobile Labs where he was responsible for building out a $3M net-new pipeline.

In 2018, Christopher was named one of InsideSales.com's Top 10 Sales Development Leaders. He has been featured on the "Make It Happen" podcast with John Barrows, Predictable Revenue Podcast, and Hubspot Sales Blog.

Associates of Chris say he is consistently pleasant, takes on all assignments with enthusiasm and dedication, learns quickly, adapts, always makes an impact, and always resolves issues in a professional and client conscious manner.

I never planned or dreamt of being in sales. About nine years ago, when I realized my dream of working in the music industry wasn't all it was cracked up to be, I regrouped and took a job as a salesman of high-end furniture. Not exactly the career I had dreamed of but that was my foray into sales.

So how does a furniture salesman in a mall end up helping a company get acquired for $173 million in 17 months? It has been a wonderful yet turbulent path full of successes, failures, and lots of learning. I have picked up secrets along the way that have helped me move up and onward.

Of all my lessons, there is one that has been instrumental for me throughout my entire career....

Do What Nobody Wants to Do and Do the Job you Desire.

There are always jobs, tasks, and duties that no one wants. They are the worst tasks that are hard, grueling, and/or tedious. Most people complain or shy away from them. When they are mentioned, people don't make eye contact or become really "busy."

I have found that when I take on these types of jobs and do them the best I possibly can, great opportunities present themselves. Proactively doing what nobody wants to do shows that you are committed and are willing to do whatever it takes. It sets you apart from the rest.

The next part of my secret is doing the job that you want before you ever have it. While you are doing the stuff no one wants to do, you should simultaneously be preparing for the job you want. Prepare for your next step so that you are ready when the opportunity comes. For example, if you are a sales representative but want to be a sales manager, you start taking on the responsibilities and behaviors of a manager.

By doing both of these things in whatever role you are currently in, you can advance and move into and even beyond the role you want.

HOW CAN YOU GET STARTED RIGHT NOW?

Here's how you can get started today.

How To Do The Job No One Wants

To do the job no one wants, you have to keep your eyes open for opportunities to step up. Look for tasks that everyone else passes on or puts off.

Billian's HealthDATA, I took on an extremely tedious and boring job. For seven months, day in and day out, I was calling 200 people per day to verify information. I did my best and was the first one in line when an account manager position for renewals opened up.

Later, while working on renewals, Billian's had put out a trial which resulted in about 100 requests per month. However, they didn't want to hire anyone to manage the leads. I stepped up and said I'd figure out what to do. Instead of hiring people, I decided we could use tools to automate the process.

I found all the tools I needed to push people from the trial into a drip campaign. It worked great.

After I left Billian's looking for a new job, I faced rejection after rejection, many due to the fact that my past sales role was in renewals and not new acquisitions. I was advised I should pivot to the tech industry. I did and was offered an opportunity with Mobile Labs.

Again, I had to start at the bottom where nobody wanted to be. But by this time, I was used to it and saw it as an opportunity to get my foot in the door. I did and learned the ins and out of sales development. It prepared me for my next role at RedLock At RedLock, we had a lead from a trade show. Nobody wanted to pursue it because they had bigger fish to fry. I took it on, kept in touch, and it snowballed. It ended up being the biggest sale I had ever made at $100,000 and the biggest deal of the quarter!

In summary, work hard at whatever you can get, seek out the crappy tasks/leads/roles no one wants, and do them extraordinarily well.

How To Do The Job You Want To Do

Next, here's how to do the job you want to do now. Start by studying the people that you desire to be, figuring out what they do well. If you aren't sure how to get started, have a conversation with someone who is excelling. A mentor. A boss. Use the information you gather to slowly start doing things differently.

For example, if I come in early on Monday and I ask my boss, "Alright, what can I do this week to enable you, or enable the team?" I'm demonstrating servant leadership. I might not be the boss, but I'm behaving like the boss. You might not be the team lead, but you behave like the team lead. I guarantee you if you do this well, you will be top-of-mind when a promotion comes around.

Work hard

Lastly, don't half-ass anything. Do everything that you do as best as you can.

When I started at RedLock on the east coast, it was hard. During the first six months, my team did horrible. I mean, we lost a lot. We only won one deal in six months. I was barely getting by and I was really depressed.

I met with our CEO, and I said, "You just gotta give me more time. I promise, 2018 will be the year of the east." I kept my head down and kept working hard. Low and behold, during the first six months of 2018, the east was the sales leader for deals won. By October of 2018, RedLock was acquired by Palo Alto Networks for $173 million!

So the key takeaway here is to do the job that no one wants to do and do the job that you desire. It will take you to where you want to go and the hard work will always catch up to you. It may not be tomorrow or the next day, but it will catch up. If you say to yourself, "Oh, nothing's working," and you slow down, it's only going to get worse. But, if you keep your head down, and just keep pushing, success will come.

Want to learn more from Chris Fago? Follow him on:
LinkedIn: linkedin.com/in/christopherfago

#65 Success Starts With the Right Attitude

RALPH BARSI

"Become aware of the goodness you pick up along the way—whether from failures, learning experiences, or successes. Share those experiences with others and leave behind a trail of breadcrumbs for people to learn from."

ABOUT RALPH BARSI:

Ralph Barsi is a seasoned veteran in the sales world with over 25 years of experience. He is currently the VP of Global Inside Sales at tray.io.

Before entering the work world, Ralph graduated from Saint Mary's College of California with a BA in Communications and also underwent the Executive Education Program at the University of California, Berkeley, Haas School of Business.

Throughout his career, Ralph has held a variety of roles working for companies such as UPS, Ticketmaster, Vertical Networks, GAFFEY Healthcare, Elsevier, InsideView, Achievers, and ServiceNow. Ralph has also volunteered at the GrowthX Academy and was a mentor for the Women in Sales Award North America.

Those who have worked with Ralph say he is a 'rare gem in sales leadership today' being the kind of leader who is 'all-in' when it comes to excelling at his craft. He is laser- focused on becoming better every single day and is described as being a thought-leader who surrounds himself with other thought-leaders. His primary assets are said to be his high energy and optimistic personality which can drive those around him to reach greater heights.

I experienced my first taste of sales as a young kid. I had a paper route and would ride my BMX bike to deliver papers every morning. Once per month, I'd have to go door-to-door to collect the checks for the customer's monthly newspaper subscriptions. I didn't know it then, but I had found my passion.

For the first 10 to 15 years of my professional sales career, I was an individual contributor. I carried the bag, oversaw territories, and collected nice commission checks. For the latter half, I've invested my time in building and scaling teams, mostly consisting of sales development reps who were relatively new to their careers.

Coaching, teaching, mentoring, developing, and nurturing future salespeople means a lot to me. Sales is my beloved profession and everyone who I coach is going to impact the eco-system. I want gems going into the profession and so I take my work to heart. While I have many things I like to impart on my fellow comrades in the sales world, below is the one I find most essential.

DEVELOP AN ATTITUDE OF GRATITUDE

When I was a younger guy, new to the sales scene, I was a bit cocky and unrefined. I would rely too heavily on my charm and wit and was less tactical about my approaches. In short, I was mostly ego. It took time and quite a few failures to learn and develop myself and I am still finding opportunities to improve every day. Throughout the process, I've discovered many secrets and strategies to drive better results but all of them won't truly help if your underlying attitude isn't right. Being so, my number one sales secret is to develop an attitude of gratitude.

What do I mean? Be thankful for the things you have, even the most simple things that are easy to take for granted. For instance, take a sip of water, and be grateful for having a fresh glass of water.

Be gracious for the people that you don't like, who you meet in your career, as well as for the people who you love and embrace. They all bring gifts in different shapes, sizes, colors, and forms, and you have to be looking for them and learning from them in order to move the collective effort forward.

Be grateful for the opportunity to generate an income today, to work with an able body and mind.

Be grateful for all that you have.

3 WAYS TO DEVELOP AN ATTITUDE OF GRATITUDE

Not feeling very grateful for your manager with a short temper or co-worker who always complains? I get it can be difficult, especially at first. If you want to start practicing an attitude of gratitude today, here are a few things you can do. In time, like anything, it will become easier and easier.

Have a Beginner's Mindset: Stop thinking only about yourself. It's not all about you. Put aside your mission, patterns, and opinions. Instead, become more curious. Inquire about what is going on with those around you and learn things as if you are required to teach what you're learning the very next day to someone. Open up your eyes and your ears a little more. Take better notes. Work to get a true understanding of what it is that you're learning before you form any opinions on it. And assume the position that you know nothing and have to learn everything from square one, even if you may have prior knowledge or assumptions on the subject.

Be Ready to Be Tested: Next, know that as you progress in your career, your belt will be tested (as we say in martial arts). If you are a black belt in sales, be ready to be tested. For example, as you grow teams, you're going to always have haters and naysayers that aren't down with your approach. They may not be down with your personality, or the way you do things. Look for the gift they're bringing to the table, even though that's tough to digest and process at times. In every situation, be ready to be tested. You can 'pass' by finding a way to be grateful and take away a learning that serves the greater good.

Be Thankful for 'Failures:' When I start thinking about failures, they're not necessarily failures. They're more just insane learning experiences. As I grow in my career, and I look back on 25 years of selling, every single company I worked for was a gift. They were gifts to me. I worked for some really tough people, and I worked for some great people. At the time, I thought some of the people were real pains in the ass, and I didn't feel great about them. In retrospect, I look back and I understand the role they played. They could have done it a little better in terms of their tone and their approach, but I appreciate what I learned from them. I don't take any of it for granted. I think they're all just great learning experiences. So look for the silver linings in the tough experiences.

By following these steps, you can cultivate more gratitude in your daily life to increase your own happiness and well-being as well as what you can give back to others and the world. It builds a strong foundation for a sales career that continuously grows and improves over time.

Want to learn more from Ralph Barsi? Follow him on:
LinkedIn: linkedin.com/in/ralphbarsi
Twitter:twitter.com/rbarsi
Blog: ralphbarsi.com

#66 If They Can Grow, I Can Grow

GERHARD GSCHWANDTNER

"For every problem under the sun, there is a solution or there is none. If there is one, go and find it, and if there is none, nevermind it."

ABOUT GERHARD GSCHWANDTNER:

Gerhard Gschwandtner is the Founder and CEO of Selling Power, Inc., the creator of Peak Performance Mindset workshops, the operator of Sales 3.0 conferences, and the author of 16 books on Selling, Sales Management, and Sales Psychology and two on photography. He is passionate about creating peak performance in business and in life.

A sales guy at heart, Gerhard established his professional reputation as a sales guru by training over 10,000 salespeople in Europe and the US. He started *Selling Power* magazine in 1982 and turned it into the world's leading sales management magazine. His mission is to contribute to the success of sales leaders with SellingPower.com, a sales intelligence platform that is visited by over 300,000 sales leaders every month.

He also runs four Sales 3.0 conferences a year (in Philadelphia, Boston, San Francisco, and Las Vegas) that attract over 1,200 sales and marketing leaders. The conferences are designed to help sales managers improve people, processes, and technology to achieve operational efficiency and greater customer satisfaction.

If that's not enough, Gerhard is also the creator of the Peak Performance Mindset workshops. These workshops are designed to help salespeople transform self-limiting beliefs into self-empowering beliefs. The workshop is delivered through 60 certified trainers that can help salespeople achieve their full potential, exceed quota, and shift their mindset to achieve peak performance personally and professionally.

Those who know Gerhard say that few people have really made an impact on the sales industry the way he has. His contributions over the years and his passion for sales have made him one of the biggest influencers in recent decades. Further, he's known as a genuine and authentic person who is making a difference in the lives of those who will listen, engage, and be open to the power of positivity.

Everything is possible. I know that from experience. I grew up in a little town in Salzburg, Austria and throughout my life have had the distinguished honor to meet some of the world's greatest movers and shakers. I've had dinner with George Bush Senior, played golf with Bill Clinton, met Oprah and even paid a visit to the President of the Dominican Republic.

No matter who you are or where you come from, I believe anything is possible if *you* believe you are capable of growing.

Belief in Growth Is the Foundation

The secret to my success has been adopting the belief that I can grow.

I found myself wondering, how did Ron Rice develop a 100 million dollar business out of suntan lotion? How can Mary Kay build a half-billion-dollar business out of cosmetics? And how did Marc Benioff make Salesforce into a $4.3 billion company?

It's because they had the thought first. They had the idea and believed in the idea and grew with the idea. You can only grow if you can apply yourself to an idea that's bigger than you.

I discovered that the human mind is an incredible growth engine. However, in most people, it is working backward, repeating the past, or, at best, idling. It is not unfolding the way it could or should.

I told myself, if they can grow, I can grow. I can grow with every insight, every interview, and every success story I hear—and I can do significantly better than I'm doing right now.

How Do You Grow?

Whether it is when you take your last breath, when you propose, or when you first see your new baby, life is filled with amazing moments. But it is also filled with a lot of problems. The only people I've known not to have any problems are in the cemetery. Life is filled with challenges. However, you can change how you respond to problems.

Here are four ways I've learned to effectively grow and live a constructive life.

Optimize Your Mindset and Feelings

Essentially, the thing you want to strive for every day is optimal cognitive and psychological functioning, meaning that your cognitive function is at a high level and you can use constructive thinking in any circumstance.

We did a study with the University of Massachusetts and Dr. Epstein found that when we gave him access to people who made a million dollars versus those who made $150k to $250k, the main difference between them was their thinking style. The successful people didn't have more education and they weren't "luckier" but they did have more constructive thinking patterns. When life gave them lemons, they would make lemonade, as they say. They had more of an automatic positive interpretation of reality.

In addition to being constructive, people also want to make themselves happy. To do so, they need to think happy thoughts and be grateful. In fact, the majority of people that have a gratitude journal are 25% happier than people who don't. Further, if you are nice to people and do a good job then they are nice to you. It's the law of reciprocity.

The highest achievers of this mindset have more social and financial success, and they are more satisfied in their relationships and lives. And it all comes down to thinking. They don't engage in twisted distorted thinking where they say life sucks. They don't make sweeping statements like that and understand that life is composed of a lot of shades of grey.

You can create the universe in your head and say I want to function optimally in my thinking but also I want to feel good so I become a good person that is nice to be around.

Understand the Four Components of the Mind

To optimize your mindset, it's important to understand that it is an operating system with four components:

1) **Thoughts**

2) **Feelings**

3) **Beliefs**

4) **Behaviors**

Thoughts create feelings; it's not the feelings that create thoughts. If you're upset, you make yourself upset with your thoughts. So if as a friend, teacher, or trainer you are working with someone who is upset, you want to figure out the underlying thought causing the feeling and help them to see how to think constructively and regain hope.

Thoughts and feelings together create beliefs and beliefs are powerful motivators that drive human behavior. So if you attempt to make a change in yourself or someone else by encouraging a change in behavior, you are treating the symptom and not the cause. If you start with ideas that are at the root of a belief and behavior, you can make a deeper impact.

For example, say a salesperson prospects every day but believes that prospecting sucks. That belief impairs their natural ability to relate to strangers and gain leads because they are coming from a negative place. As a sales manager, it's important to track down where the belief comes from. Was it a bad experience they had early in their career? Was it imprinted on them by coworkers or prior bosses? What caused them to believe that? Analyze it and replace it with a realistic constructive belief. Prospecting is a means to an end. An activity that leads to success and growth. While difficult at times, it presents opportunities. Turn the inner critic into an inner champion and the behavior will automatically change.

Be Persistent

The next part of growing is not giving up. If you tell yourself that something is impossible, it's never going to happen. But if you persist, you can bring it to reality.

After a long series of emails, I once got the opportunity to interview Terry Bradshaw. He finally said he had time two days before Christmas and we talked for three hours — laughing and telling stories. At the end of the call, I told him that all I need was a place where I could send a photographer to do a great cover picture of him. He said, "I gotta be at Candlestick Park to do the narration for the Super Bowl so send the photographer to San Fran." I agreed.

So I called the press office at Candlestick Park and asked if I could get a press pass for my photographer and they said, "What? You want what? The deadline for that was last year!" I said, "Okay, well, out of curiosity, does the San Francisco Chronicle have the pass?" They said yes, so I called the San Francisco Chronicle to get a hold of their photographer.

I asked, "Can I speak to your photographer? I have something very important that I want to share with him but I can't talk about it at this point. It's personal and business." He wasn't there but when he finally got back to me he said he couldn't because he wasn't allowed to do freelance work while on the job.

Next, I asked, "Do know the guy at San Jose Mercury News who is covering the Super Bowl?" He said he did and his name was Jose. I called Jose's office but he wasn't there. Again, I said it was urgent and important and asked for his home phone number. They gave it to me.

I called his home number and his wife answered. I say who I am and where I'm from and explain that I have an important opportunity for him that will pay $1,000. I explain that all he needs to do is take five minutes at the Super Bowl to take a picture of Terry Bradshaw. She says, "Of course, he will do that." He calls me back in a half-hour and says he'd do it.

So I connected him and Terry and it all happened.

I faced several obstacles to get the Terry Bradshaw interview in the first place and then ran into one closed door after another trying to arrange the picture. But in the end, I got it because I was persistent. No matter the obstacle, there is always a solution to every problem. You do whatever it takes, for as long as it takes until you reach your goal.

The Philosophy of Enough

Lastly, if you can grow and anything is possible, where do you stop? Do you endlessly pursue more and more and more? The *philosophy of more* always leaves you wanting. You are not free but are a slave to your money.

I have one client who has a yacht in the Caribbean, and he has 12 people to crew that yacht and they are always fighting. He says, I hate to go on my yacht and it was $100 million dollars. It's a headache and I don't want it anymore.

Another example involves Marc Benioff. He just bought this property in Maui and built a house. He has so many electronics there that the founder of Blue Wolf told me that they had to write a program for his house because he was wasting so much time managing his property.

More becomes *too much* and causes stress.

Instead, I propose the *philosophy of enough*. The philosophy of enough is related to what you need to be happy. Ask yourself how you can optimize your life in a way that makes you feel happy and so your wealth doesn't become a burden.

Make that your goal and your end game.

In 1999, I was offered $10.5 million to sell my magazine. I was elated. I was excited and I thought, "I am going to have a check in my hand for $10.5 million dollars!" Shortly after I asked, "Then what? Is that really what I want?" And it wasn't. I am not in it for the money. I was making enough money to raise three beautiful children and pay for their education. I drove a nice car. I lived in a beautiful house on the water. I had enough. And that's where the philosophy of enough helped me because I wanted to be in that zone of happiness.

In summary, it all comes down to truly believing you can grow and that anything is possible. However, that doesn't mean it is easy. To help you grow and get to the place of having your version of enough, you must learn how the mind works, optimize it to its highest level of constructive functioning, take actions to bring yourself wholesome happiness, and be persistent in whatever you decide to pursue.

Want to learn more from Gerhard Gschwandtner?
Follow him on:
LinkedIn: linkedin.com/in/gerhard20
Twitter: @gerhard20
YouTube: youtube.com/user/gerhardpsp

#67 You Can't Fake Caring

JOHN BARROWS

"When you have a genuine desire to help people
be successful, it's not selling."

ABOUT JOHN BARROWS:

John Barrows is the CEO of JBarrows Sales Training, where he trains salespeople for some of the world's top companies like Salesforce, LinkedIn, and many, many more. Before launching JBarrows Sales Training, John worked for companies such as Xerox, Thrive Networks and Kensie Partners.

John lives by his "12 Guiding Principles to Success" and is viewed as a game-changer in the sales industry. He has been fortunate to share his sales experience with thousands and feels honored to learn from them as well.

Throughout John's career, he has made an effort to put his customers first, knowing that no amount of skill can replace genuinely caring. His caring nature has made him into one of the world's greatest salespeople and a true sales guru.

Like many salespeople out there, I never dreamed of a career in sales. All I knew is that I wanted to make money; however I could go about achieving that objective was fine by me. While I was never the smartest kid, my parents taught me the importance of a solid work ethic. My mom was an artist of sorts and did art therapy; my dad was a mechanical engineer.

So from my mom, I picked up a lot of those interpersonal skills that are really important in sales and from my dad, I picked up the analytical skills that are also essential. To this day, I talk a ton about the art and science of selling—much of that influence originated with my parents.

Without a clear career path in mind though, I went to the University of Maryland where I tried a little bit of everything. My first major was art, then I went to engineering. I failed most of my engineering classes so I then went into biology and chemistry. That was absolutely awful. So I finally said, marketing is a nice mix of everything, right? First of all, it seemed a lot easier. And second, it was a nice mix of the creative side, plus the business side. Not to mention that I thought marketing would put me in a good position to make money in some way, shape, or form—which was really my ultimate objective.

When I graduated, I landed a marketing job with Dewalt Tools, which is owned by Black & Decker. My job was to drive from Maine, all the way down to Connecticut, constantly on the lookout for construction sites. When I would find a construction site, I would go in and try to get them to buy Dewalt Tools.

My job wasn't really to sell the tools, but to raise awareness of Dewalt. I had no sales quota or way to measure my success. Despite this, I actually learned a ton about sales and the importance of understanding the needs of your buyers. Instead of going straight to the foreman on the job site, as many of my peers did, I spent my time talking with the workers, learning why they used the tools they did and asking what aspects of a given tool were most important. When I did finally go to the foreman, I had all these great insights from the workers that helped support my case as to why he should consider going with Dewalt. My method was pretty simple actually but served as the foundation for my future career in sales.

As I went on to different roles at Home Depot, Xerox, and Thrive, I learned that doing well in sales was really about understanding people. It was about building rapport and finding ways to genuinely impact a person's business. Which gets me to my sales secret…

The Value of Caring

If I can offer any advice for developing sales professionals out there, it would be this: to be successful in sales you must be patient and you have to give a shit. Plain and simple.

If your end goal is only to earn your commission, you're never going to be as successful as you could be. When you get to the point of truly caring about your client, that's when you'll experience your ultimate success. A large part of that also means that you have to believe in what you're selling. If you don't see the value in your product or service, how do you expect to honestly sell someone else on it?

While you can't fake passion and true commitment, below are a few tips to keep in mind that will help you stay focused on your true objective— helping your customers succeed.

Hustle:

In sales, there are countless factors outside of your control but your effort is not one of them. As a young salesperson starting off, I was always the first person in and the last person to leave. If you're truly committed to seeing your customers succeed, working long hours won't feel like work. It will become your passion; it will drive you and motivate you like nothing else because their success will become more important than your own.

A/B Test Everything:

If I could go back in time and give my 22-year-old self advice, it would be to split test everything. For example, let's say you're selling to CIO's in the healthcare industry. Instead of using the same message on every call, come up with two different messages and make 20 phone calls using the first message then make 20 phone calls using the second. After 40 calls, see which message yielded a better response. The more data you have to inform your efforts, the easier your job will ultimately become. It will also enable you to better connect with your customers in a way that resonates with them.

Be OK With the Worst-Case Scenario:

With any decision you make, think about the worst-case scenario. If what you imagine seems acceptable, do it. I'm all about calculated risks so if I can live with the outcome of a certain action, then I know I should proceed. If I can't, then I need to re-evaluate my approach because I need to assume that my worst-case scenario is probably going to happen at some point.

At the end of the day, sales is about people and making meaningful connections. Like all aspects of life, the more you care and put in the effort, the more likely you are to see positive results. Sales is about more than merely showing up; it's about patience and truly caring about the impact you can make.

Want to learn more from John Burrows? Follow him on:
Website: jbarrows.com
Twitter: @JohnMBarrows
LinkedIn: linkedin.com/in/johnbarrows
YouTube: youtube.com/JBarrowsSalesTraining

#68 Surrender to the Work of Your Goals

MARK ALLEN

"The best dreams, the best goals are the ones we look at and go, 'That's a big hairy goal. I don't know if I can do it but I'm going to try because I think I might be able to."

ABOUT MARK ALLEN:

Mark Allen is a triathlete, six-time Ironman Triathlon World Champion, and Olympic Distance World Champion turned keynote speaker and consultant on sports business, health, and wellness.

Over the course of a fifteen-year racing career, Mark maintained a 90% average in top- three finishes and won 66 of the 96 races he competed in during that time. He was named "Triathlete of the Year" six times by *Triathlete Magazine*, and in 1997 *Outside* magazine called him "The World's Fittest Man." Additionally, in November of 2012, Mark was voted "The Greatest Endurance Athlete of All Time" in a worldwide poll conducted by ESPN and was also inducted into the Iron Man Triathlon Hall of Fame.

Now that Mark has retired from competition, he shares his stories of Ironman racing with corporate audiences across the globe. His triathlon coaching service is used in over 50 countries and he is the co-author of the award-winning book *Fit Soul, Fit Body: 9 Keys to a Healthier, Happier You.* He has also won awards for his latest publication titled *The Art of Competition.*

Those who know Mark say he is a shining example of a top professional triathlete who is a great coach and leader. He exemplifies excellence in mind, body, and spirit.

As a kid playing sports in school, I always seemed to be the last one picked for any team. People saw me as a handicap and not an asset thinking, "He can't handle the ball and he's not aggressive." There was certainly no foreshadowing that I would end up being at the top of a sport.

That goes to show that if you land in something that is a passion for you and you dedicate the time and energy, never give up, and keep refining how you do your work, you can reach that top level. However, most people that want to be successful aren't willing to do the work.

If you're an athlete, you want to be a world champion, you want to set world records. But wanting to do that and actually doing the work to achieve that level of success are two very different things. To actually become successful, there has to be a certain amount of surrender to reach your goals.

Success Is Related to Surrender

A lot of people don't associate success with surrender but as an athlete, you have to look at your goal and performance, analyze it to determine what you need to do, and then do the work day after day. The training and behavior behind the scenes are far from glamorous. And, in most cases, as you start to get close to your peak potential, the things that you're going to have to change to make that final leap to the top level are going to be things that are very hard for you to change—otherwise, you would have done them already. So you have to be ready to live what you ask for, identify what you need to do, and surrender to what is required to achieve that success.

HOW DO YOU SURRENDER TO THE WORK OF SUCCESS?

Here are five of the lessons I've learned in my life on how to surrender to the work of success.

Find Your Passion

I never had a big plan to become the greatest endurance athlete of all time. It didn't come from my parents driving me to be this great athlete. They had always tried to instill in me the willingness to work at whatever I was doing. If I had no passion for what I was doing, they'd encourage me to find something else, even if it didn't make sense at the time. And so that's what Ironman was—I was like, "I'm going to just train for a year and see if I can maybe cross that finish line." Then, I fell in love with it and became determined to win. Find something that lights you up and that you feel passionate about, first and foremost.

Create Levels of Goals

Once you find your passion and get started, I recommend you develop different levels of goals. Obviously, the big top tier goal for me was to win the Ironman, but what if my best wasn't good enough that day? Would I then lose all hope and give up? No, I needed a second goal to keep me engaged. And then, I'd need my bottom line goal, which was the one that would say, "Okay, I just want to finish the race. If I can finish the race, that will still be something that I can hold my head high about."

In sales, you're going to have your top tier goal for the year. But then have some other levels of things that are important to you that will be fulfilling. Then, if you fall behind on the big goal, you're still going to be engaged because there are achievements within your grasp.

Ultimately, I think the biggest key in any kind of success is just to stay engaged as much as you can and give the best that you can. Some days are going to be amazing, some days are going to be pretty lackluster but you can still give 100% of what you have to give on one of those 20% days.

Pace Yourself

Next, try to pace yourself, day-to-day and also over the course of the year so that you don't get into those deep fatigued, exhausted, and mind-numbing situations where you can't even fathom doing another phone call or email or meeting. Of course, high levels of success require a lot of work and so sometimes maybe you misjudge and do need a break, and that's okay. Consider it a regrouping. If you need an easy day, take it and know that you're going to regenerate and recharge yourself. Then tomorrow, you're going to relaunch much fresher, more committed, and fully engaged again.

I would do that some days. I would say, my body is just telling me I need to really back it off. And then the next day, I'd wake up fresh and ready to go at 100%. So, pace yourself, day-to-day, and also over the course of the year. And if you hit a situation where you do need to give it a break for a second, do it. Honor yourself that way, and then get back into it.

Periodically Analyze Your Performance and Adapt

Another important step is to be on the path of continual improvement. As an athlete, there are a lot of different paradigms of how you can get more fit, and it's the same with sales. There are many theories on how you can become a top salesperson. So you have to pick a few things that you're going to try and put them in play and use them over and over to see if they are effective or not. If today you're doing one theory, tomorrow you're doing something different, and the next day you're doing something different, you'll never really optimize the impact and power of that particular theory or way of training or sales.

You want to try and evolve into not only a better athlete but a better person. But at the same time, you need to give things a long enough run to be able to see if they are effective or not. In athletics, it took a whole season of me trying something before I actually knew if it was working or not.

There needs to be some consistency with what you are putting in place—not jumping from one thing to the next to the next all the time. But again, reach points where you do assess and ask if what you are doing is working or not. Are you getting faster? Are you getting more efficient and effective? If the answer is no, evolution and change will need to take place. This is an important part of the work.

View the Work as an Investment

Lastly, understand the value of the work required. In the Ironman, I had to swim 2.4 miles in the open ocean in about 15 minutes to stay on pace. That required a lot of swimming. I'd go through the holidays like everybody else and have a good time, and then by January 1 it was like, "Okay, let's get back at it now."

At the start of the year, I would hop in the pool, swim one side of the 25-yard pool, do a flip turn, and come back down the other side. Within about 35 seconds, I had seen the entire swim course that I was going to do about 50,000 more times throughout the year. I could look at all of those laps, as the most boring thing in the universe, OR I could surrender to the work and realize that with every lap, I was putting a little bit of equity in my fitness bank. Throughout the year, I'd go from being out of shape to being in decent shape to getting in good shape to achieving world-class shape, lap by lap.

In short, the keys to success are finding your passion, understanding the work, surrendering to it, continuously improving, being consistent, and appreciating the journey. It really comes down to small nuggets that lay that foundation of success. If you're looking for every day to be this incredibly exciting moment, you're going to be let down. However, if you can just keep your mind quiet, put in the work, and feel empowered knowing that you even have the guts to dream big, success will come. It may come earlier than you thought or it may come later—but it will come.

Want to learn more from Mark Allen? Follow him on:
LinkedIn: linkedin.com/in/markallen08
Facebook: facebook.com/markallencoaching
Website: markallencoaching.com

#69 Getting Back to the Basics

CORY BRAY

"Every salesperson should study sales with the same vigor and intensity as a lawyer, accountant or doctor studies their craft."

ABOUT CORY BRAY:

Cory is the co-author of four books including *Sales Playbooks: The Builder's Toolkit*, *Sales Development—Cracking the Code of Outbound Sales*, *The Sales Enablement Playbook,* and *Triangle Selling.* He's also the Managing Director of Clozeloop, a revenue strategy firm, and a founding member of the Sales Enablement Society.

Cory attended the Wharton School at the University of Pennsylvania with the goal of becoming an entrepreneur. After graduating, he joined Renegade Capital where he was an associate focused on building out analytical and process capabilities for affiliated companies.

In 2010, after identifying an improvement opportunity for Renegade Capital's sister company, Service Steel Warehouse, he led the plan's execution which earned him the role of the company's Director of Operations. He held that position for two years before resigning. However, he was recruited back one month later as a business strategy consultant. He spent five months expanding the business into another state.

It was this role that led him into founding his own consulting firm, Ateli Consulting. He ran that for a year before being recruited by CorSource Technology Group to be its Head of Business Intelligence Sales. He led the BI sales team from never having closed a deal to earning the award for BI's Partner of the Year (out of 50 partners).

Cory had the itch to move to the San Francisco area so he packed up and didn't look back. He helped Birst on a short-term five-month project as a product strategy contractor working with sales analytics. After that, he joined Ravel Law as Head of Sales where he built out sales and marketing for a year and a half.

The next stop for Cory brought him to where he is today as the Managing Director at ClozeLoop. He now shares his knowledge of management, sales, customer success, and sales enablement through his books. With four published already, he has his sights set on publishing 40.

Cory is said to be a person who is a rare combination of technical and savvy who gets things done and is excellent with internal and external customers.

When I was in my 20s, I began the Charter Financial Analyst Program, a program to earn an esteemed credential as an investment or financial professional. There are three levels you must pass which each require 200 hours of studying. It's like the bar exam for the finance industry, and over 60% of people fail each time they take the test.

I passed the first two levels and then stopped because I got a sales job. But I realized something important in that process. Lawyers have to pass the bar exam; medical doctors have to complete four years of medical school and three to seven years of residency training; accountants have to pass the

CPA exam, ethics exam (in many states), and fulfill the work experience requirement. But in sales, there's no formal training or certification.

Companies take someone who graduated with a B average, from XYZ state university with a major in political science, throw them into a sales job, and say "Go get your quota." It seems absurd to me. Sales, like the other professions, has important fundamentals that each person entering the field needs to know, understand, and execute to be successful.

Focus on Learning the Fundamentals and Practicing Them Rigorously

My secret has two parts.

First, learn the fundamentals. Develop an incredibly strong fundamental understanding of how selling works.

Second, apply the fundamentals rigorously. Don't stop until your skill, in your craft, parallels that of your friends that are accountants, lawyers, and doctors.

The first step is acquiring knowledge and the second is putting it into action the right way, at the right time. You also need to be able to apply the fundamentals under pressure.

HOW TO LEARN THE FUNDAMENTALS AND DEVELOP RIGOR

Strangely enough, sales fundamentals aren't typically taught in college. I studied entrepreneurship and only had one course in sales during my entire college education. Some salespeople are lucky enough to cross paths with incredible mentors who know the fundamentals and coach them up but what if you don't have that luxury? How can you develop yourself?

Look for Training From Your Boss or Leadership Team

First, if you are entering the field of sales I recommend choosing your employer carefully. The culture and approach to sales within a company will influence your ability to succeed. I believe you will be in the best position to sell with a company that values the development of its salespeople according to tested and proven sales principles and procedures.

If you are already in a sales position, I suggest you analyze your company and leadership with a critical eye. What sales fundamentals are they following, teaching, and encouraging, if any? Are those fundamentals conducive to success? If your boss is the type to say, "Go sit in the lobby until the contract is signed" or "Call them three times a day from three different numbers," you're learning garbage.

Instead, you should be seeking to understand what needs to get done, who are the users, and who are the influencers? Where are they at in the deal? What do you need to do to get them on board? What do you need to do to get this signed? Who is the finance budget holder? If you're just calling from three different numbers to get through, even if they do answer, you won't know the right things to say.

If you happen to be working with someone who understands sales fundamentals and applies these fundamentals with rigor, follow their example. Work backward to figure out what you should be doing today to get on that path.

Build Your Own Curriculum

In addition to finding an employer, manager, or another person to learn from, you should also take steps to educate yourself. You don't have to reinvent the wheel as there are thousands of books, courses, programs, and coaches out there that break down the fundamentals.

Ask people in sales (who you respect) if there are any resources they recommend to learn the fundamentals (prospecting, discovery, pitching, closing, follow-up, and objection handling). Research resources online. You can build your own curriculum to learn the knowledge you need and put it into action.

When taking this approach, I recommend getting granular with each fundamental. For example, if you're studying prospecting, learn to identify not only good or bad but everything in between (the best, good, okay, unacceptable, etc.) A lot of times, people live in a binary world and they're like "It's either A or B." No, there are 26 letters in the alphabet, not two.

Don't Take Shortcuts

Next, if you think somebody's ready to buy, but you haven't done everything that your sales methodologies prescribe, then you're taking shortcuts. If you skip a step and say, "I think I can skip this because this person's probably just gonna buy," a lot of times, that blows up in your face.

So for example, proposal delivery. A lot of times people just email a proposal over when they think the deal is in the bag. I challenge you to ask, "Why are we emailing a proposal over instead of scheduling a meeting?" You should be meeting in person or at least over the phone, starting off with a slide that restates all the pain that you uncovered, and tying that to some kind of financial impact.

Sticking to your sales process and not getting lazy is key to developing rigor.

Find Parallels in your Personal Life

Lastly, use other activities in your personal life to help support your mastery of sales. The thing I'm doing right now is playing pool. I work with a pool coach two hours each week who just rips me apart.

Why pool?

In chess, you need to know what to do. In golf, you generally know what to do, you just need to physically be able to do it. With pool, you need to know what to do and you need to physically do it under pressure. It combines the skills that parallel a lot of what happens in a sales conversation.

In summary, the fundamentals teach you what to say and how to say it and the rigor creates the consistency and dedication that is required for any type of success. You can develop both by seeking out mentorship from leaders and employers who understand the sales fundamentals and operate accordingly, seeking out knowledge and building your own curriculum, avoiding the temptation to take short cuts, and finding parallels in your personal life to support your mastery of sales.

Want to learn more from Cory Bray? Follow him on: LinkedIn: linkedin.com/in/ buy-thesalesenablementplaybook/

#70 Practice Makes Perfect: Becoming a Sales Artisan

LORI RICHARDSON

"Sales is an admirable profession. It takes work and effort. You need to be motivated. You need to take responsibility and remain committed."

ABOUT LORI RICHARDSON:

Lori Richardson is recognized on *Forbes* as one of the "Top 30 Social Sales Influencers" worldwide. She is the Founder and CEO of Score More Sales, a sales strategy consulting and training firm for mid-sized companies. Over the last 20 years, her team has helped mid-market technology and distribution companies grow frontline revenues by imparting success strategies that she and her team have perfected throughout their careers.

As a lifelong learner, Lori is often found at sales conferences learning the latest in how sales continues to evolve. She is also the President of Women Sales Pros, an online community dedicated to helping smart, savvy women get into B2B sales positions and sales leadership roles.

Throughout her career, Lori has approached sales like a master craftsman approaches his craft—with hard work, patience, and dedication. Continue reading to learn how you too can become a sales artisan.

Growing up, my family ran its own business—a women's apparel store that my grandmother started in Seattle, Washington. While I loved the family business, I also loved working with kids so in my early twenties, I became a teacher. Despite my passion for education, I soon learned that as a single mom I couldn't afford to raise my family on a teacher's salary so I went back to my roots and got into selling.

I explored a lot of different, non-traditional careers for women at the time (this was the 1980s after all) but ultimately landed at a technology company, selling on straight commission. I thought the tech industry would allow me to earn and support my family and believed full-heartedly when someone told me that there was more money in crumbs in tech than I would ever make in teaching. So I worked on crumbs at first. And I had to hunt my meal. And that's why I didn't make money until I started selling.

Looking back, it was a great way to get going. It's like being dropped into the deep end and being told to swim. You literally have no choice but to sink or swim.

The company I started at was in major growth mode and I was surrounded by lots of young people—male and female—just laser-focused on selling. It was a great experience and really laid a solid foundation for me to build upon. I went on to work for a company that sold personal computers, where I was the first woman they had ever hired in sales. It was the mid-1980s and we were trying to get the likes of Microsoft, IBM and Hewlett- Packard to see that there was a market for personal computers. We did a million dollars a month out of our little retail shop—it was a hustle. I eventually got promoted to sell corporate accounts, which was like the Wild West.

Through my first two decades of doing sales, I held various positions, went through some acquisitions, and even built a corporate university. What I learned over that time is that you gain from every opportunity. Every exchange, every company that you work at, all the diverse people you meet—these are all opportunities to learn and grow. So after gaining all this knowledge and experience, I decided to start my own business in 2002.

I wanted to do something where I wasn't selling and I wasn't managing—so I started a business focused on training and coaching. For me, sales has never been about making the quick deal; rather it is about adding value. And that is what I work to accomplish every day.

Why Perfecting Your Craft Matters

Having worked with countless salespeople over the years who are all looking for the ultimate silver bullet, my sales secret is quite simple: sales is a craft that requires practice to be successful. Sales is both art and science; you can't just become a sales superstar through osmosis. I've helped onboard thousands of sales reps in my time and I hear them saying the same thing over and over again. Something to the effect of, "Just give me the path that goes straight through the maze, and not all the winding around in between." But that's not how sales, or anything that requires skill, works.

Think of a craft like woodworking. I can go take a woodworking class, learn some basic things, maybe even build a box by the end of it. But I can't build a beautiful cabinet after just one class. It takes time. If you approach sales like a craft, where you work to improve little by little each day, over time you will be able to transform your simple box into a beautiful cabinet.

Steps to Mastering Your Craft

Like I've already mentioned, there is no silver bullet to becoming a sales superstar. I can't say enough about the value of hard work, patience and dedication. While those are often qualities that are difficult to quantify, below are some tips on how to go about mastering the craft of selling.

Learn Who Your Buyer Is:

This should always be your number one priority. You need a deep understanding of who your buyer is as well as who your buyer's customers are. The more you know, the easier it becomes to strike up a conversation and tie your learnings to the value you provide. It's often helpful to position how you understand their pain points in terms of how you've worked with similar clients. If you can demonstrate how you have successfully addressed the challenges they are experiencing, the more likely they are to listen to you. And all of this starts with understanding who your buyer is on a deep level.

Seek Out Support:

One of the best ways to hone your craft is to learn from your peers and to seek out helpful resources. Find out what top salespeople do (not the ones that talk and complain), but the people that are busy selling and closing deals. I also recommend joining groups like the American Association of Inside Sales Professionals (AA-ISP), where you can network and learn from people outside your company. Exposure like that is invaluable. Lastly, don't overlook the knowledge you can gain from a good book or podcast. Even as a sales veteran, I still love reading books and find time to read every week.

Set Goals:

I am a huge proponent of writing down goals. I write them down once a year and then each week, I set smaller goals to help build to my larger objective. While you may have a picture in mind of where you want to be in 10 years, goals can help crystalize that picture and make it achievable. It's also important to share your goals with members of your team who can hold you accountable. You should also ask your team members for their goals and what motivates them. After all, your team's success is your success.

Just like any craftsman or artist, being a successful salesperson takes time. If you are willing to put in the effort and invest in your craft, you too will go from building simple boxes to making immaculate works of art.

Want to learn more from Lori Richardson? Follow her on:
Website: scoremoresales.com
LinkedIn: linkedin.com/in/scoremoresales
Twitter: @scoremoresales
Facebook: facebook.com/ScoreMoreSales

#71 Crushing It With Confidence

HEATHER MONAHAN

"Fear is a liar. It's not real. It's what you create in your own mind."

ABOUT HEATHER MONAHAN:

Heather Monahan is the Founder of Boss In Heels and the author of *Confidence Creator*, the #1 business motivation and self-improvement book on Amazon. Prior to launching her own business, Heather was the Chief Revenue Officer of Beasley Media Group where she was recognized as one of the Most Influential Women in radio in 2017 before her unexpected termination.

Heather is a keynote speaker and has been featured in *Forbes*, *USA Today*, CNN, and many more. She has also been a guest on the Elvis Duran Show, Dr. Drew Podcast, and several others. Read on and discover why Heather is literally a boss in heels!

Growing up, my family did not have a lot. My mother was a single mom raising four kids. She worked three jobs to make ends meet. Everything was a struggle. At a fairly young age, I started working because I knew if I could create income, I wouldn't have to struggle as much. I started with a paper route then moved into babysitting. Eventually, I started working at a fast-food restaurant, then I got into waitressing and eventually bartending. Bartending and waitressing were the ultimate sales gigs for me. I learned if you wanted a big tip, people needed to like you—they needed to see that you were hustling, attending to their needs. So, that was really my first foray into sales—unofficially anyway.

As a bartender working through college, I remember asking one of my regulars, "How do you make so much money?" It always seemed that the hotshots driving the BMWs and Mercedes worked in sales, so that is what I decided I should do as well. Back then I was so driven by a paycheck. Money was my ultimate motivator because I had struggled so much growing up. Looking back, I wish I would have pursued my dreams and what was inside my heart. That was a lesson I didn't learn until much later in life, though. As it were, I opted to pursue the big paycheck and after graduating from college, I went to work for Gallo Winery as a salesperson.

Hustle Fuels Success

At the time, I think only one percent of Gallo's employees were female so it was a very challenging work environment. I was told by other women not to wear my hair down, not to wear skirts, and that I was sending a negative message simply being myself. To try and "fit in," I had to look and act differently than who I really was. It ended up taking a major toll on me.

Despite all of this negativity, I was so driven to succeed that I outworked everyone—seven days a week, at home, at night, and on the weekends, I hustled. I worked so hard that I became the top salesperson within a couple of months. I later became the youngest brand manager for the entire state.

While my career was really taking off, the toxic work environment became too much to bear. I was sexually harassed by my male counterparts and I quit despite all my success. At the time, I didn't have the confidence to stand up for myself so I ran away. Looking back, I wish I would have stayed and fought. Nonetheless, that turn of events led me to my next career move.

Rolling With the Punches

After Gallo, I happened to meet the owner of a radio station at an event. We hit it off right away and he quickly offered me a position with his company. I found radio sales very similar to selling wine so I was killing it in no time. To me, selling is all about the basics so more than anything, I just focused on great customer service. Within my first year, I became the #1 seller.

While my professional career was going great, personally I was a disaster. My longtime boyfriend had cheated on me and I was really down on myself. The owner of the radio station noticed that something was off with me so I confided in him. Seeing that I needed a change, he offered me the opportunity to run a new business venture for him if I got on his plane, no questions asked.

So I closed my eyes, got on the plane, and moved to Saginaw, Michigan to run this new business venture. As a city person, I never imagined living in the rural Midwest so it was quite an adjustment. My boss had bought a property of five radio stations and I was walking in as the new boss to run the day-to-day operations. As a young, female running her first operation, I had to earn respect, which was a challenge. With big expectations, I didn't have time to wait to earn respect. Instead, I just started doing what I knew how to do—selling. I began bringing in bigger deals than anyone there had ever seen and slowly I started to earn respect.

Weeding out the Villains

One of the biggest lessons I learned in Saginaw was the importance of eliminating negativity. I needed to get rid of the "villains." There is nothing more important in anyone's life than firing the villains that are holding you back and that it was I did. In order to succeed, I needed to innovate and I couldn't keep the people that had become too complacent in their roles and adverse to change.

As I progressively started to weed out the villains, we experienced more and more success. Within three years, we took a $25 million property and sold it for $57 million. After the sale, I was ready to move back to a city and soon embarked on a new journey with Beasley Media Group.

I spent nearly 15 years with Beasley and experienced great success, applying many of the things I learned in Saginaw. My time at Beasley came to an abrupt end, however, when I was terminated after a leadership change. While I was absolutely devastated, in many ways getting fired helped me find my true passion and has gotten me to where I am today. For that, I have no regrets.

Nothing Beats Confidence

Through my roller-coaster career, if I can offer one secret for true success, it would be that you need to create your own confidence. When you are your most confident self, there is nothing that will stop you.

Everyone has different challenges. Some people don't invest in themselves. Others don't celebrate their progress. Confidence is very personal so creating confidence starts first with self-reflection.

Why Is Creating Confidence Important?

Without confidence, you will never reach your full potential. You won't be able to ask for that next job. You won't go on that sales call because you're petrified someone might say no. You won't bring that amazing idea to life because you're afraid others might hate it. Creating confidence means that even though things might not go your way, you're still going to be OK. Confidence is being able to say, "What is the worst that can happen?" and being OK with the outcome regardless of how it turns out.

STEPS TO CREATING CONFIDENCE

Start With Journaling:

When it comes to confidence, everyone's baseline will be different so journaling is a good way to assess where you're at. By documenting your thoughts, you'll begin to shed light on areas you should focus on. Maybe you need to start owning your failures. Or maybe you need to identify the negative villains in your life. Whatever you're struggling with, keeping a journal can be a valuable way to help you grow and develop.

Surround Yourself With Confident People:

It's often best to learn by example. As such, try to surround yourself with people further along in their confidence journey than you. They can help be your cheerleader and show you ways you can get ahead.

Try New Things:

Trying new and different things will allow you to create confidence because you'll see, "Wow, I didn't die. I'm still alive. I'm still here. I can take on new things and new approaches and I'm going to make it." Trying new things is about getting out of your comfort zone and seeing that you can in fact survive.

In reality, there are endless ways to create confidence. Making a commitment to change is the first step. Even if you have absolutely no confidence in yourself, just remember, there is nowhere to go but up and we all have to start somewhere.

Want to learn more from Heather Monahan? Follow her on:
Website: Heathermonahan.com
LinkedIn: linkedin.com/in/theheathermonahan/
Twitter: @heathermonahan
Facebook: facebook.com/heathermonahanofficial

#72 From Home EC Teacher to Sales Expert: How a Passion for Learning Proved to be a Recipe for Sales Success

JILL KONRATH

"When I first started out, I knew nothing about sales so I became a sponge—absorbing everything I could from those around me."

ABOUT JILL KONRATH:

Jill Konrath is a B2B sales expert, an award-winning author, and a critically acclaimed keynote speaker.

As a world-renowned sales thought leader, Jill is the author of three best-selling books—*SNAP Selling*, *Selling to Big Companies* and *Agile Selling*. Her newsletters are read by 125,000+ sales leaders across the globe and her blog has been syndicated on numerous business and sales websites. With an immense LinkedIn following, Jill's work is highly regarded by peers and industry leaders alike, making her one of the world's most elite sales professionals. InsideView has recognized her as one of the "25 Most Influential Leaders in Sales" on multiple occasions. In addition, the Sales Lead Management Association named Jill to their list of the "50 Most Influential People in Sales Lead Management" in 2009, 2010, 2011 and 2012.

Jill got her start at Xerox Corporation where she was frequently recognized for her superior performance. While there, she created an assortment of sales tools, coached dozens of trainees and worked on a variety of product launches—all in addition to her sales job!

Through these experiences at Xerox, Jill decided to start her own business in 1987, a company called Leapfrog Strategies, Inc. Things were going great until 2000 when Leapfrog's two biggest clients came under fire from outside pressures, forcing them to halt all consulting contracts. Understanding that the market had shifted, Jill knew she needed to find a way to reinvent her business to stay relevant. And that is exactly what she did.

Today, Jill is internationally recognized for her fresh sales strategies and game-changing approaches that are helping sales professionals and businesses surpass their goals and objectives.

While everyone has their own story about how they got into sales, mine is perhaps one of the most unlikely ones. I first began my career as a home ec teacher. Despite my deep love for education, I absolutely hated what I was doing. Sure, home ec helps prepare students for some of life's most essential requirements, but was this really what I wanted to do with my life? Simply put, no.

Ready to make a change, I took a sick day to attend a job fair. As I visited booth after booth and was told I didn't have the skills they were looking for, I hung my head in moral defeat. As I was leaving, I had a fortuitous encounter with the organizer of the job fair who stopped me and asked how things had gone. I told him I had not had much luck. He quickly asked me to follow him and led me directly to the Xerox booth. I may never fully understand what he saw in me that day but as he introduced me to the Xerox representatives, he boldly stated, "You have to hire this person. She'll be great at sales." Three weeks later, I started working as a sales trainee for Xerox. And so began my sales career and my quest to prove that I could indeed be great at sales.

Jill's Rules for Sales Success

When I first started at Xerox, I made a commitment to myself to learn everything I could about sales in one year. I wanted to immerse myself in all things sales in order to become successful as soon as possible. Now 30+ years into my career, I've found that the guiding principles I used to hone my craft in that first year are still applicable to me today.

Rule #1—Stay Curious: No matter where you are in your career, it's important to always stay curious. Curiosity helps keep us motivated. If we're constantly asking new questions and looking at challenges as opportunities, we'll be able to maintain that drive and hunger that first ignited our desire for success.

Rule #2—Stay Humble: Humbleness, while not often thought of as a defining characteristic for a salesperson, is an extremely important quality to have. When I first started in sales, I knew I had no idea what I was doing so I constantly sought feedback from others and looked for ways to improve. Even if you've experienced widespread success, there's nothing wrong with admitting that someone else may have a better way of approaching a situation. Don't be afraid to ask for advice and seek opportunities to get input from others that have found success.

Rule #3—Put in the Time: Perfecting any skill or craft always requires one essential element: hard work. Because of my background, I've always had a passion for learning. Learning is not a passive activity and requires time and energy. If you're going to excel in sales, you must be willing to put in the time and effort.

The Power of Learning

While curiosity, staying humble, and effort are all essential qualities for a sales leader, the biggest sales secret I can offer is to ***always be learning***. I've been in sales for many years and I'm still learning. Every mistake and failure I've ever made have all been tremendous learning experiences in addition to my many triumphs. I once received a verbal beatdown from an executive assistant who didn't take too kindly to me going above her head to meet with her boss—the exchange was so volatile that I literally passed out in an office lobby. But guess what? It made for a great learning experience!

What does it mean to always be learning? While learning is inherent in nearly all things we do, to be a good learner, you need to have the right mindset. My desire to learn stems from my innate curiosity and drive to succeed. There have been several points in my career where things weren't going as I had hoped but my passion for learning ultimately helped me to find the right path forward. When I lost my two biggest clients at Leapfrog Strategies and had to reinvent my business, I kept telling myself, "You just haven't figured it out... *yet*." Instead of throwing in the towel and accepting defeat, I committed to building on what I already knew and learning how to apply my skills to my new reality. That mindset helped get me to where I am today.

HOW TO APPLY LEARNING TO YOUR SALES STRATEGY

Put Your Client First: When it comes to learning, make your client or prospect your priority. Learn everything you can about them. Obsess over their customer personas. Gain a deep understanding of their business objectives. Immerse yourself in their day-to- day needs. The more you educate yourself about your clients and prospects, the greater value you will be able to deliver.

Don't Get Complacent: Like all things in life, we have a tendency to get too comfortable in our routines, which often deters us from learning new things. Even if things are going well, I try to challenge myself and ask, "What can I do to make this even better?" The excitement of trying something new helps us to stay motivated. And motivation is hugely important for anyone in sales.

Be a Sponge: I love learning from those around me. To me, there's no better way to become an expert on a topic than to learn from the best. While you'll need to apply your own style to someone else's technique, I often find myself reverse engineering what others have done and piecing together the most applicable aspects to my own work. Try to approach all situations as learning opportunities—you may be surprised by the ideas you're able to generate.

While there are many ways to be successful in sales, I personally believe that an active desire and appetite for learning is a major key to success. Just as important as it is to always be closing, so too is it essential to always be learning!

Want to learn more from Jill Konrath? Follow her on:
Website: jillkonrath.com
LinkedIn: linkedin.com/in/jillkonrath/
Twitter: @jillkonrath
YouTube: youtube.com/user/jillkonrath

#73 It's All About the Process

MARYLOU TYLER

"Take the knowledge that you have and be very good about sharing it with others.
The more you help other people, the more confident you will be."

ABOUT MARYLOU TYLER:

Marylou Tyler is the founder of Strategic Pipeline, a Fortune 1000 sales process improvement consulting group. Her company has helped drive results for esteemed companies like Apple, Bose, AMA, Talend, CIBC, Gartner, Prudential, UPS, Logitech, Orkin, AAA, and Mastercard. She is also the author of best-selling books, *Predictable Revenue,* and *Predictable Prospecting.* Both books have sold over 60,000 copies worldwide.

Marylou specializes in optimizing top-of-funnel sales processes. Through her 7-point outreach process that is part behavioral, part predictive and part creative, Marylou helps clients implement predictable sales models to achieve maximum results.

Marylou is recognized as a strategic thought leader and innovator by audiences across the globe.

While this may or may not be a surprise, I am a computer scientist by trade. I earned my degree in computer engineering from the University of California (UC), Santa Barbara in 1981. I actually had plans to be a flight simulation coder but life took me in a different direction. Looking back now, I couldn't be happier with how things turned out.

My indirect journey into sales began soon after I graduated from UC. After getting married, my husband and I moved to El Segundo, CA where I started working at Xerox Corporation in their data center. It was in the 1980s and I worked in the data center doing operating system design. I eventually became very involved in the project management side of things, interfacing with clients and using their input to develop new design specifications. No one else on the team liked talking with our end-users so I became the default interface to take our users' ideas and bring them to life. I did this type of work for several years and eventually went into sales support. I became the technical support person for our sales reps and found that I truly loved that side of the business. With a solid start at Xerox, I went on to hold several different positions with a variety of startups and eventually branched out on my own.

While sales and computer science may seem like they are worlds apart, one common thread unites them: they are both all about following a process. As I became more sales-focused in my various roles, I continued to draw on my computer science roots, implementing processes that leveraged data to make informed decisions. This is something I continue to do to this day, and I believe, has allowed me to achieve great things.

HOW CREATING GOOD HABITS LEADS TO RESULTS

While it is difficult to boil down everything I've learned throughout my career into one sales secret, my ultimate sales secret is this: focus on habit.

To be successful, you need to engrain your process into your daily life—and your daily routine is predicated on having good habits.

THE 5 LEVELS OF HABIT DEVELOPMENT:

Desire

All habits start with desire. What is it that you want to achieve? To develop a habit, you must first start with desire. Without a passion or desire, you will have nothing driving you to change.

Repetition

The next step is to focus on the repeatable actions you should take that will get you closer to your goal. It's important to note that repetition can mean different things for different people. It could be repeating the same thing every day or maybe it is repeating the same action three times a week. Whatever your goal of repetition is, stick to it.

Discipline

From repetition, you move to discipline. How disciplined are you to do those things that are relevant and necessary in a repeatable fashion to get to your goal? If you become disciplined enough to not break the chain, you're ready for the next level.

Routine

Once you go past discipline, now you're in a routine. What are you doing routinely to build that hundred million dollar company? What are you doing routinely to get in the door of companies by prospecting?

Habit

And then finally, you hit habit. If you spend the time to work through these levels, you're going to reach your goal because you've made it a part of who you are. But you can't skip a level and expect to reach your objective. You must work through all five.

Habit Stacking

To help work through these levels, I recommend you do something called habit stacking. With habit stacking, you take a simple goal that you're trying to accomplish and progressively work up to achieve it over time. My goal was that by the time I turned 60, I wanted to do 15 pushups without killing myself. So, I had to start with one pushup. Every morning while my coffee was brewing, I did one pushup. Eventually, that stack went from one pushup to two pushups, to five pushups...all the way up to 10 pushups. Now, I can routinely do between 12 and 20 pushups without a problem.

Habit stacking is really all about alignment and taking something you already do every day and adding another step to that existing habit. It is also about consistency of effort and maximizing the return on your effort. So in my example, brewing my coffee and doing one pushup became synonymous with one another. If I was going to have a cup of coffee, I was also going to do a pushup. Tiny habits like these, when linked to the habits that you're already doing every day, will eventually break off and become their own habit. When they do, that is when you add something new to the mix. The idea is to constantly be stacking new habits on top of one another. As you stack more and more habits, they will build on one another and progressively enable you to reach your ultimate goal. The added benefit of developing habits in this manner is that as something becomes a habit, it becomes second nature and probably something you enjoy doing. But to get there, you have to go through all five levels of development.

Because of my technical background, I approach all aspects of sales as a process. Developing habits to improve your sales outcomes should be no different. If you develop and follow a sound process, the results are sure to follow.

Want to learn more from Marylou Tyler? Follow her on:
Website: maryloutyler.com
LinkedIn: linkedin.com/in/maryloutyler

#74 Failure Is Inevitable, How You Respond Is What Counts

SEAN SHEPPARD

"Be a learn-it-all, not a know-it-all."

ABOUT SEAN SHEPPARD:

Sean Sheppard is a serial entrepreneur and the founder of GrowthX and GrowthX Academy. He is also a *Huffington Post* contributor, mentor and guest lecturer. Sean has been named a "Top 20 Sales Influencer" and has successfully grown dozens of early- stage companies across a wide variety of products and markets.

At GrowthX, Sean leads market development strategy for the company's portfolio of companies. At GrowthX Academy, he shares his expertise in monitoring and adjusting revenue pipelines to help startups maximize their success.

Before founding GrowthX, Sean built and ran the sales and business development track at Tradecraft. He also co-founded the Professional Sales College to change the way the world values the sales profession through graduating the best-educated and trained sales professionals in the world.

Sean came from humble beginnings. His father was in the military during the Vietnam War and he was born while his parents were stationed in Naples, Italy. He moved all over the world during his formative years which he credits for his ability to quickly adapt to any environment.

Colleagues say that Sean is the purest example of both an entrepreneur and a leader. He is known as someone with deep experience and valuable insights across multiple industries. He is said to bring a rare charisma and positivity to any room. He is on a mission to create a better future, empower others, and help everyone grow in order to serve others to the best of their abilities.

Did you know that when you're learning to walk, you fall an average of 17 times per hour? Can you imagine trying something as an adult and failing at that rate? You'd probably want to give up. But have you ever heard of a kid that just says, "Fuck this walking business, I'm just gonna crawl the rest of my life?" No.

Every person walking learned how to go from being completely stationary to crawling to walking. I am a parent and I've watched my kids go through this. In fact, I've watched my son lose his two front teeth by tripping and smashing them into the tile of the kitchen but it didn't deter him. He got up with blood coming out of his mouth and kept trying.

This determination, perseverance, and focus is what it takes to be successful in sales and entrepreneurship.

Success Requires a Growth Mindset

My top sales secret comes down to your mindset. Period. End of story.

Everything is about understanding how your brain is wired and how that drives your emotions. It's your responsibility to manage your brain for peak and optimal performance so you can get whatever the hell it is you want—whether that be a job, a successful business, or a sale. I believe orienting your mind toward growth is key.

Why? Success is about understanding the formula of how things work and how to do them well. We are not born with the knowledge, wisdom, and ability to be masters of everything. We have to learn and practice. Just like walking, any new skill requires trying, failing, iterating, and trying again. We learn as we go.

It is how we respond to failure, resistance, friction, objections, concerns, and pushback that will determine our level of success. A growth mindset allows us to welcome setbacks as opportunities to learn, grow, and improve.

Fixed Vs. Growth Mindset

We go from a period in life where nothing stands in the way of our attempts to get what we want, to one where we are often more fixed in our ways. The fixed mindset was coined by Dr. Carol Dweck at Stanford, an Early Childhood Development Psychologist who wanted to understand when and where humans change how they respond to failure.

As we go through school and engage with society, we start to be conditioned by our environment, surroundings, and parents saying, "No don't touch that" and "No don't do this." By the time we're 17 years-old, we've heard "no" something like 250,000 times and "yes" something like 25,000 times. While it is usually coming from a well-intended place, we learn to worry about external opinions and don't want to make mistakes. We feel shame if we fail and don't want to face it. We ignore it or cover it up and, as a result, we don't learn. This fixed mindset is pervasive and ubiquitous. For every person with a growth mindset, there's probably five or 10 with a fixed mindset.

So a growth mindset and the ability to learn and adapt is everything. It allows you to acknowledge your failures and mistakes, understand why they happened, and make changes so you are better next time.

HOW DO YOU ADOPT A GROWTH MINDSET?

What if you have tendencies towards a fixed mindset? Here are five ways to reorient yourself for growth.

Embrace Failure

It's fine to be wrong and it's okay to be rejected. Not only is it fine, but it's also good. Tell yourself that one hundred times over. Embracing mistakes, rejection, and feedback are key parts to a growth mindset. Replace the word 'rejection' in your vocabulary with the word 'feedback.'

When you receive criticism, be grateful as it is an opportunity to learn and grow. If you have a manager, coach, or mentor, look forward to what you will learn because it will help you become better. When a customer says no, it doesn't mean no forever and gives you an opportunity to learn why it's not the right time and when it might be. Failure should not be shunned, it is part of the process!

Put in the Work

The truth is you can master anything even if you're not born with natural talent in that area. However, there are no shortcuts. There are faster paths, but no shortcuts. Here are the steps to mastery:

- Once you introduce a concept, you can gain competency which means you can do it on a basic level.

- Next, you can gain proficiency which means you can do it well.
- And then, ultimately, with the right amount of deliberate intent and practice (Malcolm Gladwell's 10 years and 10,000 hours), you can achieve mastery in any given area.

One of the main reasons I started the sales college and then the Academy is my belief that you don't have to be born with the gift of gab to be a great sales professional. However, you do need to invest the time and effort to get better.

Pivot When Needed

Next, the hardest thing for people to do is change. Whatever direction you're trending in, it's really easy to stay in that direction. If you're trending downward, it's really easy to stay down and it's hard to turn that around. If you're trending upward in a significant way, it's also hard to turn that around. There's a reason you see people as they get above that curve, stay above that curve and see large cycles of success.

But when you reach a point where you are trending down or remaining stagnant, don't be afraid or hesitant to change. Look at your market, position, approach, etc. and identify what you can do to turn the tide. A fixed mindset thinks things like, "This has worked fine in the past, and will be fine again" or "There is no other way but this way." However, those beliefs are not true and are rooted in fear. Be open to change and new approaches.

Think for Yourself

I like to say I love them BAs, PhDs, and straight-A students because they make great employees. I say that because they often do exactly what you tell them to. But when they start to think for themselves, do creativity and critical thought come into play? And when and where do they add value by delivering insights that business owners don't have? To set yourself apart, you have to think for yourself about what really matters to the business.

When I started in my sales job at Insight, they assigned me the classic 120 dials and four hours of talk time per day. I ignored those rules and focused on trying to target businesses that I thought had tremendous technological, transformational kinds of needs. I focused my time reading quarterly reports and 10ks, listening to interviews from CEOs, and reading publications about the leadership and what they cared about.

I used that research as a basis for trying to understand who my prospects were, what they cared at that moment, and how to talk to them in a way that would generate an honest response. Within a year and a half, I was the top rep in the entire business, selling to the global 2000. I left to join a start-up as their first sales hire that had just raised $8.5 million called Opnix.

You need to think for yourself to gain unique insights and contribute to substantial growth.

You can't be in the top 1% if you are thinking or behaving like the other 99%.

Follow a Framework for Growth

Lastly, for your growth mindset to be most effective, you need to be functioning within a tried-and-tested framework for growth. Below is the framework we follow at GrowthX.

Milestone 1: Market Discovery

The first step is discovering who your customer is right now and where they are. Answer:

- Who is your customer?
- Where are they?

- How do you find them?
- Do you have the resources to be successful?
- Is your market size big enough to hit your objectives?

Milestone 2: Market Messaging and Outreach

The second step is figuring out how to talk to your customers in a way that gets to the truth.

Your job as a sales professional is to place yourself in their shoes, to understand their role, and to learn how they're measured in that role. You need to find out what they care about and how to help them be more successful at whatever it is that they want to do. If you can do that, you can separate yourself very easily from the pack.

Milestone 3: Market Results

Lastly, continuously learn from your conversations and interactions to build a better and more complete solution.

A growth mindset is key to success in sales, startups, relationships, and life in general. Remember, personal development and professional development are inseparable in a human-centric role like sales. These five steps can help you adjust from a tendency toward a fixed mindset to one toward growth. As a result, you can set yourself on the upward path toward success.

Want to learn more from Sean Sheppard? Follow him on:
LinkedIn: linkedin.com/in/seansheppard
Website: growthx.com
GrowthX Academy: gxacademy.com

#75 Think 1,000X Bigger

KELLY ROACH

With hard work, determination, and a willingness to be consistent, every 'no' in sales can be turned into a 'yes'.

ABOUT KELLY ROACH:

Kelly Roach is a sought-after motivational speaker and sales trainer, the host of the wildly popular Unstoppable podcast (top 100 on iTunes), a phenomenal business growth expert, and the international best-selling author of *Unstoppable: 9 Principles For Unlimited Success In Business and Life.*

She has a unique story, starting as an NFL cheerleader for the Philadelphia Eagles while earning her BA from the University of Pennsylvania and working her way up to a seven- figure entrepreneur. She now provides training, coaching, and consulting to business owners and leaders looking to improve team performance, develop leadership strengths, and increase the growth and revenue of their organizations.

Kelly has been building her brand, Kelly Roach International, over the past 7+ years. Before starting her own business, Kelly was a Fortune 500 executive who built and led record-breaking teams across the US.

Clients of Kelly's say she provides valuable information and specialized training that every business in America needs to remain competitive.

Her positive insight, gracious but forceful demeanor and commanding attitude are said to be a beacon of strength for business owners looking to push their games to the next profitable level.

I came from a family with five kids. We didn't have a lot of extra income floating around so I couldn't afford to do many of the things that I wanted to do growing up. But I was the kind of kid that wasn't going to take no for an answer.

When I was 10, I wanted to get into this gym that had produced an Olympic-level gymnast so I went to the owner and said, "My parents can't afford it but I can babysit and I can come up with half the money to take classes here. Would you meet me in the middle?" Without hesitation, he said, "Yes, let's do it."

It all started from that mentality of if you can't afford it, then go out and create it. Don't just accept your current circumstances as your future ones. With hard work, determination, and a willingness to be consistent, every 'no' in sales can be turned into a 'yes'

1,000X YOUR GOALS

Now my top sales secret to all those out there trying to up their games is that you need to think 1,000 times bigger than you think is the biggest of the big. Sit down and make a dream board for your sales goals, your life dreams and correlate how your sales can create all your dreams.

Then, go out and talk to 1,000 more people than you think you need to. Do that and all of those goals, all of those dreams, will all take care of themselves. You can operate at the top of the universe, in a place where very few people are even competing with you because most don't have the nerve to think that big.

HOW TO 1,000X YOUR GOALS

How can you achieve your 1,000X goals? Here are five of my top tips:

Become the Person Capable of the Goal

First of all, think joyfully about your goals and commit to becoming the person that's capable of them. If you aren't working to become that person, you're never going to get the life that goes with it. Look at the people who are where you want to be and figure out what it will take to get there.

Remember, people meet you where you show up in life. If I show up and I have a certain level of standards and respect for myself, you're going to, in turn, be like, "Oh wow, okay. I'm going to treat you a certain way." You are going to meet me at that level because it's almost uncomfortable not to.

There's a level of professionalism you can set in every relationship where there's a standard. And it's not just about how you dress but it's the concept of being the best that you can be in everything that you do—because how you do something is how you do everything.

That's number one.

Hire Mentors

Number two, go out and find the people that did what you want to do and pay to get their help. That's been such a huge learning for me. I always have three different coaches who I'm working with on all different things.

Sometimes when you are in the midst of a situation, you can't see obstacles that will be so clear to someone who has been through it. You can cut down on months and even years of your learning curve by choosing the right mentors.

It's silly to go out and think that you have to reach your goal without following any type of blueprint for success. Every successful person is getting help from someone else that came before them.

Find the 20% that Drives the 80%

Third, we all know that the 80/20 principle lives in our lives. We can accept it or not accept it. We can think about it or not, but the truth is 80% of our results come from 20% of our actions.

Optimize your goal attainment by understanding that 20% of your actions are driving 80% of your results and then focus more of your time on the actions driving results. Ask, "How do I take this thing that's working and spend 20 hours per week on it, instead of five?"

Don't Fall Into the Mastery Misconception

Most people dabble in dozens of different things and then look around saying, "Well, I'm working so hard. Why am I not getting any results?" But they're not doing enough of anything to get real results. And many times, people prematurely make strategy changes or shifts when they are already doing the right thing to get the results that they want.

You need time executing excellently to get results. Consider that it takes 10,000 hours to master something. So when someone calls me and says they've been working so hard and it's not working, I say, "Let's peel that back a little bit.

- How many times have you done it?
- How long have you been doing it?
- How many hours have you put into it?

When you look at our frame of reference, what we think of as hard work today is distorted. A lot of times, on a scale of one to 10, we're at a zero.

You need to be honest with yourself and find out if you are actually investing the amount of time and energy in the right places to get the results that you want. If you are, be patient and keep at it. Many things are like a plant that grows underground and develops a whole amazing root system that you can't see and then all of a sudden it bursts through the seams into a beautiful plant.

Plan Your Legacy

Lastly, there are two kinds of people. The people that have spurts of excitement, optimism, and energy that fizzle out, and the people that are committed to creating a lifetime of success. The secret to consistency is playing the long game. You need to identify what you are doing in life and what legacy you want to leave behind. Once you have that, you're not running on emotional fumes or excitement, you're running on your calling. Your responsibility. Your purpose for being on the planet. And you're thinking about things in the span of where you are today versus where you want to be five,10,15, 20, 50 years from now. That's a completely different mentality and mindset.

So think bigger—1,000 times bigger. Then achieve your goals by focusing on the person you need to be and listening to mentors who have walked the path you are pursuing. Analyze yourself and your habits to identify where you are most productive and profitable and optimize how you spend your time. Understand that mastery takes patience, discipline, frequency, consistency, and 10,000 hours (at least!). And, lastly, think about what you want for your entire life and the impact you want to live and reverse engineer it. Then, you can discover an internal motivation that is unstoppable.

Want to learn more from Kelly Roach? Follow her on:
Facebook Group: www.facebook.com/
kellyroachinternational
Website: kellyroachcoaching.com
LinkedIn: hlinkedin.com/in/kellyroachint

#76 Giving a Shit Has the Highest ROI

JUSTIN WELSH

"Something was instilled in my soul and ever since I've run 100 miles an hour at everything that I want to be successful at."

ABOUT JUSTIN WELSH:

Justin Welsh is an SMB SaaS advisor, executive mentor, and former operator with more than 10 years of revenue leadership experience. He was formerly the SVP of Sales at PatientPop where he led the company from $0 to $60M in recurring revenue in just four years.

Throughout his career, Justin has held a variety of roles with companies such as PublicStuff and ZocDoc. While at ZocDoc, Justin was a 4-time President's Club winner. Through his unique experiences, Justin became a specialist in SMB SaaS sales and now focuses his efforts on helping companies develop their go-to-market strategies.

You can find Justin at some of the best SaaS events in the country. He was selected as an opening day speaker at SaaStr Annual as well as the speaker at the Global Ventures Summit. He is also a member of The Revenue Collective.

Colleagues and direct reports describe Justin as a motivating and charismatic leader who is hyper-focused on reaching goals. He is known as a person of uncompromising integrity, and someone who you want on your team when facing a problem or challenge.

My first job, fresh out of college, was as a sales rep for a large pharmaceutical company. I worked there for three years and, to be honest, never had an attachment to the product I was selling or the company itself.

If I sold a few extra thousand, or even $100,000, over my quota, it was only worth a few extra pennies in my pocket. What I started to recognize was that if I was going to invest a significant amount of my time, I needed to see a significant benefit. If I didn't, I wouldn't really care or have the drive to be successful.

You've Got to Give a Shit

It wasn't until five years into my career when I started at ZocDoc that I felt a passion and energy connected to both a brand and a product. Unlike my previous roles where I wasn't 100% ambitious or connected, something changed. A switch flipped in my mind. Suddenly, I was in the field at 8:00 AM. I was busting my butt until 7:00 PM. I was running around like crazy, slamming bagel sandwiches in my mouth, not taking a lunch break.

I made my mark there by going 104 consecutive weeks without missing my quota. I moved up by building small local teams from coast-to-coast and then eventually building larger regional teams. My last stop was reporting directly to the CEO at that time, Cyrus Massoumi, while building an ancillary product for Fortune 500 companies.

What drove my success? Why did I feel the connection, passion, and energy? Why did I start to give a shit? It came from the CEO at the time, Cyrus, and grew exponentially through the VP, directors, managers, and individual contributors. I say this in the most complimentary fashion—everybody was obsessed with being successful. I loved that environment and had never been in one like it before.

The experience caused a shift in my 24-year-old self. I was re-oriented to run 100 miles per hour toward success and became obsessed with being successful.

HOW CAN YOU START GIVING A SHIT TODAY TO MAXIMIZE ROI?

No matter where you are currently, you can start to truly give a shit and maximize your ROI. Here are some of the tips I recommend.

Find the Right Work Environment For You

Don't take the first job you're offered just because it is a job. Don't go somewhere just because your buddy is there. And don't go somewhere just to get a specific logo on your resume. Why? Because the amount of passion with which you sell something, the attachment that you have to your success, and how it benefits both you and the business, really, really matters.

To truly give a shit, you need to be incredibly passionate about the company that you join and the people you work with. If you read the mission and values and they don't speak to you, bring you joy, and excite you, don't work there. If it's a business worth being at, the people that work there are going to be insanely connected to the success of that business. You have to feel the same way or it's not going to click for you the way that it clicks for the rest of the team which isn't good for anyone.

At ZocDoc, we all knew we were changing the world. We were absolutely changing the way that people accessed healthcare. We were in the mission together, giving our best, which created trust and a strong bond.

You need to find a company that you're pumped about with a leader and team that is exciting, passionate, and obsessed with success.

Identify and Focus on the Long-Term Vision

Once you find a good work-home where you can thrive, you need to identify your long- term goal. Ask, what does this job look like in five years? What do I look like in the overall puzzle of the company? How do I move my career forward? What do I want to accomplish? How do I get there? Then, work backward to create a plan to reach your goal. Don't be afraid to get granular with 30, 45, 60, or more steps.

Even when you are passionate about what you are doing, there will be days when you face challenges. A long-term vision shifts the framing from, "Yeah, I'm on a train and this sucks," to "I'm on a train because three years from now, I'm going to be running a massive sales team at this business," or "I'm on a train right now because 10 years from now, I'm going to be the CEO of my own business."

A long-term vision will keep you motivated and tuned-in even when the going gets tough. Every planned step is working toward a bigger purpose that benefits you directly, and you will develop the habit of making progress, crossing off the steps, and being successful.

Be Relentless in Your Pursuit of Success

When I was learning the Zoc Doc business, there wasn't much in the way of resources or collateral. I was determined to figure out a path to success, even if I had to build it. Keep your mindset focused on solutions.

Outwork your peers, outwork your competitors, and invest in yourself. How? Spend time reading, learning, doing, and ingesting information. This is especially important early in your career. If you're not investing in yourself as a young salesperson, it gets much more difficult to do when you're 15 years into your career.

Stay in Tune With your Passion and Follow It

Lastly, passion and energy can plateau or dwindle. One day I got up, I was in the shower, and I just didn't feel as amped about working at Zoc Doc anymore. I identified that it was time to reevaluate where I was and if it was time for a change. It just so happened that one of the guys who was a trusted peer to me at ZocDoc was leaving and going to another company, PublicStuff, as the VP. He asked me to join him as the director of sales. The company wasn't doing well so our goal was to turn it around and get it acquired. We really ramped up revenue and that business was acquired in 10 months by a government software company called Accela. This led me to my next position as SVP of PatientPop. I encourage you to pay attention to your level of passion and engagement, and if it wanes, look for new opportunities that keep your fire burning.

In summary, my secret to success in sales is finding the right product-team-company fit for you and where you are in each stage of your life. Your work needs to fuel you and align with your beliefs. You need to feel attached to the mission and believe in the company's values. In short, you need to give a shit. When you find this right fit, you can reach your full potential as a sales professional.

Want to learn more from Justin Welsh? Follow him on:
Website: justindwelsh.com
LinkedIn: linkedin.com/in/justinwelsh
Twitter: @JustinSaaS

#77 Creating Personal Advocates

JAMES BAWDEN

"No one cares about your career as much as you, so it's important to take the wheel."

ABOUT JAMES BAWDEN:

James Bawden is a well-respected sales trainer and sales development professional. In 2018, he was voted as one of the "Top Sales Development Reps" by InsideSales.com. James also hosts a popular podcast called "The Lunch Break Podcast," where he interviews sales pros and talks about what they've learned throughout their careers, what they're passionate about, and what sales pros can take away from their respective journeys.

James' work experience began in 2008 after he graduated from a technical college with a digital/audio production degree. Although his sights were originally set on becoming a rapper, it didn't take him long to discover his natural talent and passion for sales.

Beginning in retail at Radioshack and then Verizon Wireless, James focused on developing his skills. This led him to an opportunity in B2B inside sales.

Met with a desire to increase his income, James later pivoted into recruiting with Weatherby Healthcare, a well-known and reputable company. However, after 10 months, he craved to be back in the B2B realm. He soon applied and got a job with Evalueserve where he specialized in business development. His success there didn't go unnoticed as data analytic company Cognetik soon recruited James to build their team.

Colleagues of James say he is a true sales professional who has had a profound impact on the profession. He is said to be a genuine person on and off the pitch and measures his success by enabling others. Further, he's known to always be positive, friendly, thoughtful, and a good influence in the office.

I graduated in June 2008 as the economy was crumbling. I lost my internship and at the same time, my mom passed away. It was a tough time. To make matters worse, my degree was so specific that I couldn't find a job. One day, I was looking through the classifieds for any opportunity and I happened to stumble across a sales/clerk job at Radio Shack in the mall. It kind of aligned with my degree so I applied and got the position.

I always thought sales reps were like conmen with a slick type of personality so I never had any interest in sales. But I realized I was actually naturally gifted when it came to having conversations and making people feel comfortable. I learned that sales is really about conversations and matching needs up with solutions. It was at that point that I decided a career in sales could be the path for me. My girlfriend at the time also got pregnant so the pressure was on to earn a stable income.

Around this time, someone said to me, "If you're into sales move into wireless." It wasn't long after this exchange that I was recruited by someone in the same mall to work for Verizon. That was the first conscious step I took to move my career forward. Now, 10 years and seven companies later, I have built a career in sales—and it has been quite the journey! While I have learned many helpful lessons along the way, there is one that I believe is critical to help salespeople move forward and advance professionally, personally, and financially.

Know Your Audience

My top sales secret that I think everyone who wants to advance their career should know is that you need to know your audience. Now you may think, "Okay, Captain Obvious that is Sales 101." However, I find that many people know to research and understand their audience when prospecting but they don't think about knowing their audience inside their own company.

Every day that you are working with a company, you are selling yourself or failing to do so. You are showing your co-workers, your managers, your VP, your CEO, etc. who you are, your potential, and the value you bring to the team.

Are you showing up early every day or late? Are you on social media throughout your shifts or are you focused on work? Do you bring a positive attitude every day or a negative one? Do you speak to leaders about subjects that matter to them or vent all of your frustrations to anyone who will listen?

I believe you need to constantly present the best version of yourself at all times to the people who can help you get where you need to go. To do this, you need to know and understand who those people are and what they care about.

Knowing Your Internal Audience Can Catapult Your Career

Why is it so important to know and impress your internal audience? When you do so, you gain personal advocates that will help to move you forward in your career. There were several times in my life where I felt stuck—whether it was because I wasn't making enough money, hit the ceiling of my current role, or needed a new challenge.

For example, in my second sales role with Verizon Wireless, I was excelling in sales but didn't see a long-term future in retail. The hours were too crazy and the demand for my attention never stopped—even on my days off. I was offered multiple opportunities to advance into leadership roles but I turned them all down. However, I did want to advance in my career and was passionate about sales. I tried applying for inside sales jobs online but had no luck with only retail experience.

At that time, I had been on a 6-month personal development journey and even started making YouTube videos about sales. It turns out that someone I had worked with previously, who had moved on to B2B, believed in me. He saw my video and shared it with his VP. His VP saw something he liked and recruited me over to inside sales. This opportunity never would have happened if I didn't light the fire under myself in that role. To develop myself and share my learnings. People around me took notice and one advocated for me which led me to a new opportunity.

This occurrence is a recurring theme throughout my career. Over time, I learned to purposefully study and understand those who could help me. Doing this resulted in numerous career opportunities that I never would have stumbled upon otherwise. No one cares about your career as much as you, so it's important to take the wheel.

HOW TO KNOW YOUR INTERNAL AUDIENCE

How can you start to better understand and impress your internal audience today? Like any skill, it comes more naturally to some than others. If the idea hasn't crossed your mind, don't worry, here are the steps to follow to cultivate it.

Know Who Is In Your Internal Audience

First, understand that you and everyone else within a company are being observed at all times. Your actions, your work, your attitude, your mannerisms, etc. are all being analyzed by stakeholders. That can work in your favor or against it. Being so, you need to know your role in your company and the key people with a vested interest in you.

Know What Your Internal Audience Cares About

The next step is to put yourself in the shoes of those people to understand what they want from you. Perform research to learn more about their position. Observe them and their key focus areas over time. Then, learn how to serve up what they want.

It is similar to when you are in school and you figure out what the teacher wants. Don't waste your time with a whole bunch of tasks or topics that they don't care about. They will appreciate your awareness and respect for their time. Plus, you can be more of an asset to the company and its efficient operation.

Know How to Communicate

There are many ways to convey a message. Some people don't give much thought to the options and shoot themselves in the foot. However, by understanding your audience you can speak in a way that doesn't trigger any unneeded concern.

For example, if you are a sales rep and have been feeling nervous because of a new procedure, product, or feature, you can turn to a manager for support. However, you don't want to make yourself look inept. Instead of saying something like, "I haven't made any calls in four days because I just don't get this," you could say, "Can we go through some role-playing to strengthen my confidence in this new initiative?" How you position your needs and yourself matter and will inform how others view you.

So before you ask a question or bring up a topic, take the time to plan how to communicate in a way that positions you as an expert in your field who is looking to improve or learn.

Know When You Need to Communicate

Lastly, there is a time and place for everything. Leadership teams are busy and have a lot on their plates. It's important to understand and respect that. Learn about your audience's schedule and when they are open for communications. Also, take into consideration current events with the business, personal events you may learn about, etc.

By knowing who your internal audience is, what they care about, and how and when to speak to them, you can build a positive reputation for yourself that will support career growth and personal development. This will help you from getting stuck in one position, income bracket, or company. Here's to your success!

Want to learn more from James Bawden? Follow him on:
LinkedIn: linkedin.com/in/james-bawden
Podcast: anchor.fm/james-bawden

#78 The Last One Standing

CARSON HEADY

"When you're able to be cognizant that you don't know everything it changes everything."

ABOUT CARSON HEADY:

Carson Heady is a best-selling author, award-winning Microsoft Sales Leader, speaker, management consultant, coach, trainer, and blogger. He's the author of the *Birth of a Salesman* series, which details the art of sales from interviewing and preparation to pitching, closing. and advancing your career.

He's also served in several leadership roles at companies such as Microsoft, AT&T, Verizon, and T-Mobile. He's currently working at Microsoft, overseeing partner relationships and leading enterprise account teams. As a valued expert, he has a strong social media presence with over 330,000 followers.

Carson has received many awards and honors including the 2018 USM&O and SMC Excellence Hero Award. He has also been named in the Fortune 500 Top 5% of all Sales Representatives ranking on several occasions. And, he was part of the Microsoft Gold Club for the 2019 fiscal year.

Those who know Carson say he is a visionary in sales philosophy and leadership with the ability to bring his deep knowledge, acumen, and passion to the table each day. He inspires those around him and isn't afraid to roll up his sleeves and dig in. As a result, he is known for driving lasting success for his customers, partners, and team members.

One of my favorite movies is the movie "Cocktail" from the late '80s with Tom Cruise. There's a line that says, "Never show surprise or lose your cool." In sales, we have to train ourselves to shut the brain off at times and do what we know we need to do. Commit to a course of action and execute.

Every time I get rejected or I'm working on a deal for months and they go with a competitor, it sucks. It can be crushing. But you can do two things. You can lay down and sulk or you can get up, go forward, and treat every day as a new opportunity. I make a conscious decision to maximize everything I do. I get bone-crushing disappointments all the time—it's happened my whole career. But I take the learning from that loss into that next deal and it's how I grow and develop.

Be Humble and Endure Every Situation

On your career path, there are going to be a lot of things that happen which you may or may not agree with, that you can't control, and that are unfair or unjustified. If you become the person that goes off every time you hit a bump in the road, you will cause unneeded diversions on your journey to success. Additionally, it's going to be the mark that follows you for the rest of your career. In many cases, changes or setbacks that happen today, are moot points in six months and sometimes six weeks. Things will continue to change so you need to be grounded in what you are doing and why you are there.

I've had things screw me over in roles and I've had things benefit me that shouldn't have. It's like investing in the stock market. When you invest, do you get skittish and pull your money out immediately anytime the market drops, or do you ride the wave for the long haul through the ups and downs? Statistically, it pays off if you stay the course in the stock market and the same is true in your career.

My top sales secret is if you work within the parameters, stay humble, and endure tough situations, you will be the last one standing and will be able to go wherever you want to go.

HOW TO ENDURE AND STAY HUMBLE?

When the going gets tough how do you endure through it and stay humble?

Uphold Your Part of "The Deal"

I like to say that we as salespeople have deals with our organizations. They agreed to hire the person that you sold in the interview and you agreed to the compensation, benefits, support, training, culture, etc. that they promised. If we stop being the person they hired, we default on the deal. If they stop giving us the support, training, and things they guaranteed, they default.

You have to hold up your original promise, especially when situations get tough. Obviously you applied for the job for a reason, so you may have to go back and remember why that was from time to time. A lot of times we have to transform ourselves back to that person that originally wanted the job and continue to deliver the value we promised.

Stay in Calibration Mode

Next, I am a big fan of constantly being in calibration mode. Look at each day and ask, "Okay, how can I maximize today?" Yesterday might have absolutely sucked but it's gone. Take the learnings and apply them to your process today. If you let yourself sulk, you waste another day and let your competition get a step ahead of you. So start every day anew, look at what you can control, and ask yourself how you can go to market. You can win by quickly learning from your losses.

Be Aware of What You Don't Know

Lastly, how do you stay humble, especially when you've amassed a lot of success?

When I was younger, in my 20s, I was not overly humble. There was this need in me to project this confidence that may or may not have been there. I didn't ever want my team to think that I could bleed or be vulnerable or anything like that. But as you get older, your priorities change and you realize showing vulnerability is actually a strength, not a weakness.

I now work for an organization where I am surrounded by some of the most brilliant people in the world. I walked in and it took me several months to feel like I knew what I was doing. And there are still times where I'm like, "I don't know what I'm doing." But that's the piece. You've got to get to the point where you feel comfortable going to a team member and asking for help because that is what is going to make you better.

When you're able to be cognizant that you don't know everything, it changes everything. I wrote a sales book ten years ago in my 20s and I didn't know anything about sales back then. I kick my former self to think that I knew enough about sales at that point to write a book. Now, I know that I don't know squat about sales but I know a lot more than I knew back then. We're always learning. Be honest with yourself and aware of the breadth of knowledge you have yet to learn and it will keep you humble.

Transparency wins with customers and people within the organization.

By remembering why you started with a company, consistently calibrating to optimize how you perform every single day — no matter what happened yesterday, and staying humble by remembering all there is to learn, you can endure almost any situation. Don't be swayed by the bumps in the road. As people deviate to your left and your right, you will stay straight on the path and will find yourself the last one standing.

Want to learn more from Carson Heady? Follow him on:
LinkedIn: linkedin.com/in/carsonvheady
Twitter: @cvheady007
Blog: carsonvheady.wordpress.com

#79 The Secret of Being Completely Unreasonable

JARROD GLANDT

"Will I ever be 10 out of 10? I don't think anybody's ever 10 out of 10. There's always more you can do."

ABOUT JARROD GLANDT:

Sales guru and team leader, Jarrod Glandt, is the President of Cardone Enterprises, a co- host of the Young Hustlers podcast, and an investor at Cardone Capital and Hundy App.

He specializes in business development, turnaround consulting, executive/corporate sales, digital marketing, project management, contract negotiations, and public speaking. The end goal? To help people earn millions or more annually and to get to $10 million in net worth by the time they are 35 or 40.

Jarrod earned his Bachelor's degree in business management and marketing while working as an account executive at Dominion Enterprises. He was responsible for establishing and cultivating client relationships in under-performing areas.

After two years, Jarrod moved to Americas Powersports as a Finance Manager where he worked for about two and a half years. Next up, was a five-month stint as the Director of Sales and Marketing at Fisher Auction Co. before joining Cardone Training Technologies where he is today.

Jarrod began working for Grant Cardone as a sales and marketing manager. After just three years, he was promoted to the Vice President of Sales. Now, six and a half years later, he has stepped into the role of President. Cardone Training Technologies has delivered over 36,000,000 lessons to 2,000+ clients.

Those who know and work with Jarrod say he is relentless, humble, reliable, innovative, and someone who gets stuff done. He is also known as the 'go-to' man for business development ideas and sales strategies.

When I moved to LA to start working with Grant Cardone, I didn't know anyone. I didn't have any friends, I had a new sales job, and I had never cold-called before. All I knew was that I needed to bet on this guy because our mindsets were in alignment and I wanted to make big money.

In the beginning, I struggled. I was there trying to make it but it wasn't reflecting in my actions or paycheck. I was showing up at the office at 8:00 AM when we opened and then leaving at 5:00 PM when the office closed. After 90 days, I was broke and thinking, "What am I gonna do? I am going to have to move back in with my parents. I don't want to go back with my tail tucked between my legs." It was at that moment that I decided to go all-in.

I started showing up to the office at 5:50 AM every morning so that I could call on east coast businesses when they were opening at 9:00 AM. Then I'd stay till 7:30 PM at night. I'd also come in on Saturdays. I upped my game and gave it all I could, pushing and pushing. People would ask me why I was working so hard—they would make fun of me and would tell me I was being unreasonable. I guess it all probably makes sense now.

Be Unreasonable With Your Goals

My secret to sales success is to set your goals and then get into a mindset where you are completely unreasonable (according to the status quo) in what you do to achieve them. Be unreasonably dedicated to your follow-up, to your attainment of industry knowledge, to your curiosity, and to your work schedule.

What does this look like?

- Showing up at the office at 6:00 AM and staying until 7:00 PM.
- Consuming personal development training in the morning, in the car on the way to work, and at the end of the day.
- Writing your goals down at the beginning and end of every day.
- Taking care of your physical health so that you can show up and go all-in for 13 or 14 hours a day and still have energy.

If you can work like that, it takes care of a lot.

I believe logic is a dream killer, a kick in the nuts. It will kill you because it is based on being safe and conservative while removing risk. When it comes to your goals, you need to take risks and go for them with all you have. You need to be willing to set yourself apart and to go into the unreasonable zone.

HOW EXACTLY DO YOU GO INTO THE UNREASONABLE ZONE?

You should only become unreasonable in your pursuit of a goal if it is worth it so the first step is to get crystal clear on what your goals are and how you can achieve them.

Connect To Your Goals With A Plan

Most people aren't connected to their goals.

They know they want something like, "Oh yeah, I'd like to make a million bucks a year," but it stops there. You need to dig deeper to connect with your goals. Ask yourself why you want to achieve a goal and what it would mean for you. For example, what would a million dollars per year mean for you? If you were able to do that for 10 years, what would you do? What would you have? Where would you go? Who would you go with?

Play the whole thing out. Say you want a jet. Where will that jet go? How much will it cost to operate it per year? Can you afford the maintenance and operation? Do you need to make more money? What will it mean to have that jet?

We were in Florida last year with our four-day-old baby and a hurricane was coming. We only got out of town because a buddy of mine sent his jet and flew us out. Every flight was booked on the commercial airlines. When we were leaving, I was like, "Man, there are people that aren't getting out of town." It could've been life or death. That's the impact that jet had on our lives.

People often don't take the time to actually seed all the way down to the roots of their goals, so they can't internalize them. Become unreasonably curious and interested in your goals so you can clearly define them, what they mean, and what they require on a granular level.

Follow the 10x Rule

Once you connect with your goals, you should make them unreasonably bigger.

At the heart of it, the 10X rule basically says that nobody factors in the unexpected. They set a 1X goal or target because they think that it's gonna take X amount of work, but what they don't consider are factors like the economy, a trade war, family issues, weather, etc.

For example, say you have a deal you've been working that's gonna be a multi-hundred- thousand-dollar deal or multimillion-dollar deal for you. All of a sudden, the key contact gets blown out and a new one comes in who kills the deal. It happens!

There are many unexpected factors and most people underestimate the amount of effort, energy, work, pipeline, motivation, attitude, whatever, that it's gonna take to get something done by a factor of 10.

However, if you're operating at a 10x level and you're being unreasonable with your sales activity, with the sales followup, with the sales training, with the sales leads that you're filling the funnel with, you're still going to win and come out way ahead.

Don't Give Up

Next, persistence. One of the core factors that contributed to my success and that will contribute to the majority of successes most people have is their willingness to show up to adversity—their willingness to totally fail. You need to keep doing it (whatever it is) over and over again until you get to the point where you can set yourself up to win.

What often happens is people don't show up in the first place. Those that do show up get punched in the face and about 70% of them quit right off the bat. 30% of people are still a little curious so they stay and get punched in the face again. 15% of those stay and get punched again. So people keep falling off as they continue to run into these obstacles, adversity, problems, and challenges.

Most people don't even make it to six months toward a goal. But you can if you keep coming back until you learn to dodge or block the punches. An important part of sticking through the hard times goes back to being connected to your goals. That connection has to be strong enough that trials, distractions, and challenges won't kill your belief and passion when things get tough.

The Unreasonable Question
You Should Be Asking

Lastly, the game-changing question that Grant shared with me is one that can seem very unreasonable at times but works magic on multiple levels.

"Have you seen enough to make a decision?"

We had a 60-minute presentation and I asked that question 15 minutes in. They said, "Yep." and bang, done deal.

Why waste time if the prospect is ready? Of course, sometimes I'll get responses like, "Are you kidding me? Of course not. We've only been on the call for 10 minutes." That's no problem. I say, "All good, I just wanted to be respectful of your time. If you're ready to rock and roll right now (like some people are), I want to make sure we get it out of the way fast."

65% of the time they say, "No," and get a little heated about it and 5% of the time they're like, "Uh, yeah I have, let's roll."

Of course, to ask that question you have to set the proper expectations and give the needed information. I always give them the price upfront and say something like, "Hey, we really respect your time. I just want to let you know my intention on the call is to get a deal done today with you. That's my target, that's my goal. I know we can help your business. I'm confident in it. That's why I want to get a deal done with you today. Before we do that, out of respect for your time I want to go over the pricing upfront so you know exactly what type of investment we're looking at today."

People have stopped me right there and been like, "Hey, I just want to let you know how much I appreciate that. You're the first salesperson ever that has presented me the numbers upfront." Get it out of the way so they're not thinking about it the whole time and set yourself apart from every other sales pitch they hear that day, week, month, etc.

A lot of this you may not directly correlate to daily activities initially like, "What do I do when I call the guy and he says he's not interested?" This has everything to do with that. The tactics of selling are easy if you can lock this in because the mission's big enough, the goal's big enough, the commitment is there... if you're unreasonably dedicated, everything else will work itself out.

Want to learn more from Jarrod Glandt? Follow him on:
Facebook: facebook.com/JarrodGlandtBiz
Instagram: @jarrodglandt
Twitter: @jarrodglandt

#80 Impostors Not Allowed

TONNI BENNETT

"I believe firmly that nothing is too big for you to solve just because you haven't solved it before."

ABOUT TONNI BENNETT:

Tonni Bennet is a sales consultant and the Director of Sales at Twilio Inc. In 2016, she was named a Top Sales Leader by the Technology Association of Georgia (TAG).

Tonni has held a variety of sales roles throughout her career, working for companies such as Terminus, SalesLoft, PeopleMatter, Pardot (which is a Salesforce Company), and UPS. Although her original plan was to become a lawyer, after earning her BA in Government and International Politics from Wofford College, she decided to take a break from acquiring debt to get a job. It didn't take long before she realized sales was something she felt passionately about.

Now after almost a decade, she has made a name for herself as an impactful sales leader. Tonni brings both strategic and frontline leadership to her teams. Direct reports say she values and knows how to invest in people and is one of the most dedicated, capable, and resilient people they have worked with. She is also said to have an unfailing commitment to her team and company, and an unmatched drive to succeed and innovate.

A lot of people have a preconceived idea about what a salesperson should be. Like we should be this smooth-talking persona that can overcome any objection to close any deal, kind of like the Jordan Belfort type (played by Leo DiCaprio) from *Wolf of Wallstreet*. When I went into sales, I had really no interest in it. I wasn't "that type of person" and had no interest to be. I just needed a job.

I came from a very blue-collar family, never had an example of a salesperson in my life, and didn't know anything about the tech industry. But I came into the Martech world as it was taking off and realized through a series of sales roles at different companies that it was a great fit for me.

But it wasn't about fitting into some mold. I've learned that success in sales is about finding my own voice, being authentic, and genuinely helping people solve problems.

Be Yourself and Solve Problems

What a relief it was to realize I could be highly successful just being myself. In my first sales role at UPS, I was a young twenty-something woman surrounded by 40 to 50-year- old males. I tried to imitate them at first, not really knowing what to do, and it didn't feel right.

When I got to Pardot is when everything clicked for me. I was surrounded by people my age being themselves on the phone, selling, enjoying their jobs, having exciting conversations, and actually helping customers. I was like, "Holy crap this is so fun, I want to do this for the rest of my career." I fell in love with sales. I still love that even if you sell the same products for years. Every conversation is different and every application is different.

During that time, I realized you don't need to say big words and try to sound ultra- professional. People can sense when something isn't authentic to you. Instead, when you ask questions from a place of genuine interest and you're able to then say, "Okay, based on what you're trying to accomplish, here's what we can offer"—that gets you a lot further.

HOW TO BE A GENUINE PROBLEM-SOLVER

How can you be authentic in the workplace and keep a problem-solving mindset? Here are some tips.

Solve Your Own Professional Problems

Start with being honest with yourself and solve the problems you are facing in your own world. Are you at the right company? Are you in the place where your skills will be fully utilized? Are you in the right position? Can you reach your full potential there?

For me, I moved through several companies and positions, learning every step of the way. Many times I had to leave because the company was just not the right fit for me due to the product-market fit or the culture.

Product-market Fit

At the end of the day, it doesn't matter if you're a great salesperson if you're selling a product that doesn't quite fit in the market. It's like fighting an uphill battle. A lot of your job as a sales rep is dependent on the company, the brand, the product, and if it is really providing value to the customer. If you're not providing value, then it's going to be difficult to sell. If you do, it doesn't allow you to sleep very well at night.

I recommend vetting companies thoroughly before joining them. Ask a lot of questions around what people are selling, the ACVs, what your customers are saying, and why customers leave. Do some back-channel research to really understand if the product is legit, if there is a need for it, if you will be solving real business problems, and if the company has healthy metrics.

Culture

A second factor is the company culture. The culture of a company can support you and build you up, or hurt you and hold you back. I've learned I thrive in an environment where things are transparently laid out. Further, I will work harder for you if you tell me that I am valuable and give me praise than if you give me harsh criticism. So I work well when it comes from a place of "you're valued, we love you, and we want you here." That is what motivates me. Knowing that I need a culture that provides positive feedback to thrive. It's important to figure out what kind of culture you thrive in and to find it.

Position

Third, it's important that you are in the right position. When I was applying to work at Pardot, they were offering me an SDR role. I wanted to work for the company badly but only as an account executive. I told them if I wasn't offered that position, I was going to walk. I knew that's where I needed to be. After making my case, I was given one quarter to prove myself and hit my quota or I'd be out. Long story short, I became one of the top AEs.

I would say the secret there is to be honest with yourself. If you really know and believe that you've got the skill set, and you have what it takes, fight for yourself. Fight for the position you deserve to be in. On the flip side of that, if you say, "Hey this is really far from my current skill set," then be honest with yourself about that and take the other position. Do whatever is going to set you up for success, but don't be afraid of fighting for what you think you deserve and reaching for more than someone in your position should normally be able to transition to.

I had scenarios in my career when I took jobs because of the money or convenience and it never worked out. Instead, I recommend you take positions based on a cultural fit, where the product-market fit is spot-on, and you're going to be excited and passionate about what you are doing.

Solve Problems for Your Customers

Once you work out your own situation and set yourself up for success, then it's time to focus on solving problems for your customers. I believe in partnering with a customer and figuring out what's best for them versus just selling to them.

At Pardot, customers could get a 50% discount if they signed by a certain date. It was kind of brutal and harsh. I tried my best to be genuinely interested in what a company was going through, what their challenges were, and how we could help. I would maintain the mindset of, "We just want to help you. You don't have to make a decision today. You can make a decision in two weeks. Would I like you to sign by the end of the month? Yeah, it would help me as a salesperson. However, we just want to partner with you when it's the right time and it makes sense."

My willingness to genuinely help the customer and not push too hard worked well for me. You have to push in sales, but you don't need to strong-arm customers. I think the excitement and passion that I had also helped as I was positive that we could help them on their journey. I was really genuinely excited about what we were selling because I had seen how it transformed businesses. So to help solve customers' problems, I think you need to be with the right company, you need to be excited, and you need to be willing to really partner with a customer and figure out what's best for them instead of just selling to them.

Solve Problems for Your Business

When I joined Terminus in a leadership role, I learned so much about myself and business in general. We grew to $1 million in revenue in the first year with myself and one sales rep. In our second year, we went from $1 million to $5 million with five or six people; by year three, we grew to $20 million with about 50 people. While I learned so much, the underlying themes were still to be authentic and willing to continuously solve problems.

Authenticity

How does a leader stay authentic? I am honest with my team. We've had conversations where I make it clear, I'm going to mess up sometimes. Not every decision I make is going to be great, but I tell them that they need to communicate respectfully back what's not working and we need to aerate this thing together. We're all on this mission to sell this product and make a lot of money.

Problem Solving

Problem-solving has become more difficult, no doubt. I didn't come in with a background working for an IBM or with a father who did X, which gave me a wealth of knowledge. I came in like, I've got to figure this out or someone's going to realize that I'm not qualified for this job and hire someone else. I had a network of about 10 sales leaders, VPs of sales, and CROs that I was constantly calling. I quickly learned that no one has the right answer for my business. I would take all the advice, knowledge, and tips and problem- solve to find out what decision was best for my company at this stage.

In summary, many people try to be this perception of what they think a salesperson or sales leader is and it's just not it. I believe firmly that nothing is too big for you to solve just because you haven't solved it before. You just need to be honest with yourself and those around you, take it one step at a time, think through it, figure out what works in your environment, and focus on the goal at hand.

Want to learn more from Tonni Bennett? Follow her on:
Twitter: @TonniBennett
LinkedIn: linkedin.com/in/tonnibennett

#81 Catch Fire for Education and Application

MORGAN J. INGRAM

"I believe I was able to accelerate my learning curve because I put myself out there and had conversations with people that were executives and things of that nature."

ABOUT MORGAN J. INGRAM:

Morgan is currently the director of sales execution and evolution at JBarrows Sales Training. He keeps his finger on the pulse of industry trends to consistently bring the most actionable, valuable, and relevant content to sales teams.

Morgan also hosts the SDR Chronicles podcast where he shares skills, tactics, and motivation for SDRs. He is presently a public speaker who aims to liberate people from negative thoughts. And, he is part of the Enterprise Sales GM Atlanta Chapter, a community for salespeople selling into enterprises to share, learn, network, and grow.

Talk about an active player in the industry!

Morgan earned a Bachelor's degree in Sports Management and a Bachelor of Business Administration and Finance from the University of Georgia. After graduating, he decided he wanted to be a public speaker and began his business Morgan Ingram Liberates which is still alive and well today. Meanwhile, he also joined Terminus at the beginning of 2016 as a sales development representative. After about a year, he was promoted to sales development manager. Nine months later, he left Terminus and joined JBarrows.

Morgan is said to have an exceptional presence and clarity of message which serves him in public speaking and sales. He is known for his natural ability to motivate people and deliver his ideas with poise, ease, and fluidity. As someone who has lived and breathed sales on the front lines, he teaches from experience, staying close to the realities of inside sales.

I grew up average, mediocre, going through the motions. I never really had aspirations to do anything above and beyond in my life because I honestly didn't think it was possible. My whole mindset was that to be successful, you have to be born with a special talent or a well-off family. I didn't think I had either so figured that was the hand I was dealt.

Everything changed when I was 16 or 17. My mom gave me a personal development book called 'How to Get Your Dream Job.' I read the book, took it seriously, and implemented the stuff it said to do. To my surprise, it worked and things changed. It was through that experience that I caught fire for education and application. I understood I could read books, do some of what they say, and get results.

Develop an Obsessive Hunger to Learn

With that early learning in mind, if I had to choose just one secret to help others in their sales careers, it would be that you need to develop an obsessive hunger to learn. When you become obsessed with learning, you will widen your knowledge, enable yourself to connect with a broader audience, prepare yourself to speak to your audience's priorities and concerns, and align with the wavelength of those who are levels above you.

For example, say you have studied your target market, the positions they hold, and the challenges they face. If you are at an event and meet a prospect, without even knowing what company they work for, you can have an intelligent, relevant conversation about the things they will likely care about. You can speak their language and provide more value than just going through a rehearsed script.

But you need to study and learn to become an expert.

HOW TO BECOME OBSESSIVE ABOUT LEARNING

How do you do that exactly? Here are three key steps:

Map Out Your Goals

If you want to be average and just chill, then no, this 'hunger to learn' secret isn't for you. But if you want to be number one, drive a nicer car, move somewhere more desirable, have more to pass on to the next generation, or achieve some other higher aspiration, read on. You have to do something different.

I wasn't born highly motivated. In fact, I was actually pretty lazy growing up. I really didn't care too much about anything except playing video games. I wasn't reading books. I wasn't doing podcasts. And this isn't something that I'm making up to tell a story. You can ask my friends from junior high and high school, or my family. I was a lazy person. What changed my life completely was that book that helped me realize that I had bigger aspirations and could actually achieve them.

Without goals and faith in yourself, you don't have a purpose to drive you. You're not hungry to learn because what is the point? I don't know anyone who's doing personal development work who doesn't have a big goal that they're striving for. So the first step is to identify what you want, everything you want, believe you can achieve it, and use that as your motivator. For me, it was initially to become a sports agent. Then, a public speaker. For you, it may be to earn a specific amount of money, hit 150 to 200 percent of your quota, get promoted to a new position, etc. Whatever it is, name it.

Obtain the Knowledge You Need to Achieve Your Goals

Once you know what you want to achieve, it's all about getting on the wavelength of the life you want. That is where the hunger to learn comes in. You have to do things that you may not really care about but that are important to your end goal.

I recommend reading a lot, listening to podcasts, and connecting with mentors who are where you want to be. For example, if you want to be a sales leader, shadow sales leaders and reverse engineer what they do. Read books on coaching and leadership. If you want to be a VP of Sales, read books, research, go to conferences, network, and whatever else you can do to get into the space of that position and what it entails.

The end goal is to cultivate the mindset you need to operate in the space where you have achieved your goal. The only way to do that is to passionately pursue new education and application.

Share Your Goals and Progress

Lastly, the goal itself should push you every single day. However, sharing your goal can add extra encouragement, accountability, and momentum. For the past few years, I've posted all of my goals on Facebook.

About three or four years ago, when I realized I wasn't going to be a sports agent but was going to go into public speaking, I shared it. I got on Facebook and posted, "I will become a public speaker. I'll speak on stages and I'm going to be able to do this globally. I have no idea how I'm going to do it."

Some people were like, "No way. You're not going to be able to do that. No matter how hard you work, that's not going to happen." Other people said, "I believe in you." Others were like, "That's absolutely absurd." The haters served as motivation and the supporters as encouragement.

If you don't put your goals out there, no one knows what you are doing. Then, if you don't follow through, you can always lie to yourself and say, "Oh, well I told myself I was going to lose 20 pounds this year. But it doesn't matter. No one knows so maybe next year." But if you do put it out there and say, "Hey, look. I'm looking to be number one at my company, or I'm looking to get better at sales. I'm going to attend 10 networking events this year." Now everyone's watching you. If you don't hit your goal, people are going to know and possibly ask about it, which works as a motivator.

Get Started

So where do you start? Identify three things you want to do to grow your knowledge base and achieve your goals. Then, narrow it down to one thing and do that first. Once you finish, then move onto number two. Be very targeted and focused on the one thing you really need to do at a time. Absorbing the learning, applying it, and tracking the results.

That is exactly what I did. I said, okay, I'm going to read this book first. It worked and I was like, cool, I'm going to go grab another book. Oh, that worked? Okay, cool. I'm going to go to a conference and network. But don't try to do 20 things at once because it's too much and won't be helpful. Take it at a reasonable pace where you can absorb information, understand it, and apply it. If you stay hungry and keep at it, you will gradually grow and develop your skills to the point where you can reach your next level of success, no matter what you were born with or without.

Want to learn more from Morgan J. Ingram? Follow him on:
YouTube podcast: www.youtube.com/channel/
UC5mlKms3bZLtuXapHBVp2tA
LinkedIn: linkedin.com/in/morganjingram
Twitter: @morganjingram
Instagram: @morganjingram
Email: morgan@jbarrows.com

#82 Claiming Your Space

VIVEKA VON ROSEN

"Whether you're in sales or whether you're in marketing, it doesn't matter. What you need to become is an educator."

ABOUT VIVEKA VON ROSEN:

Viveka von Rosen is Co-founder and CVO (Chief Visibility Officer) of Vengreso. She is known across the world as the "LinkedIn Expert" and is the author of best-selling books, *LinkedIn Marketing: An Hour a Day* and LinkedIn:101 Ways to Rock Your Personal Brand!

As a "LinkedIn Expert," Viveka is a contributor to LinkedIn's official Sales and Marketing blogs and has been featured in publications such as *Fast Company, Forbes, Money, Entrepreneur, The Social Media Examiner*, and many more.

Viveka takes her LinkedIn experience and transforms it into engaging and informational training that salespeople can use in their day-to-day activities. In fact, over the last 10+ years, Viveka has provided training for more than 100,000 people! She is what some might call a LinkedIn legend.

Like many people, I fell into sales completely by accident. Since my 20s, I have been a serial entrepreneur so selling was always a part of my job in many respects. What I learned early on was that I was really good at networking—face-to-face networking because that is really all we had when I first started in my career. Eventually, this thing called LinkedIn emerged, which really piqued my interest. Thinking that it may be a useful business tool, I dove in and tried to learn everything I could about it. In that sense, I guess you could say the rest is history.

When I decided to go "all-in" on LinkedIn, there weren't many people teaching or training people on how to use it as a business tool—so I decided to fill that niche. As fate would have it, one of the associations that I belonged to invited me to New York City to speak at the Waldorf Astoria in their Grand Ballroom. They wanted me to teach this intimidating group of affluent billionaires how to use LinkedIn. That was my first official speaking gig—sometime around 2007. Talk about learning under pressure!

While I have always enjoyed public speaking, I was nervous to address this particular group. With LinkedIn still being so new, and me essentially teaching myself, I worried that I didn't know my product well enough. I worried that I wasn't going to provide the information they needed. Despite my fears, my presentation was a success and led to a long term engagement with the association that arranged it. I ended up doing a lot of international events with them. In time, one opportunity led to another, which eventually led to the publication of my first book, *LinkedIn Marketing: An Hour a Day*. These various experiences ultimately led to the merger with Vengreso, where I currently work today.

Fake It Until You Make It

As I was establishing my personal brand and building up my LinkedIn knowledge, one of the biggest things I learned was that you don't have to be a subject matter expert to appear like you're a subject matter expert. When I presented to that group of billionaires back in 2007 at the Waldorf Astoria, I really wasn't an expert *yet* on LinkedIn—but I knew I was going to be.

Too often, we let our fear of not being knowledgeable enough on a topic stand in our way of progress. Even if you aren't an expert on something, commit to learning everything you can about the topic; absorb information and share what you learn. This will help build your confidence and eventually enable you to be the subject matter expert you want to be. I may not have been the ultimate LinkedIn expert back in 2007, but I am today because I made the commitment to become one.

Claim Your Space, Claim Your Expertise

When thinking about my sales secret, it's really a collection of secrets that all stem from this one idea: to be successful, you need to claim your space and claim your expertise.

Claiming your expertise will help you gain confidence, which is an invaluable trait to have. Whatever you need to do to build your confidence—do it. Whether it's learning more about your own product, or reading 100 books on digital selling—whatever you need to do to feel confident in claiming your space, make it happen.

While claiming your space is the ultimate objective, there are some other "sub-secrets" that I've outlined below that will help you to truly build your confidence over time.

Trust Your Gut:

As you begin to claim your space and people progressively start to view you as an expert, you'll begin to attract all kinds of opportunities that may or may not be right for you. Speaking from experience, be sure to do your research and trust your gut before accepting any kind of opportunity. Don't always look at every opportunity in terms of dollars. While you main gain a nice paycheck in the near term, think about the consequences that your decisions may bring in the long term. Stay true to yourself and trust your gut. Saying "no" to the wrong opportunities and "yes" to the right ones will be one of the greatest factors in propelling you to succeed.

Find a Mentor and Absorb Everything You Can:

If you're just starting out or starting in a new role, it's important to become a sponge and absorb as much information as you can. I also highly suggest finding a mentor that you can learn from within your company. If they will let you, try to sit in on calls with them. There's no substitute for learning first-hand so take advantage of all the experts around you.

Come at Everything You Do as an Educator:

This is something I always try to remind people about—don't think of yourself as a seller but as an educator. You are there to provide exactly the right information to people at exactly the right time that they need it. You are their trusted resource. You're not their salesperson. That is a very important distinction to make.

While you won't become an industry expert overnight, setting a goal to become one is half the battle. Have confidence that you can achieve your objective and put in the work to make it happen. Like I said before, be willing to fake it until you make it. Success will follow if you put in the effort.

Want to learn more from Viveka von Rosen? Fllow her on:
Website: vengreso.com
LinkedIn: linkedin.com/in/linkedinexpert

#83 The Positivity Factor

JENNIFER GITOMER

"It does not matter what happens. Whatever happens, is either creating your success or teaching you the lesson you need at the time."

ABOUT JENNIFER GITOMER:

Jennifer Gluckow-Gitomer is the Chief Executive Officer and Founder of Sales in a New York Minute where she teaches workshops on networking, customer loyalty, attitude, social media attraction, and—of course—sales.

Jennifer knew from the time she was five that she wanted to own a business and be in sales. She grew up in a successful book manufacturing business run by her mother and father and their dinner table conversations were an MBA real-world business education years before she graduated from the Olin School of Business at Washington University in St. Louis.

Jennifer jumped into sales at an early age selling Cutco knives door-to-door and working retail at Saks Fifth Avenue. Once she joined a leading Fortune 500 company, she quickly rose through the ranks as a superstar Sales Representative, National Sales Manager, and Executive Director of Sales Operations. At 29, she became the Chief Operating Officer of a test preparation and admissions counseling company.

In 2013, Jennifer found her true calling in the sales space; training and coaching sales teams and business owners on how to increase their sales and drive up their profits. To help these companies gain success, she founded "Sales in a New York Minute."

Today, she's a speaker, trainer, writer, blogger, and social media guru. Jen's trademarked advice YouTube channel, "Sales in a New York Minute," features short sales and life tips positioned to take the audience both global and viral.

Those who know Jennifer say she approaches everything with enthusiasm, she has a great depth of knowledge in sales and relationship development, and she communicates succinctly and positively. Her northeastern smarts with her New York City savvy have positioned her as the next big thing in sales.

When you lose a sale, the natural instinct is to be pissed off. It sucks, there's no denying that. Allow yourself that minute to be pissed off, but if you stay pissed off the rest of the day, you are going to lose the rest of your sales.

When I was selling Cutco knives, I sold a lot of knives but when a person wouldn't buy, maybe they were just doing me a favor by meeting with me, I would just look at it like, "Cool, I got great practice in delivering my spiel. They didn't buy anything, whatever."

Then, I would shift to focusing on what I could learn, my next sale, and my next satisfied customer.

Stay Positive No Matter What

My top sales secret is to stay positive no matter what.

Whatever happens, can help you create success or can give you the lesson you need at the time.

If you're not open to the lesson or you get all negative and pissed off because something didn't go your way, you'll miss the lesson.

You can't think straight if you're pissed off and you can't be creative.

Do you know how many times I fail per day? More than I can count.

But the more risks I take, the more I put out there, and the more I fail, the faster I can build.

So you have to stay positive.

More failures to me literally mean more success.

HOW TO STAY POSITIVE

You need to create a positive foundation in order to stay positive throughout the blows and challenges you are going to face. I do that in a couple of ways.

Find your "thing"

If you're like me, from the Northeast, most people don't look happy or seem positive. It's ingrained in them to be pissed off about people and weather and traffic. And you can go on and on and complain, but that's not going to get you the sales you need to get.

I start my morning by meditating and reading something positive.

And I go back to meditation whenever I need it.

If I need to take a 10-minute break from whatever I'm doing, I will leave the office and sit on my zen couch. I close my eyes and meditate and when I get back out of it, all of a sudden my state is different.

It may sound "woo-woo" but it works. You can go from a negative space where you're pissed off to a positive space where you can think and create.

I do crazy things too.

I go to True REST which is a saltwater sensory deprivation float tank and I go in for 60 minutes so I'm alone with my thoughts. I also do yoga which, in my opinion, grounds me.

You have to find the thing that keeps you grounded. It may not be yoga. It may be hitting a tennis ball as hard as you possibly can, running, or working out.

You have to figure out what it is for you and then you have to create the space on your calendar so you can do it consistently.

You can't look at it as, "Oh shit, I have to take care of myself now so that's a waste of time."

No.

Your body and your mind are the most important things you have to take care of every single day.

Celebrate small successes

It's also important to celebrate your successes. If someone wrote a book, a lot of times they'll say, "I'll celebrate when I sell this many copies." They keep moving the goal without celebrating milestones and they are never happy.

I've said to Jeffrey sometimes, "Aw, I didn't do this or this or this." And he'll say, "Wait, let's talk about what you did do. You launched a book and took off with this membership thing, etc."

There is a psychological effect in the brain where if you allow your brain to recognize the success that you have, it encourages you to achieve more.

You need to celebrate your wins before moving the goal, you need to find the thing you can do to help you build a positive foundation and stay grounded, and you need to put effort into shifting back into that state of positivity and productivity whenever you slip out of it. Obstacles and failures are going to come, they will come every day, so you need to be prepared with a plan to overcome them and keep going. Stay positive no matter what happens. Remember, it's a success or it's a lesson.

Want to learn more from Jennifer Gitomer? Follow her on:
LinkedIn: linkedin.com/in/jennifergitomer
Instagram: @jengitomer

#84 The One Question You Should Ask Everyone

DAVID MELTZER

"The problem isn't the product, service, or solution. It's literally the person conveying the value."

ABOUT DAVID MELTZER:

David Meltzer is the Co-founder of Sports 1 Marketing and formerly served as CEO of the renowned Leigh Steinberg Sports & Entertainment agency, which was the inspiration for the movie Jerry Maguire.

He is a three-time international best-selling author, a Top 100 Business Coach, the executive producer of Entrepreneur's #1 digital business show, Elevator Pitch, and host of the top entrepreneur podcast, The Playbook.

In his early 20s, David quickly rose to the top of his game in the business world, becoming a millionaire. He lectured around the globe and saw rapid success in every business project he touched. But something was missing, and in his 30s as a multimillionaire, he went on a rapid downward spiral that ended in bankruptcy.

It was only then that David realized, in order to revive and thrive, he needed to figure out what had made him successful in the first place. He has since emerged to realize even more rewarding heights of success in business and life.

David's life mission is now to empower OVER 1 BILLION people to be happy! This simple yet powerful mission has led him on an incredible journey to provide one thing…VALUE. In all his content and communication that's exactly what you'll receive.

David has been recognized by Variety Magazine as their Sports Humanitarian of the Year and awarded the Ellis Island Medal of Honor.

Those who know David Meltzer say he exemplifies the very best qualities of a leader and business partner. He is known as someone you can always count on to get the job done, be inspiring, and have a great time doing whatever it takes to deliver.

When I was graduating law school with no job and massive student loans to payoff I said, "God, if you can give me enough money to buy my mom a house and a car, and pay off my law loans, I will shovel shit with my hands six days per week, 12 hours per day with gratitude."

That's where my mindset was. So when I got a real job, a six-figure job, with the opportunity to make seven figures, there was no stopping me.

In nine months, I produced 10 years of what the average person would produce. Therefore, I made a million dollars, which is basically $100,000 per year for the average person. But that success came crumbling down. Now, many years later, after many life lessons, my approach to selling boils down to a simple yet powerful question.

Ask Everyone This One Question

My top sales secret is to ask everyone this one question: "Can you help me?"

Every person has about 1,000 people that they are connected to and the softest ask you can ever make is for help. The thing that people like to do the most is to help others. So you can simply say, "Hey, I sell custom suits, do you know anyone that can help me?"

Forget all the cold calls you're making and resistance you're creating.

If you ask one person per day, you could increase your network by 30,000 people every month. Now imagine if you do it every day in person, over the phone, via email, and through social media. You might get to 4 million people in your network. Even at a terrible percentage, just by asking for help, you'll have more leads than you ever could cold calling in your life.

But people are afraid to ask for help.

HOW TO ASK FOR HELP

Here are some tips to help you with your ask.

Give Value and Get Value

Asking for help requires a big shift in the paradigm of value because receiving is the biggest problem for all salespeople. We feel guilty so we don't ask. And the energy comes across as we must not have value. I ask big because I am grateful for what I receive, I add value to it, and I give it away.

I wake up every morning and I pray for 10 people I can help. I meditate.

And before I go to the gym, for one minute, I close my eyes and I dream that my room is full of $100 bills and I go out grabbing sacks and hand out $100 and ask to get $20 back.

I want to know what that feels like because I am asking for help but giving much more. There is an exchange, a flow. So I use that just like my meditation as a litmus test to know where my energy should be when I'm selling.

It's not just what I think, say, do, and believe, it's the energy I carry. People feel confident because they feel that I am giving them so much more than I'm asking for.

Understand It Makes People Feel Good

There's nothing more fulfilling to me than someone asking, "Can you help me?" and me being able to help them in some way. It makes me feel good. And if I can't, I can find someone to help which still feels good. Open your mind to the fact that you're giving and receiving. You're giving people an opportunity to make them feel good.

Respond to Spam With Asking

I recently did a video that killed it. It was on spam. My new response to every spam is an ask. Basically, if you are going to send me a message to buy and I don't know you, I'm gonna reply with, "Hey my book is launching tomorrow, do you know anyone that would like to buy or could you pass it on to a friend?" I'm telling you, I get probably 100 spams per day and I sold like 15 books from people spamming me.

Check Your Email/Message Sent Box Daily

My litmus test of how consistent I am is to go look in my sent email box to see how many emails I haven't asked in. I audit myself to see how good I am. And what happens is I will see like four emails that were obvious ask opportunities that I didn't ask, and I'll go back and follow up with an email to ask. And the conversion is very high on those. I do this every day to see what I did and then I clean it out.

Ask Every Day at Least Once

Lastly, just start asking at least once per day. There is a certain exponential value to doing something every day.

Cellular memory takes daily activity and the brain takes 21 days to build a neuro pathway, a belief. If we don't do something every day, it zeros it out and it never goes to the subconscious.

The only thing that impacts our subconscious is the conscious 10,000 thoughts/data inputs you have each day. And the only way the 10,000 thoughts have an impact is consistency.

So even if you are only asking once per day, it's better than 10 asks one day and zero the next. Set the expectation low to start and focus on consistency.

Selling With Integrity

Literally, I went from zero to hero the wrong way. Through manipulation, lying, overselling and taking value without providing it. Lying to people that I exceeded expectations. The truth is, I struggled to meet expectations because people have high expectations. Now, I fight really hard to legitimately meet and exceed expectations by utilizing gratitude, humility, empathy, and accountability. I ask everyone for the help I need while helping as many people as I can.

Want to learn more from David Meltzer? Follow him on:
Website: dmeltzer.com
LinkedIn: linkedin.com/in/davidmeltzer2/
YouTube: youtube.com/channel/
UCflt1OopRWlApMOjVgZyJ6Q
Instagram: @davidmeltzer

#85 Sell a Product That's Awesome

TOM BILYEU

"Don't over-focus on being a slick marketer; you are not going to 'slick market' your way into a billion-dollar business."

ABOUT TOM BILYEU:

Tom Bilyeu is the co-founder of Quest Nutrition — a unicorn startup valued at over $1 billion — and the co-founder and host of "Impact Theory." Prior to co-founding Quest Nutrition, Tom was the CMO of Awareness Technologies. He is also an advisor for Neurovalens.

Tom's mission has evolved over the years and is now to create empowering media and to accelerate mission-based businesses. He is personally driven to help people develop the skills they will need to improve themselves and the world, and he intends to use commerce to address the dual pandemics of physical and mental malnourishment.

Tom regularly inspires audiences of thought leaders, entrepreneurs, and change-makers at some of the most prestigious seminars and conferences around the world, including A-fest, Abundance 360, and Freedom Fast

Lane. He has also been a guest on Tony Robbins' podcast and has been featured in SUCCESS, Forbes, Inc., and The Huffington Post.

Tom describes himself as a forever student of life. His obsession with mastering skills has molded him into a well-rounded leader, battle-hardened and unafraid to fire moonshots. Those who know him say he is obsessed with driving results, has a gift for communication, uplifts those around him, and has a contagious drive and mentality for winning.

After about eight and a half years of the entrepreneurial grind, I was a C-level executive and co-owner of a tech company. I was making the most money I had ever made and I was completely miserable. I was chasing the dollar and felt completely unfulfilled. So one day I walked in the office, gave my equity back, and walked out planning to move to Greece, cut my expenses, and spend time writing, learning the language, and being with my wife.

I never made it to Greece as my partners called me on the way home and asked me to go to dinner. They told me that they could go on without me but didn't want to. I felt a camaraderie I hadn't felt, a brotherhood, and so together we realigned our goals and priorities. We were going to build something based on the passion that we would love to do every day. As a result, we sold the tech company and Quest Nutrition was born, a company built on adding value to people's lives.

What's ironic is, once we focused on adding the most value to our customers and employees, and stopped focusing on money, we made more money in a single day than our tech company did in a whole year.

Sell a Product That's Awesome

So what's my top sales secret? Sell a product that actually solves a problem. Your job as a salesperson is to really add value to people. If you break down what a sale is, it's creating something that someone wants more than the money that you're charging for it. And doing it at a price where the money you convince them to give you is more than it costs you to make that thing.

It is the most deadly simple thing but people often lose sight of the value.

So the one thing I will tell you is don't over-focus on being a slick marketer or sly salesperson. Understanding marketing and sales is very powerful but you're not going to scheme your way into a billion-dollar brand in today's hyperconnected space.

You're going to get there by being good AND selling something that's actually worth buying. Stay focused on that. That is what has allowed us to take over the industry —we sold something that was better than everything else. It's that simple.

Align your priorities with true fulfillment. Before money, I focus on adding value to people's lives, solving big problems, following my happiness, autonomy, camaraderie, having fun, and gaining mastery. Then, the money comes.

Want to learn more from Tom Bilyeu? Follow him on:
YouTube:
youtube.com/channel/UCnYMOamNKLGVIJgRUbamveA
LinkedIn:
linkedin.com/in/tombilyeu

#86 The Secret Is, There Is No Secret

SCOTT INGRAM

"Sales is an incremental process where you're going to chip away, chip away, chip away, and at some point, you may become a diamond."

ABOUT SCOTT INGRAM:

Scott is the Founder of Sales Success Media where he hosts two sales podcasts. On "Sales Success Stories" he deconstructs world-class sales professionals, and on "Daily Sales Tips," he shares a new sales tip for B2B professionals in five to 10 minutes per day, seven days a week.

Scott is also the Account Director at Relationship One, a mentor for thousands of sales professionals, and the author of Making Rain with Events: Engage Your Tribe, Create Raving Fans and Deliver Bottom Line Results with Event Marketing.

He has held various positions throughout his 20+ year career from President at Grey Matter Technologies to Major Account District Manager at ADP to Strategic Account Executive at Oracle and Certain, Inc. Now he uses the culmination of all of his experience to serve his clients at Relationship One, and host his two sales-related podcasts.

Those who know Scott say he is a rare combination of mentor, connector, leader, and synthesizer. He has a reputation for being open-minded, humble, and extremely purposeful. Further, his "Sales Success Stories" podcast comes highly recommended, hosting second-to-none guests who offer real, authentic advice that will help any sales professional grow.

The greatest people in sales are stylistically all over the place. There are few commonalities in the way they do what they do but they each have their own approach. However, one commonality that has appeared across the board is time in the saddle. There's an element of being at the same company, in the same market, role, and territory that allows individuals to develop expertise and knowledge that they can leverage to lead the pack.

Sales Mastery Is a Lifetime Journey

Sales is a craft. Honestly, I don't think there are a lot of things that you can do right this second, from a tactical perspective, that will make that big of a difference in the long term. Yes, there are things that you should do, you can do, and you need to do to expedite the process (reading books, listening to podcasts, going to events, and surrounding yourself with greatness).

But at the end of the day, sales is a long-term incremental journey that you are going to go on. You have to go through the exercises day after day, trying to get a little bit better. Once you compound that over 5, 10, 15, 20 years, that's when you're really going to have something.

HOW TO MASTER SALES

If you establish good habits and invest time in your craft daily, in time, you can become a master of sales. Here are some of the helpful habits that I've learned.

Build Relationships

Relationships are powerful. When I was first starting out, I didn't know much about business or sales. The very first client I had an opportunity to consult with was from my childhood school district. The contact there asked me how much I charge and I said $25/hour. He took me under his wing and said he was going to pretend like he didn't hear that. He was one of my first mentors and told me I was going to have a bunch of expenses and would need to charge more. I said $75/hr and he hired me.

Building the right relationships with mentors and others has been a core theme in everything I've done. You'll need different relationships at different points. And when you have a high level of hustle and optimism, people want to help. I recommend getting involved in the community, joining the chambers of commerce and rotary clubs, etc.

Keep an Even Keel

I also had a period where I had a young family, I wasn't very good at sales yet, and I was struggling with the ups and downs. I had to admit that sales is hard and it would require active mindset management. There are super high highs and horrible low lows but you have to disconnect from that part of it a bit and focus more on what you have to do each day. You've got to learn to keep that even keel and consistency and not ride the rollercoaster too much.

A helpful tool for me is consistent exercise. If I'm not working out consistently, I can't keep my head right. Two days off, and I feel a downward spiral. I wake up at four in the morning every day of the week, work out, and get an extra three to four hours of undisturbed time that most other people don't get.

Think Like an Entrepreneur

Next, sales gives you the great opportunity to run a business without taking on the risk but many mistakenly don't think of it that way. I did an interview with a 7-figure earner and he really emphasized the entrepreneurial approach. He said we need to think about ourselves as our own startups and our companies are our VCs. Companies have tons of resources for us so use them and go. Treat your territory like a franchise. That mindset is valuable.

Don't Stop Believin'

I've also learned the value of getting people bought-in emotionally through belief. In one of my sales roles, I was off to a decent start with the deals in my pipeline but I was working on an opportunity with one of the largest camera manufacturers in the world. I had been on-site, we had a series of good meetings, and we were on a good trajectory.

I painted a big vision for them to put them on a path of being a 7-figure ARR client and we were working on the first component of that for around $350,000. With two days left in the quarter, I called my buyer to check in on the status and he said, "We're not going to be able to get this done internally on time." And I had this sinking feeling of failure, like, "Man, I had this and now it's not happening."

I got to the office the next day, and I wrote the most impassioned email ever. I started telling him a story about belief and how much we believed in the success they were going to have with this partnership. And I told him a mantra we had at the company about "Don't stop believing." About an hour after I sent that email, I got a three-word email back that said, "Don't stop believing." He moved heaven and earth to get that deal done on time. And it was that transference of belief, passion, and emotion that I learned can make incredible things happen.

Get Clear About What You're Seeking

At one point in my career, I was fired. It was a time when I took a step back to identify what I really wanted and realized the importance of getting really clear about the type of organization you want to work with and the kind of audience you want to sell to.

Once I sold to people in sales and marketing, I realized those are my people. The people in the backend part of the business are much more risk-averse. I also loved tech and I realized I prefer selling for smaller organizations over larger ones, where I know I am making a difference.

Once I got clear about what I wanted, I found the perfect company where I could really excel.

Surround Yourself With the Best

Lastly, I had always heard the quote, "You're the average of the five people you spend your time with" but I wasn't fully aware of the power of that. After starting "Sales Success Stories," I experienced it.

I was having more success than I ever had and it was from the experience of learning from the best on a regular basis. And this goes back to the relationships piece. Everyone gets to hear those interviews but rarely is that the last conversation I have with those folks. They are all my mentors, some have even come on my board of directors. If I get stuck on something, I know who to call and about what.

In summary, it takes time to develop a sales skillset, you don't get it overnight or after reading one book. So many of the people that have been on the "Sales Success Stories" podcast speak about sales as a craft. You have to hone it and develop it. It's an incremental process where you're just going to chip away, chip away, chip away, and at some point, I'm not there yet, but at some point, maybe you become a diamond.

Want to learn more from Scott Ingram? Follow him on:
LinkedIn: linkedin.com/in/scottingram
Podcast: www.Top1.fm

THOUGHT LEADERSHIP

#87 The Real Price of Entry in Sales

BERNIE BORGES

"You have to know what you're selling well enough to speak intelligently about it in order to earn the respect and credibility of your prospects."

ABOUT BERNIE BORGES:

Bernie Borges is the Chief Marketing Officer (CMO) and a Co-founder of Vengreso. He has 40 years of experience in sales and marketing and is a well-respected thought leader on the subjects of content marketing, digital selling, and aligning sales and marketing at B2B companies.

Bernie graduated from Pace University's Lubin School of Business with a B.B.S. in marketing. When his parents said they couldn't afford it, he went anyway and paid his own way.

Bernie was the Founder and CEO of Find and Convert. The company helped clients across the U.S. and Canada to improve their business results through content marketing. In June of 2017, Bernie stepped away from Find and Convert, co-founded Vengreso, and took on the role of CMO. Now as CMO, Bernie works with his co-founders to drive thought leadership, lead generation strategies, and strategic messaging.

Colleagues and clients of Bernie say that he is a sought-after expert in B2B marketing with great insight and has the ability to invigorate a conference or company.

Back in the early 80's, I was 21 and working for Yourdon, Inc. selling training courses. I remember pitching data processing managers at large reputable enterprises and trying to sell them on the courses.

Now, the audience was way up there on the scale of intellect and subject-matter expert. I, on the other hand, was some 21-year-old kid. In the beginning, I have to admit that I struggled. I didn't know the lingo, terminology, or concepts well enough to have an effective sales conversation. However, by the time I left, I was a top performer.

The lesson that I learned back then, which I believe is even more relevant today, is that you have to know what you're selling well enough to speak intelligently about it so you can earn the respect and credibility of your prospects.

Make Yourself an Expert in the Eyes of Your Buyer

It is very difficult to get the attention of the buyer today, more than when I was actively selling in the 80's and 90's because we live at a much faster pace now, surrounded by digital stimuli. When you get a precious opportunity to talk to a prospect, you have to be perceived as an expert or they won't give you the time of day.

Although you may not be an expert, you have to convey to your buyer that you understand their business, their pain points, and how you can solve them. And, you have to convey all of that in a way that is convincing. Being so, it's essential to communicate at a level of expertise that enables you to have a credible sales conversation so they're willing to continue through the buyer's journey.

HOW DO YOU BECOME A SUBJECT MATTER EXPERT (SME) IN MODERN TIMES?

I'm going to go a little old school on you. In my early days at Yourdon Inc., I became more knowledgeable by talking with the subject matter experts (SMEs) who delivered the courses I mentioned above. I approached the SMEs with many questions and asked them to explain subjects in-depth. We also had these one-day overviews of the courses for prospects and I would sit in on them again and again, absorbing as much as I could. Nowadays, times have changed and we have it much easier.

Here is a list of my modern-day go-to's for increasing my level of expertise on any topic.

Listen to Podcasts

I create podcasts but I am also an avid podcast consumer. I listen to them every single day while I work out in the morning. Honestly, I don't think a day goes by that I walk out of the gym without having learned a little something.

What are my favorite podcasts?

- Mike Stelzner's Social Media Marketing Podcast (great for tactical advice that gets into the weeds of marketing and social media)
- Don Miller's Story Brand Podcast (very strategic)
- Reid Hoffman's Master of Scale (insights on how companies grow from zero to a gazillion)

- James Carbary's B to B Show (he interviews sales and marketing people about what they are doing)

For me, podcasts are a great way to obtain new information. I'm very busy so I don't have much time to sit down and read books but I can listen to podcasts while I do other things. I recommend you research podcasts from experts in the subjects you seek to master and begin listening to them regularly.

Research Topics on YouTube

I also utilize YouTube by searching for topics I want to learn about. You can find just about anything on YouTube.

Optimize Your LinkedIn Profile

Next, I would be remiss if I didn't call out the fact that every modern sales professional needs a rock-solid LinkedIn profile. One of the data points that we cite at Vengreso from the LinkedIn State of Sales 2018 report is:

"77% of buyers are looking for people who demonstrate knowledge about their industry, and 62% of buyers are looking to an informative LinkedIn profile before they'll determine whether they'll talk to that salesperson or not."

How do you make your profile informative?

- List your job history complete with dates and descriptions of your roles and
- responsibilities.
- List your education history complete with dates and degrees earned.
- Join groups related to your industry and interests.
- List your licenses and certifications.

- Include any volunteer experience you have completed.
- Add skills and ask your connections for endorsements.
- Ask connections for recommendations and post them to your profile.
- List your accomplishments in terms of projects, publications, and organizations.
- Share your interests related to your career.
- Write articles to share your industry and product or service knowledge.
- Turn your about section into a sales pitch that includes the problems you solve for your clients, how you solve them, and why they should trust you.
- Participate in conversations related to your industry and company.
- Create posts that share helpful, accurate, and innovative ideas related to your industry and company.

If you don't have a LinkedIn profile that demonstrates your expertise in a very credible way, you will miss out on sales conversations. On the other hand, an effective LinkedIn profile can help you win over clients who are on the fence.

Adopt the Expert Mindset to Maximize Sales

Being an expert for your buyers really comes down to becoming a sponge. You have to switch your mindset to a learning state and continuously seek out knowledge about whatever it is that you sell and whomever you sell to. To be honest, you will need self- motivation to want to educate yourself and the discipline to continuously pursue new knowledge. With those, you have the entire internet at your disposal. You just need to find relative information and consume it over and over again, every single day.

Want to learn more from Bernie Borges? Follow him on:
Website: vengreso.com
LinkedIn: linkedin.com/in/bernieborges

#88 Be More Than Just a Salesperson

SCOTT BARKER

"If you aren't an expert, you're like these people who are turbocharging or put NOS on their Honda Accords, you're missing the substance."

ABOUT SCOTT BARKER:

Scott Barker is the Head of Partnerships at Sales Hacker, an Evangelist and Podcast Host at Outreach, and a Board Member and the Director of Corporate Partnerships at The Integrated Fitness Society. He also consults/advises for multiple companies.

Driven by a passion for building and strengthening authentic relationships with his team and partners, Scott is a top performer in sales, business development, marketing, and team-building at B2B SAAS and media companies.

He is a self-proclaimed sales/marketing technology nerd that spends a shocking amount of time reading about up-and-coming best practices/tech in the modern selling space and is always looking for a new challenge, both in and outside the office.

Scott's career began after attending Capilano University where he studied business and commerce. He was a Sales and Marketing Representative at PortaLife Solutions where he built and maintained client relationships, supervised product testing, and engaged attendees at large events.

From there, Scott was a Sales Manager at The Global Work & Travel Co. where he holds the North American daily sales record and remained the top sales professional on the continent during his first year.

His next position was at Payfirma as a Business Development Representative followed by the same role at Media Valet. Then, in 2017, he joined Sales Hacker, where he is living his professional dream today, helping partners crush their marketing and sales goals. Scott has been credited with taking a sales process that was in shambles and transforming it into millions of dollars in closed revenue that ultimately resulted in the acquisition of Sales Hacker by Outreach.io.

Those who have worked with Scott only have positive things to say, calling him the best salesperson they have ever worked with, someone who is focused on the task and consistent when he puts his mind to something, and one of the pioneers in business development and the sales field.

When I was fresh out of high school, I decided to move to Australia on a whim. I landed a sales job and spent some time adventuring and learning about myself before I came home. After returning, I had a little trouble figuring out what to do next and ended up bartending. One night, I was serving drinks and this guy at the bar recruited me into a sales role in the travel industry. He heard my story about Australia and thought I'd be perfect.

It turns out the job involved basically selling Australian working holiday packages. Between Canada, Australia, and the UK, there is an agreement where, before you're 30, you can go and get a 1-year or 2-year visa and live and work there. We would set people up with job interviews before they got there and would take care of the first two weeks of accommodations, basically helping them to get on their feet and start their new life.

I ended up crushing it and became number one in North America and I think I hold the record for the most sales in a day. It was B2C sales, so highly transactional and was straight boiler room status — a go, go, go and drink 15 red bulls per day kind of environment. But I blew all these records and just killed it.

How? I used storytelling and had a damn good story because I had been there. It was never the nitty-gritty of the package details but painting a picture of their new life in Australia. I would talk about my time surfing and living on the beach, and this is where I first learned my number one sales secret. You have to be an expert on what you're selling, and at that time, I completely embodied what those people were looking for.

Become a Trusted Advisor

When I'm selling, I want people to get as much (or more) value from me, Scott Baker the human being, as they will from the product or service that I'm selling. By the end of the interaction, I want them to feel comfortable paying me, whatever the yearly fee is for the product or service, just to keep me as their trusted advisor, consultant, and expert in the field. My goal is to get them to see more value in me than what I am offering. The product or service is just the cherry on top.

How to Be a Trusted Advisor

To become a trusted advisor, you've first got to be the expert. That's key. If you're reading sales books before you've read every piece of literature on your technology, solution, and the problem that you're solving, you're doing it all wrong. You need to be an expert in your industry before you worry about the tweaks to your sales process. If you aren't an expert, you're like these people who are turbocharging or put NOS on their Honda Accords, you're missing the substance.

Become the Expert on Your Audience

But how do you become an expert? If you're selling to small businesses, go learn how to start a business. If you're selling to mechanics, go listen to a mechanics 101 podcast. If you sell into marketing, you have a VP of Marketing at your company, go become their best friend. You're the new person who buys them coffee every Monday and finds out about the pains and struggles in their role. Immerse yourself in the world of the people you are selling to. Read the content they are consuming. Until you become a walking Wikipedia in your industry, you shouldn't be worrying about the little sales tweaks.

Play the Long Game

Next, as you graduate in sales, the deal sizes get bigger and the relationships are longer, so playing the long game is what it's all about. Don't put the sale before the relationship—the relationship should always come first. If what you're selling is not the best fit for a prospect to buy right now and you have the choice to push it to serve your best interests or wait to serve theirs, you serve theirs. Additionally, leverage your network, make introductions, send hiring candidates your prospect's way, etc. Doing so makes them see you as valuable beyond just your product or service. That's how you become a trusted advisor versus someone who is just out there who can sell.

In short, learn as much as possible and become that trusted advisor. Embody what your customers are looking for. Deliver as much value as possible to your prospects and customers so that not only do they want to buy the product but they want to buy it faster or quicker, with urgency, because they also get you as a value-added expert who supports their growth. And, lastly, I believe in business karma. Be a good human and just do the right thing. In time, this will lead you to surpass your sales goals and build a network that will trust and support you throughout your career.

Want to learn more from Scott Barker? Follow him on:
LinkedIn: linkedin.com/in/ssbarker
Blog: saleshacker.com

#89 Own Your Expertise

PERRY VAN BEEK

"You have a field of expertise. Claim it, own it, use it, and share it. Be a thought leader."

ABOUT PERRY VAN BEEK:

Perry van Beek is a Social Selling Expert, International Keynote Speaker, LinkedIn Trainer & Coach, and the author of *LinkedIn Sales Navigator for Dummies*.

At Social.ONE, Perry's mission with his team is to help entrepreneurs and sales professionals become experts at social selling so they can stop chasing clients.

They've had the pleasure of working for companies like IHG (Intercontinental Hotel Group), Cisco, Palo Alto Networks, ABN-AMRO Bank, Oracle, ING Bank and many, many more.

Perry landed his first job in 1991 as an industrial salesman pitching equipment across Europe. After five years, the export director at the company was let go and Perry basically ran the place for seven months. He continued in the export/international business sector for about 15 years with short periods of working in asset management, real estate, and general management.

After a life-threatening heart surgery, Perry was inspired to make the most of his life by finding his true calling. This eventually led him to start his own export consulting business. After using LinkedIn to generate clients for that business, he gained notoriety for his social selling skills which led him to where he is today.

Clients say Perry provides truly fascinating information, is an inspiration, and tries everything to stay up with the latest LinkedIn trends. His methods are said to work quickly, making his coaching well worth the investment. If you want to approach your business' lead generation with a social selling mindset, Perry is the man to get you there.

In 2007, I stepped out and started an export consultancy business. I initially had a hard time getting clients but once I turned to LinkedIn, everything fell into place. I had all the clients I could need or want. However, it didn't take long for me to notice that many of my peers didn't know how to generate business from LinkedIn so I began sharing tips and tricks to help them out.

In 2009, someone asked me to speak to a small networking group of about 12 people on the subject. I showed up for that engagement and the room I was supposed to speak in was dark, dirty, and unprepared. I was a bit upset and asked the guy what was going on. He said, "That's not the room. It's upstairs now because more than 60 people showed up."

I was nervous but I gave my presentation. Immediately afterward, people came up to me and said, "You need to come help our company. We are struggling with LinkedIn." Then, they said the magic words, "We'll pay you." Three months later, I was on national television in the Netherlands as a LinkedIn expert. I couldn't believe it.

Share Your Knowledge Openly and for Free

Most people hold onto their knowledge tightly and keep it under lock-and-key. They don't want to share their expertise lest someone gain an advantage over them. In fact, when I meet most of my clients for the first time, they are very, very scared to share their knowledge. What surprises many people is that I share all of my knowledge frequently and at no cost.

Why do I openly share my knowledge?

People don't want to talk to salespeople, they want to talk to experts. Sharing your knowledge is a tool you can use to showcase that you are an expert and a thought leader. Once you are seen this way, people will be drawn to you like a magnet. And when you have a following that trusts and believes in you, it is much easier to sell anything, which in my case is direct access to me.

Why not charge for both the knowledge and the direct access to you?

By sharing your knowledge for free, you cast a wider net and bring in more people. For example, if you have a course and you sell it for 100 euro per head to 1,000 people, you're doing really well. You've got $100,000 in your account. Great. But what if you give it away for free and you get 100,000 people to take it? Now if out of those 100,000 people, two percent signs up for your monthly coaching (2000 people) at $20 per month, you're looking at a recurring monthly income of $40,000. After one year, that's $480,000. And it doesn't have to be monthly coaching, it can be whatever product or service you are offering.

The real value is not in the content you create from your knowledge, but it can draw people to you who you can then provide real value.

HOW-TO SHARE YOUR KNOWLEDGE

How can you get started creating content from your knowledge base and using it to drive your audience to you?

Understand Your Expertise

At speaking engagements, I often ask my audience how many of them are experts. If I have about 100 people in the room, five or 10 people usually raise their hands.

I tell them, look at your network. Who knows more about your field of expertise than you? Even just look at your own LinkedIn connections. How many LinkedIn connections do you have and how many know more about your subject than you? Maybe one or two? That makes you belong to the top one percent. Then, I ask again how many people in the room are experts and everyone raises their hand.

You have a field of expertise. Claim it, own it, use it, and share it. Be the thought leader.

Don't Be Scared

Many people feel apprehensive to share their knowledge because they are worried about what people will think. I say don't try to please everyone. If you want to please everyone, go sell ice cream. Believe in what you say and just share it. Don't be afraid to have an opinion. If you think someone may not like it or feel unsure, forget it. You will attract the right people. Sometimes you may have to say sorry and that's okay. I say just take your stance and start sharing. It will be worth it.

Share Existing Content

You may be wondering, how you are going to create enough content to consistently share your knowledge. I learned this the hard way but you don't have to create all the content yourself. There's so much good content out there and you can share that too, but not without putting some effort in.

Everyone says content is king and I like to add that context is queen. When you share content, tell why you are sharing it and your opinion on the matter. Mixing original content and shared content can make it much easier to become a thought leader.

Use Various Channels

Lastly, I found my niche using LinkedIn when I was starting my business and I think it is a great place to share professional knowledge. However, don't limit yourself to one platform. Right now, I am actually transitioning a little bit away from just LinkedIn. I still love it, but I'm seeing that email marketing is really growing fast again. So keep your options open and don't limit yourself to one platform.

Own Your Expertise and Share Your Knowledge

In summary, my top sales secret is to share your knowledge frequently and openly. Figure out what you know, develop an opinion, share it, and don't be scared. Then, eventually, you will become a thought leader and you can monetize your position whether it's by granting people direct access to you or positioning your products and services to them.

Want to learn more from Perry van Beek? Follow him on:
LinkedIn: linkedin.com/in/perryvanbeek
Twitter: @perryvanbeek
Website: socialone-en.mykajabi.com

#90 Own Your Voice and the Rest Will Follow

AARON ROSS

"Comfort is the enemy of growth."

ABOUT AARON ROSS:

Aaron Ross co-founded PredictableRevenue.com in 2008, a software and consulting company that accelerates outbound sales using the Cold Calling 2.0 process that added $100M+ in extra revenue at Salesforce.com.

He has published two best-selling books under the Predictable Revenue umbrella: *From Inevitable to Impossible—How Hyper-Growth Companies Create Predictable Revenue!* co-authored with Jason Lemkin, and *Predictable Revenue: Turn Your Business Into A Sales Machine With The $100 Million Best Practices Of Salesforce.com,* co-authored with Marylou Tyler.

Aaron is also a highly-ranked international speaker. He is well-known for combining 'big picture' inspirations with hyper-tactical takeaways.

His career began after graduating from Stanford with a BS in Environmental Civil Engineering. Aaron then spent four years working in mergers and acquisitions and product marketing before founding his first company, LeaseExchange.

After two years, Aaron shut down and liquidated his business and joined Salesforce.com. He wanted to learn about sales and was willing to start in an entry-level position to do so. It didn't take long for him to work his way up to the Director of Corporate Sales and then Senior Director of Corporate Development and Acquisitions.

After four years at Salesforce, Aaron moved to Alloy Ventures for one year as an entrepreneur/expert-in-residence (EIR), before founding his second business, Predictable Revenue. And the rest is history as they say.

Aaron now lives in Los Angeles with his wife and nine children, and (usually, but not always) keeps a 25 to 30-hour workweek. He is well-known as a creative, insightful, positive, and innovative individual. His concepts are said to contribute immensely to businesses and his principles have helped to shape the inside sales and marketing industry as a whole.

When looking at any kind of sales transaction, the bottom line is people buy from people. If you're a salesperson who's kind of drone-like, going through the motions with nothing extra to add, you're not going to be very successful.

Whatever job you do, you need to have a voice and presence. It's in the way you talk about the things you care about, how you see things, and what you are most interested in. You may think, but I don't know what my voice should sound like. Well, not many people do right out of the gate.

Most people have to kind of figure it out over time and I have a unique approach to help you hone in on your unique voice and perspective.

Commit to Creating Content Regularly and Speaking About It Publicly

My number one secret to sales is committing to content publishing and public speaking. When you are speaking in front of people and publishing content regularly, it forces you to think about what people want to hear and what you have to share that is interesting. Doing so can help you figure out where your special powers are, where your extra areas of interest or talent are, and how you can add extra value and create new things. Knowing these things can help you get a promotion or new job, come up with new ideas, and/or build a larger audience.

How to Find and Share Your Voice Through Content and Public Speaking

With modern technology, anyone can write up an article or make a video and share it through social media. The trickiest part of this secret is sticking with it. When you're nervous, busy, afraid, or lazy, you can't give up or drop off. Each person is different so the approach will vary but here are four tips I recommend.

Identify Your Why

There's no job or activity that will be great every day. It doesn't matter what you do, you're going to have days that are up and days that are down.

Even with parenting. I have nine kids and there's definitely days and times where I'm just like, "Oh, this sucks." However, there's an undercurrent in which I know what I am doing is important so I still love, appreciate, and stick through it in the hard times. If you don't have that driving "why" in what you are doing, it's likely you're going to end up giving up when the going gets tough.

So, identify what drives you, whether it is to grow in your career, provide for your family, make a name for yourself, or something else. Write it down, create visual reminders, and keep it top-of-mind so you stay on track through the ups and downs. Creating a reputation for yourself will require the courage to speak up and the patience and diligence to stick with it for years.

Set Public Deadlines as a Forcing Function

Next, you need a forcing function, which is something that makes you want to do things when you don't want to do them.

Imagine two friends who both want to lose weight. They both join the gym but the second friend also commits to run a half marathon two months down the road and announces it on social media. Who do you think is going to be more driven to lose the pounds?

By creating public announcements about your goals and deadlines, you create an external accountability force that helps you to work toward your internal goal. You involve other people who are going to be wondering how you are progressing and if you achieve what you said you would.

I recommend you choose strategic dates and times to publish and speak and share them publicly. After one is done, set another one. Once you set a date, you have to figure it out. There were many times in my career that I would decide to speak before I knew what the topic was because I knew I needed to do something. I would post, "On the 25th, I'm gonna have a conference call" and It would force me to think about what I want to say, who I'm going to invite, and what I want them to take away from the message.

Doing that, even a couple of dozen times over a few years, really helped crystallize what I was doing into fewer ideas that were more focused. And, it also helped me to grow my audience and skills.

Create Live Speaking Events

When speaking about your content and work, it is best to do it live (online, in a webinar, over the phone, in-person.). While it is okay to create a video in advance, there's an element that you miss with recorded content. Going 'live' shows who you are, unedited. It also creates urgency as people can't view it 'live' at any time, it is just this once. Further, it gives you the opportunity, in many cases, to interact in real-time with your audience which provides them with immense value.

Learn From Your Mistakes

Lastly, as you begin to put yourself out there, you are bound to make some mistakes. When I was 26 working in product management, I hadn't done much public speaking. I gave a talk in front of a couple of partners and made a few jokes about sex, politics, and religion which did not go over well. It was definitely embarrassing and one of my more painful public speaking lessons but I didn't stop. I took note of the problem and was more careful about what I would joke about when speaking publicly. No matter what happens, look for the learnings from it and keep going.

Success in your sales career depends on using your strengths and skills to differentiate yourself from every other sales professional out there. You have to step out of the mold and discover who you are and what you have to say. Too many salespeople get stuck in the script and become kind of drone-like. Use content creation and public speaking to share your unique value with the world while also honing in on your areas of expertise and opening doors for your future.

Want to learn more from Aaron Ross? Follow him on:
Business Website: predictablerevenue.com
LinkedIn URL: www.linkedin.com/in/aaronross

#91 Content Sells

SARAH SCUDDER

"I am growing my company by building out a marketing team, not a traditional sales team. I believe creating content is the future of sales."

ABOUT SARAH SCUDDER:

Sarah Scudder is the President of Real Sourcing Network (RSN), a respected columnist, and a podcast host. She was named one of the 40 under 40 Trailblazers by the *North Bay Business Journal*.

Before beginning her career, Sarah attended Sonoma State University. She double- majored in Business Administration and Economics and minored in American Multicultural Studies and Marketing.

After graduating, she took on the role of Chief Growth Officer at The Sourcing Group. While Sarah had no formal sales training, she was highly motivated to succeed. She researched the market and identified a niche that she thought would be the most profitable for the company. After about six years, she increased the company's value from $3 million to $13 million.

Following her success with The Sourcing Group, Sarah decided to launch her own business. Now her startup, Real Sourcing Network, is taking a non-traditional approach to print and marketing services.

Sarah's colleagues say that she is one of the smartest, most ambitious, diligent, competent, and creative professionals they have ever met. She is said to have an impressive understanding of cutting-edge sourcing and procurement concepts, as well as a far-reaching network of connections throughout the supply management universe.

The world has changed dramatically in the last three years and newsflash: people no longer need or want to be sold to! Traditionally, you would contact prospects in your target audience and would have a limited time to pique their interest. Now, thanks to the internet, buyers, and consumers are constantly doing their own research and want to self-educate.

With this shift, our role in the sales process has changed. Prospects are contacting us after they already know about our offerings. So should you just sit around and wait? Of course, not. You need to expand your business's reach through marketing. You need to become an authority in your industry, make your brand known, and establish thought leadership.

But how exactly can you do that?

Don't Invest Your Time in Selling, Invest Your Time in Marketing

My belief is that marketing is now sales. Below are the strategic marketing actions I have taken to grow my businesses.

Find Your Niche

First things first—you need to find your niche. Figure out what you do well and target a specific market or buyer. In my first role at The Sourcing Group, I didn't have the resources to give everything to everyone and couldn't target 10 verticals; I had to choose one.

I did a great deal of research and decided to target restaurants because they spent a lot of money on printed materials (uniforms, brochures, menus, flyers). Many national restaurant chains had over 100 locations which I knew could be huge deals. I was right and they were the key to my company's successful growth.

Create Content

Once you have your niche, you need to create a content strategy to reach your audience in all stages of the buying cycle.

Here are some of the types of content you can create:

- Whitepapers
- Email newsletters
- Articles
- Blogs
- Landing pages
- Social media posts
- Ebooks
- Webinars
- Infographics
- Case studies
- Long-form content
- Template and checklist downloads
- Videos
- Round-ups
- Slideshows
- Collaborations
- Q and A's
- Interviews
- Press Releases
- Product News
- Comparisons
- Step-by-step guides
- How-to guides
- Research reports

Your content should be present across multiple channels and should inform your audience throughout their research process. Within the content, don't hard sell your company or product but instead focus on providing valuable information that prospects will be looking for. Also, set up ways to gain your prospect's contact information (e.g. email address at the very least) in exchange for your content.

At RSN, we mail out a quarterly magazine to 1,500 heads of procurement and we have an electronic newsletter that goes out to 8,000 procurement executives. Our magazines feature four articles, three written by us and one by an outside consultant, and each article is the result of an interview. We interview people who are succeeding and who we want as clients. In the process, they get to know our company and our value, allowing us to sell without selling.

Additionally, we build a meaningful relationship with each interviewee by learning about their story and sharing it with our followers. In addition to publishing the articles in the magazine, we also publish and promote them online through our social media channels. Further, others in the procurement industry want exposure through our magazine so they sponsor it in order to be featured. As a result, we don't have to pay for it which further increases the value.

Where can you get content? At RSN, we don't have content writers on staff, so we have found agencies or freelancers to help us. If you can't hire content writers and need to do it yourself but aren't a writer, I recommend blocking out 30 minutes every day to learn how to write.

I am not a naturally gifted writer but I decided that writing articles about my industry to help build my authority and share my ideas was a must. I did as I said above, writing for 30 minutes every day and published my work on LinkedIn which anyone can do for free. Over time, I started reaching out to editors to tell them that I was interested in writing for their publication. I would tell them why they should pick me and would send examples of my work.

In my first year, I got picked up by three publications. Of course, not everyone says yes but media companies are always looking for fresh new content. Now, I write for several publications each month and I share them on my website and social profiles.

Another important factor is helping your content reach as many people as possible which you can do through paid advertising and search engine optimization. We use Hubspot to manage our outbound processes and have someone whose specific job is to manage analytics and make everything flow. I firmly believe content planning, creation, disbursement, and management is where all businesses should be placing a bulk of their investments.

Network In-Person

In addition to content, in-person networking is important. What kind? Start with industry events. Now, I don't recommend setting up a booth as I think that is a waste of time and resources but you should attend the events. Go and connect with people. You can then get follow-ups, people in your pipeline, and people you can send your content to.

At RSN, we actually host events, too. Additionally, we are also hosting one-day seminars with keynote speakers, breakout portions, and lunch.

Making face-to-face connections is highly impactful and can help you to broaden your reach and earn advocates for your brand.

Find Connectors

The next piece is finding connectors who can help you build your network and thus raise awareness about your brand. One of the biggest mistakes I made in my first role at The Sourcing Group was working too hard to get meetings. Later, I figured out that interactions go much more smoothly when you are introduced to a new contact by a mutual connection. Now I spend time looking for connectors, well-connected people who are in my industry and who can connect me with other people.

Once I find one and we come to an agreement, I send them a list of 100 prospects and ask them who they know. I constantly email and call them and they make introductions for me throughout the year. Further, I have a script I send them so the introduction takes zero effort. I make it so easy that they can't say no. Oh, and make sure to always follow up and say thank you. Maybe even send a gift if it was a bit more work than usual.

Diversify Your Target Mix

One last tip, diversify your targets. Those big national restaurant chains I mentioned before are targets I refer to as 'whales.' They are huge and highly profitable but they have longer sales cycles, take longer, and are harder to close. When deciding which prospects to pursue, you shouldn't focus exclusively on the 'whales.' You need a mix in your pipeline and I recommend 25% whales, 50% mid-market, 25% smaller type prospects.

I hope my experiences and tips can help to boost your sales performance even though they are not in line with traditional sales tactics. Times have changed, especially in the past three years, and we must change too. I believe in taking advantage of the tools we have to make the most of the evolving marketplace. Remember, content is KING.

**Want to learn more from Sarah Scudder? Follow her on:
LinkedIn: linkedin.com/in/sarah-scudder-marketing-
services- procurement-guru
Website: rsnetwork.com
Twitter: @sscudder**

#92 Growing Your 'Volk' (aka Tribe)

STRING NGUYEN

"Be you, it's not business-to-business,
it's people-to-people."

ABOUT STRING NGUYEN:

String Nguyen is a proven video expert and a three-time Top Voice on LinkedIn where she grew her following from zero to 30,000 followers in a little over a year! Most recently, she founded The Trusted Voice— a company that helps regular people including thought- leaders, salespeople, marketers, and entrepreneurs to become video influencers online.

A little about String, pre-LinkedIn. She graduated from RMIT University, earning a Bachelor of Design in interior design. After graduation, she worked as an interior designer for about three and a half years but didn't feel fulfilled in that role. She decided to pivot and start her own online business, String Story Media, where she would collect and develop stories that inspired various art projects.

Now, just over 11 years later, String's company has evolved as she is now a global brand ambassador and provides social media strategy and video production services. Additionally, she launched The Trusted Voice in November of 2018.

Those who know String says she provides the insights needed to improve your online marketing and even double the size of your email list in one month. She is known to be generous with her time and a great resource if you want to learn how to communicate with your audience in a genuine way. Oh, and she loves fried chicken!

Marketing online isn't business-to-business anymore, it's person-to-person and everyone is now a media company for themselves. You can control your narrative and you can control how you position yourself. But what is the best way to market yourself, show who you are, and drive sales?

Go All-in On Video

My top sales secret is to go all-in on video. That means creating video content on a regular basis on at least one channel whether that be LinkedIn, YouTube, Instagram, or another. It engages people, allowing you to share your energy and message with your audience face-to-face so they can see and feel who you are.

A lot of people think they have to put on this professional face of a 9 to 5'er but you don't. Be true to yourself and be authentic — even be awkward and show your personality! That's why I use fried chicken. I love it and I tie it into my brand. It actually helps people relate to me.

If you're thinking you don't have time for video, it's true that it can be a lot of work but you can still do it. Just find out where your Volk is (more on that below) and go all-in with video on that channel.

HOW TO GO ALL-IN WITH VIDEO

I've created the 7 V's to help you use video to become a trusted source in your niche.

Vision

Find your vision. It's not a goal but your role in the world. The thing that you wake up thinking about every morning. What kind of impact do you want to make with your life? What is your legacy? That is your starting point. All of your videos should tie back to it somehow.

My vision is to increase creative vibes. We all work so much that we might as well do something that we believe in and are passionate about. My message is not about working for the man, it's about finding your own creative satisfaction. I count how many creative vibes I get per day (along with how many fried chicken nuggets I get), and I share my creative vibes with everyone.

Values

Next, establish your values. There are two types; personal and business. Your personal values are your moral compass. Business value is the value you provide to the world and your unique selling proposition. Define both.

Volk

Volk is a German word that basically means your tribe. To build a community, you need to create content that resonates with your volks. So the more you understand who your volks are and create for them, the better your content and results become. They will eventually see you as a go-to channel that will solve their problems.

Voice

What is your key message to the world? We all have topic pillars but you can't wear 100 hats. You want to have three key messages so people come to you for those. This will help you cut through all the content out there and be memorable. Further, when people are ready to consume your message, it will already be ingrained in them because you have repeated it over and over.

Visuals

Your visuals include how your brand is presented. Most people think of their logo but with video, it is also your face. Unless you're a twin the world, there's no one else that looks like you or has your personality. People will begin to associate you with your brand and the value you provide. And you become a differentiating factor for your business.

Validation

This V is about ensuring your approach is working. Check in to ensure you have goals that align with your vision and to see if you are growing or not. You don't want to invest so much energy creating a media company if you're not hitting your marks.

Victory

Make money! Once your volks trust you, monetize by providing products and services!

There you have it the 7 V's. Now, I'll answer some of the most frequently asked questions about making video content.

What if I'm Nervous About Getting in Front of the Camera?

I get it. I didn't even show my face in my first viral video. It causes all of our internal fears of ourselves to be projected onto the world. How I got over it was just doing it and practicing. You can train yourself to be more confident just like with anything else. So use repetition to drain out the fear.

What If My Videos Suck?

When you first start out, you are literally showing your bad side. But the hilarious thing is you do one shitty video, two shitty videos, three shitty videos, but when you get up to your 10th one, it will be better. And you keep on doing the same thing and people literally follow your journey. When you start out with a shitty video but get better each time, people will gain respect for you.

How Can I Get Started Right Now?

Go on Instagram and make a video today. It can be short and you don't even have to talk or show your face. Then, do it every day. It takes 60 days to make a habit. You can start by sharing things that aren't you— like your house or your cat. But then start to show your face and start talking like you are talking to a friend on the other side.

It's okay to be awkward but you don't want to make people uncomfortable on the other side. Your energy is literally being shed onto the other person. People mirror you. If you're closed, they will be closed. But if you are open, people will be open and you can begin to grow your following.

These are my 7 V's and top tips to help you to become THE trusted source for your area of expertise using video. Need help? You can message me on LinkedIn with questions and I will answer because I want to help as many people as possible!

Want to learn more from String Nguyen? Follow her on (and message her about fried chicken to show her your "in" her tribe): LinkedIn: linkedin.com/in/stringstory Twitter: @StringStory Instagram: @stringstory

#93 Love What You Do or Don't Fucking Do It

JEFFREY GITOMER

"I'm the 'King of Sales.' How did I get that title?
I named myself."

ABOUT JEFFREY GITOMER:

Jeffrey Gitomer, the "King of Sales," is an international sales trainer, keynote speaker, and best-selling author. Jeffrey has written 13 best-selling books, spoken at 2,500 corporate events, and shaped the world of sales over the last 25 years.

Jeffrey is known across the globe for his critically acclaimed books including The Sales Bible, Little Red Book Of Selling, and his newest book, Get Shit Done. Jeffrey and his wife, Jennifer Gluckow, are also the hosts of the popular podcast, "Sell or Die." He is also the author of a syndicated column called "Sales Moves," which is read by millions of salespeople each week.

Jeffrey has traveled the globe helping sales teams master how to discover the buying motive and he has taught tens of thousands of students through his Gitomer Online Learning Academy.

Jeffrey's keynote talks are electrifying and unlike any others. He provides answers, informs, challenges, and inspires salespeople, sales teams, and sales leadership teams for hundreds of the largest and most successful companies in the world including Coca-Cola, BMW, Salesforce, and many more.

Known as an active salesman — Jeffery is not just a teacher and a writer, but also a do-er, making sales calls every day to stay sales-relevant both online and face-to-face. He is also a proud husband, father, grandfather, and dog owner.

You can't get into sales just to make a lot of money.

If you do, you'll hate what you do every day. And you'll come home, throw shit around, drink beer, and watch Netflix every night like a fool.

You have to find what you love to do. What you love to sell.

I love what I do.

I go to sleep sober every night.

I wake up between five and six o clock every morning and I sit in my favorite chair. My chair is worth 10 million dollars because it is the chair that I do all of my writing.

Every morning, I write, I read, I prepare, and that causes me to think and create.

I've done those five things for 25 years—every fucking day.

Doing What You Love

So how do I do what I love? Read my book, Get Shit Done.

But the bottom line is people have too many diversions. Your phone dings more than it rings. If you're a woman, you don't need to know that your high school boyfriend got a little fat on Facebook. If you're a man, you don't need to see the latest meme your friend posted.

You don't need notifications on your phone. I get texts and that's it. No other notifications and sometimes I even turn the texts off.

Because I do things on my time. Not when people put urgency on me. I do important things, not necessarily urgent things, and delegate everything else.

I'm an idea guy, I'm a writer, I'm a sales guy and I'm a speaker. Anything else is a waste of my fucking time. Find what you love and focus on only doing that. Make time for that and turn off or delegate everything else.

Create Your Own Competitive Advantage

Once you're doing what you love, if that's selling, you have to walk into a sales call with a competitive advantage or you'll lose every time.

It's not something that you have that the competition doesn't have.

It's something that you're great at that the customer considers important or valuable.

For example, I'm great at sales, there's a lot of people out there that say they are great at sales. But they only read The Little Red Book of Selling and I fucking wrote it.

The challenge is how are you different or perceived as different or more valuable than your competitor?

You don't have to downgrade or bad mouth the competition. You have to be perceived as different or better. And you better have social proof to back up your case.

There's a way for every business type to do this that's different but the bottom line is, you have to be perceived as an industry standard. You have to be the standard-setter, not a follower.

I'm the "King of Sales." How did I get that title? I named myself. No one else took it. I took it.

So find what you love, find what sets your offer apart, and go all-in on it.

Want to learn more from Jeffrey Gitomer? Follow him on:
LinkedIn: linkedin.com/in/jeffreygitomer
Personal Website: gitomer.com/king-of-sales/
Company Website: gitomer.com

#94 Own Your Destiny

TRISH BERTUZZI

"If you don't put in the time, effort, energy, and focus to make yourself successful, it will never happen."

ABOUT TRISH BERTUZZI:

Trish Bertuzzi is the Founder and CEO of The Bridge Group, Inc., a best-selling author, and a LinkedIn Top Sales Voice (2018 and 2019). At the Bridge Group, Trish and her team help B2B companies build world-class Inside Sales teams. Since 1998, they have helped over 400 companies to build, expand, and optimize Sales Development and Inside Sales.

Trish shared her expertise in her book, The Sales Development Playbook: Build Repeatable Pipeline and Accelerate Growth with Inside Sales, which was a best-seller in the sales and selling management category on Amazon from 2016 to 2018.

Through a combination of hard work and timing, Trish and her team's research and ideas have been featured on Inc.com, in Forbes, by associations like SLMA and AA-ISP, and across more than 68 sites in the sales and marketing world.

Trish was recognized by the American Association of Inside Sales Professionals as "Consulting Provider of the Year" from 2013 to 2017 and was named a Women Sales Pros Advisor in 2019.

Those who have met and worked with Trish describe her as a brilliant sales strategist, trainer, and visionary. Many say she is THE leader to be connected with if your organization cares about Inside Sales.

I didn't get my first sales job until I was 27. I was a single mom. It was back in the day of the three-martini lunch and I was waitressing at Kent's Steakhouse in Framingham. The executives would come in every day and I'd wait on them. If you know me, you know I'm far from being shy so I would give them shit and we had a great relationship.

One day, an executive told me, "You are rude, obnoxious, arrogant, and hungry—you should be in sales." I said, "Well, give me a job." And he did. So I went to work selling paper lead lists over the phone. Old school.

I didn't get why people said sales was so hard. I thought it was easy and I loved selling over the phone, I loved the product, and I ended up being the number one rep. The number one rep they eventually fired.

They fired me because I was a pain in the ass. I thought I knew everything about everything. It was their worst nightmare. And I learned, it doesn't matter if you're the top performer. If you're not a team player, you're gone. So I got fired and I deserved it. I was an asshole. I thought I could get away with whatever I wanted because I was crushing my numbers. Just not a good corporate citizen. So I got what I deserved.

But you pick yourself up, you dust yourself off, and you go get another job.

So I humbled myself a bit and got another job in telemarketing. I did really well and I convinced them to let me build a team. And when they got a new tech product, I told them I could sell it over the phone, and I did. And then I built a team for that. And then I went to another tech company. And then I moved to another one and became the VP of Sales.

One day in 1998, I had a moment where I realized there was a problem in the industry. Executives thought reps just pounded the pavement and

547

revenue shot out the other end. I thought I'd start a consulting company to teach them how to build world-class inside sales teams. I figured if it didn't work, I'd just get another job.

There's a quote by Margaret Shepard I find true—"Sometimes your only available form of transportation is a leap of faith." Well, it worked and I've been doing it ever since.

Take Ownership Of Your Success

The number one sales secret that I believe is key to success is understanding that nobody owns your success but you.

Nobody.

I see new salespeople and they're like:

"We don't get any training."

"Yeah, they didn't teach me how to do that."

"I was going to watch that webinar but then I got busy."

Okay. It's not up to your company to make you successful. It's not up to your family to make you successful. It's not up to your boss to make you successful.

It's up to YOU to make you successful.

If you don't put in the time, effort, energy, and focus to make yourself successful, it will never happen.

So full circle, who is to blame? You.

The only person who owns your success is you.

How Do You Take Full Responsibility For Your Success?

- Assume responsibility for everything.
- If your company doesn't provide training, train yourself.
- If you don't have enough leads, find a way to get the leads.
- If you don't know something, figure it out.
- If you get fired, own it, and learn from it.
- If you see a problem, fix it.
- If you need an opportunity, create one.

Everyone loves to blame someone else for their problems.

Don't.

I developed this skill because I didn't have options. There were not fabulous resources that are available today when I started.

I took responsibility for everything even before I had my own company. I did it when I was a telemarketing rep. I'd say to the field guys, "How do you get them to think about it this way?" Or, to this day, I still do this, if I'm on the phone and I'm talking to a prospect and I can tell we are going nowhere, they are not grooving on me, I stop and I say, "What about my message is not resonating with you? Can you help me understand?"

And a lot of times they will tell me whatever it is that I didn't articulate that would've made them pay attention. And that's a learning experience.

I took responsibility for learning the craft of sales and you have to do the same.

And learning isn't just reading a book or going to a conference. It's interacting with your buyers and asking questions both when it's going well and when it's not.

I'll end with an example. Jill Konrath is a fabulous author. I read her book, Selling to Big Companies, and I thought, "Oh my god, this is changing my life." So I tracked her down. I called her. And now I consider her one of my closest friends. Do not be afraid to ask. Do not be afraid to learn. Do not be afraid to do what you need to do to be successful. You'll be amazed. If you don't ask, you don't get it. But if you ask, sometimes you get and it's a blessing.

You can do whatever you want as long as you work hard and earn it. You don't deserve it. You don't hang out long enough so it happens for you. You earn it.

Everyone is going to screw up. You just have to forgive yourself. Try not to make the same mistake again and keep going.

Want to learn more from Trish Bertuzzi? Follow her on:
Twitter: Trish Bertuzzi (@bridgegroupinc)
Website: bridgegroupinc.com
Linkedin: linkedin.com/in/trishbertuzzi

NETWORK RELATIONSHIP MANAGEMENT

#95 End the Battle Between Sales and Marketing

TODD WILMS

"Those that can make the mental shift to align sales and marketing will be successful, and those that can't, are ultimately going to fail."

ABOUT TODD WILMS:

Todd Wilms is the Silicon Valley marketing leader who has helped numerous top-class brands get to the top level. He is the founder of Founders Place, a FractionalCMO for numerous companies. He is also a #1 Amazon Hot List author, a keynote speaker, and an angel investor.

Todd uses his experience from PayPal, eBay, PeopleSoft, SAP, Neustar, and Verisign to help founders, entrepreneurs, and startups conquer the marketplace. He's also part of the Consultant's Collective, a group of executive consultants who help organizations innovate, transform, and improve performance.

Todd earned his BA in Psychology from Butler University and his MBA from The George Washington University. Throughout his career, he has served as the Worldwide Director of Marketing at Emptoris, Head of Social Strategy at SAP, Head of Corporate Communications and Digital at

Neustar, and VP of Corporate Marketing at Verisign. Along with running Founders Place today, he is also on MOCCA's Board of Directors, fundraises for Help Refugees, and volunteers for #Mobility4All.

Those who know Todd say he understands marketing in today's rapidly changing context and offers counsel that is well thought out and carefully considered. He is known to lead with humor, kindness, creativity, and heart, and to be someone who uplifts others wherever he goes.

Many leaders unintentionally pit their sales and marketing teams against each other, wasting precious time, energy, and resources on an endless (and unproductive) fight. Your company may have this problem if you are hearing arguments like this:

"Well, I drove them to the event." "Well, I met them at the event."

"Well, I followed up with a great piece of content." "But I met them in the room and sold them."

"Yes, but I delivered the final webinar that got them to sign on the dotted line."

The truth of the matter is, both sales and marketing contribute to the buyer's journey and are responsible for bringing in customers. But as the departments fight to take credit or point the finger, they sink the ship.

Sales and Marketing Need to Align for Success

The majority of organizations struggle with this us vs. them, sales vs. marketing battle and it does more damage to the forward momentum of an organization than anything else. You can put the right resources, time, and energy together but if those two teams are competing instead of finding the best way to connect and interact with customers, the company is doomed.

The problem in many cases can be traced back to attribution. Leaders often ask, "Who is it that ultimately drove the revenue?" And when you put ownership on one group or the other, it is a zero-sum game, somebody has to win and somebody has to lose. So sales and marketing teams end up arguing over who brought in the customer, who is driving revenue, and who should get more of the budget.

Sales and marketing leaders need to understand that the organization needs both of them and they are most powerful when in full alignment. It's not a "you vs. me" but a "sales and marketing vs. the goals and the competition" situation. Leaders have to set the atmosphere as one of unity where goals are set, measured, and compensated to motivate the teams to work together.

It sounds so simple, like a "duh" moment. You may ask, "Well aren't we doing this already?" But no, most organizations are not. It's why CMOs have an average tenure of 18 months and why you're shifting through chief revenue officers every 24 months.

HOW TO ALIGN YOUR SALES AND MARKETING TEAMS

Aligning sales and marketing starts at the top. Here are some tips on how to combine the two forces for greater success.

Put Attribution in its Rightful Place

First, I'm not saying leaders shouldn't look at attribution. It's important to know what actions are driving results. But that information shouldn't be how the success is measured. It doesn't indicate the sole method that closed a sale anyhow. No one goes to a show one time, meets you and buys. They have likely had seven or eight other things happen behind the scenes that drove them to that point. So leaders should know the attribution report and understand it, but shouldn't hang their hat on it or speak about it to the teams.

Set United Goals

Instead of focusing on attribution and who closed the sale, organizations need to focus on the bigger company goals that both teams can work towards. It can be managing certain KPIs, pipelines, bookings, revenue, or whatever your business needs to prioritize at the moment.

For example, say a goal is a certain number of bookings. Both teams should be signed up to own that piece, both on the hook for it. Now, internally, behind closed doors, leaders can look at attribution, who did what, who brought the deal in, but ultimately what they're measuring and speaking about is if the team is achieving the goal for bookings as a whole. And compensation should be aligned respectively.

Transparent Proactive Discussions

The next part is about taking the time to have proactive, transparent discussions. The heads of sales and marketing need to sit down together and discuss the goal. They also need to identify all the things that are working at present, the things they haven't considered yet, and those they may want to experiment with. I'm a big fan of experimenting. You've always got to try and find where the edges are.

This should be an opportunity for either leader to voice if they need more from the other. For example, the sales leader can say, "You're not providing on SEO, what's going on?" Then, the marketing leader can say, "Okay, how much of that is accurate and where do I need to improve?" And then the marketing leader can ask, "Hey, why aren't your SDRs doing more outbound calls?" And the sales leader can say, "Well, they don't have the right content or scripting."

Address the concerns honestly and openly upfront instead of pointing the finger later. Both leaders are responsible for voicing what they need from the other. The goal and the true task at hand is to effectively maximize goal attainment together.

Make United Decisions

Lastly, once you both are on the same page with the goal, the needs, and what's working/ not working, you can make educated decisions as a collective unit.

For example, marketing may want to build a great new website and work on the face and voice of the company. However, after talking with sales they find out that other priorities need to come first. They identify that outbound sales are down because they need more scripts and content. Marketing would need to focus on that content first and then circle back to other priorities. Without communication, the budget would get spent in silos which don't necessarily support each other and the greater good of the company. So the details, priorities, and plan should be hashed out together.

Alignment, even at that first step, is a river. It's the source of the Mississippi. If you don't get that fixed, everything else will be impossible to resolve because the foundation isn't right. On the flip side, every time I've worked with co-leaders who have this kind of transparent, honest, radical relationship, I've seen them uncover opportunities for meaningful revenue growth.

So remember, organizational leadership has to align sales and marketing. The teams cannot be fighting. Don't make it about attribution. Nothing is done in one touch. It is a collaborative effort toward the greater good of the company so both teams need to work together toward shared goals.

Want to learn more from Todd Wilms? Follow him on:
LinkedIn: linkedin.com/in/toddwilms
Website: Foundersplace.co

#96 How Much Is Your Network Worth?

AMY FRANKO

"I really believe that the value of my relationships directly impacts the sales results that I can accomplish."

ABOUT AMY FRANKO:

As a strategic sales expert and keynote speaker, Amy Franko built a successful B2B sales career working for major two major tech companies—IBM and Lenovo. In 2007, Amy pivoted into entrepreneurship and launched a training company called Impact Instruction Group. At Impact Instruction Group, Amy built a book of business that included Fortune 1000 clients and has consistently sold 5-to-7 figure engagements since launching the business.

Her expertise is widely shared on social networks, and in respected publications such as *Top Sales World, Selling Power, TD Magazine, Training Industry, Training Magazine, Accounting Today,* and *CLO Magazine.* Amy has been featured on several elite sales podcasts as well as in *Entrepreneur, Forbes,* and *O Magazine.*

Her book, *The Modern Seller,* is an Amazon best-seller and was named a top sales book of 2018 by *Top Sales World.*

I started my career doing traditional B2B sales, with the bulk of my time spent in the technology space. I worked for major players like IBM and Lenovo, which proved to be a great learning experience for me. I worked a variety of accounts—big to small—and saw firsthand the value of building relationships. That is how I spent the first 10 years of my career. Then I decided to make a major pivot.

Around 2007, I decided to venture out on my own and started my own consulting practice. It was terrifying but exhilarating at the same time! During the first 10 years of my career, I had always known I wanted to lead or start my own company—I'm not sure where that desire came from but I think it had always been with me. The right opportunity came along to make the change and I remember thinking, "I don't want to look back in 10 years and say I wish I had given it a shot." That was the last of the catalysts that I needed to say, "Okay, I'm going to leave this B2B selling behind."

I still remember the day that I called my boss to quit my job. I was so scared. I probably dialed the number and hung up three or four times. Even though I knew I was ready to take a chance on myself, putting my plan into action required a few pep talks. Looking back, while there are most certainly things I would have done differently, I have never regretted my decision to follow my passion.

It's All About Social Capital

As I launched my new business, I had to learn a whole new set of skills in order to be able to grow and expand my business. While I was great at building relationships with the clients I already had, I needed to expand my network if I wanted to succeed. This is where my sales secret comes into play—for entrepreneurs and salespeople alike, I encourage everyone to focus on building your social capital.

I like to think of social capital as the collective value of our networks. Some modern sellers and modern selling organizations really get the value of social capital. They know that their relationships and networks have a real, tangible value that helps fuel their success. In building my business, I found that the bigger my goals were, the more I needed the support of my entire network to accomplish them.

At its core, I believe social capital is all about leveraging your network to accomplish your goals; it's also about helping others to achieve their goals and objectives. Through these kinds of symbiotic relationships, everyone wins.

HOW TO BUILD SOCIAL CAPITAL

I like to think in frameworks so for me, the first step in building social capital is to define what your most significant business development or sales goal is for the year. Once you define that goal, it is much easier to start thinking about the relationships you need to build (and add value to) in order to help accomplish your objective. We never accomplish a goal entirely by ourselves so the sooner you accept that, the easier it will be for you to start building your social capital.

As you reflect on your primary goal, you then need to ask yourself, "What are the types of relationships that I need to be building?" This might be with strategic partners. Or it could be with different centers of influence, both inside an organization and outside of it. You can then start to look at who you know or who you are connected to within those networks.

Putting Social Capital into Practice

Let's says your goal is to break into a certain industry, with the primary objective to land four or five cornerstone clients in that space. It's important to note that you want your goal to be something tangible and focused that you can wrap your head around. If your goal is too broad, you'll have a more difficult time developing steps to achieve it. Once you have clearly defined what it is that you want to accomplish, you can now start digging deeper into "the who" can help.

Taking your list of four or five cornerstone clients that you want to break into, focus on one at a time. Within each individual organization, look at who the decision-makers are, the centers of influence, external strategic partners, etc. From there, build a list of 3—5 people that would be helpful for you to form relationships with. Now, you're not trying to build relationships with hundreds of people, but rather a small, important subset. Doing this helps make the entire process much more manageable and actionable.

Asking for Introductions

Once you have a list of names, now you need to consider who in your existing network can help connect you with the people you want to meet. LinkedIn is an ideal place to start and can be a great channel for seeking introductions. But you need to be really smart and strategic about asking for an introduction.

Every time you ask someone to make an introduction for you, make it as easy as possible for them to introduce you. Give them two or three bullets they can use to minimize the amount of work they have to do. Not only will they appreciate the help, but it will also leave nothing to chance.

Social Capital Is a Two-Way Street

While social capital can be an extremely valuable means of reaching your business objectives, it is vital to remember that social capital is not all about taking. You must be willing to give at the same level you take. In my experience, I have found that people are constantly looking for connections to ideas, people, and resources—the more generous I am with my network, the more value I get in return.

If I can leave you with one parting thought, it would be to always have the courage to ask. Every time I pushed myself out of my own comfort zone and simply asked for what I needed, I was always pleasantly surprised by the response I received. Don't be afraid to ask for help and always do your best to return the favor.

Want to learn more from Amy Franko? Follow her on:
Website: amyfranko.com
LinkedIn: linkedin.com/in/amyfranko

#97 Get Out of Your Silo

MAX ALTSCHULER

"Build your brand. Build your network. Get out there.
Share, help, engage with other people who are sharing
and helping. Get out of your silo. Meet people whether
it's on LinkedIn or local meetups, or conferences,
or whatever. That's your modern Rolodex."

ABOUT MAX ALTSCHULER:

Max Altschuler, Vice President of Marketing at Outreach.io and Founder of Sales Hacker, is a serial entrepreneur, mentor, investor, and established thought-leader. In just under a decade, he has built three multi-million dollar companies, published two books, keynoted conferences globally, and been named a top sales expert by Salesforce and Inc. He has also been featured in industry-leading publications such as Forbes, The Harvard Business Review, Money, The Huffington Post, and Entrepreneur.

Max's first big mark on the scene was at Udemy where he built the supply side of the marketplace, which was recently valued at over $1 billion. Shortly after, he helped develop AttorneyFee which was acquired by LegalZoom. Since then, he has helped launch three highly successful media companies; CMX, SaaStr, and Sales Hacker. SalesHacker was recently acquired by

Outreach at the end of 2018, and Max joined the new team as the VP of Marketing.

In his new role, Max is utilizing his extensive knowledge of marketing to sales professionals to extend the company's reach in the sales community. Additionally, he helps millennials to navigate their careers and is a startup investor/advisor who helps over 50 seed and series A stage B2B companies with marketing, sales, non-technical recruiting, and fundraising.

As one of the original sales hackers and a "jack of all trades,' Max Altschuler is dedicated to making an impact in the sales community. He has continued to grow throughout his career, taking on new challenges, and accomplishing greater and greater feats. Meanwhile, he gives back to up-and-coming entrepreneurs, travels the world, and spends time with his girlfriend and two dogs.

As far back as I can remember, I have always had an entrepreneurial mindset. While in elementary school, I found my parent's candy stash on top of the fridge and snuck it into my room. No, I didn't eat it all or hoard it away. Instead, I pitched the goods to my fellow students on the school bus—and quickly sold out!

That was my first taste of entrepreneurship. In the 10 years since college, I have built multi-million dollar companies and drove growth to help multiple businesses get acquired, including my own company Sales Hacker.

But what is the key to my success? What nuggets of wisdom can I impart? There is one key thing every single salesperson should be doing regardless of where you are in your career. You have to get out of your silo and build your network! I'll break down why networking is key, how I did it, and the four actionable steps you can take to start as soon as today.

Grow Your Network and Stay Top-of-Mind

A key to my early success was learning how to outsource services at a low cost and sell them for more, collecting a margin on the difference. Another was learning to scale myself, whether through outsourcing or automation. However, nothing has been more impactful for me than networking and staying consistently engaged with my connections.

No matter where you are in your sales journey, whether entry-level or trying to level up into the 9-digit club, the larger and more engaged your network, the more doors you open for yourself. It's not just about garnering followers but building meaningful, mutually- beneficial relationships.

Networking Propels Your Sales Career Forward

Networking is instrumental to a successful sales career because it gives you credibility and creates opportunities. The more well-known you are, the more trusted you can become. As a result, your connections will turn to you when they need your product or service. Further, they will refer their connections to you. Once it gets going, it becomes self-perpetuating.

By publishing books related to my niche, writing articles for national outlets, keynoting conferences, joining focus groups, interacting on social media, and more, I have been able to build a powerful network that knows and trusts me. I continuously nurture my network and help it in any way I can. As a natural consequence, I can match needs up with solutions which is the essence of sales. This has helped me on every level from building the network of educators on Udemy to building and selling Sales Hacker. Build your network, and opportunities will come which propel your sales career forward.

HOW TO EMPOWER YOUR SALES THROUGH NETWORKING TODAY

A network doesn't pop up overnight, and if it does, it's not authentic and won't be powerful. You have to decide that you are going to invest your time, energy, and effort into building connections, make a plan to do so and then follow through on a daily basis. At first, you may feel like you aren't making any progress but remember it takes time and repetition.

Here's how to get started.

Create Valuable Content

A great way to build your network is to regularly publish content online. You can publish on your own blog, on a company blog, on LinkedIn, on Medium, or even self-publish a book on Amazon. Share your story, what's happening in your industry, and the actionable takeaways people can apply to their life. I do a lot of writing and find that it helps to clarify ideas because you can pull out the emotion and make your message very clear. After doing so, you are left with very effective teaching materials.

Repurpose Your Content

Once you have really great content, use it to create a variety of microcontent pieces. For example, take key messages out of a blog and turn them into quotes that you share on social media. Make a slideshow of the content to share on Slideshare. Record a podcast in which you elaborate on topics from the blog, or even create a course. Transforming your content in various media types will help to further engage your audience and provide them with more value (while saving you time).

Engage on Social Media Platforms (Especially LinkedIn)

Join social media platforms such as Facebook and LinkedIn and create profiles that represent who you are and the value that you offer. Connect with people in your industry whether influencers, clients, suppliers, competitors, or authorities. Engage in conversations about industry topics. Like, comment, and share posts. Provide meaningful input. Create your own conversation-starting posts. As you build a reputation for yourself, you can establish trust and credibility with potential clients amongst others.

Network In-Person

While networking online is very impactful, supplementing that activity with in-person networking will help your efforts. Attend industry conferences, local meet-ups, mastermind groups, and whatever else you can to engage with people in your professional community. I can't tell you how instrumental these connections have been to my career. I was part of a group from which several of my businesses were built. So get involved, be open, and go in with the mindset of helping as much as you can!

While it can take time to gain traction with your network, it will slowly build and gain momentum. For me personally, if someone sends me a generic message asking for a 15-minute phone call, I wouldn't take it. However, if that person is consistently responding to my posts, asking questions, and providing meaningful input, I am going to eventually notice them and appreciate their engagement. If I meet them in person at an event, that solidifies their presence in my mind. Then, if an opportunity arises that the person is a fit for, they will be more likely to hear about it. Approach connections with the mindset to offer value, rather than to gain something. If you focus on helping as much as you can, your efforts will be repaid in time and in many forms.

Want to learn more from Max Altschuler? Follow him on:
Website: maxalts.com
LinkedIn: linkedin.com/in/maxaltschuler
Instagram: @hackitmax

#98 There Are No Shortcuts to Sales

TYLER LESSARD

"You should be sweating the details."

ABOUT TYLER LESSARD:

Tyler Lessard is the Chief Marketing Officer at Vidyard, former Chief Marketing Officer at Fixmo, former VP of Global Alliances with BlackBerry, and alumni of the University of Waterloo. He has over 15 years of experience in B2B sales enablement, content marketing, branding, and video.

As a marketing, product, and business development executive, podcast host, and chalk talker, Tyler is passionate about customer-centric problem solving, creative storytelling, and data-driven marketing.

He has been recognized as a "Fearless 50 Marketer" and won the 2018 B2B Marketing Innovators Award for Buyer-Focused Marketers, the B2B Killer Content Award, and the Top Video Marketing Blog Award.

Those who've worked with Tyler say that he's passionate about everything he does. He is clever, creative, positive, and has a great sense of humor. His partners say he offers great advice, fresh ideas, and is selfless in his approach to marketing.

As a proud Vidyardian and activist in the movement to make B2B marketing great again, here he shares his top sales secret.

I began my career at Blackberry as a software developer but quickly discovered that, with my engineering background, I had unique knowledge to bring to the table. Further, I had a small special gift which was my ability to effectively explain our developer tools and get people excited about them. When the opportunity came up to work with developers and build a developer ecosystem, I took it.

I would proactively go out to other teams, different channels, internal development teams and ask them, "Are there places I can help you by delivering this message?" I found the value I could offer and put myself out there to be of service.

In sales, you should be doing the same thing. Identify the special gift you have that you can bring to the table. Is it your ability to communicate, tell a story, or do you have an infectious passion and energy? Whatever it is, you can use that value to engage the right people within your industry, build relationships, and improve your sales performance.

Build Authentic Relationships and Offer Value

My top secret to sales and marketing is pure and simple to me. It's all about how well you can establish a connection with people. How well you can build rapport. How well you can build trust. And how well you can deliver value through education, solving problems, or whatever your special gift may be. It's a combination of value and relationship. Whether I'm wearing my marketing or sales hat, this has been the number one secret for myself and the folks that I see successful around me.

Relationship building matters more now than ever because of how businesses operate and sell in the digital landscape. People are inundated with messaging through ads, emails, social platforms, text, and various other channels and they are skeptical. The natural instinct now is to ignore and exclude messaging until they are ready to go out and have a conversation.

So, as salespeople and marketers, it's important to think about how we can establish a more personal, trusted, and authentic relationship with potential buyers. That's what's going to set us apart from the million other automated messages or hundred other sales reps that are still in the dark ages sending haikus and asking if you're stuck under a rock.

Now it's about authenticity, being personal, and building a relationship to stand out. It matters more than ever because most marketing is still impersonal.

HOW TO BUILD VALUE-DRIVEN RELATIONSHIPS TODAY

Where do you start to build value-driven profitable relationships that drive sales?

Find the Right People

The truth is, you can't get hyper-personal and build meaningful relationships with individuals if you are trying to do it with 10,000 people at the same time. You have to be smart with how you prioritize your time and who you're going after.

To do that, you need to identify your ideal potential buyer. How? Coordinate with your marketing team, research social feeds, and use whatever tools are available to you in your role.

In my experience, activity scoring is often used to find the best prospects. Initially, we thought if someone read five pieces of content and downloaded two, they were the holy grail of prospects! Turns out that wasn't true. They may just be a two-person agency that loved the content. It's not just about the activities.

We began putting equal, if not more, weight on demographic and psychographic information like job title, role, company size, industry, etc. and that has proven to give us a better prediction of our ideal buyers.

Whatever tactic you decide to use, prioritize the people that have the highest propensity to ultimately convert.

Do the Research

Once you find the right people to build relationships with, you have to learn everything you can about them. I always say you should be sweating the details. Try to go one step further than most would go and learn as much as you can about the business and the individual. Also, look for connections you may have to the people. There are lots of great tools that can help you find connections. For example, do you have someone you know on LinkedIn who has a relationship with the person? An introduction through a connection is a much warmer way start to a relationship than a direct cold outreach.

Form the Connection

Next, decide how and where you are going to approach your targets. Further, decide if you think they are ready to buy now or if you want to prime them for buying later on down the road.

If your prospect is not showing signals that they are really in the market but you know it's the right company and right person, I might start with a more authentic "I genuinely want to connect with you and share great stuff with you" on LinkedIn. And then I won't start selling to them for a few months.

Sometimes you have to be patient as a sales rep and think four quarters in advance. If you're just thinking about the next 30 days, it's easy to put too much pressure, too fast. "Let me know if you ever want to have a quick chat about this," can be a much better way to start a relationship than, "Hey, nice to meet you. Do you have 15 minutes next Tuesday at 5:45 pm?" While sometimes you may have to do the latter, it should be more of an exception than a rule.

Provide Personal Value

Lastly, it's hard to build a lasting relationship if you're not providing any type of value to the other party. Think about your personal and business relationships. In your personal life, you may be offering security or companionship. In business, you have to understand how you can help, not only helping their business succeed but appealing to the prospect personally.

Find out, as an individual buyer, where they are in the organization and how they relate to others. Reveal not only how you are going to help them get better results but how they are going to learn something new, do something awesome, and/or accelerate their career. When you do this, people get connected, they believe you are trying to help them succeed as an individual, and they get behind you.

Relationship building, both internally and externally, has been key to my success. When you have a relationship built on authenticity, transparency, and integrity, people trust you and want to do business with you. There are no shortcuts there. It's something that takes time and requires patience but pays back ten-fold in the long run. I hope that these four steps can help you to improve the relationships you have with your prospects and clients and level up your sales results.

Want to learn more from Tyler Lessard? Follow him on:
LinkedIn: linkedin.com/in/tylerlessard
Twitter: @tylerlessard
Vidyard blog: www.vidyard.com/blog

#99 Empower Your People With a Blueprint for Success

KHARISMA MORASKI

"Properly enabling and empowering your people is really the difference between giving someone a fish and teaching them to fish on their own."

ABOUT KHARISMA MORASKI:

Kharisma Moraski, Head of Global Sales and Emerging Business at ServiceRocket, is an experienced and strategic GTM leader that loves driving revenue growth. She is passionate about women in technology, customers, problem-solving, new team development, emerging technologies, and scaling organizations for success.

With more than 18 years of experience in sales and operational leadership across various industries, Kharisma has become a well-known name in the sales leadership world. Her career began as a retention supervisor at one of Capital One's call centers. It was there she led her first team to success by exceeding client retention while providing excellent customer service.

From there, she was an Inside Sales Manager at J. Crew, a Customer Operations Manager at Pitney Bowes, and then a Sr. Manager of Sales at Network Solutions, Healthy Back, and Trulia. In the following years, she held Head of Sales roles at Syncplicity by Axway and Clari, and then stepped into VP of Sales roles at Kaseya, Hustle, and then Conversica. Most recently, she has joined the team at ServiceRocket.

Kharisma is also an MVP member of Modern Sales Pros, the world's largest community for leaders in sales, operations, enablement, and related disciplines, and was named one of the Top 35 Most Influential Women in Sales in 2018. Those who have worked with her say she understands her book of business, is very good at managing the team through a thoughtful sales process and, most importantly, knows how to coach teams to over- achievement.

I began my career working at Capital One and it was a pivotal time for me. It was there that I discovered my passion for inside sales and realized that I could be a fantastic sales manager who drives performance through others. The funny thing was, I learned what to do through someone who showed me what not to do.

Sales Management 101: What Not To Do

I started on the phones at Capital One, basically an SDR type of role, where we literally used the phone book. We were retaining customers and doing outbound cold calling to gain new ones. I was part of a team and I moved very quickly from an SDR to what would be considered an inside quota-carrying role. I was always the first or second person on the board every month.

Not long after I started, Capital One started a mass hiring initiative and the performance across the teams dropped dramatically. The rep-to-manager ratio was skewed and off- balance and many people were in onboarding mode. I noticed there were three or four people on my team who were sitting in the bottom 75% but just seemed to need some help and direction. I spent time working with them in the following weeks, sharing my knowledge, and one of them actually ended up beating me the next month. Not only that but all of them ended in the top 10% of the company.

Our team had been sitting around fifth or sixth and we moved up to second but I personally dropped down to fifth from my top spot. After that outcome, I remember sitting with my manager and he was telling me that I had had a really bad month. I explained to him that I had been helping to lift up the team members and showed him those results. He said that wasn't my job and I needed to stay first or second on the board.

I remember thinking that a good manager would see what I did and wonder how he could use it to help the entire department move forward. It was then I thought I should think about management because the right person should understand the importance of empowering people to move the team forward as a whole.

Empower Your People With a Blueprint for Success

Now, coming up on two decades later, my top sales secret which I first learned all those years ago, is to empower your people with a blueprint for success. If you focus on your people (sales team) and if you properly enable and empower them, they will do what is right for your customers, and your organization will achieve phenomenal results in sales. When I was at Conversica, we had an SDR team that hadn't received as much attention as they needed. I came in, we enabled them, and they improved 100% over the previous quarter.

If you are not focused on your people, if you're not giving them the blueprint to success, and if you are not enabling them properly to execute that blueprint for success, you are going to fail. If you fail, you are failing yourself and your people. So focus on your people, focus on giving them the right blueprint, enable and empower them properly, and then get out of their way. You will have amazing results.

HOW TO START EMPOWERING ON YOUR PEOPLE

How do you focus on your people, enable them properly, and empower them? Here are some tips and tricks I use.

Share Your Blueprint for Success

It starts with the blueprint. What does that mean? It is what every person needs to do every day to hit their goals. You should know how many inputs or active leads and sequences each person needs to be successful. If you aren't measuring that on a weekly basis and your people don't know what that is, then you are not enabling them properly to be empowered for success.

For example, if you are supporting SMB, you might tell them, "You need 220 active leads in sequence at any given time. You need to have five conversations per day. Of those five conversations, you need one that will convert. If you're not converting at that rate, we're going to role-play." If the metrics aren't met, you know some type of coaching action needs to be taken.

Empowerment Through Self-Discovery

The next part is empowerment which comes from a leader's relationship with their team and their coaching. As a leader facing a problem with a sales rep, I first identify whether it is a skill or a will issue. If it's a skill issue, I can help. If it's a will issue, I can't help and won't try. People with issues rooted in a lack of will are coached out of the business quickly as they can turn the environment toxic. So, first, people need to have the desire to be there and to be successful.

When people are having skill issues, I use a method called "questioning for self-discovery"—aka seeking to understand. What that means is I ask questions until the data becomes their own. A question I would ask is, "If you were in my shoes, dealing with this level of performance, what would you do?" I prompt them to come up with solutions. If I just tell them they need to improve and they aren't hitting their goals, they will come up with reasons to justify falling short. However, if they realize inside themselves that they need to improve, then they will make changes.

Once you do that enough, people start asking themselves those discovery questions when their performance is falling short. Then, they come to me with possible solutions instead of me initiating conversations where I am guiding them to identify the problem.

I focus on getting my teams to a level where they hold themselves accountable for their own performance versus me holding them accountable. Once they get there, they are self-sufficient, they are completely empowered, and we also have our next generation of leaders in the pipeline. It's really the difference between giving someone a fish and teaching them to fish on their own. When you have a team of people with this mindset, you'll be unstoppable.

Want to learn more from Kharisma Moraski? Follow her on: LinkedIn: linkedin.com/in/kharismamoraski

#100 Leverage Your Sphere of Influence to Select Prospects

JAMIE SHANKS

"Everyone has a sphere of influence and most of a person's network is made up of like-minded people. You can tap into their network."

ABOUT JAMIE SHANKS:

Jamie Shanks is the CEO of Sales for Life, a Social Selling training program for mid-size and enterprise companies. Jamie is focused on enabling millions of sales pros to move from analog to digital selling.

He is a social selling expert and the author of two best-sellers, *Social Selling Mastery*, which was #1 on Amazon's Hot New Releases in Sales and his newest book, *Spear Selling*, which was released in January of 2019. He has been named #34 on Canada's Profit Hot 50 list, one of 37 Top Sales Experts by *Forbes* and Quota Deck, and one of the Top 25 Sales Influencers by *Inside View*.

A true pioneer in the space of digital sales transformation, Jamie has trained over 300+ companies and 100,000 sales and marketing professionals around the world. With clients such as Microsoft, Sprint, Oracle, and numerous others, he is the CEO of the leading Social Selling Management Consulting and Training Company in the world.

Jaime began his career as a sales rep at BMO Nesbitt Burns while earning his Commerce Degree from the University of Ottawa. From there, he attended the University of South Australia to earn his MBA in International Marketing. In the following years, he worked as a consultant for CRESA Partners, and a Director of Business Development for both Captive Channel Corp. and Firmex Inc. In 2010, he founded Shanks Group Inc. which was a full-service inside sales agency, and two years later, Sales For Life was born.

Those who know Jamie say he is a true thought leader in the area of modern sales techniques who has one of the best sales training companies out there today. He and his team are said to inspire B2B sales teams and drive results through fantastic techniques and effective guidance.

After about a decade in sales, I came up with a theory and that one theory became the foundation of Sales for Life. It was my flux capacitor moment. The realization was that salespeople, more often than not, focus on the wrong accounts during pipeline creation and business development. They shotgun their message to all the accounts they can find in their target area or vertical, using a blanket-style approach. However, a smarter, more effective way to target accounts is by harnessing the asymmetrical competitive advantage of relationships.

Tap Into Your Social Sphere of Influence

The process of account selection should leverage the relationship strength of you and your company. Meaning, everyone you know has a sphere of influence and most of a person's network is made up of like-minded people. You can tap into the networks of the people you know to gain access to warm leads. Instead of blindly reaching out to account after account, you can get a warm introduction from someone who already advocates for your brand. By doing this, you increase your odds of getting through to have a conversation and are starting with your foot in the door.

My first client at Sales For Life took a bet on me and gave us $2,500 to do a workshop for their global salesforce. After the job was complete, I wanted to gain access to their network for more potential clients. I drew their logo in the middle of a piece of paper and used LinkedIn to map out the people connected to that company that we could prospect as future clients.

From there, I asked my client for introductions to three people in their network. Happy with my service, they said yes and made the connections. I was able to share the story about how I had helped that first client and how I can do the same for them and it worked. I continued this process with each client I had and, long story short, we went from our first $2,500 local client to $400,000 in sales and global clients by the end of the first year.

This theory changed my account selection process, not only for me but for my customers.

It effectively takes one happy customer and turns it into 10.

Start Using Relationships as an Asymmetrical Advantage

How can you get started with this theory today? Here are four key step steps.

Identify Existing Untapped Advocates

Work with your team to identify every existing account that you have that has strong advocates and relationships. Customers who are happy with your product or service. If you are an account executive and you don't have those relationships but your customer success department does, that's not an excuse. Go get them. Do what it takes to build a list.

Collect the Data You Need

Acquire the data you need to help you identify people that are within your advocate's sphere of influence (three per advocate). Pro tip: On LinkedIn, you can actually go in and look at a person's connections and organize them by the companies they work at. Examples of connections that might turn into clients include anyone who used to work at their company but that has left and gone to another company, past customers, their competitors, partners, vendors, friends of key stakeholders, etc. Then, fill in the gaps in the data, emails, mobile information, social network information as you'll eventually need to engage them.

Make the Ask

Next, approach your advocate and ask them if they will broker an introduction with three people. Tell them why you want to meet the connections and provide them with a script they can use to make the connection. This makes it as easy as possible for them and ensures that the prospect receives the message you are trying to send.

Tell Relevant Stories

Lastly, when you get a chance to talk with the contact, you need to have a compelling story to push them off the status quo. It must be centered around your advocate and their sphere of influence so tell the story of working with companies that highly correlate to these people's universe.

Here's what this might look like:

Imagine that you are a past customer of mine who was thrilled with my product; an advocate. I would look into your social network to see everyone you're connected to (I use LinkedIn) and would identify three people that I want to be connected with. Any more than three is greedy. I would then give you a prescriptive play. I'd say, "I would like an introduction to Sheryl, Susan, and John for these reasons, is that possible?" and I'd ask how well you know them. I'd have a few names lined up for back-up in case you didn't feel comfortable making an introduction to my first three picks. If you say yes, I'd then give you a message to send to the people so it's easy for you to make the connection. Then, I'd have a compelling story ready for when I get the chance to engage with that client.

And then you just rinse and repeat.

Relationships that lead to referrals give you an asymmetrical competitive advantage. On the same note, your competitors can have connections or relationships that can put you at an asymmetrical competitive disadvantage. For example, if a contact for an account is an ex-employee of your competitor who is still connected with the majority of the team, they will likely go with your competitor's solution. You need to determine which accounts are green flags and which are red flags. That doesn't mean you don't sell to red flags, it means you minimize your efforts against those accounts because you have a disadvantage. By investing more of your time up-front in the planning stage (80%) to find the accounts you can get warm introductions to, you can use your sphere of influence to disarm prospects and more effectively earn business.

Want to learn more from Jamie Shanks? Follow him on:
LinkedIn: linkedin.com/in/jamestshanks
Website: salesforlife.com
Twitter: @jamietshanks

#101 Stop Selling and Start Doing Business

WILL BARRON

"You've just got to do the right things for long enough and success comes."

ABOUT WILL BARRON:

Will Barron is the host of the Salesman Podcast, the world's biggest B2B sales show in the world that reaches over 20,000 sales professionals per episode. It's a top 100 iTunes business podcast that has won many awards from iTunes and gets over 800,000 monthly downloads!

Will has interviewed more than 400 people to dig deep and understand the "hows" and "whys" of their successes but how did he get where he is today?

Will earned his Bachelor's Degree in Chemistry and started his career in a medical device sales role. He was slightly better than average but wasn't crushing it per se. About four years ago, he decided to seek out content online to learn how to improve but instead of finding answers, he found a gap in the market. It was then he started interviewing salespeople for his own benefit. His following gradually grew and, now, he has the biggest B2B podcast in the world.

Listeners of Will's podcast say it is nothing short of life-changing. He is universally respected by sales leaders globally for his insights, practical advice, and ability to ask the right questions.

The sales industry is rapidly changing. The role that people were doing five years ago does not exist anymore. Transactional salespeople, if you're reading this and you can close a deal on one or two phone calls, you need to look for a more complex sales role, because your job isn't going to exist in another five years. It's all just changing and the sales secrets of sales aren't about selling anymore. They are about being a great business person.

BECOME A BUSINESS PERSON, NOT A SALESPERSON

We need to stop being salespeople who are just one-way pushers asking for our prospect's time. Instead, we need to have engaged, meaningful conversations and relationships. If someone doesn't want to talk to us, there are plenty more prospects out there. We don't need to spam people and piss them off. Instead, we can use our insights, networks, and dealmaking skills to engage the right people and bring in bigger deals.

HOW TO BECOME A BUSINESS PERSON

There are multiple elements involved in becoming a business person but I distill it down to three core elements: sharing insights, networking, and dealmaking.

Sharing Insights

Many people currently lead with a long consultative approach where you ask a prospect a list of discovery questions like "What keeps you up at night?" and "What are your biggest pain points?" Then, you repeat all you've learned, which they already know, back to them.

Instead, I suggest leading with an insight into the prospect's market, company, or self that makes them think, "Oh shit, I didn't know that." When you give people insights that they don't know, you get their attention, they take you seriously, and they often want to hear more.

To give meaningful insights, you need to know about your prospect's vertical, market, and company better than they do in some way. How do you do that? Time in the same industry, research, and paying attention will help to give you an edge.

Further, reach out to your internal resources. If you don't understand how your customer's business works from a financial perspective, then you need to speak to your CFO. They should know all these things off the top of their heads. If you're selling to marketers, as I do, and you're not sure of the trends or the pitfalls of what's coming up next year, you need to speak to your marketing team and get insights from them. All the information that you need, if you're with a company of any caliber, is all available internally.

Networking

Step two is building and leveraging a network. Something all business people do.

In my sales role, I was selling to surgeons predominantly. They were the big loud-mouthed people that would get the deal going on the back end. And I built a network of connections and stories over 10 years. When I didn't know the answer to something or someone internally didn't know the answer, I could go "Oh, I'll ask the surgeon in Germany who's developing these products. I'll get him on the phone." The surgeons all had heroes within the space and I knew a lot of their heroes, so I made the introductions and my network exploded.

That's a way that business people, rather than salespeople, add value. If you don't have a network, how can you grow one as fast as possible?

Help people. In my experience, if I help 10 people, 9 people don't help me back but one person does substantially more than the 10 could as a collective. And you want to be going up the value ladder while also helping people who are a step behind you.

How do you start? Spend time networking and helping out. Just ask people, "Can I help you?" For example, if someone said to me, "Hey, you know, we were chatting before about gear and recording equipment?" Then, I could say, "Yeah, that's right, I'm going to send you a massive email in a minute with all the pictures, data, and gear that I'm using here. And hopefully, that will help you improve your quality." Then, when someone tells them, "Holy shit, your show is looking amazing." They will say, "Oh, Will Barron helped us out with that." It all comes back around.

And that compounds the longer you spend in an industry. It's a lot harder when you're jumping around from sales role to sales role, company to company, as you don't have the opportunity to make those connections. So try to find a vertical and invest in it.

Nowadays, deals come from people who know that you can help them, especially as you go up the value chain, as opposed to people who think you're a good person and they want to spend time with you on the golf course. So, you need to build your network and provide them with value.

Be a Legitimate Dealmaker

Rather than just trying to push a product, be a dealmaker. Don't just focus on your sale, think about how you can actually help your network by matching them with solutions that make sense for you both. If you're providing insights and networking, you will have buyers coming to you wanting to make deals.

And it's also about building and creating momentum. If you were to interview Richard Branson or anyone who's of that caliber in the business world, you'd be so wrapped up in everything that's going on, that you'd just get driven forward organically. There's no "Hey, just checking in to follow up..." emails or nonsense like that. So that's what a dealmaker brings to the table.

PUTTING IT ALL TOGETHER

Now, here's an example of how these three elements can come together.

Say, I am selling imaging systems and am in the hospital with Surgeon A and I'm observing him. He's working really well and everything is going smoothly. Then, I visit Surgeon B and he is struggling and has loads of damaged endoscopes. They're getting broken all the time and slowing down his work process. So from my experience, I gain the insight that Surgeon B is making some mistakes and could change a few things to work more efficiently like Surgeon A. I share this insight with Surgeon B and he says, "Who are you to tell me what I'm doing wrong, young whippersnapper?" or whatever nonsense they would use in good old Britain.

Then, I pull in the networking element and say, "Well, do you want me to introduce you to this other surgeon I observed this morning who had no broken endoscopes? We can solve your problem and show you how to clean your devices without breaking them. We need to do some training on how to properly clean these endoscopes." That is where you render the value scale of keeping someone as a customer on board for long periods of time. That's your dealmaking.

In summary, you need to step out of the mindset of selling, doing cold emails, and making cold calls. and elevate yourself to the level of a business person. If the company that you're in doesn't allow you to do that, change companies to one that will.

Four or five years in, people will know you. If they haven't done business with you after five years and you've not been spamming them or cold calling them, but have been giving them insights and helping them out with different things. You've been making introductions. You've shaken their hands at a couple of industry events. Well, that 400th time you call them to say, "Hey I just found this and I think it might be useful for you," then you get that huge deal which makes it all worth it. So compounding is the best way to describe it.

Your sales career compounds over time. You come up with stories, anecdotes, people who couldn't help you in one organization are now the decision-makers in another organization. It's a grind, but I think the end result—especially after that five-to ten-year period, that's when you start crushing it.

Want to learn more from Will Barron? Follow him on:
Podcast: www.salesman.org/category/podcast
LinkedIn: linkedin.com/in/willbarron

#102 Teamwork Makes the Dream Work

DAYNA ROTHMAN

"It's not your own individual game. We as leaders have to set ourselves up for success by building a team that can support and drive our visions."

ABOUT DAYNA ROTHMAN:

Dayna Rothman is a leader of all things marketing and sales. She is the author of *Lead Generation for Dummies,* the creator of top content strategy courses on Lynda.com (over 1.3 million views), a seasoned marketing speaker, and one of the Top 25 Women in Revenue.

She is currently the Chief Marketing Officer at OneLogin, after climbing the corporate ladder in record time and making positive impacts at multiple industry-leading companies over the past decade.

Dayna moved from Connecticut to California in 2009 and earned an Executive MBA from Golden Gate University. She then entered the marketing world at Blue Wolf as a marketing generalist, performing everything from writing blogs to running her own marketing programs. After about a year, she was recruited to Marketo as a Senior Content Marketer where she spent three years learning the marketing fundamentals.

Her next stop was a role as Director at EverString, where she was promoted to Senior Director and then VP of Marketing in under a year. She then moved on to become the VP of Marketing and Sales Development at BrightFunnel; then Chief Revenue Officer at SaaStr; and later, the VP of Marketing at Mesosphere before joining OneLogin as the current Chief Marketing Officer.

Dayna's areas of specialization include demand generation, marketing analytics, mid- funnel acceleration, content, brand, social, web, SEO, marketing operations, events, sales development, and closing sales.

She is an invaluable marketing leader, manager, and mentor. Those who have worked with her say she is an intelligent, hard-working and strategic marketing professional who brings structure to companies while positioning teams for success.

I credit Marketo for a lot of the marketing fundamentals I learned and my ability to take over different roles in marketing. But more than that, it was there I learned about the power of bringing the right people together. The marketing team was very much like a machine that drove that business forward and it was exciting to be part of that.

One of the most valuable building blocks for me was when Marketo's co-founder at the time, John Miller, required everyone in the marketing organization to be an expert in some aspect of marketing. He wanted us to go out and speak, do podcasts, write, and build our personal brands. He really pushed me to go out and speak at conferences. While it no doubt elevated the Marketo brand, it also uplifted and empowered each member of the team, making us each develop and become recognized experts in our respective fields.

Marketo didn't just put out the content itself, it built a team of experts that exponentially increased the content and influence which drove the brand forward and made it unstoppable.

BUILD A TEAM THAT CAN SUPPORT AND DRIVE YOUR VISION

Much of my success has been based around building teams. I've learned how powerful it can be to hire the right people and effectively manage and mentor those people over time.

I've even had my teams move with me to new companies.

For me, the key has always been about being hands-on and in the trenches. I never manage from an ivory tower. I always make a point to understand what's going on in the day-to-day happenings and I keep my skill set very relevant. I'm still in technology and using all the tools regularly.

So my secret to success as a sales and marketing leader is to develop a strong team that supports you and one anther. It's not just your own individual game. You really have to set yourself up for success by building up people that can support you and help drive your vision.

HOW TO BUILD A STRONG TEAM

So how do you build a strong team?

Identify the Roles

First up, identify which roles are absolutely necessary. For example, if I'm starting out from scratch, I need somebody for demand gen, somebody that's running content, somebody that's doing design, someone doing events, etc. You need to cover all the key functions.

Gauge Skill Sets

Next, identify the soft and technical skills needed to make your team successful.

Technical Skills

The technical skills you can very easily determine from a resume.

However, I always keep in mind that there are people out there that don't have years of experience doing something but bring something else to the table that gives them the potential to be really unique. I was that person when joining Blue Wolf.

After graduating with my MBA, I thought marketing sounded interesting so I applied for an open position at Blue Wolf without any prior experience. They really liked my background and the potential of me, versus the fact that I didn't have all that crazy experience. If they would have only looked for technical skills experience, I would never have had a chance.

Soft Skills

Identifying soft skills can be more difficult to gauge. However, you can gain insight from the way people answer interview questions.

For example, I always look for a person's ability to be agile and humble. I need people who can collaborate with the team, have an idea that's collectively owned, think on their feet, and push the collective agenda. It's also important that they can take criticism and feedback constructively, rather than getting defensive and dismissing it.

With this in mind, during interviews, I ask questions about how candidates would manage a hypothetical task and who they would include in the process. A lot of people don't necessarily know who to include, they exclude the right people, or don't think about how to work with other members of the team to make something happen. That's a red flag for me. You can also offer them feedback on the interview and observe how they receive it.

Lead by Example

Lastly, you have to be the expert, the thought leader, and the mentor for your team. Work hard to stay on the cutting edge of industry trends, knowledge, and technology, and inspire the team forward. You can't impact them from the top or when you're disconnected. You have to be in there, driving them with passion, and lifting them up. Together, as a united team with a shared purpose, you can achieve much more than any individual can alone, no matter how great their skillset.

Want to learn more from Dayna Rothman?
Follow her on:
LinkedIn: linkedin.com/in/daynalrothman

#103 How I Book A-List Guests on My Podcast

JORDAN PARIS

"There's a reason behind every line and it's rooted in human behavior and communication."

ABOUT JORDAN PARIS:

Jordan Paris is the Host of Apple's #15 Podcast, Growth Mind University, the author of two books, and an entrepreneur who has been featured by Forbes, Entrepreneur, Yahoo! Finance, NASDAQ, Market Watch, Men's Health, and more— all by the young age of 22.

While still in high school, Jordan began bussing and serving at a restaurant called Firebirds Wood Fired Grill. He made decent money for his age but learned an important lesson— he should never take a job or have a boss again.

Jordan was inspired by a family friend, Steve Jordan, who was a personal trainer to celebrities like Arianna Huffington and Jordan Belfort. He reached out to Steve in the summer of 2016 to ask if he could work for him for six months at no cost. Steve agreed and Jordan shadowed him and learned many fundamentals of business and branding.

By January of 2017, Jordan was certified as a personal trainer with the National Academy of Sports Medicine and he built a client base over the next few months. Meanwhile, he was also earning his BA in entrepreneurship and entrepreneurial studies at the Florida Gulf Coast University and founded a web development agency that summer.

In March of 2018, Jordan started the Growth Mindset University podcast and began writing his first book by the same name. On May 17, 2018, Growth Mindset University (the book) was published on Amazon.

Jordan is curious by nature and is open to being wrong or saying, "I don't know" as he knows it means he can learn something new. He believes that maintaining a child-like innocence is key to living a good life. He is known to be purpose-driven, goal-oriented, and an impressive podcast host who is a natural conversationalist with great delivery.

Alex Banayan wrote one of my favorite books called the Third Door. Once I finished the book, I immediately reached out to him to be on my podcast. I went through all my usual emails and follow-ups but heard nothing, radio silence.

I really wanted him on the show so I went through my exact same process again. I started with the same initial cold outreach email and a nice message that said P.S. I know this is the second time I sent you this message so if you need me to back off, just let me know.

He finally responded simply saying, "Let's do it =)."

After seven to eight months of pursuit, I was thrilled but he didn't book a time. I sent him another message asking him to pick a day but again, radio silence.

He finally proposed a few days and times and then we had to do some shuffling around because of things that popped up on his schedule but we made it happen.

That was one of my toughest closes.

The Secrets to Booking A-List Guests on my Podcast

When I first started my podcast, I had a 100% close rate. However, I wasn't booking anyone well-known, busy, or "important." Once I got a few bigger name guests, I set my sights higher. While my close rate dropped from 40% to 50%, the guests I was landing were much more impactful.

I share all of my secrets to a successful podcast in my recent book The Podcast Playbook but here are a few of my core practices to landing guests.

Learn Human Behavior

First, learn about human behavior, where humans came from, how we operate, our nature, and our tendencies.

Read books like:

- *The Laws of Human Nature* by Robert Greene
- *Sapiens: A Brief History of Humankind* by Professor Yuval Noah Harari
- *The Ellipsis Manual* by Chase Hughes
- *Captivate: Use Science to Succeed with People* by Vanessa Van Edwards
- *How to Win Friends and Influence People* by Dale Carnegie (price of entry)

Getting a base understanding of human nature is important if you want to learn how to do this whole process better. It enables you to engineer human behavior.

Cold Outreach Email Templates

Next, I have email templates of initial cold outreach emails with several follow-ups.

They are very personal and strategically planned. There's a reason behind every line and it's rooted in human behavior and communication—my favorite things to study. I've also iterated and improved upon them as time has gone on.

Here's an excerpt from the book to give an example of one of my emails. This was to Rand Fishkin, someone I've been following for many years who I reached out to over summer.

Dear Rand,

I'm sure you receive quite the abundance of emails so this will be quick.

I've been a long time user of Moz which has been invaluable to my business. Thank you for creating it. Now having recently discovered SparkToro fake follower audit tool, I am having a ton of fun with that.

I'm 21 years old and have interviewed James Altucher, Mark Manson, Kevin Rudolph, Evan Carmichael, Dan Locke, and others. I'd love to add you to this mix and create something special.

My show Growth Mindset University is all about learning the lessons we should have learned in school but didn't to help people succeed in this progressive new age of business.

And the honor would be entirely mine to host you. We can promote Lost and Founder and SparkToro.

Do you want to propose a few dates and times or is it easier to go ahead and secure your spot really quickly on our calendar?

Again, totally get how busy you are so even a short reply would be great.

Cheers to manufacturing amazing,

Jordan

Line one is a static sentence that acknowledges that the recipient is busy and their time is important.

In the next paragraph, I show them that I care, I've been impacted by their work, and I have a high level of respect for them. You don't want to overdo it here, just one to three lines.

Next, I say who I am and show my credibility (yes, I name drop). Past credible guests give the person I'm reaching out to an opportunity to be associated with these names.

Then, I say what my show is all about and that I want to help them promote them.

I finish up with an elaborate double-binding question that gives them the illusion of choice when in reality, both outcomes are favorable to me.

And then, an extremely subtle guilt trip to boost response rates again, saying I totally get how busy you are so even a shorter response would be great. It's like saying, I know you're too busy for me.

And a unique ending.

All of this combined together provides for a very high response rate.

Relentless Contingency Plan

Next, I have a contingency plan. If a person doesn't answer my first email, I put a note in my calendar to follow up several times after over a six month period. And sometimes, like with Alex Banayan, I repeat the whole cycle again if I don't get an answer in the first six months.

It actually works better if they do respond to one of your emails but say no, then you respond and make an appointment in your calendar to follow up three to four months down the line at which point they will know who you are.

Be Coachable

Lastly, be coachable. Always keep studying, learning, and listening. I know it's in my best self-interest to be coachable and to know what I don't know. That approach enables me to improve and amplify who I am and my platform infinitely.

In summary, the top sales skills that have helped me grow my podcast guest list include setting out to learn about human nature, crafting strategic cold emails based on that knowledge, following up relentlessly, and always keeping a coachable mindset.

**Want to learn more from Jordan Paris? Follow him on:
LinkedIn: linkedin.com/in/jordantparis
Website: jordanparis.com
Growth Mindset University: jordanparis.com/
growth-mindset-university-principles/**

#104 Obsess Over What You Can Control

COLLIN CADMUS

"If I was going to the bathroom or getting a drink of water, I'd be thinking about the talk time I was missing."

ABOUT COLLI CADMUS:

Collin Cadmus is a talented thought leader, gifted negotiator, and a fierce sales executive. He is currently a Consultant and Advisor at his own company, Collin Cadmus, LLC where he helps startups build and scale world-class sales organizations. If you need guidance through go-to-market or building and scaling your sales efforts, he's your man.

Collin earned his Bachelor's of Science Degree in Business Management from Johnson and Wales University in 2008. After mastering retail management at CVS, he entered the world of software sales and quickly went from being a top salesperson to building and leading large sales organizations. He went on to hold sales leadership positions at SinglePlatform, Doctor. com, and Aircall.

Collin has hired and trained over 200 salespeople, collectively generating over $40 million dollars in recurring revenue. He is well-known as a leader who operates with transparency and who is willing to "get in the trenches" with his team. His ability to extend trust to his teams, foster a fun working environment, and implement key processes, has helped him to drive significant revenue wherever he goes.

Obsess Over What You Can Control

When you take on the burden of carrying a quota as a salesperson and have a number to hit every single day, every single month, it comes with a lot of pressure. And because there is no perfect product, selling environment, manager, or training program, it is very, very easy for your mind to naturally start to try and find excuses and reasons for failure. Maybe your Salesforce glitched out or something else happened. But every second that you spend even just thinking about that stuff or getting distracted is a second away from executing.

Focus on What You Can Control

My top secret is to forget about all of the uncontrollable elements and distractions. Instead, you need to focus all of your energy, your mental energy, your physical energy, every hour of your workday on things that are 100% under your control. If you do that and plan your schedule accordingly, you will be significantly more successful than the people who don't.

You need to train your brain to focus on and only on the things that are 100% in your control. Even people who are great at focusing on the controllable elements, need to be reminded of it. We all have relapses. Even me, the one sharing this secret. There will be moments where my brain starts to go to an excuse—it's a natural instinct and so you have to train yourself to identify that you are slipping into that mindset and readjust. And I think for a great manager, sales leader, or CEO, your job is to constantly stay focused on reminding your team of this mindset.

It's actually a hell of a lot of fun and really enjoyable to work around people who focus on overcoming obstacles and it's miserable to work with those that don't. And whichever mindset you have is contagious.

HOW TO FOCUS ON CONTROLLABLE ELEMENTS

What are the controllable elements and how can you focus on them?

Identify What Is Controllable

Start out by writing a list of the things that are 100% in your control that will have the greatest impact on the success in your role.

Let's say you are an SDR. Things under your control probably include:

- Making a lot of cold calls
- Researching the right people
- Cranking out a bunch of emails
- Making LinkedIn requests

It's basic sales activities. You know what those things are. Most of the time, they are pretty straight-forward.

Think Before You React

Next, when you notice you are coming up with excuses for subpar performance, train yourself to notice and stop. Think before you react and especially before spreading that excuse into somebody else's mind. Instead, think about a way to overcome the obstacle and still meet your goal. Often times, you will realize within about 30 seconds of reflection that an issue is "uncontrollable" and can be disregarded.

Manage your Schedule

Thirdly, you need to manage your schedule so your work time is focused on your controllable elements.

Say you have to make 100 cold calls today and you make two calls now and then check your texts, then you make another call and check Facebook, the day is pretty hard to tackle and your cold calls are probably going to suck.

But if you come in and say, "From 9 to 11, I'm going to make 20 cold calls to the east coast. My notifications on my phone are off. My Slack is closed. And I am only singularly focused on those 20 cold calls right now." You become significantly better at your job and that's how you can get the inputs and outputs to be very predictable. Then you know if I just stick to this schedule, I'll hit my numbers.

So block out your time and staying disciplined. Be sure you put the breaks you need into the schedule. Maybe you need to walk to the coffee machine after those 20 calls. But then you get back to work.

As a leader at my company, we give a recommended daily schedule to the SDRs here. But we give them flexibility, we don't micromanage it. Some may find that something else works for them. However, if their performance starts slipping, that's when we use it to guide them back to what we know works.

Want to learn more from Colin Cadmus? Follow him on: LinkedIn: linkedin.com/in/collincadmus/

CONCLUSION

Thank you for investing in this book.

Everything I learned and documented in this book has changed my life, and I hope it will do the same for you.

Now that you have finished reading this book, the only way for you to increase your sales is to start applying and using these sales secrets today!

Production over perfection is the key to success. Paralysis by analysis doesn't generate more sales.

Taking action, prospecting, pitching, closing, learning, optimizing, improving, and getting better every day maximizes sales.

So now it's time to get to work, you got this!

Last, if you enjoyed this book, please help me help others by giving this book a review on Amazon.

I read every single review that is written and it's the fuel to my fire to go all out to maximize your success.

BONUS: If you screenshot your Amazon review and DM me the picture or email it to me at brandon@seamlessai.com, I've got a special gift for you that I know you will love.

Thank you and I look forward to helping make this next year your biggest and best yet!

My Best To Your Success,
Brandon Bornancin
CEO & Founder
Seamless.AI
The World's Best Sales Leads
brandon@seamlessai.com

ACKNOWLEDGEMENTS

Sales Authors:

I want to thank all of the other sales authors out there who have impacted me beyond measure. Each of you has virtually educated, mentored and empowered me to maximize my sales success.

I am forever grateful for everything that all of you have taught me as a result of taking the time to write books of your own. I love learning from other sales experts in the industry and I'm so thankful that you took the time and energy to share your expertise and advice. I read hundreds of sales books in my early sales career and my success wouldn't be a reality without you sharing your sales wisdom with the world. I am so thankful for you.

To The Readers:

Thank you to all the salespeople, marketers, entrepreneurs, recruiters, and anyone else reading this book working hard to maximize your sales success. My mission in life is to positively impact a billion people and to help you connect to opportunity faster than ever before.

Without you taking the time to read this book, or investing in and using our sales software at **Seamless.AI**, we would never be able to accomplish this mission. This past decade I have poured my heart and soul into helping salespeople, marketers, entrepreneurs, and recruiters to maximize their sales success and will continue to do so for the rest of my life.

I am forever grateful to you for buying a copy of this book, taking the time to read it, learning from it, and for writing positive reviews on it. I can't wait to hear about your success stories at **www.presidentsclubaward.com**.

This book is dedicated to all of its readers. May it help you reach your full potential and maximize your sales success every single day.

Thank you so much for believing in me and supporting my efforts.

CONNECT WITH ME

Personal website: www.brandonbornancin.com
Linkedin: www.linkedin.com/in/brandonbornancin
YouTube: Brandon Bornancin YouTube
Instagram:@brandonbornancinofficial
Twitter: @bbornancin
Email: brandon@seamlessai.com

The World's Best
Sales Leads

Find Emails and Phone Numbers For Anyone.

Made in the USA
Middletown, DE
27 December 2021